D0874375

GENERAL JAMES WOLFE

# THE
# SIEGE OF QUÉBEC

## AND THE CAMPAIGNS IN
## NORTH AMERICA
## 1757 – 1760

by
### CAPTAIN JOHN KNOX

EDITED AND INTRODUCED BY

### BRIAN CONNELL
### MAPS BY K. C. JORDAN, F.R.G.S.

Pendragon House of Mississauga
1980

# THE SIEGE OF QUÉBEC

Copyright 1976,
The Folio Society

ISBN 0-88761-008-0
All Rights Reserved

THIS EDITION WAS PUBLISHED
IN 1980 BY PENDRAGON HOUSE
LIMITED.
PRINTED IN CANADA BY WEBCOM.
TEXT SET IN 12 PT.
FOURNIER TYPE.

## THE PENDRAGON CANADIANA SERIES

**Canadian Libraries.** *2nd edition. H. C. Campbell*

**James Cook: the Opening of the Pacific.** *Basil Greenhill*

**A History of the War of 1812.** *Gilbert Auchinleck*

**Over The Top!** *John Meek*

**The Siege of Québec.** *John Knox*

## THE PENDRAGON HOUSE GROUP

2525 Dunwin Drive
Mississauga, Ontario
L5L 1T2, Canada.
416-828-0400

47 Main Street
Old Mystic, Connecticut
06372, U.S.A.
203-536-1163

2595 East Bayshore Road
Palo Alto, California
94303, U.S.A.
415-856-6353

Penmenner Road
Lizard Town, south of Helston
Cornwall TR12 7PG, England.
The Lizard 741

# Contents

# Maps

# Illustrations

# Introduction

IT HAS LONG BEEN a favourite and dangerous boast that the British army loses its battles but always wins the war and the peace. This is no philosophy for a nuclear age, nor was it true, for a particular and significant reason, of the French and Indian War in North America from 1756-60, the transatlantic counterpart of the Seven Years War in Europe. After initial and severe reverses, when the inadequate militia forces of the separate British colonies, with increasing regular support, very nearly succumbed to the organised power of the French in Canada, massive reinforcements from Britain won all their battles, including Wolfe's decisive capture of Quebec. They won the campaign comprehensively. The French surrender was total and complete. Most of North America became British. Strategically and politically it was a disaster.

The colonies, united in interest and victory as never before, saw their opportunity. The cordon the French had drawn round their settlements from New Orleans, up the Mississippi, through the Great Lakes and down the St Lawrence to the Atlantic, had been irretrievably broken. The government in London sought to maintain control of the territory west of the Appalachian range which had hitherto formed the boundary of the colonies. Their American subjects sought land, furs and prosperity in the vast lands of the Ohio, the Mississippi and the Missouri and surged westwards.

For a century and a half, whether Puritan refugee in New England, Cavalier expatriate in Virginia, German fugitive from the Thirty Years War in Pennsylvania or convict in Georgia, they had built up an independent existence on the basis of thrift, hard work, land settlement and intermittent frontier skirmishes against the French and dispossessed Indians. They had functioning local assemblies a hundred years before Britain's 1832 Reform Bill Parliament. They were nominally and administratively subordinate to the British Crown, which appointed governors, judges and customs inspectors. They were only allowed to trade with Britain and her Caribbean dependencies, but otherwise they were left very much to their own devices. Now that they were free from external threat, they began to formulate their own challenge.

Twice previously, the disunited and disjointed colonies had

exerted themselves with some success in their own defence. In 'Queen Anne's War'—the counterpart of Marlborough's campaigns in Europe—and in 'King George's War'—the extension of the War of the Austrian Succession in the 1740's—they had held their own against the French with little aid from regulars sent from Britain. In 1746 a motley force of colonial militia had even captured the great French fortress of Louisbourg on Cape Breton Island at the entrance to the St Lawrence river, only to see it handed back at the peace. The third encounter was a very different matter. In the end, Britain had to send some 40,000 regulars across the Atlantic, but when the home country tried to present the bill after the war in the shape of organised taxation and customs dues, the ungrateful colonists fought the measures with ingenuity and contumely. 'No taxation without representation' was their cry and with a continent for the taking at their back, their defiance grew in confidence and ended in rebellion.

What the Americans know as the French and Indian War is remembered chiefly in Britain for the isolated encounter at Quebec between Wolfe and Montcalm. Yet it was a continental war, fought over immense distances and trackless forest country by small armies hundreds of miles apart, out of contact with each other and precariously in communication with their home governments. Reports, requests for supplies and reinforcements often took six months to cross the Atlantic and receive a response. The French, fighting on interior lines, held the initiative. Before the Seven Years War broke out in Europe, they had renewed their pressure on the frontiers of the British colonies. Their raiding parties, including the Indians they always organised better than the British, harassed fur traders and settlers. The Colony of Virginia sent a reliable militia major, the young George Washington, into the Ohio country as far as Fort Duquesne, now Pittsburg, to remonstrate. He was rebuffed, and in a second expedition, repulsed. A mixed force of militia and regular reinforcements from Britain, under General Braddock, was bloodily defeated. Another expedition of colonial troops to hold the one British outpost on the Great Lakes at Oswego barely survived the winter and was hounded back in the spring of 1757.

The colonies were at bay. The French in Canada, a pyramidal feudal society, with every settler liable to be called to arms, a colonial army under the Ministry of Marine, had been heavily reinforced by regiments of regulars under the command of the Marquis de Montcalm. He began to press south and east from the Great Lakes and Montreal. Although the population of French Canada was perhaps a fifteenth of the British colonies, they were integrated and organised and the British were disorganised and divided. Frantic calls for military aid deluged London.

At home, the incompetent Newcastle was making way for the magisterial Pitt. Even during the interregnum of confused government, the call for aid was heard. Somehow, between the competing demands of Europe and America, regiments were found to send across the Atlantic. Some came from Ireland and were brought up to strength at Cork. They included the 43rd, whose officers included a lieutenant named John Knox. His military career remained modest, but he wrote a Journal of the Campaigns in North America which is the one totally authentic account of the stirring events from 1757-60, during which the British turned the tide and after further disasters, defeated the French.

The basic strategy remained that imposed by geography. There were only three routes into New France from the British colonies. One was to re-establish a presence on the Great Lakes across the Ohio valley or along the River Mohawk and then strike east to Montreal. The second was to strike north up the Hudson valley and along the length of Lake Champlain, again to Montreal, and the third was to capture Louisbourg and thrust up the St Lawrence river past Quebec.

Knox and his 43rd Regiment found themselves part of the third prong, although his Journal includes accounts provided by fellow officers from the other theatres of operation. At first, the 43rd had to help secure the territory of Nova Scotia, called by the French Acadia, held by the British since the previous 'Queen Anne's War'. The population was French, nominally neutral, but actively hostile. The key point was the port of Halifax, rendezvous for the transatlantic convoys of British reinforcements. The 43rd endured the frozen winters of garrison duty, then, as the balance of military power shifted, formed part of Wolfe's expedition to Quebec, suffered the subsequent siege by the French, and pushed west to Montreal in 1760 for the grand reunion of the three isolated prongs of the invasion forces under General Amherst at the French surrender. Knox's Journal is the personal account of the campaigns and the victory.

Little enough is known about Captain John Knox, and such personal facts and history as have emerged had to be culled nearly a hundred and fifty years after his death from parish records, the

Registry of Wills and Military Despatches. There are no contemporary references to his Journal, although there were several rival accounts of the French and Indian War, written by others of higher rank and influence and less dedication to comprehensive accuracy.

Knox was born in Ireland. His family was clearly of Scots plantation worker stock. He was the third son of John Knox, merchant of Sligo, of whom it was said in a brief family memorial that he was always distinguished for revolution principles (that is to say, against James II) and a warm fidelity to the House of Hanover. Of Captain Knox's early life, nothing has been discovered except for the related fact that an uncle, who became a clergyman, was educated at Strabane by a Mr Ballantine and matriculated at Trinity College, Dublin, as a pensioner student.

The author of the Journal first appears in a public record as a volunteer in the War of the Austrian Succession. For his gallant conduct at the battle of Val he was presented in 1749 by the Duke of Cumberland with an Ensigncy in the 43rd Regiment of Foot, with which he was to serve during the campaigns in North America. In 1751 he married Jane Clare, of Cork, a lady of some independent fortune, whose affairs were sadly mismanaged by a trustee. That year, Knox purchased a Lieutenancy in the 43rd, and three years later he is recorded as having petitioned for his pay during three months' absence from duty spent prosecuting his wife's defaulting trustee.

His personal history from 1757-60 is interwoven with that of his regiment and the part it played in garrison and combat against the French in America. On his return home he was promoted Captain of an Independent Company of Foot, soon to become the 99th Foot. But this regiment was disbanded in 1763 and the captain went on half-pay. There followed a period of a dozen years with Knox grumbling to the Secretary of War, Lord Barrington, about his lack of preferment, in spite of the declared interest in his favour of the Countess of Shelburne. It was not until 1775 that he obtained the command of a Company of Invalids at Berwick.

By now embittered, unrecognised and unrewarded, Knox sank into petty military squabbling with his superiors. Relationships with his junior officers deteriorated. A Lieutenant Simpson complained about his captain's conduct and was called upon to make a proper submission. Knox's querulous requests for further promotion were answered tersely: 'Promotion is for officers who belong to the active corps. Officers of Invalids not being in that situation, are not promoted in the service, but enjoy the honourable ease they have so well merited.'

By the end of 1777, the affairs of the military establishment at Berwick had clearly reached a nadir. Queries came from Lord Barrington about the pay and exemption from duty of certain Invalids and dissatisfaction between the officers had reached a point which required Barrington to write: 'I am to acquaint you, it is the king's intention that those matters should be enquired into and determined by a Reviewing General in the Spring.'

Knox was in no condition to stand the continuing strain. Banished to the periphery of military activity, his contribution to the history of the army to which he had given his life unrecognised, enmeshed in the conflicts of a miniscule command and beset by his straightened circumstances, he surrendered. The threatened investigation preyed on his mind, and, in the opinion of his wife, hastened his end. The only reference to his death is an entry in the *Gentleman's Magazine* for 1778: 'Captain Knox, Captain of an Independent Company at Berwick, Feb. 8.'—We do not even know how old he was.

His widow was left with an income of £26 a year. Her appeal to the War Office for assistance elicited the reply: 'The Compassionate Funds is confined to officers' widows and orphans who have no other provision.'

At some period during his time on half-pay Knox produced his masterpiece. It was published at his own risk and expense in 1769 and sold by 'W. Johnston in Ludgate Street and J. Dodsby in Pall Mall'. The work was dedicated by permission to Lt-General Sir Jeffrey Amherst, who had been Commander-in-Chief in America. The printed list of some 200 subscribers is headed by William-Henry, Duke of Gloucester and George, Prince of Mecklenburgh. A generous proportion of Irish names and addresses is nevertheless leavened by the names of a number of fellow regimental officers and such grandees as Field Marshal the Marquis of Granby; John, Duke of Bedford; Lord Barrington himself; the Earl of Clanricarde (two sets); Earl Cornwallis; Major-General Keppel MP and Colonel William Howe MP, who had commanded the Light Infantry at Quebec. In his own introduction, the author is disarmingly modest:

'The end proposed, at least professedly, by all publications, is *Instruction*, or *Entertainment*. That I have any prospect of affording either, by a recital of facts, so recent as to be universally known, may possibly be a question with many. But the answer is ready. Though the facts, here recited, are known now, how long will that knowledge continue, if they are trusted meerly to memory? . . . I hope to afford the most sublime of all entertainments to the generous mind, placing before him past scenes of glory, in which he has either shared personally, or shall share in the review, by patriotic sympathy: and the most profitable instruction which history can give, by shewing the steps which have led to success; the true advantage of experience. We know to act, by knowing how others, in like situations, have acted before us . . .

'Every brave man is naturally curious of the events of war. *Britons*, in particular, must be fond of knowing every circumstance that contributed to wrest the empire of *North America* from *France*, and add it to the Crown of their beloved Sovereign. To this great *point* of blending pleasure with profit, *utile dulci*, I found my pretensions solely on the sacred basis of truth. Let facts speak for themselves, I represent them faithfully as they were. The praises, therefore, which on a review of great actions will irresistibly burst from an honest heart, cannot, must not be imputed to any design of flattering the illustrious Actors. They are the debt of gratitude. They are no more than justice, the inviolable laws of which would oblige me to reprehend with equal impartiality; but to the immortal honour of all concerned, rarely, most rarely indeed does any cause of reprehension exact that painful duty.

'Every other particular, in the execution of this undertaking, is submitted to candour, which will reflect, that the life of a soldier has but little leisure for study.—That the Flowers of Rhetoric seldom grow amid the thorns of War. The several occurrences, recited in the following work, which happened in the parts where I did not personally serve, were communicated to me, by some of the brave Officers present, with whom I had the honour of corresponding; and on whose judgement and veracity I could depend. But my principal debts of information are due to General *Sir Jeffrey Amherst*, Colonel *Amherst*, and General *Williamson*, *of the Royal Artillery*, for the *orderly books*, and authentic accounts of different events, with which they condescendingly assisted me, to compleat this work.'

Knox writes much better than he chooses to admit. He is no great stylist and the construction of his sentences is sometimes slipshod. But there is a marvellous immediacy in his description of battle scenes, the country through which the army passed and the life of the settler communities, together with observant and accurate descriptions of the fish, animals, birds and vegetation. Both the dangers and excruciating boredom of garrison life and the excitement of active campaigning bring out the best in his terse and authentic account. Anecdotes abound and many minor characters are vividly illuminated, like old Killick, the master of one of the transports taking Wolfe's army up the St Lawrence, who refused to allow one of the captured French pilots to touch the helm of his ship. Senior officers tend to be treated with proper deference and the French uniformly as villains, but then Knox had his eye on promotion. It was his misfortune that even glossing over the incompetence of some of his commanders was no substitute for the influence he lacked.

The two volumes of his Journal, published in 1769, are a triumph of the printer's art and a pleasure to see and read to this day. In handsome format, beautifully set in large type on superb quality paper, the original edition must have been exceedingly expensive to produce and Knox cannot possibly have made money out of it. It would qualify as a luxury publication to-day and only the proliferation of 'f's' for 's's' betrays its age.

It is also an extremely rare collectors' piece. Although long known to historians as the most invaluable source book on the campaigns of the British expeditionary forces in North America from 1757 to 1760, it was rescued from public oblivion by the Champlain Society of Canada in a subscribers' edition in 1914. This was edited in three volumes by the considerable historian of American affairs Arthur G. Doughty. It is a monument of turn of the century scholarship, every reference checked, rechecked, traced to its source, footnoted and indexed. There are maps of all the campaigns, illustrations culled from the museums of the world and lengthy biographies of participants, major and minor. For all this minute and praiseworthy care, the edition is almost unreadable. On a good many pages there are not more than half a dozen lines of text and thirty or forty of footnotes.

I have returned to the original, uncluttered version. Errata have been corrected and Knox's own informative footnotes incorporated in the narrative where appropriate. Brief biographies of some of the main protagonists, mainly based on those provided by Doughty, are included in the index. I have cut Knox's original text by about half. He was something of an encyclopaedist and scores of pages of formal orders, states of the army, articles of capitulation, casualty lists and repetitive detail of minor troop movements and garrison minutiae interrupted the flow. I have concentrated on the essential and the exciting, the colourful and the descriptive. I have retained some of his archaic spelling where it embellishes and does not confuse. Knox has no individual chapters. The present division is mine, together with necessary summaries and introductions to set the scene.

BRIAN CONNELL

NOTE: Knox's inconsistent spelling of place names has been followed in the text. The newly drawn maps use the most usual or the more easily identifiable form.

To

SIR JEFFREY AMHERST

Knight of the Honourable and Military Order of the Bath

Colonel of the Third and Sixtieth Regiments of Infantry

Lieutenant-General in the Army

and late Commander-in-Chief of all His Majesty's

troops and forces in North America

this Work is inscribed with great respect

by

his much obliged and obedient servant

JOHN KNOX

*City of Gloucester*
10 *May* 1769

# I

# The 43rd goes to War

*Frontier skirmishing had escalated into minor pitched battles between the British and French in North America a good year before the outbreak of the Seven Years War in Europe. Major George Washington with a force of militia had been bundled out of the Ohio valley in 1754. When they advanced again the following year with a small army of regulars hastily sent from England under General Braddock, they were bloodily repulsed from Fort Duquesne, now Pittsburg. That year the French sent a reinforcement of seven crack regiments to Canada under an experienced commander, Baron Dieskau. He led part of them in a mixed force of colonials and Indians south across Lake Champlain to the head of its appendage, Lake George. There he met with the spirited resistance of 3,000 New England and New York militiamen, was defeated and captured.*

*Another force of colonists had moved west and reinforced the British post at Oswego on Lake Ontario with a fort and garrison. In 1756 the French sent two more regiments of regulars to Canada and a new commander, the Marquis de Montcalm. His first act was to capture Oswego and send its defenders tumbling eastwards. The British colonies were now at bay. In 1757 the invasion routes would be wide open. During the winter William Pitt formed his first short-lived administration. War had broken out in Europe, but he galvanised the Horse Guards into finding regular reinforcements for North America. Seven regiments were made available from the Irish establishment, the second battalion of the first, or Royal Regiment of Foot, the 17th, 27th, 28th, 43rd, 46th and 55th Regiments. They were assembled in the vicinity of Cork, equipped as an expeditionary force and brought up to strength. Their commander, the Earl of Loudoun, had preceded them across the Atlantic. Serving in the 43rd was our diarist, John Knox.*

O N 25 APRIL 1757 a large fleet appeared off Kinsale, supposed to be those expected to transport and convey the troops, which are under orders of embarkation for foreign service. The troops were compleated by draughts from other regiments, mustered, and embarked in great spirits; together with their baggage, stores etc, and this business was so well conducted that there was not the least confusion or accident happened. Our fleet kept well together until 20

May, when they separated in a fog; but the weather clearing up the day following, they were discovered a great way to leeward; upon which the admiral shortened sail, and threw out signals to keep together and come down under his stern.

On the 22nd, the wind was exceeding high, with thick foggy weather and a very rough sea: the fleet once more separated, *and we lost them.* About two o'clock PM we spied a sail at a great distance standing towards us, whereupon we shewed our Admiralty colours, and she then hoisted a British flag and came down under our stern to speak with us; she was a merchantman bound to the West-Indies, and had, with many others, rendezvoused at Cork for the benefit of convoy: we made reciprocal inquiries when either had seen the fleet, and which way they stood? The trader informed us that he thought they stood to the southward; that, seeing six or seven sail in that quarter, he would follow them, and recommended the same to us; but the master of our transport, though an expert and experienced seaman, took a contrary measure, and steered northward, telling us he knew we were bound to Halifax, that he had made the voyage frequently before, and was certain, by keeping that course, we were more likely to recover the fleet, but he proved mistaken: for, a few days after, the commanding officer, seeing no likelihood of rejoining them, insisted on the captain's opening his secret instructions, which he and the rest of the transports had received at Cork; and, thinking it proper to comply herewith, he perceived he was directed, 'in case of separation by bad weather etc, to make the best of his way to Halifax, in Nova Scotia: which, at first discovery, he would find to be a reddish-coloured land; and also to keep well to the southward in his course'.

Notwithstanding these orders were positive, he ventured to deviate from them, and continued his course to the northward. The truth I believe was, our ship was a *letter of marque,* and a stout (though heavy) sailor; mounted seven carriage guns (which she could fight under cover) besides a great many swivels, with plenty of ammunition; and his cabin was well furnished with small arms and cutlasses; he had a good number of able hands on board, and our detachment (including, however, a few women and children) amounted to about one hundred and forty persons: therefore I believe the true motive, under these flattering circumstances, of our captain's counteracting his orders, was the hopes he entertained of picking up a prize; and our commanding officer, suspecting this to be the case, as he could not interfere in the sailing of the ship or the business of its master, gave orders for the soldiers' arms to be flinted in readiness, and a cask of ammunition to be laid in a handy place of safety, where it might readily be come at in case of necessity.

There happened little remarkable in this voyage, except chasing several sail in our course, bringing to, and clearing ship two or three times to fight, when we thought we might expect resistance; but it so turned out, that we neither met with enemy or prize.

We saw every day great numbers of whales, grampusses, and porpoises, together with variety of sea-fowl, particularly penguins, which were numerous; they are about the size of young geese, have a thick skin covered with short feathers resembling down, much valued for its exquisite softness and white colour; but they are not sufficiently fledged to take flight; our attention, however, was more agreeably attracted by several mountainous islands of ice, which, at a distance, appeared to us like land covered with snow; we perceived the air felt exceedingly cool while they were in our neighbourhood; and they were indeed remarkably curious; it happened to be fine moderate weather when we came up with them, so that we were not apprehensive of running foul of them; one in particular was within less than a quarter of a mile of us, and, for my own part, I thought I should never have been tired with viewing it; we computed it to be near a mile in length, and it did really appear like a barren mountain or rock, with a North-American winter's cloathing; every eye saw different beauties in this immense heap of ice, and one of the officers had time to draw a sketch of it with his pencil, there being little wind abroad; and the view it made on paper was extremely grotesque and pleasing.

At our arrival upon the banks of Newfoundland on 27 June, we spoke with a fishing schooner of New-England, who informed us that he heard several French men of war and transports had arrived at Louisbourg near three weeks ago; I remember we inquired of him what latitude we were in, for it was then, and had been for a few days, such foggy weather (endemial to all the North-American coasts) that we could not take an observation; but the poor simple fellow knew nothing of the matter, having neither quadrant, log nor even a compass on board; and told us he did not know the use of them, for that the fishermen of his country never troubled their heads about any thing more than an hour-glass and a sounding lead.

The weather cleared up and we saw a large topsail vessel a-head, crowding all the sail she could to come up with us; we hereupon once more cleared ship, our men were quartered, and every thing was in readiness for action; they endeavoured to get the wind of us, for, our soldiers having white linings to their uniforms, and their cloaths

19

being turned outside in for cleanliness, according to the custom of
troops at sea, the captain of the sail concluded for a certainty that we
were a French transport bound to Louisbourg, and had lost convoy;
this ship proved to be a Massachussetts privateer, and having taken
a prize the day before, which he had sent into Halifax, and there
being at this time many of his prisoners in our view upon deck,
dressed in bag-wigs and sharp-cocked hats, we were for some time
as strongly prepossessed with a notion of his being an enemy; and as he
mounted twenty-two carriage guns, we concluded some mischief must
ensue, though we were one and all determined not to visit Cape
Breton without the company of our friends who left Europe with us.

As to his colours, though he shewed us British, we paid no regard
to them; but, at length coming a little nearer, our captain, seeming
now somewhat dubious, hoisted our admiralty jack and went forward with his trumpet, still however keeping the wind of him, and
haled him; the other soon put us out of suspense by favouring us with
his history, and accounting for the appearance of French men upon
his deck; then, inquiring if we were bound to Halifax, offered us his
service to convoy and pilot us into the harbour: which we taking
kindly, invited him to dine with us, and proposed hoising our own
boat for him at dinner-time; but, the wind freshening with a lumpy
tumbling sea, we mutually agreed to postpone the civility to another
opportunity. In the afternoon we happily escaped running foul of
the privateer, by the carelessness of his and our helmsmen: the
American was immensely terrified, and, instead of exerting himself
as a British tar would do in the like imminent danger, fell upon his
knees to pray; whereupon the captain of our transport was obliged
to give directions with his trumpet for the guidance of both ships,
till at length, by exerting the greatest activity, we cleared him; and
this accident gave the New-England-man such a dislike to our company, that he bore away and left us.

On 30 June we fell in with Sir Charles Hardy's fleet, with the land
forces under the Earl of Loudoun from New-York, and bound also
to Halifax, which had very fortunately escaped falling into the hands
of a much superior one of the enemy, that had cruised in search of
them for many days before, under the command of Monsieur de
Beauffrement, who had very luckily sheered off to Louisbourg, in
consequence of intelligence he had received from a fishing schooner
of Boston, who had heard, and either thought it was true, or wished
it so, 'that we had twenty sail of the line and a great number of land
forces just arrived from Europe, now lying in Chebucto [Halifax]
harbour.' The fleet were doubtful whether we belonged to them,

though many of them thought they had not seen our ship before: however, we took no notice of them, but slipt into the harbour in the crowd, and came to an anchor off the town of Halifax, about the length of a musket-shot from (or as the sailors say, 'nigh enough to chuck a biscuit on') shore.

This voyage we performed in seven weeks and five days, and, though we had a good deal of rough, blowing weather, with thick fogs to sour our passage, yet upon the whole we esteemed ourselves peculiarly fortunate; the duty of chaplain was performed by an officer, who read the service of the church every Sunday upon deck, when the weather permitted; and was very decently attended by the greatest part of the men and women on board: one circumstance, however, though it may appear trifling, I cannot omit on this occasion: the master of our ship, who was a very sober moral man, always attended divine service with great decorum, and answered the responses with much devotion; but, if unfortunately (which was sometimes the case) the attention of the man at the helm was diverted from his duty, and consequently the ship yawed in the wind, or perhaps was taken a-back, our son of Neptune interrupted our prayers with some of the ordinary profane language of the common sailors, which, immediately following a response of the Litany, provoked some of our people to laugh, seemingly against their inclination; while others remained steady and attentive to their devotions, looking upon such uncouth interventions, though seasonable at that time, as the mere effects of custom, and I am persuaded they proceeded from no other motive.

Upon our anchoring in Chebucto harbour, our commanding officer went a-shore, and waited on his excellency the Earl of Loudoun, who, with Major-General Abercromby, expressed great pleasure at our arrival, with the information they received of the fleet and reinforcements we had parted with at sea; and his lordship said, *We staid so long he had almost despaired of us*; but, being assured our delay proceeded principally from an obstinate set of contrary winds that had retarded us in Ireland above two months after our arrival at the port of embarkation, his lordship seemed pleased.

On 1 July troops from New-York, disembarked and incamped on a rough, barren, and rocky piece of ground, on the WNW side of a steep hill of a considerable height, which covers the town of Halifax on that quarter; this new settlement is on a declivity, on the opposite side, hanging like seats in a theatre, down to the water's edge; which view of the town from the river, with an incampment of the grenadiers from the 40th, 45th and 47th regiments formed on the hill

close by the citadel above the town, together with the neighbouring
verdant woods on every side, and some few buildings on George's
Island (which is commodiously situated for defence as well as ornament), affords one of the most delightful prospects that can possibly
be conceived. The troops in camp consist of the 22nd, 42nd, 44th,
48th, 2nd and 4th battalions of the 60th, or Royal Americans; their
establishment is one thousand men each, with three subaltern
officers, and four serjeants per company. I was sent ashore in the
afternoon to mark out ground for our detachment to incamp on.

On 11 July the commander-in-chief reviewed a battalion of the
Royal Americans: in the firings, a ball was discharged from the
center, which wounded one of his lordship's orderly Serjeants in the
arm, but, upon the strictest scrutiny, it appeared to be an accident;
it is however remarkable, that an affair of the same kind happened
before, though not in this camp, as his excellency was reviewing
another battalion of this corps, by which a lieutenant was killed, who
stood very near to his lordship.

We have had most violent rains, with thunder and lightning,
which renders our camp very uncomfortable. A body of rangers,
under the command of Captain Rogers, who arrived with the other
troops from the southward, march out every day to scour the
country; these light troops have, at present, no particular uniform,
only they wear their cloaths short, and are armed with a firelock,
tomahock or small hatchet, and a scalping knife; a bullock's horn
full of powder hangs under their right arm, by a belt from the left
shoulder; and a leathern, or seal's skin bag, buckled round their
waist, which hangs down before, contains bullets and a smaller shot
of the size of full-grown peas: six or seven of which, with a ball, they
generally load; and their officers usually carry a small compass fixed
in the bottoms of their powder-horns, by which to direct them when
they happen to lose themselves in the woods.

One of our twenty gun ships, who was reconnoitring the harbour
of Louisbourg, brought in a prize on the 20th after a stout resistance
on the part of the enemy; she is a sloop of sixteen guns, bound from
Quebec to Louisbourg, where she was to have left her lading of
ammunition and provisions, and then to have returned to Europe;
by this prize information is received that the enemy have divided their
fleet between Cape Breton and the capital of Canada, being apprehensive that our menaces against the former are only a finesse to
cover our real intentions of proceeding up the river St Lawrence to
attack Quebec.

One hundred days baggage and forage money was issued out to

the troops which came last from Europe, at the rate of six pounds five shillings sterling to each subaltern and staff officer, and seventeen pounds ten shillings to captains and field officers.

On the 24th, the picquets of the line, with a working party from the army, marched to the left of the camp, where the intrenchments were thrown up; they were formed into distinct bodies; one half carried on approaches, while the other defended; frequently sallying out to obstruct the workmen, when the covering parties attacked, repulsed and pursued them, making many prisoners: which afforded much mirth to a numerous crowd of spectators. This is in order to make the troops acquainted with the nature of the service they are going upon; also to render the smell of powder more familiar to the young soldiers; and is to be continued till farther orders; one man was slightly wounded in the thigh at the trenches, but, upon inquiry, it appeared to be accidental: there are frequent councils of war held at the headquarters.

On the 29th, four sailors, who had walked a little way into the country, were attacked by a party of the enemy, suspected to be Indians; two of them were found dead and scalped, and the other two are missing; this is supposed to be a small scouting party, sent here in order to take a prisoner for intelligence; in consequence of this accident an officer's guard from the line was ordered to mount at Point Pleasant, near that place. Advice is received by a tender that three ships of war were off the land, coming to reinforce our fleet; that they took a large rich prize laden with money, arms and other presents to the Indians in alliance with the enemy; that she came from Rochelle, and was bound to Quebec. Weather variable, sometimes vastly hot and clear over-head; at others, cold with fogs and high wind; and the changes from one extreme to the other are very sudden. The troops continue every morning, for several hours, their counterfeit attacks on the trenches, and are greatly pleased with this kind of exercise, as every incident is shewn to us by the generals and engineers that can almost occur upon actual service; the army are in great spirits, and seem zealously impatient to realise and change the scene to Louisbourg. Great quantities of fascines, hurdles and gabions are daily making, and drawn to the wharfs in the town, in order to be put on board proper ships, by the sailors of the fleet.

The artillery, stores and other heavy baggage of the army (except their cloathing and camp equipage) were embarked on 1 August, and the troops have received orders to hold themselves in readiness to march on the shortest notice. The army was formed into the following brigades.

*First brigade*

Royal 44th, 55th, 28th: to be commanded by Major-General Hopson.

*Second brigade*

17th, 46th, 2nd battalion 60th, 42nd: Major-General Abercromby

*Third brigade*

22nd, 48th, 4th battalion 60th, 43rd: Major-General Lord Charles Hay.

*Reserves*

The 27th regiment with a detachment from the 40th, 45th and 47th, to consist of 700 men, are to be commanded by Governor Col. Lawrence.

The detachment of the Royal Artillery, consisting of about 370 men, officers included, is commanded by Lieutenant-Colonel Williamson.

All the troops embarked the next day by brigades, at the different wharfs appointed for them; a boat full of soldiers of the 43rd regiment overset; the men were happily all saved; but a few arms and some ammunition were lost. The transports at this embarkation are much more crowded than they were at leaving Europe, on account of some vessels being discharged, and others employed in carrying fascines, gabions, flat-boats, with other stores, for the expedition. The state of the regiments as they embarked, viz. Royal, 700 rank and file only, having been very sickly; the other six regiments, who came last from Europe, at 668 each; and the six regiments from New-York, at 980 each; which, together with the detachment of 700 from the 40th, 45th and 47th regiments, amount (exclusive of the artillery-men, marines and 500 rangers) to 11,288 effectives: hence it appears that, since this army last embarked at their respective ports, if they were then actually complete, they have suffered by sickness etc, and perhaps a few by deaths, to the amount of 612 men.

Orders are issued to the masters of transports to be particularly careful of their wood and water, and, according as either is consumed, to have it replaced from shore, while we remain in the harbour.

The admiral with the fleet are to proceed to Louisbourg, and endeavour to decoy that of the enemy out of their harbour; and transports, with their convoy of frigates, are to remain here, and wait the event.

A large French schooner is brought in on the 5th which was taken by the Gosport man of war off the Banks of Newfoundland; she was bound from Cape Breton to France, and her business was to carry

intelligence; when she struck, she pretended to throw a packet
overboard; but, upon searching her, a small bag was found in an
unsuspected place, under a parcel of dry fish, which contained letters
to the French Ministry, 'acquainting them with the arrival of their
fleet at Louisbourg, consisting of twenty-two ships of the line,
besides frigates; and that, exclusive of a garrison of 3000 men, they

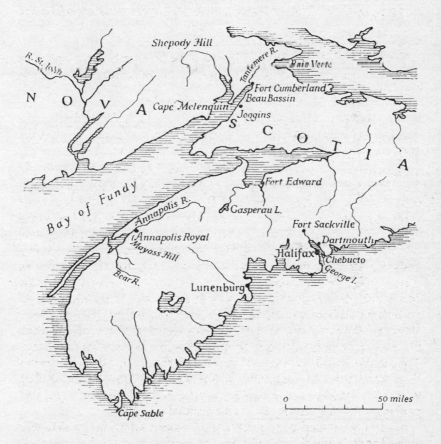

have an army of 4000, intrenched up to their necks, with twenty-five
pieces of cannon (of different dimensions) and three mortars, in
order to oppose our descent; that their fleet and army are in great
spirits, and provided with every thing necessary for a good defence'.

The intelligence obtained by the French schooner has obliged us
to alter our measures; the expedition is laid aside, and all farther
design of acting offensively to the eastward, for this campaign, is
given up.

Some malevolent spirits have contumaciously endeavoured to propagate a general discontent by insinuating that the foregoing intelligence is the result of a refined piece of policy in the French; and have taken upon them to alledge that it was not intended the prize schooner should proceed farther than the latitude wherein she was taken by the Gosport; but the army in general, as well as all sensible people here, entertain too just an opinion of the commander-in-chief to give the least credit to such infamously absurd assertions; being assured his lordship is not to be diverted from an enterprise of such consequence by any finesse the enemy are capable of.

The Royal and 28th regiments are ordered to disembark and return to camp; the fascines, hurdles, gabions etc are likewise landed upon George's Island, having no occasion for them at present. The 27th, 43rd, and 46th regiments are ordered to hold themselves in readiness to sail at a moment's warning, upon an expedition up the river St John, in the Bay of Fundy, under the command of Governor Lawrence; after which these corps are to be sent to garrison the forts of Annapolis Royal, Fort Cumberland (called by the French Beau Sejour) and Fort Edward (formerly Pisaquid) all in this province: which, with the troops at Halifax, are to remain under the command of Major-General Hopson: the rest of the army are to proceed with the Earl of Loudoun to the southward, and the fleet are to sail and cruise off Louisbourg.

It is to be observed, that the troops in North America are daily supplied with ship provisions (independent of their pay) from his majesty's stores, according to the Earl of Loudoun's regulation, which bears date at Albany the 21st of September, 1756;

*Rations per day*

A Colonel 6, Lieutenant Colonel 4, Major 4, Captain 3, Lieutenant 2, Ensign 2, Chaplain 2, Adjutant 2.

Chief Engineer 5, Engineer in ordinary ranking as Captain 3, other Engineers as Subalterns 2, Director of the Hospital 5, Clerk of ditto 1, Master Surgeon 3, Surgeon's Mate 1.

Quarter Master 2, Surgeon 2, Mate 1, Serjeant 1, Corporal 1, Private 1, Drummer 1.

Master Apothecary 3, ditto's Mate 1, Matron 1, Commissiary of Stores 3, Clerk of ditto 2, ditto Overseer 1, Extra Clerks 1, Artificers 1.

The artillery are to be served with provisions in the same manner as the rest of the army, the commanding officers as majors; and to draw four rations *per* day. A lieutenant-colonel or major commanding a battalion may draw six rations each: no officers are to receive money for their provisions; what he does not take in kind, at the regular times of issuing, to be a saving to the government. A ration is a certain proportion of provisions or forage: a soldier's allowance *per* week is seven pounds of beef, or, in lieu thereof, four pounds of pork, which is thought to be an equivalent; seven pounds of biscuit bread, or the same weight of flour; six ounces of butter, three pints of pease, half a pound of rice; and this is called seven rations.

With regard to the currency of money, the dollars (says the Earl of Loudoun in this day's orders) together with all the other denominations of that species, are to be issued out to subsist the troops, as they are remitted by the government; that is to say, the dollar at 4s. 8d. and the rest in proportion. Throughout this province the dollar passes for five shillings, which is called the currency of Nova Scotia.

Our men take great quantities of fish over the ships' sides; they are chiefly mackerel and pollock: our transports are now much crowded and, there not being sufficient berths or accommodations for the number of men on board, we are obliged to have recourse to the following expedient: 'A man from each berth mounts guard every day on the main deck, with a serjeant and corporal; and they remain above, for the better convenience of the rest below, until they are relieved; there are several sentinels posted both fore and aft, who have orders given them with respect to fire and candle; also with regard to boats going from, or coming to the ship, to prevent spirituous liquors being brought on board, and likewise the smoking of tobacco'. This guard is superintended by an officer, who is obliged, as the troops are served with an allowance of rum instead of beer, to see the same issued out every day, and mixed with water; each soldier's daily proportion is a gill of this spirit, with three of water.

The prices we paid for the following articles of provisions were, beef and mutton six-pence *per* pound; veal from one shilling to one shilling and six-pence; fresh butter (scarce and very indifferent) sixteen-pence; milk four-pence *per* quart; a loaf of good soft bread (about three pounds and an half) one shilling; most kinds of fish, and particularly lobsters, in great plenty; but the demand for them was such as rendered them much dearer than might be expected.

The town of Halifax is large: the streets (which are not paved) are tolerably regular and of a good breadth; but their houses, upon a nearer view, are mean and do not display any great knowledge of architecture, much less of taste, in those who erected them; which in general, together with a capacious church, are of wood and covered with the same materials. Great allowances must nevertheless be made for a settlement still in its infancy, and the inhabitants, together with the troops, have had incredible difficulties to struggle with: one circumstance however is to be regretted, namely, that the settlers who are of different countries (as well as religions) have no great inducements to continue here, the country about it being entirely rude and not worth cultivating: consequently as their chief prospects of gain, and dependence for support, are by the sale of slops, haberdashery wares and liquors to the navy and army (which is a precarious trade), the inhabitants can at best be only reputed sojourners; for, as their profits upon these several articles are immense, so it is natural to suppose they will remove to some less inhospitable climate, where they may enjoy their wealth more to their satisfaction, or lay it out to good advantage in land and agriculture.

Their batteries, citadel and other fortifications are of timber, these being thought sufficient to protect them against an Indian enemy; but the channel of the river is well defended by a respectable battery on the eastern shore, and by several others upon George's Island; there is also a post at the head of this river, where there is a small picketed fort, called Fort Sackville, occupied by a party of regulars; this is about twelve miles from Halifax.

They have here great variety of excellent fish, the staple commodity of this country and its dependent islands: as for the other necessaries and conveniences of life, they must be indebted for them to New-England, the other provinces to the southward, and to the mother-country; but I must not omit that Chebucto or Halifax harbour is one of the finest in the whole world for depth of water, good anchorage and safety: they have a royal dock here, with all the conveniences for the largest first-rate ship to heave down and careen; moreover, it very rarely happens that this harbour is frozen up in the winter; for which several reasons, it is the rendezvous of all his majesty's ships in America, and is frequently resorted to by others from the West-Indies, whenever they have occasion to undergo any repairs.

# II

# In Garrison at Annapolis

*The reinforcements from England were dispersed to the different theatres of war. Some of the regiments were sent north from New York to hold the line which led to Fort William-Henry, the redoubt which had been built on Lake George on the site of Dieskau's defeat. Some were designated for the siege and capture of Louisbourg on Cape Breton Island. The remainder were to hold Nova Scotia in garrison, with its precious naval base of Halifax. This thankless task fell to the 43rd.*

*The French called the territory Acadia and had colonised it. At the peace that terminated 'Queen Anne's War' half a century earlier, the colony had been ceded to Britain. The French settlers remained, obstinately loyal to their Catholic religion and former masters. Although they took a nominal oath of allegiance, they were constantly exhorted by their priests and the French from Canada to commit acts of hostility. In 1756, their behaviour had become so intolerable that most of the population was rounded up and deported down the eastern seaboard of the British colonies as far as Georgia. Enough remained, with the Indians and backwoodsmen from Canada, to form raiding parties which rendered the British hold tenuous. A string of forts was built along the Bay of Fundy leading up to the narrow isthmus connecting Nova Scotia with the mainland. As the 43rd prepared for the bitter winter ahead nothing but ill tidings came from the other theatres of war.*

At SIX O'CLOCK on the morning of 16 August, fine weather though very sharp, a signal was made to unmoor, and the whole fleet and convoy sailed soon after; about ten, we met an express sloop from Boston, with dispatches to the Earl of Loudoun, importing that the enemy had laid close siege to Fort William-Henry; whereupon a signal was made, and the fleet came near and lay to. A council of war was held on board the *Winchelsea*, in consequence whereof two the the regiments that had been destined to sail with us up the bay, viz. the 27th and 46th, were ordered to proceed with his excellency to New-York, and an express was sent back to General Hopson at Halifax, to embark the 28th regiment, and send them immediately after us. There being a detachment of the former of these corps stationed on board the *Success* to serve as marines, which consisted of a lieutenant, two serjeants, one drummer and sixty rank and file, the same was instantly ordered to be relieved by the like command from the 43rd regiment, and this unpleasant service fell to my lot; the removal from one ship to another in a trifling cock-boat, the wind blowing fresh with a short tumbling sea, rendered it very disagreeable, and more so still as I had not time to take some live stock, good liquor or sweet water with me, which we had on board our transport in plenty, and they were wanted on board the *Success*: this circumstance I had much cause to regret during the remainder of our voyage. About five o'clock, every thing being now settled pursuant to this change in affairs, the several squadrons made sail, Lord Loudoun's to the southward for New-York; Admiral Holburne's to the eastward for Louisbourg; and Captain Ourry's for the Bay of Fundy.

The expedition up St John's river is laid aside for this year, and, it being apprehended that the enemy may attempt this autumn to strike *a coup* in this province and try to recover Fort Cumberland, we are to proceed thither without delay. Mr Ourry being desirous to see my detachment exercise in the marine way—which is nothing more than, after firing over the ship's side, to fall down upon one knee, so as to be under cover, and load again—we performed these firings repeatedly for an hour: the men were formed into three divisions, two upon the quarter-deck and one upon the forecastle, facing the starboard side of the ship, and then fired, right, left and center; afterwards several vollies were discharged, and the men acquired great applause from Governor Lawrence and our vice-commodore.

On the 20th we spoke with a sloop from New-York, bound to Halifax with stores and provisions, and a bag of letters for the Earl of Loudoun: by him we are informed that the inhabitants of the province where he came from are under the greatest apprehensions, lest Monsieur Montcalm should pay them a visit; by his accounts, the French army at Fort William-Henry amount to almost 15,000 men; that the provinces had levied an army of 22,000 to stop their progress, some contributing a fourth, and others a sixth man; I observed that Governor Lawrence paid little regard to any of this intelligence, either respecting the enemy, which he thought extravagant; or the new levies, which he seemed to have no great opinion of for immediate service.

About one o'clock on the 24th we made Chepordie [Shepody] Hill, said to be the highest land in Nova Scotia; it bore NE and by N at the distance of seven leagues; Cape Orage [Enrage] likewise in view, stood north, and here the bay is about seven miles over. At four o'clock Cape Melenquin [Meringouin], on the north shore, lies NW and by N of our course, a pleasant prospect everywhere: here the bay is not above three miles over, and the banks on each side are of the finest verdant green. About an hundred and sixty yards from each shore are delightful woods, seemingly as if arranged with-design, and much resembling the artificial groves, without any under growth or incumbrance below, which one frequently meets with about noblemen's and gentlemen's seats in Europe; here the water is of a turbid colour, and not unlike the Thames at London.

About six o'clock we sailed through the Joggen [Joggins], and soon after came to an anchor in the Bason, called by the French with much propriety, Beau Bassin, about five miles from Beau Sejour, now Fort Cumberland; the rest of our squadron joined us in less than an hour, and anchored also, where an hundred sail of the line may ride in safety without crowding; and, from the time we entered this bay, we found water enough everywhere for a first rate ship of war. The governor and our naval commander lost no time in going ashore under a discharge of fifteen guns from the *Success*; my young mar-ines were drawn up on this occasion, not with their fire-locks, there not being room to handle them properly, but with cutlasses belong-ing to the ship; and, upon the governor's landing, he was saluted from the fort also with fifteen guns.

His excellency and the commodore returned on board early the next morning, and the transports were ordered up nearer to the fort for the convenience of landing the regiment and the baggage of the officers: upon this occasion the *True Briton* had a fortunate escape, for, when the tide left her, she lay athwart a creek, and thereby en-dangered the breaking her back; however, by disembarking the detachment in order to lighten her, she was got off without receiving any damage, and the men were sent on board again; here the tide rises to the height of sixty feet and upwards. I was ordered ashore this day, to assist the quarter-master in marking out ground for the regiment to incamp on; which we accordingly executed under the cannon of the fort, leaving a proper space on our right for the 28th regiment, hourly expected: here we found a detachment, equal to a battalion, from the 40th, 45th and 47th regiments, under the com-mand of Lieutenant-Colonel Wilmot, who entertained the governor and his company with great hospitality; at nine o'clock in the evening, I returned with the governor and commodore on board the *Success*.

The 43rd regiment disembarked and incamped the following day; fine weather until after night-fall, when it set in for rain, which continued incessantly for the space of twenty-four hours, with great violence, accompanied with thunder and lightning. My detachment was ordered on shore from the frigate; we were five hours rowing against wind and tide, and the rain never ceased; the men were much to be commiserated, not being able to change their cloaths; and our camp was a perfect swamp; as my party was landed without the governor's knowledge, he ordered it to be replaced by the like numbers from the troops in garrison.

A deserter is arrived from the island of Cape Breton, who says, 'that a large body of troops from thence are preparing to invade this province': when the 28th regiment joins us, we are to intrench our camp. There is a large blockhouse here, advanced about a quarter of a mile NE of the fort, upon the skirts of the wood leading to Baye Verte (or Green Bay) which is occupied by an officer, two serjeants, a gunner, a drummer and thirty-two rank and file, to prevent any surprise to the garrison from that quarter; this house is an excellent fortress against musketry only, constructed of large square timbers, and consists of three floors or stories; the first is twenty feet square, the middle one twenty-two, and the upper twenty-four feet; there are port-holes in each face of the second floor for cannon, there being two six pounders, on ship carriages, mounted and always ready loaded. Each of the two upper floors project, or extend, two feet beyond the apartment immediately below them, with round holes at certain distances about eight inches diameter, through which to fire musketry or throw grenado's, in case the enemy should attempt to fire the house; besides these, there are numbers of loopholes in each face for the service of small arms, which of course render it an airy habitation to those who are to defend it. The officer has orders to maintain this post to the last extremity; for this purpose, he is provided with a week's provisions and a large quantity of ammunition, both for his cannon and musketry. Such is the barrier to most of the forts and garrisons in America, where an officer and thirty men may make a noble defence against any numbers whatsoever, provided there are no artillery brought against him, or that the enemy do not attempt to fire it with arrows, which, I am told, has been practised by the savages heretofore, where there have not been any ordnance mounted to oblige them to keep their distance.

A detachment is gone out to cut and make fascines and pickets for intrenchments, that are to be thrown up here with all expedition: we are credibly informed the enemy threaten to come and retake this fort: at night the blockhouse was alarmed by one of its advanced sentries, who is posted in the skirt of the wood; he fired his piece at

THE TOWN AND HARBOUR OF HALIFAX IN NOVA SCOTIA

a man as he imagined, who was advancing towards him; however it appeared to be a mistake, and is rather supposed to have been a wild dog or fox, with which the forests here are much infested.

The 28th regiment came to an anchor on the 30th in the bason from Halifax; near to which place a body of French and Indians have lately shewed themselves at Dartmouth, on the opposite side of the river. The 28th regiment disembarked the day following, and incamped on the right of the 43rd; by them we are confidently assured that a large corps of regular and light troops are upon their march to retake this fortress, and are commanded by Monsieur Boishébert [de Boishébert] a famous partisan, who is lieutenant for the French king in this province, where I find, by the following manifesto he has resided for some years:

'We, the officer commanding for the king, on the river St John, and in all French Acadia, and their dependencies.

'As sordid interest, rather than any other motive, induces the Acadians to expose themselves to the apparent danger of being taken by the British, and that we have recent examples of the risks which worthless subjects incur, who are perhaps taken.

'For this cause we command all the Acadians not to leave their habitations, or places of residence, without our permission, under any pretence whatsoever.

'And we promise a reward of fifty livres (about two pounds, five shillings, sterling) to any person who shall advertise us of such transgressors for the future; and we admonish these last, under the penalty of three hundred livres, to be levied upon their goods and chattels, besides causing them to be transmitted to Quebec as rebellious subjects and prejudicial to the public good.

'And we command all captains of militia to circulate and publish these our orders on all their rivers and districts.

'To three of these presents we have fixed the seal of our arms (viz. three ducks regardant) that no person whatsoever may plead ignorance.

'Given at our camp, this twentieth day of December, 1755.

BOISHÉBERT.'

Our commodore has received a letter from Admiral Holburne, who was returned to Chebucto (Halifax) from Louisbourg, wherein he informs him that he looked into the harbour with his own ship, and reckoned eighteen capital ships of the enemy's, some of which were much larger than many of those under his command; and he is of opinion there could not be less than seven thousand men intrenched along shore; that he drew up his fleet in the bay, in order of battle; but the enemy would not come out. The admiral has recommended it to the commodore to repair, without loss of time, to Annapolis Royal, as he thinks he will be safer under the cannon of that fortress than here. A council of war has been held in the fort, upon the measures to be taken in case the enemy should put their threats in execution. Our men load their arms now upon all duties, and the sentinels have orders not to suffer any person to pass them in the night, without giving them the countersign, or second watchword.

The 28th and 43rd regiments moved their camp on 1 September nearer to the glacis of the fort, in order to render it more compact; for this purpose they are confined to closer distances than usual, in larger armies and incampments; as the men are growing sickly, by reason of the wetness of our camp, they are ordered to bed their tents well with the boughs of spruce for want of straw, and the officers have got boards to floor their markees: it is inconceivable what quantities of mice we have on this ground, insomuch that one can scarce walk a few paces without seeing or treading on them; they burrow under the decayed roots and stumps of trees that formerly grew here, and I am told they have been frequently eaten by the French inhabitants, as well as by our troops, when fresh provisions have been scarce: I am likewise assured that the soldiers have also fed upon dogs and cats under the same circumstances. We are tormented here, both day and night, with myriads of musketa's, which are so immensely troublesome, that we are obliged to have recourse to various expedients to defend ourselves from them.

We have begun this day to intrench our camp; for this purpose some officers who had served in the Netherlands during the late war (of which I was one), were this day appointed overseers of his majesty's works at three shillings *per* day each, which is to be continued while we are employed on that service; a few expert serjeants from each regiment are also employed to lay fascines and instruct the soldiers, who are each to be allowed one shilling *per* day. Our troops and sentinels are ordered to be very alert and circumspect, some parties of the enemy having shewed themselves from the shore to our ships in the bason; a small number of these fellows came here on the 20th ult. before our arrival, and carried off above sixty head of black cattle, and some horses that were grazing within less than a quarter of a mile of the fort.

The weather cool and windy, with frequent showers: between detachments, fatigue and camp duties, the subalterns, non-commissioned and private men have very little time for rest; a reserve from each regiment, consisting of a captain, lieutenant, ensign, and sixty rank and file, with serjeants and drummers in proportion, mount every evening at retreat beating, and patrole the camp every night continually.

Another deserter is come in from Cape Breton; he says, 'the enemy expect to subdue this province to the French arms before the severity of the winter sets in'; our works go on vigorously. The country here is infinitely preferable to that about Halifax, and there are many vestiges, everywhere, of the industry of the pretended neutrals, its late inhabitants. Between nine and ten o'clock on the night of 5 September, a detachment of the troops, in camp and garrison, under the command of Lieutenant-Colonel Walsh, with a company of rangers, were ordered to proceed to Gasperau, and Baye Verte, as well to reconnoitre the country as destroy the roads and bridges and render them as impassable as possible; they have taken three days' provisions with them. Baye Verte lies eastward of this fort, at the distance of about thirteen miles; and it is from thence we expect the enemy will visit us, if they should put their threats in execution.

The detachment returned two days later all safe and well: they destroyed eleven bridges, cut trenches in many parts of the road, burned three large boats and a schooner that lay at anchor in the bay; they neither met with men or cattle, nor could they discover any human tracks in any part of the country where they have been: the weather is now dry and warmer than of late.

A sloop arrived from Halifax on the morning of the 8th; in her passage here, she called at Annapolis Royal, whence we are informed that they had lately sustained a great loss at that place, by a party of the enemy who came down, took away all their cattle and burned several store-houses; that the garrison were so weak, as to numbers, that they could not venture to sally out and pursue them: by this vessel we also learn, that some corps of new-raised Highlanders were arrived at Chebucto.

By a letter which I have received, from a brother officer at New-York, dated 13 August, I have the following information of the fate of Fort William-Henry and of its late garrison:

'Lieutenant-Colonel Monroe commanded there with about two thousand men, composed, by detachments, from the 35th regiment, the 60th and a body of the New Jersey Militia; part of which were entrenched in the lines adjoining to the fort: on the third instant, an army under the Marquis de Montcalm (Captain-General and Commander-in-Chief of the French forces in Canada), consisting of eight thousand regulars and militia, some artillery, and fifteen hundred savages, invested the place and cut off every communication, by which there was the least appearance, or possibility, of the garrison or trenches being reinforced, either with men, ammunition or other stores. Colonel Monroe contrived to convey several letters to General Webb, who had retired to Fort Edward with five thousand men, to wait for farther succours, which had been promised by the several provinces; but, these supplies not being arrived or likely to come in proper time, the general transmitted a letter to that effect to the colonel, recommending it to him to make the best terms he could for the troops under his command.

'This letter was intercepted by the marquis on the morning of the ninth, and was sent by him, without delay, to the commanding officer of the garrison, accompanied with a peremptory demand of the surrender of the place, under pain of his not having it in his power to prescribe bounds to the savages if he did not immediately comply. The gallant colonel, thus mysteriously forlorn, after making spirited defence, was thereby compelled to surrender on the same day: by which, the troops under his command are restrained from farther service against the enemy or their allies for the space of eighteen months from the date of the capitulation; we had about three hundred, of every rank, killed and wounded during the siege; the loss of the enemy is uncertain, but, by accounts from deserters who came to Fort Edward on the 8th, their loss could not then be less than twelve hundred men; this my dear friend (continues my correspondent) is a great number to lose in so short a time, and where there was no action; but the French general has acknowledged he never saw artillery better served than those of the garrison were. After the troops had marched out (which they were allowed to do with the usual honours of war), the savages, who before had been flattered with great hopes of plunder and scalps, notwithstanding the escort which our troops had to conduct them in safety to Fort Edward, and in sight of the whole French army, fell upon the poor fellows with the most barbarous rage, rifled the officers of every thing they had, even to their shirts; and basely butchered several hundreds, neither sparing women or children; Colonels Monroe, Young, and a few officers, with about three hundred men, retired to the French army, and put themselves under the marquis's immediate protection; how this intricate affair, the inactivity of our forces, and this flagrant breach of faith on the part of the enemy, will be received

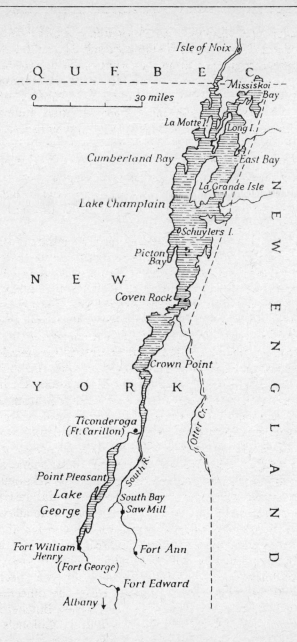

at home, time only can evince. I returned here yesterday from Fort Edward; we are all in confusion in these parts, as you may well suppose: it is said the enemy have demolished the fort, and levelled the lines; if they should advance farther into the province, etc, etc. Postscript. Several of the Indians did not use fire-arms, some of our people being killed and wounded with arrows, in the use of which those brutes are reputed very dexterous.'

I immediately waited on Governor Lawrence, and shewed him this letter, as he could not receive any authentic accounts before; he told me he had got some letters from the southward, by the way of Halifax, brought by this same sloop; but mine contained more particulars, and he was heartily sorry to believe our advices of that shameful disaster were too true.

We proceed at our intrenchments with great diligence, and without intermission even on Sundays: the working hours are from six to eight, from nine to twelve, and from one to six in the afternoon; the men are assembled by the ringing of a bell at the fort. The troops of this province are supplied with spruce beer, which was first introduced, during the late war, in the garrison of Louisbourg when we were in possession of it; and then the molasses were issued from the stores gratis, this liquor being thought necessary for the preservation of the healths of our men, as they were confined to salt provisions, and it is an excellent antiscorbutic: it is made of the tops and branches of the Spruce-tree, boiled for three hours, then strained into casks, with a certain quantity of molasses; and, as soon as cold, it is fit for use.

When we were incamped at Halifax, the allowance was two quarts *per* day to each man, or three gallons and an half *per* week, for which he paid seven pence New-York currency (equal to four-pence and $\frac{1}{12}$ sterling), as by the Earl of Loudoun's regulation of the 5th of July last. Here the soldiers are obliged to draw five pints *per* day, or four gallons and three pints *per* week, for which they are charged nine-pence half-penny currency of this province (equal to eight-pence and $\frac{23}{28}$ sterling). The paymaster of the 43rd regiment assured me that the spruce account for that corps, in the space of about seven weeks, amounted to eighty pounds currency.

During the night of 20 September we were alarmed in our camp by two shots fired on the swamps to the left of our ground; the guards and pickets turned out, and we stood to our arms until it was clear day-light in the morning; this was occasioned by some of our rangers, who took the advantage of a moon-light night to lie in waiting for wild ducks, which, with most other kinds of wild fowl, are in great plenty here, though not to be got at without risk.

The reinforcements of Highlanders, mentioned before to have arrived lately at Halifax, consisted of two new-raised regiments; an unlucky accident lately happened to one of their private men, of which the following are the particulars; a soldier of another regiment, who was a sentinel detached from an advanced guard, seeing a man coming out of the wood, with his hair hanging loose and wrapped up in a dark-coloured plaid, he challenged him repeatedly, and receiving no answer (the weather being hazy) he fired at him and killed him; the guard being alarmed, the serjeant ran out to know the cause, and the unhappy sentinel, strongly prepossessed that it was an Indian, with a blanket about him, who came skulking to take a prisoner or a scalp, cried out, *I have killed an Indian, I have killed an Indian, there he lies, etc* but, upon being undeceived by the serjeant, who went to take a view of the dead man, and being told he was one of our own men and a Highlander, he was so oppressed with grief and fright that he fell ill, and was despaired of for some days. In consequence of this accident, most of these young soldiers, being raw and unexperienced, and very few of them conversant in, or able to talk English (which was particularly his case who was killed), these regiments were ordered to do no more duty for some time; at length some of the inhabitants having crossed over to Dartmouth to cut fire-wood, they were attacked by a party of the enemy, and several were killed and scalped: whereupon a large detachment of these Highlanders were immediately sent to take post and remain there; which will effectually secure the town on that quarter, and inable the settlers to provide fuel during the approaching winter without any farther apprehensions.

A Frenchman has appeared on horse-back (with a white uniform, supposed to be Monsieur Boishébert) on the shore westward of our fort; the *Success* frigate rides within less than a quarter of a mile of that place, and this day gave him a gun, upon which he thought proper to disappear, and, at the same time, there was a great shout heard from the adjoining woods.

We have at length finished all our works, and the late garrison, with the 43rd regiment, are ordered to embark their baggage on Monday 10 October, and themselves on the day following: the 28th regiment, with a company of rangers, are to remain here this winter; a detachment of three hundred men from that corps, under their own major, were ordered out this afternoon to scour the country as far as Baye Verte, to discover if any thing has happened in that quarter since the last command had marched that way. Two of the number of oxen, stolen by the enemy last August, deserted their new masters, swam across Tantamere river, and once more put themselves under the protection of the British flag. There being now no farther attendance required from the officers who had been appointed to inspect the king's works, they were this day paid off, with a polite compliment for their service.

The embarkation of the baggage is much favoured by the weather, which is warmer than it has been for some time past. This forenoon the above command returned to the fort: on Sunday evening (the ninth) they got upon the tracks of men and horses before it was quite dark, and soon after came upon an abandoned camp, with fires still burning; wherein they found a bottle of milk, a British pork barrel, some flour, a small leather bag of balls and buck-shot, also a fire-lock, which, by the marks, appeared to have formerly belonged to a man of the ranging company, who, with an officer and twenty five men, were way-laid and made prisoners some weeks before our arrival here; the night coming on apace, and the ground being advantageous, the major occupied this camp, and immediately posted his sentinels, giving all necessary orders on this occasion.

About midnight a party of the enemy (as is surmised) returned to reconnoitre the disposition of the detachment, but, being nearer to one of the sentinels than they had suspected, he, upon hearing a rustling noise in the bushes, gave an alarm by discharging his piece as near, as he could form a judgement, to the place the noise proceeded from; this was instantly repeated by the rest of the sentries round their post. The party immediately stood to their arms, and the men fired so furiously, some one way and some another, that it was with difficulty their officers could restrain them; whether any fire was returned on the part of the enemy is uncertain; there were no shouts nor yells heard, therefore it is concluded if any were there, they were surprised and stole off, seeing our party so numerous and well situated; the detachment remained under arms until it was clear day-light, and the sentries were doubled, the officers continually visiting them.

In this affair, very fortunately, there were none killed, though four men were slightly wounded (I presume by the impetuous firing of their own comrades). By the number of tents or wigwams which the enemy left standing, and the pressure of many bodies upon the beds of spruce where they lay, with various other circumstances, it is conjectured that they were not a small party; but, being, as I said before, taken unawares at the first appearance of so uncommonly large a detachment, they retired to some of their fastnesses, flattering themselves that they would be pursued (for these fellows will not fight without some apparent advantages); they were, however, disappointed, for, as soon as it was light enough to march with precaution, the commanding officer, pursuant to his orders, directed his course by a different route, back to the camp.

This affair has been variously represented, and some circumstances have been told that I think are not probable, therefore I omit any mention of them; however, what I have here related I have collected from my materials, and I believe it to be as near as possible to the state of the case. The enemy never fire a single ball, for they always load with six or seven smaller ones (which are called buck-shot) besides their usual musket-ball; and it is agreed by every body there was no such shot fired that night. That the enemy had been in, and occupied that camp, previous to the command's marching out, I give intire credit to: but, at the same time, I am inclined to think the sentinel, who first fired, was rather alarmed with his own apprehensions, and perhaps a breeze, just at that instant, springing up, caused a rustling noise in the bushes, which increased as the wind continued.

Upon the whole, by all that I can learn from the British inhabitants of Nova Scotia, and officers, as well as rangers, who have lived long in this country (and to which I may now add my own subsequent experience), I am induced to believe, if there had been so small a number as twenty of the enemy, and our party even six hundred instead of three, they would actually have given a fire, raised their accustomed savage shout, and then fled: for they are very enterprising and clever in those woods; their hatred of the English is implacable, and their revenge beyond conception; therefore, if one or two of those poor misguided wretches were there, when the first shot was fired, they came as spies, and must only have withdrawn themselves to their main body, as I have already observed, with the hopes of decoying the detachment to a post more suitable to their own humour and manner of fighting; for there is no other consideration could have prevailed on them, at that time, to desert their camp and the present opportunity.

The 43rd regiment embarked on the 12th, after a great deal of trouble, and many delays on the part of the masters of transports, who were very tardy in sending their boats for them, insomuch that the regiment was obliged to march and countermarch the marshes, to keep the men in motion until the evening; for they were above ancle-deep in mud and water, besides being exposed to the inclemency of very tempestuous weather.

About two o'clock in the morning of 14 October we got under way, with the advantages of wind and tide, which rendered it pleasant sailing; between eight and nine, made the opening or entrance of Annapolis river, which is about half a mile over; the current here is very strong. Upon the entering of the headmost ship several signal shots were fired, in the woods on the larboard-side, by the enemy who are watching our motions and reconnoitring our force; about ten we came to an anchor, in a spacious fine bason, off Bear Island; here we met the *Enterprise* man-of-war of forty guns, stationed in this river for the safety of the fort, at the distance of twelve or thirteen miles. This bason at the broadest part is about four miles over, but it is not uniformly so; for in other places it is not above a mile as you approach Goat Island, and then the river narrows to the fort, to the breadth of about twelve hundred yards; and shrinks from that upwards, to half a mile. On each side we see the ruins of habitations, and extensive orchards well planted with apple and pear trees, bending under their weight of fruit; beyond these are dark, thick woods, and high mountains all round. The garrison not being quite ready to receive us, we remained at anchor until the morning of the 15th, weighed between nine and ten, and worked up to the quay in less than four hours; we found the *Success* at anchor in the road. We landed our baggage on the 16th, and the six companies disembarked and marched into quarters, where there are tolerable barracks both for officers and private men.

The principal orders, which the commanding officers of the forts and garrisons in this province have received from the governor, are, 'That, in case either should be attacked, they are reciprocally to reinforce and assist each other'. How this can be complied with, I own I am at a loss to conceive; for there are no roads through the province, which is in general one continued rude wilderness, abounding with innumerable rivers and impassable swamps; and these garrisons are an incredible distance from each other; the only communication then must be by water, which for some months of the year is bound up with frost; but, if that was not the case, we have neither sloop, schooner, galley or barge on this river, whereby we might even transmit an express upon any pressing occasion; there are two or three old crazy canoes on the shore, of little or no use; nor are there any vessels stationed at any of those forts, except a province sloop and schooner, one of which is, for a few months of the summer season, at Fort Cumberland, who makes two or three trips back and forward to Chebucto and, for form's sake, looks into the bason of this harbour; but her principal station, and the schooners', is at Halifax, whence they serve as runners to Boston, or elsewhere, for intelligence, or on any emergency.

The old garrison embarked for Halifax, and with them two Indian captives, a brother and sister, who passed by the names of Clare and Anselm Thomas; they are of the Mic-mac nation; she is comely and not disagreeable; her complexion was not so fair as the British, nor yet so dark as the French in general are; her features were large, with sprightly black eyes, hair of the same colour, thin lips and a well-shaped nose; I believe she may be about twenty-three or four years of age, not taller than five feet five inches; somewhat Dutch-built, but was very sprightly, and had much of the French in her manner and behaviour. Their family have been converted to (what is commonly called) Christiantity, as may partly appear by their names, but I have a stronger reason for this suggestion, by their having crucifixes; Clare had one of silver, that hung down from a large bunch of beads which she wore about her neck; Anselm's was made of wood and hung by a leathern string from a button-hole of his coat; their cloathing they got from the officers of the garrison, except a turban the female had on her head, and a pair of paltry pendants from her ears: these, I am told, were her own.

When I first went into the room where they were confined, the sister rose up from her seat, approached me eagerly, and saluted me after the French manner. The brother, who was neither so fair nor so tall, came towards me in a fearful skulking manner, grasped one of my hands, and shook it with great emotion, accompanied with an unintelligible jargon: he was a mean-looking fellow, not so sprightly as the other; yet he was well proportioned, and seemed to be active, but he had not the engaging openness of countenance of Clare, nor could I discern the smallest resemblance between them. These Indians were not very talkative; I spoke to them in French, and they answered me, but what they said was so low and thick that I could not understand them; I am told their language was a mixture of their own mother-tongue and of French; in a second visit, which my curiosity led me to make them, Clare made a sign to me for pen, ink and paper; these I accordingly procured for her, and she instantly filled one side of it with a writing, or characters, which are to me unintelligible; I have it now before me and, though there are some letters in it apparently similar to part of our alphabet, yet it is utterly impossible to make any discovery from it.

Some months ago this man and woman, with two other brothers, came to Mayass Hill [Maillard's Hill] within a mile of the garrison, under a flag of truce: an officer with an interpreter were immediately sent out to inquire their errand, and to invite them in, which they accordingly accepted of. They said—'they belonged to a settlement at Pan-nook [Penhook], in the country of Lunenburg (which lies to the eastward of us, about three or four and twenty leagues) and that they were sent by their father to treat in behalf of their family and the rest of their tribe; that they were desirous of burying the hatchet and becoming true friends to the English, with whom they now hoped to put a final period to all animosities; and, if we did not chuse to trust and employ them as allies, prayed that they may be reputed and treated hereafter at least as neutrals'. So eager were they to be confided in, that Anselm and Clare voluntarily proposed to continue here as hostages, while the other brothers should go to Pan-nook, for their father and one or two other chiefs of their nation, the better to convince the English of their sincerity.

Having got a favourable answer and reception, the two brothers accordingly departed from the fort with some trifling presents, and directed their course towards Lunenburg, in order to procure, through the channel of some acquaintances they had there, a British escort to conduct them either back to this garrison or to Halifax: in their journey they called at Pan-nook and, upon their favourable report to their father, he and two other chiefs accompanied them towards the German settlement before-mentioned; but unluckily, in their march thither, they were way-laid by an accidental party of our people, who knew nothing about them, nor the errand they were going upon; in this affair the father of Anselm fell; the rest betook themselves to flight, and the party not pursuing immediately, as they did not yet know the number of the Indians, gave the old chief time to recollect himself and escape also. This had such an effect on the Sachems and their companions, who concluded it to be the result of treachery, that they thought it in vain to renew their sollicitations and (no doubt vowing revenge at a proper season), persuaded that the English were a faithless people, they resolved to return to their habitations and remain quiet until they should hear the fate of Clare and Anselm.

These circumstances being yet unknown to the commanding officer here, except an imperfect account brought, within this fort-night, by a sloop from Fort Edward in this province, viz. that a scouting party of the enemy had been way-laid near Lunenburg; that one old man was killed (this was supposed to be the father of these captives) whom the rest carried off before our people could venture upon a pursuit, etc and, the two brothers not returning pursuant to their promise, it was concluded they must have been the suspected enemy, and therefore it was resolved that Anselm and Clare should be detained and brought to Halifax, there to be disposed of as the governor should think proper.

As I was very particular in my description of these savages, I thought it necessary to account for the manner in which they fell into our hands. The detachment we relieved here was commanded by a captain, and consisted of eighty effective men, besides artillery-men, to the number of ten, including their officer, who is a lieutenant. They made a very shabby appearance (I mean the infantry) and did not trouble themselves much about discipline, nor were they regularly cloathed; their officers seemed to be a good deal ashamed; but I think great allowances should be made for troops, situated as they were, who were worn out with hard labour and watching, and who rather looked upon themselves in the light of slaves or, at best, of rangers doomed to perpetual banishment. The regiments stationed in Nova Scotia have suffered much in all respects by their long confinement in this province, and their being subdivided (the very bane of discipline to a corps) into small detachments to garrison so many different places; but, at length, by the arrival of an army this year at Halifax, the appearance, as well as regularity, of these European troops, and the out-parties, from the other regiments, being relieved and called in, raised an emulation among them immediately, upon their junction: they gradually improved, soon discarded the ranging party coloured cloathing, and re-assumed the air and spirit of expert regular forces. There is nothing can be more prejudicial to his majesty's service, and it can be no advantage to the mother-country, in many respects, to suffer troops, or people in public employments, civil or military, to reside long in any of those remote garrisons or countries; I could point out some judicious reasons in support of these sentiments, but it is no longer requisite; they are, or seem to be, at this time (*Anno* 1768) obvious to the ruling powers, and wiser measures are now adopted.

I must, however, intreat the reader's patience to attend to what I am going to relate, as it is not altogether foreign to the subject, and, I have been frequently assured, is matter of fact. There is an old French gentlewoman here, of the Romish persuasion, whose daughters, grand-daughters and other relations have, from time to time, intermarried with officers, and other gentlemen of this garrison whereof some of the former's were of respectable rank; the ladies soon acquired an influence, the spirit of the soldier and the characteristic of a good officer were gradually changed, and succeeded by rusticity; the women, in short, did as they pleased, provided they would indulge their good natured husbands in a pipe and a chirping glass extraordinary in the evenings.

The private men, whether on guard, or employed, at the government's expence, in patching the decayed works of the fort, have been sent for to dig up gardens, or do some other business, for the inhabitants of the town, and, after earning an extra shilling, repaired to a public-house to drown the cares of the day in the seasons of good fellowship, regardless of their duty, or the work they had, perhaps, been engaged at in the morning: if an officer ventured to call one of these delinquents to an account, the answer was, 'I was sent for to finish a job of work for Madam ———'; and, if the soldier was confined, the old gentlewoman ordered him to be released by her own authority, which was deemed sufficient, and no farther inquiries must be made into the matter. I am also assured that this good lady has actually presided at councils of war in the fort, when measures have been concerting to distress the common enemy, her good kindred and countrymen. The simple relation of these matters now a-days, appears very extraordinary: but, I believe, I may venture to assert that they are no less to be relied on.

I called at this gentlewoman's house one morning soon after we had been settled, and, seeing a young man in blue cloaths, with a soldier's hat and lace on his head, I supposed he was an officer's servant, and therefore directed my eyes towards him and his hat, to try if he would take the hint; but the poor lad, though in soldier's pay, was an idiot: his father had formerly been an officer of rank in much esteem here, and was married to one of her daughters; she, seeming highly offended at my viewing her grandson so stedfastly, said, 'I might look at him, but she could assure me he was a ———'s son, as good as myself, etc, etc.' I unfortunately replied that I supposed he was the son of a French militia ———' or words to that effect. I cannot describe her wrath at this answer; she could no longer contain herself, and, after venting a great many choleric expressions, she concluded with this speech, *Me have rendered King Shorge more important services dan ever you did or peut être ever shall; and dis be well known to peoples en authorité.* To which an officer, who accompanied me, answered, *Very true, Madam; I suppose it was in council.* He was going to add something more, but the lady grew so outrageous that we found it was time to decamp. All measures, however, in consequence of these connections, have been long since changed by deaths and removals; I shall therefore proceed to a description of this famous fortress, which has had the honour of being, if not under the jurisdiction, at least the influence of this sage and able female counsellor.

Annapolis Royal is of a quadrangular form, and stands on an artificial height, which, with the ramparts, are raised by loose sandy earth faced with timbers; it is situated close to a pleasant river, which takes its name from the garrison, and lies S E of the entrance leading from the Bay of Fundy, at the distance of somewhat better than four leagues. It has four bastions or batteries, one at each angle; it has one gate, a draw-bridge and two barriers, with a fosse, a covered way and a good glacis; the curtains, to the east, west and south, are flanked by ravelins or half-moons; and to the north, by the river; with the town running eastward along the shore, which is protected, at the upper extremity, by a blockhouse, built on a peninsula called Hog Island; and on the S S W stands another, leading to the country, to prevent any surprise on that quarter.

Under the north curtain, on the level of the covered way, is a barbet battery faced with brick, and well situated; it mounts six twenty-four pounders pointed down the river, and a thirteen-inch mortar; behind this battery, in the ditch, stands the powder magazine, whose communication with the garrison is by the sally-port. The fosse, or ditch, which is dry, is very broad and of a proper depth, in the center whereof, between the scarp and counterscarp, stands a wall of palisadoes ranged close together. The garrison mounts about thirty pieces of cannon, mostly twelve and nine pounders, with some smaller ones, and several mortars of different calibers; but the works are in a ruinous condition, there are no communications between the body of the place and the ravelins: these last seem to be entirely neglected; and the timbers that face the scarp of the ramparts are so decayed that they, as well as the sandy foundation, are gradually mouldering away.

The works were formerly much more extensive, but it was found necessary to demolish some, in order to render it more compact for the small force which could only be spared to garrison and defend it. Within the fort, besides the barracks, some of which are much out of repair, are arsenals, store-houses, work-shops, an armoury and a new building, not near finished, which is intended for a casemate to contain 300 men. I dare say a draught of this place, thrown into perspective, would appear very respectable, but I am sorry I cannot say it is so in reality. A stranger would naturally expect, on coming here, to see a complete fortress and a better town—if he considers that Annapolis Royal has been in the possession of the British crown since the year 1714, when it was ceded to us by the treaty of Utrecht. The houses of the village (for it does not deserve the name of a town) are mean, and in general built of wood; and, though it is much inferior to Halifax, the inducements to settle here, with respect to the country about it, are infinitely greater; there is a good deal of clear ground here, within view of the fort, which, however, at present lies disregarded, as it can neither be cultivated, nor even converted into pasturage, in safety: on the opposite side of the river, and on the SSE and SW quarters the lands are high and covered with dark thick woods; but on the west side of the fort, beyond a small rivulet called Allen's River, are the ruins of settlements and regular planted orchards.

Our new garrison consists of the six companies of the 43rd regiment, amounting to about four hundred and fifty men, all ranks included; a fort-major, a lieutenant of the Royal Artillery, a bombardier, two gunners and ten matrosses. There is also an engineer here, who with the artillery officer (generally a lieutenant fireworker), a clerk of the cheque and a store-keeper, form a board or committee, and constitute the civil branch of this garrison: they derive their authority from the respectable Board of Ordnance at home; and under their inspection are the works, barracks, arsenals, stores of various kinds, armoury, and the superintendence, as well as payment, of all the artificers, and others employed in the king's works, in like manner as in all his majesty's other forts and garrisons: besides these gentlemen before-mentioned, there are about fifty men fit to bear arms, composed of inhabitants and a few artificers who are in constant pay.

A detachment of one captain, two subalterns and 126 rank and file, with serjeants and drummers in proportion, are ordered to be in readiness to embark in sloops hired for that purpose, to proceed down the river to a place called Fort Faggot, to cut fire-wood for the garrison: the men are not to be relieved until they have done cutting, but the officers will be relieved every week; the men are to be paid at the rate of two shillings *per* cord, and to be allowed rum every day at his majesty's expence. Hitherto, when the troops in garrison were few in number, they were supplied with this article from Boston, and other parts of New-England, at the rate of thirteen, fourteen and fifteen shillings currency (of this province) *per* cord, which was brought here by sloops and schooners; this circumstance would scarce gain credit in Europe, when people are told at the same time that the forts and garrisons in this province are surrounded by forests of all kinds of excellent wood, fit for fuel: but then it also remains to be told that, though we are said to be in possession of Nova Scotia, yet it is in reality of a few fortresses only, the French and Indians disputing the country with us on every occasion, inch by inch, even within the range of our artillery; so that, as I have observed before, when the troops are not numerous, and cannot

ANNAPOLIS ROYAL

venture in safety beyond their walls, the necessity of importing fire-wood from other places appears obvious.

The officer of the guard having demanded candles for his own and his men's use, it was a matter of great surprise to the fort-major, who declared that, in the many years he had been in office here, there never was a candle asked for before, for that the officer of the guard usually passed his time, when on duty, in his own quarters or else-where in the fort; and that, moreover, there was no fund to supply that contingent; but the commanding officer convinced the fort-major (who was a reasonable, genteel man) of the necessity of candles upon guard, and assured him he should expect the duty of this garrison to be executed very differently, in future, from what (by his account) it had usually been. Accordingly three candles, of about twenty to the pound (the price of this article, here, was from eight-pence to ten-pence *per* pound), were produced, which were insuffi-cient, but, upon complaint being made, proper lights, and more of them, were soon after granted (as is customary in all other countries) as well to the main guard as the block-houses.

Some horses, which the enemy stole from the inhabitants of this place last summer, appeared, on Mayass Hill, near two miles from hence (this eminence is the utmost limit of our clear, open ground south of the fort); two or three officers, with a serjeant and twelve men, went out to intercept their retreat to the woods; but they were so shy and wild, that the party found it impracticable; so they returned without them.

Another party of volunteers, consisting of officers and soldiers, seeing the horses before-mentioned return to the hill, went out in the afternoon, divided themselves and, after some coursing, got between them and the woods; whereupon a few signal shots were discharged by the rabble under their cover, and they set up a hideous shout; as the party approached the garrison with their prize, two of the enemy appeared on the skirt of the wood and fired their pieces, hoping thereby to draw our people after them into a snare; but the officers having, at their setting out, received positive orders to keep clear of the forests and thickets, they returned with their booty, being eight in number, and drove them into the fort.

The inhabitants came the following day to the commanding officer, claimed, and made a formal demand of, the horses brought home yesterday; the officers, being immediately sent for, transferred their right to the soldiers of the party, and the colonel was desirous that some small gratuity might be given to the men, to encourage them to go on such kind of services hereafter; especially as these

D

claimants acknowledged they would not have ventured themselves for their horses without a good party to sustain them (because they have had frequent experience of the enemy skulking in hollow ways, and under the sides of banks near to the hill, for several days, to take a scalp or a prisoner); at length the colonel, seeing the honest burghers would neither pay salvage, nor reward the men in any respect, gave them up their horses that there might be no room for preferring a complaint against an officer or soldier under his command.

The garrison contracted with a merchant to supply them all this winter with beef and mutton at four-pence *per* pound; pork and veal (as long as the latter can be got) at six-pence; milk, which is a scarce article, we pay for at the rate of three-pence *per* quart, and eggs from eight-pence to one shilling *per* dozen; the want of soft bread is supplied by sea-biscuit from the stores; these we soak in water, then divide them and lay them before the fire to dry or toast; we have no butter except what we are supplied with also from the stores, which is generally very rancid, notwithstanding it undergoes various operations to render it eatable: wine and spirituous liquors are not unreasonable, and in general much better (because free from adulteration) than in England.

On 3 November, all the men off duty were sent to the orchards eastward of Mayass Hill, for a quantity of apples for the garrison; two captains, a lieutenant, two ensigns and our chaplain went as volunteers, and obtained a covering party which, with town's-people, artificers, etc. completed our command to about fifty armed men; as soon as we passed the barrier, a corporal and six men were advanced to scour the country. After we had reached the orchards about three miles from the fort, the covering party were ranged in such manner as to prevent any surprise, while the rest filled bags, haversacks, baskets and even their pockets with fruit; a most grateful treat to our poor soldiers in particular, so long accustomed to a salt diet, without any vegetables. After we had sent these men back to the garrison with their agreeable lading, the armed party divided themselves into two separate bodies to take a tour through the country for a few hours; our plan was to pursue different routes, mutually promising to come to each other's assistance in case of being attacked: we agreed to meet at a particular place by the river-side, which our guides had fixed upon; and the first who should reach this rendezvous were to whistle three times and wait a reasonable space for the other; and, if the whole should not unite in half an hour, the division that should reach first were to cut three large notches in a tree with a hatchet, then return to the orchards and wait until the remainder should join, marking, at different places, a tree to serve as a beacon or guidance to the others.

Accordingly, one division directed their course by the river-side, keeping however under cover, while the other struck into the country to the southward. After we had reached the appointed rendezvous, which is computed about eleven miles from Annapolis, the signals were made, but no answer returned; we even waited long beyond the appointed time, and made several kinds of noise, yet had no prospect of our companions; two of the artificers, contrary to orders, fired at some ducks (which, being killed on the water, were carried down with the current) and the great reverberating report of these two shots was not even productive of any signal on the part of the rest of our detachment; so that we returned to the orchards by the same way that we had before taken, following our own marks we had left on the trees. We posted a few sentinels, and then made fires to warm us; but it was near two hours before the other division rejoined us, and, through some mistake of their guide, who had bewildered himself in those forests, they were not able to make the appointed rendezvous.

Upon our junction we compared notes; the river party saw some tracks of horses, and found some ordure quite fresh, which appeared to be human; however, from various circumstances, we rather believed it to be that of a bear, to which it is said to have some resemblance. The division who had directed their course to the southward saw no tracks of man or beast, neither did they hear the two shots that were fired, nor any other noise; their guide seemed shy every step he took, from which they concluded he was frightened, and thereby misled them. The French have been at great pains here in clearing and planting these orchards, and, indeed, finer-flavoured apples, and greater variety, cannot in any other country be produced; there is also great plenty of cherry and plumb trees; but the fruit were either gathered, or had rotted and fallen off. These people have left large patches of clear ground, with tufts or small patches of spruce trees at certain distances, which in winter, or bad weather, served their cattle for shelter, and now themselves for ambuscades, when they are disposed to way-lay our people; the branches of this tree are large and bushy, forming a thick cover: there are various kinds of it, some whereof grow up into timber, and others are dwarfish; this last species is that which favours their barbarous stratagems, being as impenetrable to the eye as a brake of furze.

We met with the ruins of several habitations, and many vestiges of industry; where the country was cleared, the soil appeared to be tolerably rich and good, and the grass inconceivably long, with great plenty of it, though very coarse. Upon the return of the first division to the orchards, for they lie in sight of the fort, the soldiers off duty were again sent out with sacks and a pair of horses, which we loaded and returned to our garrison by a different route from that we had taken in the morning, wherein we found some difficulties, such as swamps, thick underwood or brush etc which, together with a violent snow that fell at the same time and beat in our faces, soured our excursion and rendered the latter part of the day disagreeable and very fatiguing.

On 13 November arrived the *Swift* schooner from Halifax, last from Fort Cumberland; the master informs us that a few nights ago a party of French and Indians came down and cut away a sloop that lay at anchor in the creek at the head of the bason; she was about sixty tons burden; that there were only a man and boy on board when the enemy came and took possession of her, they being asleep in the cabbin: that they worked her up Chepordie river; but, being immediately pursued both by land and water, by a vigorous sally of regulars and rangers from the fort, the rabble set fire to and abandoned her; the party came up with her before she was much damaged, and had time to save some sugars and other articles that lay in casks in the hold. About two hours before this happened, Mr Arbucle, the master, carried on shore twelve hundred dollars he had brought for the subsistence of the garrison.

As this is neither the first nor second act of this kind that has happened since we recovered that part of the country, it is surprising some effectual means are not taken to prevent such flagrant insults; for, if the enemy were to become masters of a trader or two, they would in a short time reduce Fort Cumberland to great streights; a good block-house with a couple of guns erected on a convenient spot (of which there are many) and surrounded with a stout palisado work, would prevent such accidents for the future, be a great defence to the inhabitants, and also contribute much to the safety of their cattle when turned out upon the marshes, this creek being very little short of an English mile from the garrison. We likewise learn that, since we left that place, the enemy have been so troublesome as to appear in small parties of two or three, in different places round them; that the rangers are always sent out when they have the impudence to shew themselves; but, as it is impossible, by the situation of that place, to make a detachment from the fort without their knowledge, there is no coming up with them; for, before they can reach the skirts of the wood, the rabble may be at two miles distance.

The wood cutters and covering party returned on 22 November to the garrison from Fort Faggot, and made as droll and grotesque an appearance as a detachment of Hungarian or Croatian irregulars, occasioned by the length of their beards, the disordered shape of their hats, and the raggedness of their party-coloured cloathing; for some had brown, others blue watch-coats (buckled round their waists with a cartouch-box strap) and some were in their threadbare uniforms; in short they had very little of the British regular about them, and it could not be otherwise, the kind of service whereon they had been employed duly considered; but I have said enough on this subject before, respecting troops long stationed in this province, who must in a great measure lay aside the uniformity of the clean, smart soldier, and substitute, in his stead, the slovenly, undisciplined wood-hewer, sand-digger and hod-carrier.

A sloop arrived the following day from Boston with stores; by whom the colonel has received an order that the officers and men must be provided with all manner of camp equipage and necessaries by the first day of March next. This affords great pleasure, as it opens to us a prospect of being relieved and going upon service with the army, the ensuing campaign.

We see frequent fires, on the north side, in the woods up the river. The *Sea Flower* sloop from Biddeford (New England) arrived in ballast, last from Fort Cumberland; he says all is well there; being asked his reason for coming up, as he had no packet or any thing else for us, he replied that, suspecting bad weather and a contrary wind, he ran into the bason and intended to come to an anchor; but, seeing a great smoke in the woods and seven or eight canoes on the shore, he concluded it would not be safe to stay there; herein we see one of the bad consequences of not having a vessel stationed here for the protection of this river.

Six officers and a party of soldiers, all volunteers, amounting in the whole to thirty armed men, went out on 1 December to scour the country; as their route was through the orchards to the eastward of Mayass Hill, we took all the officers' servants and other men off duty, loaded them with apples, and sent them back to the fort; after which, the day being pleasant, we agreed to extend our walk and take a view of the country; we soon got upon the tracks of cattle, which we easily discovered by the snow on the ground; and, when we had marched about five or six miles, we came upon human footsteps: some of them had the impression of a *moggosan* or Indian

53

slipper (moccasin, mockasin, molkasin, morgisson, mogasheen, mackassin, mocsen; in the New Hampshire provincial papers of 1704 the spelling is mockasin.)

The reader is desired to observe, as he will frequently meet with this epithet in the course of this work, that these slippers are generally made of the skin of beaver, elk, calf, sheep, or other pliant leather, half dressed: each *moggosan* is of one intire piece, joined or sewed up in the middle of the vamp, and closed behind like the quarters of a shoe; they have no additional sole or heel-piece, and must be used with three or four frize socks, or folds of thick flannel wrapt round the foot; they are tied on the instep with thongs of the same leather, which are fastened to the joining behind, and run through the upper part of the quarters; they are exceeding warm, and much fitter for the winters of this country than our European shoe, as a person may walk over sheets of ice without the least danger of falling: the meaner sort of French and Indians make them of a tougher and thicker leather, but the heads of tribes, and better kind of French, affect a more gay, dressy sort, with very broad quarters to them, that turn over like the deep or broad neck of a shirt; and this part, as well as the vamp from the toe upwards, is curiously ornamented with narrow slips of red cloath, covered with white, green, and blue beads sewed on in various whimsical figures.

We also got upon the tracks of horses, and found some of their dung before it was cold, and afterwards some pieces of apples indented with human teeth which had not yet changed their colour; from these and other circumstances (needless to be recited) we had reason to think the enemy had discovered us, and were retired to one of their fastnesses: these are generally on a road or path by which they expect their enemy must pass; however we still marched on and, coming soon after upon fresh footsteps of men, we halted our party, animated our soldiers, and charged them not to suffer themselves to be surprised or terrified by shouts or yells: they promised, 'they would not yield an inch, but would stand by us like good soldiers'.

Accordingly we advanced in excellent order, following the enemy's steps to a house or cabbin in the center of a clear piece of ground, about ten miles from the garrison; we found the door was fast and, not seeing any key-hole or other mark on the outside by which it was secured, we naturally concluded that it must be bolted on the inside, and that we had now caught some of the river vermin in their own trap; whereupon we surrounded it, and called to the enemy, in French, to open the door and surrender; but, receiving no answer, we declared we would instantly set fire to it—and immediately one of our men, more impatient than the rest, with some difficulty forced the door and rushed in with his bayonet only in his hand; it is not to be wondered we received no answer to our menacing challenges, for the birds were flown.

It was not a dwelling, but a store-house, and was partly under ground; there were three rows of shelves on every side of it, covered with long wheaten straw on which lay a choice collection of apples; the floor was likewise covered with straw and fruit, which were the best we had met since we came into the country; there was nothing else in the house, except a few pair of wooden shoes and a small vessel resembling an half peck. As soon as the detachment had filled their pockets and haversacks with part of their plunder, we set fire to the house, and only tarried until we saw it past all recovery; while we were thus employed, our guide examined the field and discovered in the snow the tracks of a small party of men, which he followed as far as he could with safety and came back to report to us; he told us he knew which way the enemy were gone; that their route led to a mill, where there was a river, and (to use his own words) 'as wicked a pass as any in the country'.

We consulted whether there was no possibility of taking a tour, so as to come on the back of them in that place? He answered in the negative, the day being so far advanced: so we agreed it would be most prudent to avoid any night-work, and accordingly, directing our guide to re-conduct us by a different path to Annapolis, we proceeded on our return by a lower road, where we perceived many footsteps up and down the country, and three or four scattered huts; these we looked into, but, finding nothing in them, we would not lose time by staying to burn them; we did not meet with any thing remarkable until we had reached the back of the orchards, which was about three miles and an half from our garrison, and SSE of it; and there we discovered in a close thicket an abandoned camp, and from many circumstances they could not be fewer in number than fifteen or sixteen, nor was it long since the enemy had been there, as plainly appeared by the small trees they cut down for fuel; while we were viewing and making our observations, we heard a noise, when immediately a dog barked, and howled afterwards as if silenced by force; this being an advantageous place, we formed our men and stayed above half an hour in hopes they would return to their camp; our guide and three men advanced together about two musket-shots' distance from us, towards the place whence the noise proceeded; and by his account they had been lately here, for he saw their tracks every-where, and was persuaded they had withdrawn themselves either to increase their numbers, or in the hopes of decoying us after them to a place where they thought they might give us a *coup de surprise* with greater safety; this not being improbable, and the evening drawing on a-pace, we repaired to the fort without any accident or other remarkable occurrence; we found all our friends uneasy about us, as we had been expected to dinner; and, had we continued out much longer, a detachment was to have been sent in pursuit of us.

Upon finding the enemy still numerous in Nova Scotia, for I always apprehended they, or the greatest part of them, had been seized and sent out of the province, I was naturally induced to make some inquiries on that subject; and the only information I could receive was that forty-eight families, who formerly resided and were well settled on this river, had retired with their effects to the mountains and other inaccessible places, to wait the event of the war; they were generally reputed neutrals, and were assured that, if they would take the oath of allegiance to his Britannic Majesty, and swear neither to assist, traffic nor correspond with the French, their allies or the subjects of France in Canada, they should not be molested; but this they obstinately declined, whereupon, fearing compulsion might be used, or rigorous measures taken with them, they thought it safest to withdraw; and now, in order to procure a livelihood, they are obliged to have recourse to robbing and plundering, and the Governor-General of Canada has taken them under his protection by placing an officer among them, supplying them with arms and ammunition, and rewarding them for scalps and prisoners.

On 6 December, a party of soldiers and artificers went over the water to cut some wood for firing; they had no covering party, as it was not conceived the enemy would presume to molest them within the range of the cannon of the fort; about twelve o'clock, when they were refreshing themselves at dinner, they were surprised by a party of Frenchmen who posted themselves on a rising ground and fired at them; there were not above three or four of our people that had arms with them, who precipitately betook themselves to flight towards the water-side, the ground being there clear and open; one of our best grenadiers was killed on the spot; six men were made prisoners with Mr Eason, the master-carpenter of the garrison.

The troops in the fort were instantly alarmed; a captain, two subalterns and seventy men were ordered to go over to the assistance of the party and in pursuit of the enemy; however, there not being any barge, flat or boat on the river to ferry such a number over (for there were only a small whaleboat and an old crazy canoe on the shore), the detachment was countermanded for the present: two officers went voluntiers, and took over with them a serjeant and twelve rank and file; but even this, for want of proper boats, was attended with delay; as soon as they had all crossed the river, they proceeded into the woods and tracked the enemy and their prisoners, some of whom they believe are wounded, for they traced their blood above two miles from the place where the wood-cutters had been way-laid; the officers, being injoined by the colonel not to go too far, returned and brought with them the corpse of the grenadier, who was stripped of every thing except his breeches, but they had not time to scalp him.

The enemy returned to the same place in the evening, fired a *feu de joie*, and set up a shout; whereupon a detachment of two captains, two lieutenants, two ensigns, four serjeants, two drummers and one hundred rank and file, with four guides, were ordered out to scour the country and endeavour, if possible, to cross the river above, not only to recover the prisoners, but also to give a sensible check to the rabble for their insolence; we were reinforced by a captain, an ensign, three young gentlemen cadets, some townsmen and a few soldiers, who all turned out voluntiers, which augmented our command *to one hundred and thirty armed men*: we marched out in the dusk of the evening, and immediately it began to rain, and continued until it was dark, and then it poured heavily for some hours; the darkness of the night obliged us to halt several times until our guides, with an advanced guard, went forward to find out the road, which the thickness of the woods and the obscurity of the night rendered difficult; the rear of our detachment lost themselves and, as soon as they perceived it, one of the officers fired two shots as a signal to halt the van, who had by this time reached the fording-place at Saw-mill-creek (a small river about fourteen yards over), and here, the marsh being spacious and clear, we halted until the whole should join.

It is conjectured these two shots alarmed the country, but there was no avoiding it, and it was a pre-concerted signal: in the space of half an hour the remainder of our detachment came up, and we then waded the creek, which luckily was not above knee-deep, for as this, as well as the main river, is always considerably swelled by the tide of flood, so it would not have been passable at high water, which would have retarded our march and put us to great inconvenience: as soon as we had all crossed over, we halted, to put our men in good order, and then proceeded briskly, the country being open, until we reached Joseen's village, distant about seven miles for Annapolis;

and, finding it impracticable to proceed farther by reason of many trenches and other obstructions in the roads, we retired to an adjacent field, where stood the ruins of an old house and some wooden fences adjoining to it; here it was agreed to lie on our arms until morning. It had hitherto rained very hard, but the weather cleared up by the wind's shifting to the north-east, and it blew fresh with an intense frost, inconceivable for its sudden transition from soft rain and its severity: we did not venture to make a fire, lest the enemy should be farther alarmed; and, as we were all wet and the night so extremely cold that we could not sleep, we refreshed ourselves with victuals and drink, and walked about for the remainder of the night with our arms in our hands.

As soon as the day had dawned, our detachment was formed, and we set forward, directing our course under cover of the woods as much as possible, to avoid being discovered: about nine o'clock we crossed two branches of Barnaby's river, which is about twelve miles from the garrison: the ground leading to the fording-place is high and woody on this side, and very low on the other: the descent is a narrow, winding, steep road, opposite to which, after you pass the river, is a thick orchard inclosed with a fence of boards between five and six feet high: this flanks the pass on the right hand, and the remains of a large saw-mill and offices the left. Here we had some expectations of meeting with the enemy, it being reputed a dangerous pass; for, as the planks wherewith the orchard is inclosed are not laid close by two inches, these spaces would well answer the service of musketry; so that, after we got down the hollow road and passed one arm of the river, a dozen tolerable marksmen within-side of this fence would do great execution among us, while as many more might run down from the thickets which were a little higher up, possess themselves of the precipice behind us, and a fewer number also occupy the old houses to the left, and thereby get the detachment between three distinct fires.

This is so feasible that it would not admit of any doubt of effectual success; and my reason for being so particular, in my description of the place, will be known before the return of our detachment to the garrison; having met with no annoyance here, we vainly flattered ourselves we had stolen a march upon the enemy, and that we should soon surprise them in their settlements either on this or the north side of the main river. We continued our route through very difficult and disagreeable forests, some rough and others swampy; and, about one o'clock, we crossed Renne Forêt bridge, another defilé that afterwards proved fatal to many of our party. We came now upon the tracks of moggosans, and also of some horses, which it was evident, by the snow or sleet that had fallen this morning, were quite new; thereupon we quickened our pace until we arrived at Peter Godet's, about twenty-four miles from the fort; it is the first fording-place called the Freshes. Here it was intended we should cross the river Annapolis, fall upon the enemy's settlements, and return by the road they had taken with their prisoners on the 6th instant; but, from the depth of water and mud, it was not possible.

We saw three horses on the north side, which we were of opinion were those we had traced, and had with their riders swam over the river: finding we were disappointed here, we possessed ourselves of a thicket on an eminence to the right of the road (it being too late in the day to attempt any thing farther, and we had neither halted or refreshed since we left Joseen's Village this morning). This is called Godet's Village. Here we incamped, and indulged ourselves with fires: we made beds of spruce tops laid in a circular form, with a fire in the center, and shaded round the windward side with larger branches: thus we lay after the manner of the Indians. We posted a proper number of sentinels, who were relieved every hour, and the subalterns visited them every quarter of an hour: their orders were to challenge every body, and oblige them to give a countersign, which was Brest, for we too sanguinely flattered ourselves, by intelligence we had received from Boston, that this port and harbour were under British colours.

After we had secured our camp, and rested ourselves, one of the officers and Mr Dyson, our principal guide, with a serjeant and twelve men, were ordered to try once more if they could wade the river, but with no better success than before. In their making this attempt, several signal-shots were fired by the enemy on the opposite side. In the evening we made a third attempt to ford the river, and found it utterly impracticable. In returning through a thicket to the eastward of our camp, we made a prize of thirteen sheep, which we instantly killed and divided among the detachment, reserving only one for the officers and guides, which we roasted after the Indian manner, and afforded us a comfortable repast; but we unfortunately paid dear for it the next day.

As soon as it was light, our commanding officer called all the officers and guides together, and consulted on the measures next to be taken; the result of which was that we should proceed farther up the river, and endeavour to find out a fording-place where we might cross over to the north side: accordingly we marched about six miles higher up, to a place called Bernard Grotet's, alias Peter Bernard's.

Here we hoped to succeed, but we were again disappointed, the river being uniformly of the same breadth as it is opposite to the garrison; and the higher up we marched, the more rapid did we find the current. We took a view of the country, and saw a great deal of clear ground seemingly fertile: we found a neat small painted canoe, which we staved and sent adrift: opposite to it on the north shore lay a more ordinary one, with many tracks of human feet on the mud at both sides. Here we consulted again about our farther operations; and, upon inquiry, we discovered that the detachment had neither bread, rum, wine nor any other refreshment, except a few joints of French mutton our soldiers had got in their haversacs; that many of our men were lame and foundered, as were also some of the officers, and the whole command exhausted with the preceding day's and two nights fatigue. Under these circumstances it was resolved to return homewards.

Our guides, being examined about the situation of the country and roads, declared they were as great strangers to these parts as ourselves, and that they had never been so high up before. Moreover, that they knew of no road, nor would they undertake to reconduct us to our garrison by any other than that which we had taken. This being the case, and we now above thirty miles from Annapolis, there was no room for hesitation, or time to delay: so we resolved to return. Three horses were picked up in our way, and we marched about ten miles unmolested, which brought us to René Forêt river, a most dangerous pass, about twenty miles from the fort.

Here we were suddenly attacked with a dreadful shower of ball and buck-shot, seconded by as horrid a yell as ever I heard. This, with our commanding officer's being shot dead on the spot, and all our advanced-guard (except three or four) cut off, who had got over the bridge, threw our men into some confusion, and made them fall back, repeatedly crying out, *Retreat to the plains*. This we were compelled to submit to as they were not above an hundred yards behind our rear, the center of which was still within reach of the adjacent forests, if the enemy had thought proper to follow and line the skirts of them; but this they did not venture to do, contenting themselves with destroying the advanced-guard who were under the bank below them, and shouting all the time according to their custom. When we had reached the plains, or more properly a tract of cleared ground, the next officer in command detached four subalterns with small parties to the skirts of the woods, forming a kind of square; while he, with the remainder in the center, consulted with the guides and the officers who were volunteers about the measures to be pursued in our present dilemma.

These gentlemen and Mr Dyson were not long coming to a resolution, and it was agreed upon to force the pass and dislodge the enemy: whereupon the parties were called in, the whole was drawn up in a rank intire (for hitherto we had marched two deep), and the officers took their posts; but, before we moved off, a trusty serjeant was sent forward to the hollow road, to possess himself of every thing the deceased officer had about him; which he gallantly performed, regardless of the enemy's fire and noise, for they plainly perceived what he was doing, and endeavoured to make him desist; but he persevered until he had got the captain's laced hat, watch, sash, fusil, cartouch-box, pistols, and his purse with nearly thirty guineas in it; all which he faithfully accounted for. This brave fellow, a North-Briton, by name Cockburne, was justly rewarded with five guineas, and the captain's hat.

In this small space of time the officers went from right to left, animating the men; and particularly the commanding officer harangued them very coolly on the occasion. Every thing being now adjusted, and our soldiers, by the example of their officers, in good spirits, we moved forward to force this detested pass, which I shall here describe. 'The enemy lay concealed to the right and left of the road, on a prodigious steep hill covered with trees impenetrable. This hill was on the opposite side of the bridge, and a-head of our line of march: they had a breast-work before them of stones and felled trees; at the bottom was the river, which discharged itself into that of Annapolis, and is between forty and fifty feet broad: over it were thrown, by way of bridge, two planks of timber laid close together, both making eighteen or twenty inches in breadth, so that one man only could go over abreast, and there was no hand-rail. These timbers were supported at each end by by piers of earth and stones, and were elevated about twenty feet above the water. The ground we were on was high, and led with a descent through hollow road to the river-side, where we received the enemy's fire, and there the marsh was flat, clear and open. On both sides of the hollow way were dark thick woods, and the road took a turn to the right with a gradual rising, and three steep steps to the bridge; on the other side, the road inclined to the left, and ran serpentine up the hill, with dark forests on each side,'

Such is situation of this defilé, which our detachment forced their way through about eleven o'clock this morning, in the face of a heavy fire, where a more resolute party of fifty or sixty men might repulse ten times their numbers with inconceivable loss; and this shews that, though the enemy's plan was well concerted, it was ill supported; by the time that the commanding officer, volunteers and guides, with the van, had gained the opposite side of the bridge, there was a little halt or stop for the space of a minute; which they perceiving, called out to their companions, and huzza'd. The officer who brought up the rear answered them; which encouraged our men to advance boldly and pass the bridge, not however without farther loss, as the rabble still repeated their fire. Upon the van's marching up the hill, they saw the enemy sculking and running from the right to the left; whereupon they briskly ascended, followed them into the woods on the left, chased them from their ambush, and gave them a close fire in their flight: by this time the whole had got up the precipice and, when they found themselves in this situation, their ardour to pursue was inconceivably laudable: but the enemy were gone off, we could not tell where; they knew the country, and we were strangers to it.

Therefore the commanding officers halted, to have the men's arms examined, and properly loaded: then consulting farther with Mr Dyson, he gave it as his opinion, in the hearing of the soldiers, 'that since the rascals were gone, they intended to meet us at Barnaby's river and mills (before described), where they would undoubtedly way-lay us a second time, and dispute every inch of the country to Annapolis; that we had better push on and secure that place before them, for that there was no other road for us by which we could return to the fort'. This speech was delivered so clear, with such emphasis, and, as I said before, expressed in the hearing of the men—who had a great opinion of this gentleman in particular, and of our other guides, on account of their knowledge of the country, as well as of the enemy and their peculiar manner of making war—that, after what had already happened, it would have been in vain to think of pursuing other measures; therefore it was agreed to move forward with all expedition, and endeavour to get before the enemy: but, coming to a part of Barnaby's river that branched out in two places, we crossed the left arm of it and forced a road over a steep swampy hill, which, however, was so deep as to take us up to our knees, and it was with difficulty some men could be pulled out of it, even with the loss of their shoes. By this course we shortened our road considerably, and avoided that dangerous defilé at the mills we had so much apprehended.

When we reached Comeau's village, within eight or nine miles of our journey's end, the ground being clear and open beyond shot (or reach) of any thickets, the wounded men we brought with us begged to have a halt, which was granted for half an hour; and, in this interim, we were agreeably surprised with a sight of one of our officers (who had been a volunteer on this unlucky expedition), two guides and eighteen of our soldiers, whom we had given up, concluding they were among the other sufferers at the place of action; this gentleman told us that, seeing these men submit to the influence of one of the guides who headed them, it occurred to him that it was not improbable but a way might be discovered whereby to cross Forêt river higher up and charge the enemy either in flank or rear, while we engaged them in front, and therefore took the command of this party; but, finding it impracticable to succeed, and hearing the fire we made at the bridge, he hastened to our assistance, fought his way over the pass without any loss, after giving the enemy who had returned there two regular fires on the top of the hill to the left; and perceiving, by the loss of blood from some of our wounded men who were able to march with us, that we had directed our course homeward, he made the best of his way after us. We arrived at our garrison, between five and six in the evening, much harrassed (as may be well supposed) after a march of about thirty miles, without any refreshment since the preceding night; we did not meet with the least annoyance, though we nevertheless took every necessary precaution.

Our loss in this expedition amounted to one captain, one serjeant and twenty-two rank and file (six of whom we brought back with us), besides twenty-four firelocks, sixteen bayonets, twenty-three cartouch-boxes, one drum and a number of axes, hatchets, camp-kettles, etc. etc. It is difficult to ascertain what number of the enemy engaged us, but, by the weight of their fire, we conjecture they were not less than forty, or more than fifty; and, from several circumstances, we conclude they may have about twelve killed and wounded. It was an inconceivable mortification to us to leave so many disabled men behind us; but alas! what alternative had we in our present situation? We were not prepared to lie out another night, and we were this day expected at the garrison; we had neither liquor nor provisions of any kind; therefore, under such circumstances and at this rigorous season, it might have proved a matter of some difficulty to keep our soldiers steady, or under discipline: they seemed, from this day's experience, to be fully convinced that they were by no means a match for the rabble in the woods; the opinion of our guides and others who accompanied us seemed to have more weight than any thing their officers could say; so that, in such a dilemma, there was an absolute necessity of returning to the fort as fast as possible, to give our poor fellows time to recollect themselves.

The officers and volunteers exerted themselves as much as men could do, and indeed the generality of the detachment behaved well; some, it is true, were restless and foolish, but they were young, strangers to woods and bush-fighting, and, as this was their first bleeding, every allowance ought to be made for inexperienced soldiers, especially when obliged to act out of their own proper sphere.

A French and English advertisement was put into a tin canister, with two pens and an ink bottle; and the same was tied to a pole with a white flag, and erected upon Mayass Hill; the contents of it were to offer a ransom to two hundred dollars (fifty pounds currency) for Mr Eason the master-carpenter, who was made prisoner on the 6th instant; the enemy are desired to give an answer in six days, conveyed in the same manner, with a red flag displayed instead of white: the commanding officer has passed his word for the punctual payment of the money and the greatest security and honour to the person or persons who shall deliver the prisoner and demand the ransom.

The garrison has been regularly served with spruce beer since our arrival here, which is to be continued; the paymaster of the 43rd regiment assures me that this article brings in a revenue of twenty pounds currency in the space of nine days, which is above 800l. *per annum*; and this is exclusive of what is expended by the officers.

We have had the most whimsical weather that ever was known in any climate; and the inhabitants say it is right Nova Scotia weather; one day it will freeze hard, change towards night and rain incessantly for five or six hours; this is succeeded by snow, and afterwards by frost; let what wind will blow, it rains, snows and freezes alternately from every point: and we are not many hours certain of our weather. Notwithstanding the rigour of the season, the *Gens de Bois* are almost every day hunting and shooting on the opposite side of the river, even within the range of our guns; which sometimes provokes us to give them a shot.

By the end of January the ground is become so slippery that it is dangerous to stir out of doors: the troops, throughout this province, are obliged to have recourse to various expedients to prevent meeting with accidents by falling: some by wearing coarse stockings over their shoes, with an additional sole or two, of thick frize or other woollen cloth; some wear moggosans; and others again use what are by us termed creepers, which are an invention calculated for the hollow of the foot, that buckles on like a spur; it is a small plate of iron an inch broad, with two ears that come up on both sides of the shoe between the ankle and instep, with a stud on each of them, for the leathers: from the two extremities are four stout points turned downward, to the length of two thirds of an inch, which, by the weight of the person who wears them, are indented in the ice; this contrivance is actually necessary, and prevents many fatal accidents.

I think I may say with great truth, I never felt any thing equal to the rigour of this season in February; one would be inclined to suspect that a climate so much upon extremes should not be healthy; however, the inhabitants here are remarkable for their longevity, and it is rare to hear of any person's dying of acute disorders; the reader may observe that we have been in some measure prepared by many almost insensible gradations (as in other northern climates) which usher in the intense and most severe cold. I am credibly informed that there are not any settlements of the enemy nearer than sixteen or eighteen miles to our garrison, and yet these skulking wretches are so amazingly hardy that they scarce pass one day without scouring the environs of this fortress, which they daringly make known to us by their repeated signals, especially upon the arrival, or sailing of a vessel, or of a detachment marching out: there is a sloop that came up to-day, who is bound to Fort Cumberland with king's stores, etc. She has made many efforts to work up the bay, but, from the quantities of floating ice, was as often compelled to put back; at length, finding it impracticable to get there, she steered for the entrance of Annapolis, and came to an anchor in the bason between Goat Island and the Scots Fort; he soon after sent his boat a-shore for some wood and water, and, at their landing, two signals were discharged in the woods very near them, whereupon they instantly took to their boat and returned to their ship: upon their report to the master, he prudently took the advantage of the tide of flood and brought his sloop up to the wharf.

If these rabble could have lain quiet, they might have way-laid the two men, manned the boat and seized the vessel, which would have proved a noble prize; and it could have been accomplished without any danger, for there was only a cabin-boy with the master on board; the consequences of such a capture, which would have put them in possession of this navigation, must have been of the highest prejudice to his majesty's garrison.

A serjeant's party, with two guides, went out in order to take off a dozen head of black cattle that appeared on Mayass Hill; they took the lower road to the orchards, with an intent to get round to the skirts of the wood behind them; but the cattle were soon alarmed and, instead of turning that way to gain the cover, as was expected,

E

they directed their course a-cross a small rivulet called Allen's river,
and got off to the westward; the men could with ease have shot some
of them, but were restrained by the serjeant, in hopes that a more
favourable opportunity might soon offer to surprise and take the
whole: the party returned to the fort without making any discovery,
and reported that they never saw such plenty of hares and partridges
as the orchards and adjoining thickets now abound with.

As I have already more than once observed, that the troops are
obliged to pay extravagant prices for every European article they
have occasion for, I think it will not be improper to particularise
some of them; and, in order to set these matters in the clearest light,
I propose to draw a parallel between the prices here and what I could
have bought the same articles for in Ireland; I would say in Britain,
if I were acquanted with them; but, for several years before I left
Europe, the regiment was upon the Irish Establishment.

| Articles | Prices Currency of Ireland | Currency and Prices } N. Scotia |
|---|---|---|
| Ordinary coarse shirts | 3s. 6d. to 3s. 8d. to 3s. 10d. | 8s. |
| A better kind | 4s. 10d. to 5s. 8d. | 10s. |
| Soldiers' linnens per yard | 1s. to 1s. 3d. | from 2s. 6d. to 3s. |
| Common woollen yarn stockings | 11d. to 1s. 1d. | „ 2s. 2d. to 2s. 6d. |
| Ordinary worsted ditto | 1s. 6d. to 1s. 10d. | „ 3s. 6d. to 3s. 9d. |
| Ordinary cheque linnens | from 10d. to 1s. | „ 2s. 2d. to 2s. 6d. |

Besides the foregoing, they pay here 1s. 10d. per lb. roll-tobacco;
and leaf from 10d. to 1s. Scots snuff from 2s. 6d. to 3s. per lb. Hard
soap from 10d. to 1s. Lump sugar from 1s. 3d. to 1s. 6d. Ordinary
powder 10d. Common brown sugar 6d. Ordinary smoking pipes
from $\frac{1}{2}$ to 1d. each; and a better sort $1\frac{1}{2}$d. to $2\frac{1}{2}$d. each. Dutch pipes
6d. Threads, needles, pins, tapes, flannels, coarse woollen cloths,
nails, bolts, locks, hasps, garden tools, with all manner of haberdashery and stationary wares, bear the same proportions.

We were reduced to great straits in our manner of living, having
nothing to eat, except the store provisions, and sometimes a little
thin starved beef, much inferior to some that I have frequently seen
condemned and burnt publicly in well-regulated market-towns in

Europe. In the times of the greatest plenty, which I have ever seen since I came into the country, a soup made of the king's pease, with a piece of pork in it, composed the principal dish in our bill of fare; and, indeed, we should have made a very indifferent repast without it. Our constant drink, for these two months past, has been spruce beer or bad cyder, qualified with as bad rum: wine we have almost forgot the flavour of; roots, or any kind of vegetables, milk and eggs, we are intire strangers to.

A little before the wooding-party marched out on the morning of 20 March, some of the enemy came to Mayass Hill with a flag of truce, but, the weather being hazy and their flag rather small and ill-coloured, the sentinels did not immediately discern them, which they perceiving, instantly fired two shots. The fort-major then pushed out at the head of the wooding-party with a napkin fixed to a pole, and demanded their business. They seemed shy, and un-willing to trust us; but the major, advancing singly, took off his hat and waved it towards them to advance in like manner into the plain (for as yet they kept among stumps of trees and uneven ground, where our people have been daily wood-cutting); upon which one of them came forward, and acquainted the major that they had not discovered our flag with the canister (which was hung out on the 18th of December last) until yesterday; that the written paper was so defaced, it was not altogether legible; therefore desired to know what it had contained: on being told it was a proposal of two hundred dollars for the ransom of Mr Eason the master-carpenter, whom they made prisoner on 6 December, he answered that he supposed there could be no objection, and requested that the form and terms should be again reduced to writing.

This, he was told, should be complied with; and, upon being ordered to wait for it, and the major's turning from him, he humbly intreated in the name of his party that they might be supplied with some *l'eau de vie* (meaning brandy or rum) and some tobacco, which were accordingly promised. In an hour's time the paper was sent to them, with a basket containing a few pipes, some tobacco, one gallon of rum, some cold meat and biscuit; for all which he seemed very thankful, yet nevertheless answered evasively to the various questions that were put to him. Being asked how soon we might expect an answer, he replied, that their commandant lived a great way from hence; therefore he could not pretend to say when an answer would be returned. We inquired the meaning of the tracks of rackets, which were discovered some days ago near the wooding-place: and he gave us to understand, that, seeing constant fires there, three or four of their people came down, *merely to gratify curiosity*, and to see what we had been doing.

Those whom I saw were a raw, hardy, active yet mean set of fellows, and as meanly cloathed: one of them had a firelock and cartouch-box of the 43rd regiment, and another had a band and bowling to his hat of our soldier's lace. They were asked how they could presume to come before us with our spoils about them? To which, notwithstanding our hospitality, *they gave no answer than an impertinent shrug*. We desired to be informed what they did with all our prisoners, as well the wounded men as the others that were not wounded. To this they replied—'Gentlemen, we have a great way to go, and beg we may be permitted to depart; as to such of your people who have fallen into our hands, we took as much care of them as we have done of ourselves.' So saying, they once more thanked us for our civility, bid us adieu, and retired to the woods.

On 29 March two sail of ships were discovered to cross the bason below and run up Moose and Bear rivers, which being unusual for British ships, a boat that had lately been fitted up was sent down for intelligence, and to watch their motions. The boat returned, and brought up the masters of the two vessels; they came from Fort Cumberland, and are bound to Boston; by them we are informed there is an embargo laid on all the ports of New-England, New-York, Halifax, etc etc; we hear of great preparations for opening the campaign, that there are more troops expected from Europe, and that the province of Massachusetts are raising a large body of provincials to co-operate with the regulars; the masters of these sloops say that all is well at Chegnecto, and also at Fort Edward and Fort Sackville, where they have lately been: these men farther add that it was reported at Boston, *that the particular department of the New-England troops, this campaign, would be the reduction of Canada*; this was matter of great mirth to us, and an officer, who was present, humorously replied, *And let the regulars remain in the different forts and garrisons, to hew wood and dig sand, etc then the French will be finely humbled in America.*

On the morning of 1 April two shots were discharged on Mayass Hill, and a flag of truce was hoisted, upon which the fort-major, with an officer and fifty men, marched out under a white flag: the enemy did not seem so shy as they were on the 20th ult., we demanded of them their errand, and they answered, *They came to know whether we would exchange prisoners with them?* They offered four men for the two Indians, viz. Clare and Anselm Thomas (as mentioned under 17 October last); the persons who appeared to us were the father and brother of the two captives, with a Frenchman; but we could discern there were others in the skirts of the woods, at a distance behind them: the old Sachem was told that we had heard he was dead, being shot by an accidental party of our people, who were ignorant of the particulars of his own and his family's case and resolutions, etc. to which he replied there was sufficient cause for such a rumour, but that he himself was most culpable.

Upon this we interrogated him, and related to him what we had heard of the matter; to which he answered—'It was not so, for he was actually, at that time, with an English party; that he grew diffident of their sincerity, and, being suddenly seized with a panic, he slipped behind them, with an intent to make his escape; that the English turned about and fired at him, which he avoided by falling prostrate on the ground, and from thence he supposed our people might have thought he had been killed.'—This chief appeared to be an honest, chearful, well-looking old man, much resembling his daughter, though of a swarthier complexion: he was meanly dressed, and not at all like an Indian; his son, who had also a good open countenance, was habited quite in character, with a turban on his head, adorned with an extravagant number of beads and feathers of various colours, which these creatures much affect and are very fond of.

They were told that Clare and Anselm were both well at Halifax; upon this they took leave of us, retired to the woods and made fires for themselves; our party returned to the fort. An hour had scarce elapsed, when the enemy appeared a second time on the hill, waving their flag, which obliged the fort-major and his party once more to march out; being desired to answer precisely what business they came upon, the Frenchman (or rather Canadian, which, by the multiplicity of buttons on his coat and his leathern cue to his hair, he seemed to be) replied—'to see if you will barter with us for our furs, and give us tobacco and *l'eau de vie* in exchange'. The major told him we would neither traffic nor carry on any correspondence with his majesty's enemies. We conversed near an hour with them, and the Indians expressed an inclination to come into the fort, and, we believe, would have been prevailed on, were it not for the great influence their French companion seemed to have over them: we inquired if this party did not belong to the same people who came to us on the 20th ult. to treat for Mr Eason? The Frenchman first pretended ignorance of that business, tho' he afterwards contradicted himself, and was obliged to confess it. Colonel James invited these people to come into the fort and surrender, assuring them of generous treatment, adding, 'we have all kinds of provisions and rum, and you shall have the same allowance with his majesty's troops'. Monsieur politely thanked him, said they were in want of provisions, and that he would impart our kind offer to the rest of his friends. Upon their departing, the fort-major, by order, told the Frenchman, 'that at present he and his companions were quite safe, for that we should always pay due honour to a flag of truce; but, for the future, they must not presume to appear on trifling errands, except they should come determined to surrender or to bring Mr Eason the master-carpenter to be ransomed, otherwise they might be assured we should treat them as enemies'; the major farther added, 'that we took very ill their making fires in the woods within the precincts of our garrison, and that it was highly impertinent': to which the fellow replied, 'it was the savages'—and pertly subjoined this old trite evasion, 'we cannot be accountable for the conduct or actions of the Indians'.

The next morning, between eight and nine o'clock, two shots were fired on the opposite side of the river, which attracting the attention of our sentinels, they discovered a large party marching from the woods towards the shore; the officers having dark-coloured cloaks and the soldiers brown watch-coats on them, at the same time the weather being remarkably hazy so that they could not easily be distinguished by the naked eye from the enemy, we were a little alarmed, and the artillery officer received orders to discharge all the guns he could bring to bear on them with grape-shot; but the commanding officer, fortunately coming out with a perspective, discovered them to be an English party, and instantly as his orders were ready to be executed, he countermanded them; the adjutant was immediately sent over, and soon returned with a captain of the 43rd regiment, who, with a lieutenant, ensign and sixty rank and file, had been detached from Fort Edward in order to escort our engineer thither, on his way to Halifax, whence he is to proceed with the army to Louisbourg.

This command left their garrison on the morning of the 28th ult, and the officers compute that they have marched about one hundred and twenty miles; they met with several habitations of the enemy, and about ten or a dozen straggling Frenchmen, in different parts of the country, who, on first discovering our people and so unexpectedly from that side of the province, ran off, as if terrified, and hid themselves: for, such a visit being (I am told) almost unprecedented, they were not prepared, especially as they could not be certain but there might be other detachments out, either before, the better to secure the defilés and thereby reinforce the party; or else behind, in order to execute some secret service, perhaps to their utter extirpation from the country. The Acadians did not appear armed, and the captain, being ordered to make the best of his way to this garrison without any unnecessary delays, took no notice of them, especially as they did not presume to molest him. In point of weather, our visitors were very fortunate; for, before the last of them could be ferried over the river, there came on the most violent storm of snow that ever I saw, which blew about in such clouds that the oldest people here express the greatest surprise at it: before night it was so deep as to obscure our windows, and then our soldiers were all turned out with shovels and lights, in order to make communications throughout the fort and to clear the batteries, sentry-boxes and ramparts; though every man off duty was employed, this was a work of some hours, and, had it been neglected, we should all have been barricadoed in our houses before morning.

We had the satisfaction to receive many European letters by this detachment, being the first since we sailed from Ireland: we learn that General Abercromby is appointed commander-in-chief and is to conduct an army that is to act by the lakes; that Major-General Amherst and Admiral Boscawen are to command an expedition against Louisbourg, and that the Colonels Lawrence, Wolfe, Monckton and Whitmore, are appointed brigadiers upon this service; all the lieutenant-colonels of regulars, serving in North America, are promoted to colonels, in order to give them the rank of the Colonels of militia or provincial regiments: we are farther assured, that one French ship of war, and several transports with troops and stores that were bound to Louisbourg, have been intercepted by Admiral Coates; that Sir Charles Hardy is arrived at Halifax, and Commodore Durell at New-York; moreover that Admiral Boscawen was daily expected at Chebucto with the fleet, on board of which are several regiments from Britain and Ireland.

It is said the Earl of Loudoun is gone back to England, and that Major-Generals Lord Charles Hay and Hopson, with Colonel Webb, will return by the next opportunity.

# III

# Ticonderoga and Louisbourg

*The year 1757 had brought unmitigated military disaster to the British in North America. Montcalm stood triumphant on the headwaters of the Hudson. The western frontier in the Appalachians was harried by Indian raiding parties who murdered settlers and burnt homesteads. Louisbourg stood inviolate at the entrance to the St Lawrence.*

*But the tide of war was changing, imperceptibly as yet. More British reinforcements crossed the Atlantic, bringing the strength of the regulars above 20,000, with a similar number of colonial troops brigaded, trained and equipped, although still of doubtful value. The Royal Navy had at last established command of the sea and Montcalm received scant reinforcements and few supplies. The administration of French Canada was riddled with corruption and this started to tell on the morale of the troops.*

*Britain was still looking for successful generals. The combination of Major-General Jeffrey Amherst and his principal brigadier, James Wolfe, was to succeed in the renewed onslaught on Louisbourg. Abercromby, chosen to force his way up Lakes George and Champlain, led his army to calamitous defeat at Ticonderoga.*

MILD SEASONABLE WEATHER these two days, mornings and evenings raw and cold, with fogs. Yesterday, 22 April, being in company with some of the inhabitants, I was told that, when the French were settled in this town and neighbourhood, though the better sort of them generally behaved with tolerable decency, yet the poorer sort, being employed as servants and workmen, took frequent occasions (which however never passed unpunished) of being impertinent in displaying the fruits of the good education they had received; for, in driving a team of oxen, if an officer, or other British subject, passed them in the street or road, they instantly called out to their cattle by the names of *Luther, Calvin, Cronmere* (meaning Cranmer) etc and then laid most unmercifully on the poor beasts with their whips or clubs, as if they had in reality got these eminent men under their hands.

Some of the transport sloops arrived on the 28th, and the rest, hourly expected, the day following. Mr Proctor, the agent, and Mr Winslow, the commissary, came passengers; by them we are informed that one company will remain at Fort Edward, and the other three, with the like number from hence, are to relieve the 28th regiment at Fort Cumberland, who are to proceed with the army on the expedition to Louisbourg; that three companies are to remain here, and that the major will be sent by the next opportunity to command this garrison. This intelligence is not only a great disappointment, but an unspeakable mortification to the 43rd regiment, *thus doomed to an unsoldierlike and inactive banishment*: the cause of this hard fate, we are told, was in consequence of orders to the commander-in-chief from England, 'that one intire regiment should garrison Annapolis Royal and the other forts in this province'; and his Excellency made choice of the 43rd for this service, on the sole account of their being the most complete as to numbers, and the youngest corps in Nova Scotia.

Three of our companies embarked on 1 May, and fell down the river; the colonel embarked in the evening; he is to command six companies and a detachment of rangers at Fort Cumberland; upon his stepping into the boat he was saluted with eleven guns, according to the custom of most garrisons abroad. Our present force of every rank, including the detachment of Royal Artillery, amounts to two hundred and twenty-five men: and, if occasion should require, we can be reinforced with about seventy artificers and others from the town.

The transports sailed the next day, and the *Hawk* sloop of war came up to the wharf to clean; at ten o'clock this night, as some of the town's-people were fishing in their ponds, they were near being surprised by some of the enemy in a canoe, whom we conjecture to have been laying night lines on the north shore; and, perceiving a light which our people had with them, they had the presumption under cover of a thick fog to make towards it, but were luckily discovered and obliged to put off hastily to prevent an alarm; it is suspected they were desirous to take a prisoner in order to procure intelligence of our present strength, as the sailing of so large a detachment from hence could not escape their vigilance.

Late on the night of the 12th arrived a sloop from Fort Cumberland, with Major Robert Elliot of the 43rd regiment, who is to take the command of this garrison: to-day, at his landing, he was saluted with eleven guns, which were answered by the swivels of the sloop, in which he took his passage. The transports with the 28th regiment came to an anchor in the bason; the wind, being contrary, obstructs their pursuing their voyage. Several representations have been made of the ruinous condition of the fortifications of this garrison, the insufficiency of the number of troops here to defend it, the necessity we are under of sending parties almost two miles off to cut fire-wood, and of our soldiers being obliged to carry it that great length of way, at the risk of their lives; the pressing necessity we are under of forwarding the king's works; and that we have neither flats, boats, barges, schooner or other vessel on the river, by which to protect the navigation; or, if invested, to inable us to detach advice to any other fort or garrison in the province: and, lastly, that our paymaster has not money sufficient to subsist the regiment for the ensuing muster.

We are credibly informed, that upwards of forty letters for the officers and soldiers of the 43rd regiment lately lay at the post-office at Halifax, and the postmaster, not knowing how he should be repaid the postage of them, or where to forward them to, transmitted them back to New-York, by which means it is not improbable but they may all miscarry; it is an unlucky circumstance that some regulation is not set on foot to prevent such disappointments happening to the troops throughout America, and those particularly who are doomed to exile in the miserable fortresses of this remote province. It is well known, that, during the late war in Flanders, there was a postmaster-general to the British army, whose office was always at the head quarters; and all letters, whether forwarded by the packets to Holland, or tranmitted by private ships or otherwise, were regularly sent to the army and duly distributed to the respective regiments; it is almost incredible what sums have been paid for single European letters by officers and soldiers, and the unnecessary extravagant expence that has been incurred by their travelling over almost every part of British America, before they have reached their proper owners.

We are now tormented much by musketa's and a small black burning fly: they give us no quarter either by day or night; if I mistake not, the author of Lord Anson's memorable voyage says, that the musketa's are very troublesome in South America during the day-time; and that they never bite after sun-set: the case is very different in this part of the world, these insects being exceedingly more teazing by night than they are by day. There are a number of birds that fly about here after sun-set, called musketa hawks for their living on and destroying the musketa's; they are of the falcon kind, of a dark grey colour and a little larger than a blackbird; they are numerous, according to the quantity of their prey, and fly so low and steady as to be a good mark to be shot at.

Here follows an extract of a letter from Halifax to our commanding officer, dated 30 May 1758.

'The fleet, amounting to near two hundred sail, sailed on the morning of the 28th instant; before we lost sight of them, they were joined by the *Dublin*, on board of whom was Major-General Amherst, who immediately went on board the admiral; exclusive of the army, there are near *eighteen hundred marines* on board the fleet, which you are sensible will be a good reinforcement to throw into the trenches, after the troops have landed and cleared the way for them. The admiral has nineteen ships of the line, exclusive of the *Dublin*: and the *Devonshire*, with the *Pembroke*, who are in this harbour, will join the fleet as soon as their men recover. There are also nine frigates, two fire-ships and a great number of sloops to assist, as occasion may require; so that we hope we may soon expect to hear good news from the eastward, etc. etc.'

The gardens and the country are now in great beauty; if an European was to visit us at this season, who had never wintered in America, it would be almost impossible to persuade him to credit the extreme length and severity of our winters, and he would be inclined to think all he had heard and read of this climate was fabulous; it is really astonishing to behold the length of our grass and the forwardness of the fruit-trees, as well as of vegetation in general, in the short space of a very few days.

A vessel from Fort Cumberland put in here on 17 June, by her a letter was received, acquainting us that on the 18th ult. three deserters from the enemy came and surrendered there to the commanding officer; they brought their arms with them; one is a Swiss, the second a Hollander, and the third a native of France; they belonged to the regulars, and their uniforms are faced with blue. They report, that they came from the island of St John (near Cape Breton) that their people were starving for want of provisions, and that Monsieur Boishébert was actually gone to Louisbourg with a great number of men from this province; being asked how many, they answered between three and four hundred.

In consequence of repeated reports made by the officers who daily visit the barracks, 'that the soldiers have no bedding to lie on (what they had being worn out), that the windows are in a shattered condition, and the roofs of these caserns are so faulty that the men can scarce keep themselves and their arms dry,' the commanding officer has made frequent representations of these grievances, yet to no purpose: the answer, made by the gentlemen who have the management of these matters here, is to this effect: 'We cannot do any thing without orders from England, the barracks are not worth repairing, they ought to be condemned, etc.'

The detachment here is daily at exercise, nevertheless our time passes away very heavily; and, when the calendar does not furnish us with a loyal excuse for assembling in the evening, we have recourse to a Free-mason lodge, 'where we work so hard that it is inconceivable to think what a quantity of business, of great importance, is transacted in a very short space of time'.

Fresh provisions have been scarce with us for some weeks past, so that, when we are not so fortunate as to take fish, we are reduced to eat salt beef and pork from the stores; a circumstance much more disagreeable in summer than in winter. Our commandant has made a partition of all the clear ground, on Mayass and Babinot's-hills, within the range of the advanced blockhouse; and all hands are now employed in cutting and saving hay, against the arrival of cattle from New-England, for the ensuing winter.

We begin to be impatient for news from the eastward and southward; this morning our major, desirous of taking a view of the country, ordered an officer and thirty men to escort him; we were accompanied by Mr Dyson, and proceeded as far as Saw-mill-creek; we marched out, and returned by different routes; scoured the orchards and all the adjoining thickets without making any discovery, except some horse's dung which was quite fresh: we tracked the horse to the creek, where we could perceive he had crossed over, so that we conclude he was mounted by one of the enemy, who might be detached as a spy to watch our motions, and, having discovered our party, had retired to alarm the country. The orchards abound with apples, pears, cherries, currants and some raspberries; the grass, on these grounds, is not less than three feet in length, though of a strong coarse kind; nothing can equal the beauty and fragrance of the forests at this season, where there are strawberries and other spontaneous fruits in great plenty; the detachment returned, about four o'clock in the afternoon, a little fatigued, for the heat of the weather was intolerable; though of this we cannot complain every day.

On 2 August arrived a sloop from Boston with sheep and black cattle, a most agreeable freight as we have been much distressed for fresh provisions for some time past; several letters were brought by this vessel, among which I received two with the following authentic intelligence:

'Camp before Louisbourg, June 16th
'The fleet arrived safe in Gabarus Bay on the 2nd, 3rd and 4th instant; and, by a perverse series of bad weather, we could not land

before the eighth; which we fortunately effected, after encountering dangers that are almost incredible: we are now intrenching our camp, but cannot yet land any artillery, by reason of the high wind and great swell upon this coast. Brigadier Wolfe (whom, I have heard you say, you remember in Flanders) has performed prodigies of valour, and has, within these few days, taken post at the light-house point, which is opposite to the island battery. To give you my own private opinion, I think General Amherst (whom I have also heard you mention) seems, by his great prudence and steadiness, to be well calculated for the American service; I thank God I am well, and when we have reduced this garrison—which now I make no doubt of, for I think the worst is over—if I am alive and able, shall transmit you, according to my promise, a faithful narrative of all our transactions, etc etc. We hear constant skirmishing in the woods in our rear, between our light troops and the Indians, etc. I have requested an officer of the navy to forward this by the first opportunity to Halifax or Boston.'

My second letter is as follows:

'Fort Edward, 11 July 1758.

'I thank God I can inform my dear friend that I am alive, and that is all; on the 6th instant a division of our army, under the gallant Lord Howe, fell in with an advanced party of the enemy, whom we routed; but his lordship was killed, and is deservedly lamented by every individual. On the 8th we attacked the French army who were strongly intrenched at Ticonderoga, and, after reiterated efforts to no purpose, we were obliged to give way with very considerable loss. The remainder of our army retired to our old camp near Lake George, where we left them; the wounded officers and soldiers were sent off without delay for their recovery, some to this place, and some to Albany, where I received your letter of the 6th of February last, two days before we marched from thence: I have not time, nor am I well able, to say more at present, as I write in great pain from a bad wound I received in my left arm; when I am better, and more at leisure, you may depend on my punctuality in writing you as particular a relation of this unhappy attack as I possibly can.— Adieu.'

By the foregoing sloop we learn from Philadelphia that the forces under Brigadier Forbes advanced very successfully towards Fort Duquesne, and that, from the precautions he takes, affairs are like to go well in that quarter.

On 7 August a breach is discovered in the palisado fence on the lower end of the marsh, contiguous to a place called the French dock, where there appear many tracks of moggosans on the mud: whence we conclude the enemy came last night to steal away our cattle, pursuant to their custom; that place has been their constant rendezvous on such occasions, and the unevenness of the ground favours their scheme, so as to render them unperceived by either of the blockhouses; it is not to be doubted but these fellows saw the supply we received by the last sloop; and, in order to disappoint their views, for the future, a proclamation is issued from the fort ordering all the cattle to be housed immediately upon the first gun firing in the evening.

A schooner arrived, from Boston, on 20 August; by this vessel we had the satisfaction to receive a bag of letters, some from Europe, and others from the southward; but none from the eastward: among those which I got, was the following one from my friend in the commander-in-chief's army, dated Albany, 29 July 1758.

'I scratched a few lines to you on the 11th instant, from Fort Edward, and, as I wrote in great pain, I think it was scarce legible; such as it was, shall be glad to hear it reached you safe: in a few days after I dispatched it to you, my fever abated and I was judged to be out of danger; for some time, however, it was apprehended I should lose my arm; as all my baggage remained here since last winter, I obtained leave to remove to this place, knowing I could be better accommodated here, than in my confined situation at Fort Edward: in my last, I promised you a particular account of our unhappy storm of the 8th instant; it is a mortifying task, but you shall be indulged as I know you are curious after every occurrence.

'It will be needless to have retrospect to any events preceding the 4th of this month, as there was not any thing remarkable, except preparing for the expedition and embarking our provisions, stores and artillery; the latter were mounted on floats or rafts, for the protection of our armament upon the lake and to cover us at our landing. On the 5th, the whole army, amounting to about sixteen thousand men, embarked likewise; our transports were batteaus and whale-boats, and in such numbers as to cover the lake for a considerable length of way, as may well be supposed; we proceeded soon after in great order and, as I was in one of the foremost divisions as soon as we were put in motion, I think I never beheld so delightful a prospect. On the 6th, we arrived early in the morning at the cove where we were to land: here we expected some opposition; but a party of light troops having got on shore, and finding all clear, the whole army landed without loss of time, formed into columns, and marched immediately; upon our approach, an advance guard of the enemy, consisting of several hundred regulars and savages, who were posted in a strong intrenched camp, retired very precipitately, after setting fire to their camp, and destroying almost very thing they had with them; we continued our march through dark woods and swamps that were almost impassable, till at length, having lost our way, the army being obliged to break their order of march, we were perplexed, thrown into confusion, and fell in upon one another, in a most disorderly manner.

'It was at this time that Brigadier Lord Howe, being advanced a considerable way a-head of us with all the light infantry and one of our columns, came up with the before-mentioned advanced guard of the enemy, whom we also suppose to have lost themselves in their retreat, when a smart skirmish ensued, in which we were victors though with some loss; trifling, however, in comparison to that which the army sustained by his lordship's fall, who was killed at the first charge, and is universally regretted both by officers and soldiers; the enemy suffered much in this rencounter, being very roughly handled; and we made many men and several officers prisoners.

'On the morning of the 7th we marched back to the landing-place, in order to give the troops time to rest and refresh themselves, being by this time not a little harrassed, as may well be conceived: here we incamped, got a fresh supply of provisions and boiled our kettles; we had not been there many hours, when a detachment of the army (to which I belonged) were sent off under Colonel Bradstreet, to dispossess the enemy of a post they had at a saw-mill, about two miles from Ticonderoga; but they did not wait for us; for, upon receiving intelligence by their scouts of our approach, they destroyed the mill and a bridge that lay a-cross the river; the latter we soon replaced, and lay upon our arms until the evening, when we were joined by the remainder of the army.

'I wish I could throw a veil over what is to follow; for I confess I am at a loss how to proceed. Our army was numerous, we were in good spirits, and, if I may give you my own private opinion, I believe we were one and all infatuated with a notion of carrying every obstacle, with so great a force as we had, by a mere *coup de musqueterie*; to such chimerical and romantic ideas I intirely attribute our great disaster on the 8th, in which we were confirmed by the report of our chief engineer, who had reconnoitred the enemy's works, and determined our fate by declaring it as his opinion that it was very practicable to carry them by a general storm; accordingly, the army being formed and every thing in readiness, we proceeded to the attack, which was as well conducted and supported as any bold undertaking ever was. But alas! we soon found ourselves grossly deceived—the intrenchments were different from what we had expected, and were made to believe; their breast-works were uncommonly high, and the ground in their front, for a great length of way, was covered with an *abbatis de bois*, laid so close and thick that their works were really rendered impregnable. The troops, by the cool and spirited example of the general, made many eager efforts to no purpose; for we were so intangled in the branches of the felled trees that we could not possibly advance; the enemy were sensible of this and remained steady at their breast-works, repeating their fire, which, from their numbers, was very weighty, and, from a conviction of their own safety, was served with great composure. Such was our situation for almost five hours, when, at length, finding our loss considerable and no prospect of carrying our point, we were ordered to desist and retire.

'The army retreated to the ground we had occupied on the preceeding night at the saw-mill, and the wounded were sent off to the batteaus without delay, where the remains of our shattered forces joined us early on the ninth, and the whole re-embarked, and continued our retreat to Lake George; there we arrived the same evening and incamped. That place is computed to be about thirty miles from Ticonderoga (though I believe it is more) and fourteen from Fort Edward, whither, as also to this town (from which I now write) all the wounded were sent the next day. Our loss is indeed very considerable, as you will see by the inclosed return. The valiant Colonels Donaldson, Bever, and Major Proby, with many other of our friends, I am heartily sorry to acquaint you, are among the slain. So that what we find so feelingly expressed by the poet is here fatally versified. For,

> *How many mothers shall bewail their sons!*
> *How many widows weep their husbands slain!*

What loss the enemy sustained, or if any, it is impossible for us to be able to give the least account of; they did not attempt to pursue us in our retreat. Let me hear from you upon receipt of this packet, and, if any thing should occur in the farther course of this campaign, you shall hear from me again; but I presume, the French general will cut out such work for us, as will oblige our forces to act on the defensive.'

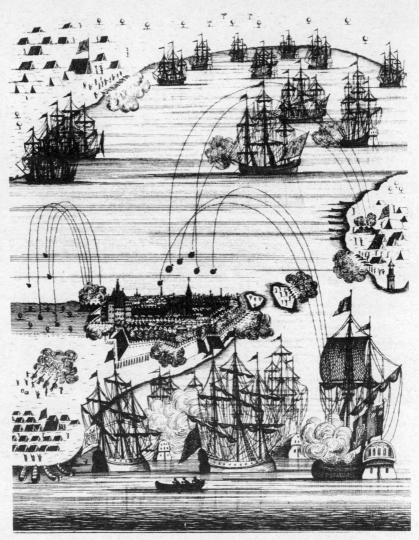

THE BRITISH CAPTURE OF LOUISBOURG

| Loss of the Army before the lines of Ticonderoga, July 8, 1758. | Regulars. | | | Provincials. | | |
|---|---|---|---|---|---|---|
| | Killed | Wounded | Missing | Killed | Wounded | Missing |
| Brigadier-Generals | 1 | | | | | |
| Colonels and Lieut.-Colonels | 2 | | | 1 | 3 | |
| Majors | 4 | 2 | | | | |
| Captains | 5 | 26 | | 1 | 6 | |
| Lieutenants | 10 | 28 | 2 | 5 | 9 | |
| Ensigns | 5 | 9 | | | 1 | |
| Engineers | 1 | | | | | |
| Adjutants | | 1 | | 1 | | |
| Quarter-Masters | 1 | 2 | | | | |
| Serjeants | 14 | 44 | 1 | 4 | 15 | 1 |
| Rank and file and Drummers | 424 | 1005 | 27 | 75 | 206 | 8 |
| Total | 467 | 1117 | 30 | 87 | 240 | 9 |

Total: Regulars and Provincials          1950

Our little garrison are daily employed in cutting wood and digging sand; there cannot be greater slaves than our poor soldiers are here; yet they patiently submit to it, as their officers take their share of the burden, and in hopes of being yet relieved and of joining the army; undoubtedly our lot here is very mortifying, and a natural propensity to variety, peculiar to military men, renders it much more irksome; to this I may add the great scarcity of books for our entertainment, which we often lament; and, in short, the want of more manly employment and rational amusement serves to heighten our discontent.

On 6 September a sloop arrived from Boston and, as soon as she came near to the wharf, the troops and town's-people eagerly ran down to inquire for news: every soul was now impatient, yet shy of asking; at length the vessel being come near enough to be spoken to, I called out—'What news from Louisbourg?' to which the master simply replied, and with some gravity—'Nothing strange'. This answer, which was so coldly delivered, threw us all into great consternation, and we looked at each other without being able to speak; some of us even turned away, with an intent to return to the fort. At length one of our soldiers, not yet satisfied, called out with some warmth—'Damn you, Pumkin—is not Louisbourg taken yet?' The poor New-England man then answered—'Taken! ay, above a month ago, and I have been there since: but, if you have never heard it before, I have got a good parcel of letters for you now.' If our apprehensions were great at first, words are insufficient to express our transports of joy at this speech, the latter part of which we hardly waited for, but instantly all hats flew off and we made the neighbouring woods resound with our cheers and huzzas for almost half an hour. The master of the sloop was amazed beyond expression, and declared he thought we had heard of the success of our arms to the eastward before, and had sought to banter him.

Among the letters that were now handed on shore, I had the satisfaction to receive my wished for packet; but shall postpone any notice of it until I have inserted some extracts of the general orders that were published before the army sailed; at landing; and in the course of the siege, viz.

'Halifax, May the 12th.

'The standing orders of America are to be given to Amherst's regiment, to Anstruther's when they arrive, to the artillery and to any detachments that may be ordered from the fleet, whenever they join the army. The regiments intended to serve upon the expedition against Louisbourg, under the command of Major-General Amherst, are

'The 1st, 15th, 17th, 22nd, 28th, 35th, 40th, 45th, 47th, 48th, 58th, 2nd and 3rd battalions of the 60th, and 78th of Highlanders.

'The Brigadiers-General are Whitmore, Lawrence and Wolfe.

'Lieutenant Isaac Barré, of the 32nd regiment, is appointed a major of brigade to this army . . .'

The fleet and army sailed from Halifax on 29 May, and had the happiness to meet the *Dublin* off the harbour, on board of whom was General Amherst, commander-in-chief of the expedition; after their arrival in Gabarus Bay, his excellency published the following orders from on board the *Namur*, being the admiral's own ship:

'3 June, 1758.

'The army is to land and attack the French in three different bodies, and at three different places. All the grenadiers and detachments of the right wing land upon the right, in the bay, within the White Point. The detachments of the left wing land in two little bays, about a mile and an half to the left of the White Point. The light infantry, irregulars and Highlanders are to land in the fresh water cove, in order to take the enemy in flank and rear, and cut some of them off from the town. Men of war are ordered to each of these places, to scour the coast, and protect the troops at their landing. The grenadiers are to be drawn up, as they lie in their brigades, upon the right of the right attack, and to rendezvous in a line behind a boat with a red flag, in which Brigadier Wolfe will be. The detachments of the right wing are to assemble in a line, as they are in their brigades, behind a boat with a white flag, where Brigadier Whitmore will be. The detachments of the left wing are to rendezvous in the same manner, behind a boat with a blue flag, where Brigadier-General Lawrence will command. The Highlanders, light infantry and irregulars are to rendezvous to the right of the island, lying before the fresh water cove, and to be ready to row into the cove when the signal is given; the signal to row on shore will be three guns from the *Sutherland*, repeated by the admiral. Although the Highlanders, light infantry and irregulars are a separate attack upon the left, yet, when they land, they are to consider themselves as a part of the left wing, and immediately under the command of Brigadier-General Lawrence . . .

'The signal to prepare to land:—A red flag, with a blue cross at the foretopmast-head of the *Sutherland*, and to be repeated by the *Namur*.'

'*Namur*, 4 June

'As the surf is so great that the disposition for landing in three divisions cannot take place, and as the men-of-war cannot be carried near enough to the shore of the bay, within the White Point, to cover the landing there, the general (not to lose a moment's time) has thought proper to order that an attack be made upon the little intrenchments within the fresh water cove, with four companies of grenadiers, followed by the light infantry and irregulars, who are to be supported by the Highland regiment, and those by the remaining eight companies of grenadiers, that no body of men, regular or irregular, may dare to stand a moment before them: these detachments are to be commanded by Brigadier-General Wolfe. The detachments of the left wing, under Brigadier-General Lawrence, are to draw up, as was before ordered, behind the frigates of the center attack, in readiness, if the weather permits, to run ashore upon the opposite beach; or, if not, to follow the grenadiers when it is judged necessary. The right wing to draw up to the right, as in the orders of yesterday, opposite to the bay, that is, on this side of the White Point, to fix the enemy's attention or to follow the troops of the left wing when they shall receive orders for that purpose. The boats of this division are to keep out at a mile and an half or two miles' distance from the land, extending in a considerable length of line.

'As the grenadiers will now assemble towards the left instead of the right, the captains must be attentive to the red flag in Brigadier Wolfe's boat, which is to be the center of their line, and range themselves accordingly. The detachments of the right wing must have the same attention to Brigadier-General Whitmore's flag, and those of the left wing to Brigadier Lawrence's flag, and the whole to assemble at their different posts immediately after the signal is made to prepare to land. The four oldest companies of grenadiers are to attack first; the Royal and Forbes's, under the command of Lieutenant-Colonel Fletcher, in the little bay upon the right; Amherst's and Whitmore's, under the command of Major Murray, in another little bay upon the left. The field-officers and captains of these four companies of grenadiers will receive their particular instructions from Brigadier Wolfe. After the grenadiers are landed and have taken post along the intrenchment, the light infantry are to land, push forward into the wood and force the enemy's irregulars to retire.'

'The enemy's coast was one continued chain of posts, from Cape Noir to the flat point; some works were thrown up, and batteries erected at the most accessible places; all the cover from these intrenchments to the bottom of the bay, was full of irregulars. From the 2nd instant (which was the day the fleet came to an anchor) to the 7th inclusive, they were reinforcing their posts, strengthening their works, cannonading and bombarding our ships, and making every preparation in their power to oppose the landing. The enemy, at first, behaved with great steadiness, reserving their fire until the boats were near the shore, and then poured in upon them with all their cannon and musquetry; they were commanded by Monsieur Colonel St Julien. At the landing, two captains, two lieutenants and seventy French grenadiers were made prisoners; and the general reaped some advantage by the garrison's cannonading our troops in their pursuit, as they thereby pointed out to him the distance whereby he could incamp his army with safety from the range of their artillery.'

I shall now proceed to the contents of my long-expected packet, with my correspondent's account of that important expedition.

'Louisbourg, 30 July 1758.

'I have the happiness and pleasure to transmit to my old acquaintance the agreeable news of this fortress, island and dependencies having surrendered to our arms the 26th instant; and, as I know you are compiling a Journal, I herewith, pursuant to my promise, inclose you some particulars of the siege, and the principal terms of the capitulation, for that work; which I hope, at some time or other, to have the perusal of. I had the pleasure to write to you, on the 16th of June; but, as I have never since laid eyes on the midshipman who had it in charge and promised to forward it, I despair of your having received it. This has been the work of several days, and I have not time to send you any returns, except that of our loss during the siege; or to subjoin any thing more at present, being much hurried.—I thank God I am in perfect health, though greatly fatigued; and therefore request my friend will excuse me.—When more at leisure, or if I remove hence, you shall hear from me again; I hope the papers that accompany this letter will fully answer your purposes, and I shall be happy, ctc etc etc.

'We had variety of weather, and generally very unfavourable until the sixth of June, on which day it was intended the army should land at a place which General Amherst and our brigadiers had before made choice of: for this purpose the signal was thrown out and the troops got into their boats; but, the wind rising soon after with a prospect of angry weather, at the same time a lumpy sea running with a very frightful surf on shore (rolling many degrees worse than you and I have seen it in Yarmouth Roads or elsewhere) and a fog at the same time thickening, it was not thought practicable to disembark at that juncture, and we were all ordered back into our ships.

'The weather continued obstinate until the morning of the eighth, when we were again ordered into the boats, the swell being abated, and the wind more moderate; the frigates at the same time edged in shore to attack the enemy's intrenchments and to cover the landing. After the ships had been some time engaged, a signal was made for the troops to put off, and they rowed up and down, making feints, as if intending to land in different places and thereby divert the enemy's attention from any one particular part of their coast: this in a great measure answered our wishes, and Brigadier Wolfe (whose flag-staff was broke by a swivel shot) pushed ashore, with his detachment, under a furious fire, and landed upon the left of the enemy's works, then briskly engaged and routed them; the remainder of the army followed the example without loss of time, landing almost up to their waists in water. The ardour of the troops, in this enterprise, is not to be conceived nor parallelled; many boats were destroyed, and several brave fellows drowned: yet our whole loss at landing, I am well assured, did not exceed one hundred and ten men of all ranks, killed, wounded and drowned.

'The enemy fled with great precipitation, and Brigadier Wolfe pursued them almost to the gates of the town, with the light infantry, rangers, Fraser's Highlanders, and the grenadiers of the 1st, 15th, 17th and 22nd regiments. I can only account for the unsoldier-like behaviour of the enemy on this occasion, by their apprehensions, perhaps, of being cut off from the garrison by some or other of the divisions whom they suspected would land elsewhere for that purpose; and of being thereby hemmed in between two fires: they were very well intrenched in a circular form round the cove, were numerous, and had many pieces of ordnance mounted, from twenty-four pounders downwards, with some mortars, etc which were all well served. These, as you may suppose, with their intrenching tools, stores, ammunition and some provisions, fell into our hands: they had some Indians among them, for we found the corpse of one of their chiefs, a stout fellow with uncommon large limbs and features; he had a medal and crucifix of silver, both hanging by a chain from his neck.

'Though many lives were lost in this descent by the oversetting of the boats, occasioned by an uncommon great surf, yet, I believe, we benefited by it in a very eminent degree, for, when the boats were lifted up by the violence of the swell to a considerable height, the enemy's shot, which would problably have done execution had we been upon even water, passed under us: and in like manner some flew over us in our quick transition from high to low; this is the only reason that I can assign for our not losing more men by the enemy's fire. The weather continued rough and unfavourable, so that we had no communication with our fleet for several days; consequently, having no tents on shore and a very short allowance of provisions, our situation was far from being comfortable.

'On the night of the 11th, the enemy destroyed the grand battery which is opposite to the harbour's mouth, and retired into the town; in consequence thereof, Brigadier Wolfe received orders to march with a large detachment, and take possession of the Light-house Point, which, with the island battery, form the entrance of the harbour. We have an incredible deal of labour on our hands, cutting and making fascines, gabions and hurdles; intrenching our camp and posts, erecting blockhouses, throwing up redoubts, making roads for our artillery through a vile country, partly rough (worse, if possible, than the ground we incamped on last year at Halifax) but in general swampy; advancing our lines or approaches, constructing batteries, and skirmishing continually with the rabble in the woods round our camp, who are very troublesome neighbours: such are the employments of the army, often by night as well as by day; such the toils we have to encounter in the progress of this enterprise; yet with inexpressible pleasure I behold the zeal of the troops surmounting every difficulty, in all which they have noble examples before them in our general officers.

'On the night of the 19th, Brigadier Wolfe opened on the island battery, which however was not silenced until the 25th; he also quieted the fire of a frigate that gave us much annoyance. We then (for I was upon that service) got orders to rejoin the army with our artillery, and leave a small detachment with some ship-guns at the point to prevent the enemy's repairing their works and batteries on the island. On the 26th, a party of the enemy sallied out and attempted to destroy one of our blockhouses by fire, hoping thereby to favour a *coup* they had projected (as we surmise) of greater importance; but they were disappointed and beat back to their garrison with some loss. A command of marines were landed for the first time, and took post at the cove, which is to be relieved from the fleet. On the night of the 30th we had a small alarm from that quarter, the marines having apprehended an attack from the savages and other irregulars. The enemy sunk four ships in the harbour's mouth, to obstruct the channel and prevent our fleet's going in; the troops are growing sickly, particularly the New-England-men, their disorders mostly the small-pox.

'July the 1st.

'A part of the enemy skulked out, to procure some firewood (as 'tis supposed); they were instantly drove back to the town by Mr Wolfe's detachment: deserters are daily coming out to us; they are mostly Germans, say they were basely betrayed and forced into the French service: the enemy's ships in the harbour continue to annoy us considerably.

'July the 9th.

'A strong *sortie* was made by the garrison; and, though their men were shamefully drunk, yet they surprised some of our troops, and a smart rencounter ensued; but some companies of grenadiers, coming up, soon put an end to the fray, and repulsed them with the loss of an hundred killed and wounded; most of the latter were taken prisoners; many of them in their retreat threw down their arms, which we also recovered; we had about forty men and officers killed and wounded.

'July the 11th.

'Brigadier Wolfe is now about seven hundred yards from the west gate, whence he has damaged the town considerably with his shells; he is erecting a battery of four thirty-two pounders and six twenty-four pounders: our most advanced lodgement is not six hundred yards from the garrison. The making of roads for our artillery has been the most painful of our labour and, though now almost completed, they must nevertheless undergo daily repairs: the weather does not generally favour our operations. General Amherst is indefatigable; he visits our outposts, batteries and other works every day; and is continually concerting plans and reconnoitring new places from which he can most sensibly insult the enemy's works and accelerate the siege.

'July the 15th.

'Some rockets were thrown up by the Lighthouse detachment, as a signal to the fleet of some ships stealing out of the harbour; which were answered by Admiral Sir Charles Hardy's squadron, who instantly put to sea.

'July the 21st.

'Three of the enemy's ships in the harbour took fire and were burnt down to the water's edge: we cannot say whether this disaster, which was preceded by a great explosion on board one of them, was accidental or designed. Several batteries are now playing upon the town, and others are still to be erected. We fire both day and night with great spirit, and have done so for some time.

'July the 22nd.

'Three new batteries were opened this day with good success; one of them mounted mortars only; it soon demolished the citadel, which I saw in flames for several hours.

'July the 23rd.

'This evening a long range of buildings (which I am told are the barracks) were set on fire by our shells, and burned with great rapidity; we have now brought our approaches so near, as to be able to beat off the gunners from the enemy's bastions with our musketry.

'July the 24th.

'The enemy's fire is by no means so spirited as for some time past. Some hundreds of seamen were sent on shore, to assist in forwarding the new batteries.

'July the 26th

'Last night the admiral sent a body of sailors, with the boats of the fleet and a proper number of naval officers under two captains (whose names I cannot learn) to take or burn the remainder of the ships in the harbour, as they considerably annoyed us and retarded our operations: this service was well performed, and with very little loss; the *la Prudente*, of seventy-four guns, being a-ground, they burnt her; the other, which is a sixty-four, they took and towed into the north-east harbour. To-day the garrison proposed to surrender; they demanded the same terms which had been granted to the valiant Blakeney at Minorca; but, being told they must submit at discretion, they at length found themselves under the necessity of complying; and the whole island of Cape Breton, the more fertile isle of St John, together with their inhabitants, are all comprehended in the treaty.

'The day following Brigadier Whitmore (who is to remain governor) took possession, placed guards at all the gates, arsenals, magazines, etc and received the submission of the French troops by grounding their arms on the parade in his presence. Eleven stands of colours are fallen into our hands, which, with all the prisoners, are to be sent to England: they amount (I am told) to almost 6000 men. We have got immense quantities of stores of all kinds, with some ammunition and provisions, and a respectable artillery: the enemy have now, both by sea and land, sustained a fatal blow in America. Mr Amherst has displayed the general in all his proceedings, and our four brigadiers are justly intitled to great praises; Mr Wolfe being the youngest in rank, the most active part of the service fell to his lot; he is an excellent officer, of great valour, which has conspicuously appeared in the whole course of this undertaking. The troops behaved as British troops should do, and have undergone the fatigues of this conquest chearfully and with great steadiness; the light infantry, who are inconceivably useful, did honour to themselves and to that general who first saw the necessity of forming these corps.

'The troops have suffered considerably by sickness; but, though I am told so, I find, upon inquiry, the loss has been mostly among the rangers and New-England artificers, to whom the small-pox has proved very fatal; the greatest unanimity has subsisted throughout this whole armament both naval and military, and Admiral Boscawen has given us all the assistance that could be wished for. I went into town yesterday, and found the place in such ruin that I was glad to return to the camp without any delay. Never was artillery better served than our's; they have distributed their destruction to every corner of this fortress with great profusion. Our adjutant has obliged me with the following return of our whole loss, which has not been equal to what might have been at first expected.

'A list of the killed and wounded at the siege of Louisbourg.

| | K. | W. |
|---|---|---|
| Colonels | ... | 1 |
| Captains | 2 | 4 |
| Lieutenants | 8 | 16 |
| Ensigns | 2 | 3 |
| Sergeants | 3 | 4 |
| Corporals | 8 | 5 |
| Privates | 149 | 320 |
| Drummers | ... | 2 |
| Total | 172 | 355 |

*N.B.* Of the Royal Artillery one Gunner and three Mattrosses killed, and one Corporal, Gunner, and three Mattrosses wounded; which with the Rangers are also included.

Total killed and wounded, 527.'

# IV

# The French Confined

*The season was too far advanced for further major campaigning. The British victors at Louisbourg vented their spleen by laying waste the French settlements on the lower St Lawrence. The subsidiary expedition under Colonel Forbes into the Ohio valley redressed previous defeats by capturing and holding Fort Duquesne, renamed Pittsburg. The third avenue into Canada was open and French resources were becoming stretched. The 43rd Regiment was condemned to another miserable winter in the Bay of Fundy, but the spring of 1759 saw them released to serve under Wolfe in the definitive campaign of the war. Knox kept his pen active.*

THIS MORNING, 7 SEPTEMBER, at five o'clock, I commanded a large detachment to the forests SSE of our garrison, in order to cut down wood for a *feu de joie*; a parcel of carts belonging to the town's-people (which had never made their appearance since the arrival of our regiment, being carefully housed up) were sent out on this occasion, attended by their respective proprietors. Having discovered the remains of a fire still burning, we concluded some of the rabble had been sculking there; and, to prevent a surprise, the detachment was subdivided, and marched by two distinct roads into the woods in order to scour the country; we did not proceed above a mile, when, making no farther discovery, the whole rejoined and marched back to our ground, where, after having posted the proper sentinels, with a serjeant and twelve men advanced a little way—to defeat any attempt by these *gens de bois*—we set to work and, in the space of a few hours, loaded thirty carts with timber and under-wood. We set fire to the forest in seven different places, and returned to the fort: had there been any wind abroad, these fires would probably have cleared a large tract of ground, which was our desire; but they died away before the evening.

At noon the garrison marched out to the covered way: thirty-five guns were discharged from the ramparts, answered by twenty-one swivels from each of the blockhouses, and by three vollies from the troops. This evening the New-England artificers raised a large pile of the wood that was cut and drawn for the fort in the morning, and in the center of it erected two masts to the height of sixty feet, on the tops of which they fixed a barrel of pitch: at night-fall a rocket was thrown up as a signal for some fireworks to be played off, that had been prepared by the gunners; and for lighting the pile, etc which was done amidst the joyful acclamations of the troops and town's people of all ages and both sexes. One shilling per man was advanced to the soldiers, and the officers, with other gentlemen, repaired to the commandant's quarters, where an entertainment was provided for them, as elegant as the place would admit of; his majesty's health was drank with three cheers, and a discharge of twenty-one guns: all the barracks and town were illuminated, and the night was concluded with great festivity and general good humour.

On 23 September arrived his majesty's sloop of war, Captain Rogers, from St John's river; by whom we learn that Brigadier Monckton, with the 35th and second battalion of Royal American regiments, a detachment of the royal train of artillery and a large body of rangers had arrived in that river on Saturday the 16th instant; that they landed without opposition, hoisted British colours on the old French fort, were repairing it with all expedition, and building barracks for a garrison of three hundred men. This gentleman adds that, upon his ship's first entering that harbour, he saw three of the enemy; that one of them fired his piece up in the air as a signal, and then they ran off into the woods; that the brigadier is making preparations to proceed farther up the river with a parcel of armed sloops and schooners, in order to destroy some storehouses and an Indian settlement that are about twenty-five leagues up that river, beyond our New Fort. This is the service that was intended to be performed by Brigadier Lawrence with the 27th, 43rd and 46th regiments in August 1757; but was prevented by two of these corps being ordered to proceed with the main body of the army to the southward, upon the news of the unhappy fate of Fort William-Henry.

Captain Rogers says that some prisoners who were taken at Louisbourg gave information that, if our expedition there had miscarried, the enemy were determined to make themselves masters of Annapolis Royal, Fort Cumberland, and Fort Edward; after which they proposed to surprise and burn the town of Halifax; and all these gallant feats were to have been performed before the expiration of this autumn. By a letter which the commanding officer here was favoured with from Brigadier Monckton, we have the following particulars: that Sir Charles Hardy, with seven ships of the line and the three following regiments under Brigadier Wolfe, viz. the 15th, 28th and 58th, were gone to destroy all the French settlements on the river St Lawrence as high up as Gaspée bay; that four hundred rangers and regulars, under the command of the major of the 35th regiment, were landed at Cape Sable in order to rout the Indians and others from thence; and that two armed sloops keep cruising off that cape for the major's service, and to prevent the vermin from getting off in their canoes. The brigadier said he had intended that we should send a detachment from hence, to assist those at Cape Sable, in case the inhabitants had directed their course this way; but, recollecting the weakness of our garrison, he laid that project aside, and has sent orders here to keep close and not suffer the soldiers or inhabitants to stray to any distance. Our major was also favoured with the following disposition of the troops, viz. the 22nd, 28th, 40th and 45th regiments are established at Louisbourg; the 15th, 58th and 3rd battalion of Royal Americans, commanded by Governor Lawrence, at Halifax; the 1st, 17th, 47th, 48th and Fraser's Highlanders are gone to Boston to proceed to the army.

The *Ulysses* sloop of war sailed for St John's harbour: the fort-major was sent to Brigadier Monckton, to give him a true state of this garrison respecting its almost defenceless condition, together with our barracks, soldiers' bedding and many etceteras correspondent therewith, particularly the difficulties we undergo in the article of firing, and the want of candle-light for the troops here during the winter-season. A sloop arrived here from Old York with timber, planks and boards for the new fort at St John's river. Also a schooner from Boston, with cattle, liquors and vegetables, for the same place. By this last vessel we have the pleasure to learn, that Colonel Bradstreet was detached from Lake George with three thousand men, composed of regular and provincial troops, besides a body of savages, to Lake Ontario, in order to undertake the demolition of Fort Frontenac, where the enemy had a grand magazine; that the colonel landed within a mile of the fort on the 25th of August, without opposition; and the garrison surrendered on the 27th, consisting of one hundred and twenty Regulars, forty Indians and Canadians, with a few women and children, who are all prisoners of war. They had in this fort sixty pieces of cannon and sixteen mortars of different calibres; an immense quantity of provisions, stores and ammunition for the French troops, their barbarous allies, and their numerous forts SSW and SSE of Frontenac. The colonel also made himself master of nine armed vessels mounting from eight to eighteen guns, which was all the naval force the enemy had on the Lake Ontario; that these vessels were richly laden, insomuch that the article of beaver-skins and other furs are valued by the French at seventy thousand louis-d'ors.

We are likewise informed that our troops have burned and de-stroyed the fort, provisions, magazines, stores, artillery, and all the vessels except the two largest, on board of which the colonel had removed the skins and other most valuable prizes: that the enemy have sustained a fatal blow by this expedition, and the consequences will be very great to us, as it will not only facilitate Brigadier Forbes's operations against Fort Duquesne and the country of the Ohio, but also (as it is supposed) defeat the designs of the enemy against our forts and settlements upon the Mohawk river. This enterprise does great honour to General Abercromby, as well as to Colonel Bradstreet, who so gallantly executed it.

We have the pleasure to hear that all the French families who lived in the remote parts of the island of Cape Breton and St John, are daily repairing to Louisbourg with their arms to submit to the general's mercy. By the disposition his excellency has made of the forces since the reduction of these islands, and the different services on which they are employed, the most effectual measures are pur-sued to extirpate the enemy from this province, and to disable them from ever making any figure in this part of the world. By all accounts the French troops pretend they were as well pleased to deliver up Louisbourg to us, as we are at the success of our arms. They were greatly terrified with the apprehensions of a storm, and the con-sequences that would probably have followed. They also feared lest our Highlanders should not give them quarter; and that the army in general would make reprisals for the inhuman infraction of the capitulation of Fort William-Henry. These reasons, together with a consciousness of their having acted an ungenerous part in the course of the siege, by discharging nails, hinges, latches and all kinds of old iron from their guns, where there was no scarcity of fair shot, was a sufficient cause for their suspicions and fears. *Thus conscience makes cowards*, etc.

The Volontaires Etrangers, that composed part of their garrison, were originally raised for the King of Prussia's service; but, being betrayed and sold to the French king, they were sent to America and arrived at Louisbourg a short time before our invasion of that island: a great many of the private soldiers are entertained in our troops at their own request, and have promised to serve us faithfully, from principle, against the French, to whom they express having a natural and unalterable aversion.

A plot was discovered at Halifax, before Brigadier Monckton left that place: some Dutch settlers were to have assisted a detachment of Regulars, Acadians and savages, under Monsieur Boishébert, to surprise and fire the town, and in the confusion to butcher all the troops and inhabitants; a cellar full of arms was discovered, and some of the conspirators were hanged. A night or two after the detection of this horrid affair, a great smoke was seen in the woods behind the town, which alarmed the garrison; the guards turned out, the troops repaired to their posts, and continued under arms for three nights; till at length the French partisan, finding no signal made for him, concluded the enterprise was discovered and, therefore, thought proper to remove himself, and his barbarous accomplices, to some other quarter.

Vessels are continually running between this port, Boston, Halifax, and St John's, now Fort Frederic; from the latter of these places our fort-major is returned; he says that new fort will be a strong compact place, will mount twenty-one pieces of cannon, from fours to twelve pounders, besides several mortars, swivels and wall-pieces; and that the barracks for the garrison are almost finished. Brigadier Monckton had detached a small reconnoitring party of rangers up the country; they proceeded to the distance of eighty miles, keeping the course of the river; and at their return reported that they saw several large settlements, with fields of corn still standing, but did not discover any of the enemy. The prisoners that were at Fort Cumberland have been sent down to Fort Frederic, to serve as guides and pilots on the river St John; they have informed the brigadier that Boishébert was expected to be at this time at the head of that river, with five hundred regulars and militia, and two hundred savages; but that upon the approach of our armament they will retire, except they have lately received orders from Monsieur de Vaudreuil (Governor-General of Canada) to act otherwise.

Brigadier Monckton and the forces are gone up the river from Fort Frederic; this intelligence is received by a brig from thence, who was dispatched here for provisions, iron work, a forge and bellows, etc etc and also for some smiths and carpenters. Troops that are confined to the retired forts in this country lead a very insipid, disagreeable kind of life; soldiers are naturally fond of variety and activity; the want of a good collection of books is a very sensible loss to the officers, and the constant sameness in all we hear and see is tiresome, one day being the dull duplicate of another. When we left Europe in 1757, the general prevailing opinion was that the reduction of Cape Breton would put a final period to the war in America; that Louisbourg would be garrisoned by New-England troops, and that the army would return to Great Britain, to be employed on other services; these political sentiments, how shallow soever they may appear, were frequently impressed upon us by people of high rank and authority who ought to have known better: and to them only can be attributed the neglect paid by the officers of each corps to the purchase of a good regimental library, for their entertainment as well as improvement. I earnestly recommend it to my military brethren to pay strict attention to this circumstance for the future.

This situation of affairs has induced the officers of this garrison to address Major Elliot by letter, requesting him to transmit our sentiments to Colonel James and to intreat he will apply to the commander-in-chief without loss of time, in the name of the whole corps, that the 43rd regiment may be employed with the army in the ensuing campaign. This has produced a discovery of a circumstance which has been hitherto preserved with great secrecy, viz. that the whole regiment will meet at Fort Cumberland by the latter end of November, until which time our application may be postponed.

An officer at Fort Cumberland writes to his brother here, that the regiment is to be imprisoned this winter at that place, and that the colonel is in daily expectation of us; in consequence of this certain information, we have packed up, and prepared for our removal. On 19 November some guns were heard from the bay, which, we conjecture, are to notify the return of Brigadier Monckton and the troops from the upper part of St John's river to Fort Frederic; we are in hourly expectation of being relieved by a detachment of the 35th regiment. Some transports arrived on the 22nd with part of the relief from the new fort; Lieutenant-Colonel Fletcher came on shore in the afternoon, and was saluted by eleven guns.

The remainder of the detachment sailed up the next day, amounting in all to five companies; the establishment of the regiment is one thousand men, and the adjutant assures me they do not want above eighty men to complete the ten companies, which is a trifling number considering the services whereon that corps have been employed these seven months past. The other half of the regiment is stationed between Fort Frederic and Fort Edward, three companies at the former of these places, and two at the latter; the battalion of Royal Americans, that was employed with the 35th, are sailed under Brigadier Monckton to Halifax: the rangers are cantoned throughout the province as usual, and the light infantry, which were composed of chosen men from the different regiments, are returned to their respective corps.

The three companies of the 43rd embarked on 25 November for Fort Cumberland; but, the wind being contrary and blowing hard,

ADMIRAL SIR CHARLES
SAUNDERS

GENERAL JAMES
MURRAY

GENERAL ROBERT
MONCKTON

we were detained here for several days: we were very fortunate in not being able to sail immediately, as we have thereby escaped some very bad weather and a great storm; we have now a hard frost, and the air is inconceivably cold.

We weighed on 1 December about eight o'clock, and attempted to get out into the bay; but not consulting the proper time of tide, we were obliged to put back and come to an anchor: about noon we weighed again with the tide of ebb, and little wind falling, with an agitated sea occasioned by conflicting currents, our transport missed stays, and we narrowly escaped being wrecked upon a lee shore, where the vessel would probably have been dashed to pieces, the western side of the entrance being a complete ledge of rocks. The master instantly fell upon his knees, crying out 'What shall we do? I vow, I fear we shall be all lost, let us go to prayers; what can we do, *dear* Jonathan?'—Jonathan went forward, muttering to himself 'Do —I vow, Ebenezer, I *don't* know what we shall do any more than thyself'—when fortunately one of our soldiers (who was a thorough-bred seaman, and had served several years on board a ship of war, and afterwards in a privateer) hearing and seeing the helpless state of mind which our poor New-England-men were under, and our sloop driving towards the shore, called out, 'Why, d—— your eyes and limbs—down with her sails, and let her drive a——e foremost; what the devil signifies your praying and canting now?' Ebenezer, quickly taking the hint, called to Jonathan to lower the sails, saying, 'he vowed he believed that young man's advice was very good, but wished he had not delivered it so profanely'. However, it answered to our wish; every thing that was necessary was transacted instan-taneously; the soldier gave directions and, seizing the helm, we soon recovered ourselves, cleared the streight, and drove into the bay stern foremost.

The next day about noon we arrived safe in the bason of Fort Cumberland after an agreeable passage and moderate weather; as our quarters were ready for us, we landed immediately and marched up to the fort; they have had frost and snow here invariably these six weeks past, and the cold is so intense that we are at once sensible of the difference between this climate and that of Annapolis. Our arrival here gives great pleasure to our friends, as they have been under apprehensions, for some time past, of a visit from the enemy, who threaten to come and retake this fortress, or destroy it by fire. Soon after we had disembarked, it blew very hard, which was succeeded by a great snow storm.

The colonel is ordered to provide the regiment with flannel

G

under-waistcoats and leggers, or Indian stockings; here follows a description of them: leggers, leggins or Indian spatterdashes, are usually made of frize or other coarse woollen cloth; they should be at least three quarters of a yard in length; each leggin about three quarters wide (which is three by three) then double it, and sew it together from end to end, within four, five or six inches of the out-side selvages, fitting this long, narrow bag to the shape of the leg; the flaps to be on the outside, which serve to wrap over the skin, or fore-part of the leg, tied round under the knee and above the ankle with garters of the same colour; by which the legs are preserved from many fatal accidents, that may happen by briars, stumps of trees, or under-wood, etc in marching through a close, woody country. The army have made an ingenious addition to them, by putting a tongue or sloped piece before, as there is in the lower part of a spatterdash; and a strap fixed to it under the heart of the foot, which fastens under the outside ankle with a button. By these im-provements they cover part of the instep below the shoe-buckle, and the quarters all round; the Indians generally ornament the flaps with beads of various colours, as they do their moggosan or slipper; for my part, I think them clumsy and not at all military; yet I confess they are highly necessary in North America; nevertheless, if they were made without the flap, and to button on the outside of the leg in like manner as a spatterdash, they would answer full as well: but this is matter of opinion.

The rigour of the winter here is inconceivable, yet every body is remarkably healthy; the air is quite serene and the sun shines almost every day; perhaps that benign luminary is concealed from us once in four, five or six days, when a snow-storm sets in, which, however, does not continue above twenty-four hours, and then we have clear weather again.

Our retired situation here does not afford constant materials for my pen, which (as the reader may suppose) is the reason of my passing over many days in silence. A large bear rushed out of the woods between the gibbet and the blockhouse; he seemed to be hard pressed, whence we conclude he was hunted by the enemy: he afforded us excellent sport for almost an hour, and several pieces were discharged at him; but at length, directing his course towards the bason, he escaped by swimming a-cross the bay.

Our principal amusement here is skating; the marshes, having been overflowed before the frost set in, afford us now a scope of several miles: a quantity of coals and wood were laid in here before our arrival from Annapolis; but, being almost exhausted, the ranging company are now employed in providing fuel for us: the allowance to each fire-place is 'one quarter of a cord of wood and two bushels of coals, weekly, for forty weeks; or half that allowance for every seven days through out the year'.

The weather inconceivably severe, continual frost and snow; the latter is several feet in depth and sets in with thick drifts and high wind: it may seem a paradox to say it rains frost, but that is actually often the case in this country. On 20 January two soldiers walked out a few miles on the road leading to Gaspereau and Baye Verte, and, seeing a man lie dead at some distance before them, they returned instantly, and apprised the commanding officer therewith: a serjeant and eighteen men were detached with a hand-sleigh to bring home the corpse; so little did we apprehend any danger, that the officers have been out daily for some time past, either walking, shooting or riding. In the evening the party returned, and brought with them the remains of one of our best grenadiers, who was stripped of every thing except his shirt and breeches, and had two different parts of his scull scalped.

The rolls of the companies being immediately called, it appeared that one serjeant and three privates of the rangers, together with seven of our soldiers, were missing; and as they were seen going out to cut wood this morning (contrary to repeated orders) we suspect they are either killed or prisoners with the enemy.

The whole company of rangers went out this morning to scour the country towards Baye Verte: they returned in the afternoon, and brought with them a sleigh which our unhappy sufferers had taken out with them, and on it were laid the bodies of four of our men and one ranger, who were killed and scalped; the rest are still missing: at the place where these unfortunate people were way-laid, there was a regular ambush, and designed probably against the rangers who have been out for some weeks cutting and cording wood for the garrison, and seldom missed a day except the weather was uncommonly severe, which was the case yesterday; and their not going was providential, for they are generally too remiss upon service, and so little did they suspect any danger that the half of them went out without arms, and they who carried any were not loaded.

The victims were fired at from the right side of the road, being shot through the right breast; all were wounded in the same place except one who had not a gun-shot about him, but was killed by a hatchet or tomahock across the neck, under the hinder part of his scull; never was greater or more wanton barbarity perpetrated, as appears by these poor creatures who, it is evident, have been all scalped alive; for their hands, respectively, were clasped together under their polls, and their limbs were horridly distorted, truly expressive of the agonies in which they died: in this manner they froze, not unlike figures, or statues, which are variously displayed on pedestals in the gardens of the curious. The ranger was stripped naked as he came into the world; the soldiers were not, except two who had their new cloathing on them; these (that is the coats only) were taken: I am told this is a distinction always made between regulars and others; the head of the man who escaped the fire was flayed before he received his *coup mortel*, which is evident from this circumstance that, after the intire cap was taken off, the hinder part of the scull was wantonly broken into small pieces; the ranger's body was all marked with a stick and some blood in hieroglyphic characters, which shewed that great deliberation was used in this barbarous dirty work. The bloodhounds came on snow-shoes or rackets, the country being now so deep with snow as to render it impossible to march without them; they returned towards Gaspereau, and we imagine they came from Mirrimichie, there being no settlement of them (as we suppose) nearer to us on that side of the country.

Our men were buried this afternoon and, as we could not break or stretch their limbs, the sleigh was covered intirely with boards, and a large pit was made in the snow, to the depth of several feet, where they are to remain for some time; for the earth is so impenetrably bound up with frost that it is impracticable to break ground, even with pick-axes or crow-irons; their funeral was very decent, and all the officers attended them to the burying-place. Our men appear greatly irritated at the inhuman lot of their friends, and express the greatest concern lest we should not permit them to make reprisals whenever a favourable opportunity may offer. In these northern countries, any people that happen to die after the winter sets-in are only left under the snow until the beginning of summer, for spring I cannot call it, there being no such season in this part of the world.

With respect to fresh provisions of any kind, it is also customary to kill them about the middle of November, and leave them in an airy out-house or other place where the frost will soon affect them; so that there is nothing more common than to eat beef, mutton or poultry in March or April that were dead five months before: hares and fowl, as soon as killed, are hung up in their skins and feathers, and without being drawn, until they are wanted; at which time, by steeping them (or any butcher's meat) for a time in cold water, and not merely immerging as some writers and travellers aver, they become pliable and fit for any purpose that the cook may require.

One captain, one subaltern and sixty men of the 43rd regiment have been under orders these few days past to attend, as a covering-party, on the rangers, while they are employed in wood-cutting; but, the weather being at present so uncommonly severe, they cannot stir out; this is to be continued for the remainder of the winter, whenever it can be found practicable. The frost is so intense that many of our soldiers have had their noses, ears and fingers nipped or frost-bitten; for which there is no other remedy than to have the part affected well rubbed with snow by a warm hand, and to keep clear of fire.

Nothing can equal the extreme bitterness of the season; yet our detachments are every day out at the wooding-place. All manner of provisions and liquors freeze with us; even rum and brandy do not escape the rigour of this winter: the officers prefer sleeping in blankets, sheets being too cold for this northern climate.

The whole month of February does not afford any materials: the weather still invariably the same; the inclemency whereof is not to be expressed; yet our wooding-parties are constantly employed on that fatiguing service, and the fuel, when cut, is drawn home by the soldiers on sleighs; the rangers forming the van, and scouring the woods on each side of the road, while some regulars bring up the rear. At the place where our poor fellows were lately waylaid and butchered, the enemy constructed an intrenchment of three faces, with logs of timber, in such manner as to flank the road and enfilade the approaches to it; on the outside of each face were felled trees, with the tops laid outwards. From these precautions it appears their malice was levelled against the rangers, with whom they probably expected and intended, after the first surprise, to have maintained a skirmish.

One day early in February the sentinels could scarce keep their posts; many of them were so much affected that it was found necessary to relieve them: two, who had been so ill as to be hardly able to speak, had each of them an half pint of good rum poured down their throats, which recovered them instantly, but was not sufficient to intoxicate them: they were both remarkably sober men, and had frequently been rallied by their comrades for their ab-stemiousness. I mention this circumstance to shew that it was not from habit, or the force of custom, that these men were not in-ebriated by such a quantity of spirituous liquor; for it is certain that every man, even the most temperate among us, can drink more wine or stout punch at this rigorous season before he becomes innocently chearful, than he can at any other time of the year, or in a more moderate climate, with decency. It is the opinion of the settlers, who have passed many winters in this province, and several years in this remote part of it, that this is the most severe winter they ever remember to have seen in Nova Scotia.

Provisions of all kinds are now grown scarce, and those issued from the stores are very indifferent: our men can neither get rum or spruce, and the captains have not money to subsist them. With respect to some of the articles of the king's provisions, the men are put to short allowance through scarcity: even the officers are sensible of these calamities.

A sloop, which has been frozen up here all this winter, has now got off by the assistance of the high tides, and sailed to Boston for supplies of all kinds for this garrison, and to hasten up any other vessels she may meet with, whether consigned to this or to other places. A small party of the enemy appeared in the skirts of the forest to the left of the blockhouse next to the marsh, where the officers have been skaiting for the greatest part of this winter when the weather permitted.

The sun is now so warm, and has such great effect upon the snow, that the sleighs will not run; so that the very disagreeable service of cutting and drawing wood can no longer be performed, to the inexpressible satisfaction of the poor soldiers and rangers: and, as the ice in the center of the bay is broken up, we give many a wishful look that way, hoping soon to have ships—agreeable news—and plenty for the time to come.

I never saw such great plenty of wildgeese and ducks, and in such numerous flocks, as at this time; by which we look upon the winter to be almost at an end: the wind is now fair for vessels to come up, and the bay is tolerably clear of ice. On 5 April, about two o'clock, to the inconceivable pleasure of this garrison, a sail appeared at the Joggen, and soon after another came in sight, both which came up in the evening. These vessels, with two others bound for this port, have been for several weeks at Annapolis Royal, waiting until the weather should break up: they made many efforts to come sooner, but were put back by contrary winds and floats of ice in the bay.

By the aforesaid vessels we have at length received a confirmation of the great success of the army under Brigadier Forbes, the enemy having burnt and abandoned Fort Duquesne on 24 November last, which the general took possession of, on the evening of that day, with his light troops, and his army arrived there on the 25th: the

French retired towards the Mississippi, being deserted by their Indian allies, who have since put themselves under our protection. Incredible are the hardships which that army have undergone in the course of the campaign; but, when success crowns our endeavours, it makes ample amends for all our toils, and inspires us with fresh vigour for farther enterprises. Our accounts of that large tract of country bordering on the river Ohio are extremely pleasing.

As soon as Brigadier Forbes's army had reached Fort Duquesne, he set about the necessary repairs, and, having rendered the place as defensible as possible, he garrisoned it by two hundred and forty Highlanders from Colonel Montgomery's corps, and fifty of the Royal Americans: the remainder of his forces he marched back to Philadelphia; but, before he took his departure, he conferred on his new conquest the name of Pittsburgh, in complement to that super-eminent statesman, the right honourable William Pitt Esq; by whose great abilities, excellent conduct and the most steady exertion of the reins of government, our affairs, particularly in this new world, have assumed so prosperous an aspect.

Another smaller fort, dependent on this, situated on a branch of the Ohio, the brigadier also honoured with the epithet of Ligonier, to perpetuate, in some measure, the just sense which he and the British forces entertain of that experienced general's high merit and long faithful services. By our farther accounts from that quarter, the late French garrison had perpetrated the most unheard-of barbarities upon all our prisoners: in the ruins of the fort are found pieces of human skulls, arms, legs and other relics of their brutality, which were half burnt; after these monsters of butchery had sated them-selves with this savage and unchristian treatment of some unfor-tunate captives, on the parade within the fortress they gave up the remainder to the Indians, who, according to their custom, toma-hocked and scalped them, one after another; and all this in presence of the unhappy sufferers, who remained to be the last victims of their rage and cruelty. Fort Ligonier is garrisoned by a detachment from Pittsburgh, which is relieved weekly or monthly, at the discretion of the commanding-officer.

We also learn that General Amherst is making vigorous prepara-tions for an early campaign; that the provinces are raising many regiments; and that his excellency, to avoid that confusion which would otherwise happen, as well as to encourage the provincials and to keep them under some kind of regularity, proposes to form all his batteau-men into companies of fifty each, under proper officers, who are to raise their own men for their commissions; likewise the drivers of ox-teams and waggons are to be under the like regulations, and the whole army, destined for the service of the lakes, are to rendezvous at Albany, about the latter end of this month.

On 14 April Colonel James had the pleasure to receive orders from the commander-in-chief (through Brigadier Monckton) for the 43rd regiment and Captain Danks's company of rangers to hold themselves in readiness to embark on board such transports as shall carry troops here to relieve them; that the rendezvous of the army, which is intended for an expedition up St Lawrence river, under the command of Major-General Wolfe, will be at Louisbourg; this argreeable intelligence soon flew thro' the garrison, and nothing but continual huzza's were heard for some hours from the barracks, and were repeated in the evening by the soldiers assembled at roll-calling, when each honest heart gladdened, which diffused itself conspicuously in every countenance.

As we are now about to depart from his majesty's province of Nova Scotia, where the forty-third regiment have had the misfortune to undergo an inglorious exile of twenty-two months and upwards, separated not only from the busy active world, but likewise from those scenes of honour in which, I can venture to affirm, every man, both commissioned and private, most ardently wished to have shared, I shall proceed to a review of our service and employment therein, to which I shall annex an historical account of the country, its soil, produce, etc etc and this shall be done in as concise a manner as possible, that the reader may not be detained from occurrences of much more importance.

The occupation of the troops in this desert province, and particularly of the forty-third regiment, since our leaving Halifax (the capital thereof) in 1757, does not afford any great entertainment, and still less subject for speculation; for, besides the ordinary duty and defence of the forts they have occupied, cutting and providing wood, digging and drawing coals and sand, throwing up retrenchments, erecting redoubts of timber, and scouring the country in the environs of our respective posts, often with some loss on our side and great barbarity on the part of the enemy, compose the affairs which have ingrossed both our time and our attention; to this I may add the distress we were often exposed to for fresh provisions and liquors, and the constant apprehensions we were under, from the very indifferent state of our fortresses, of a surprise from our inhospitable neighbours on every side, which obliged us to exert the utmost vigilance and circumspection while we continued here;

our exclusion from the world, for the space of two long winters, by the rivers, bays and harbours being bound up with frost, together with our confinement within very narrow limits, and without even the benefit of riding, shooting or being able to partake of any other healthful exercise in safety, rendered our situation inconceivably irksome and disagreeable to men naturally fond of and accustomed to activity; our discontented reflections, under all these circumstances, may be better conceived than expressed.

The government of Nova Scotia was merely nominal until the year 1747, when a settlement was established by the then governor, Cornwallis, on the west-side of Chebucto harbour, called Halifax (before described) and is now the metropolis: here are two houses of assembly, called the upper and lower; the former is composed of the lieutenant-governor and council, who, with the governor, are all appointed by the king; and the other is formed of the representatives, who are chosen by the freeholders; to whose choice, however, the governor has it in his power to object.

Though this province is situated in a very favourable part of the temperate zone, yet its winters are at least seven months long, four of which are almost insupportably severe; we are strangers here to the spring, that delightful season of the year in other countries; the winter being immediately succeeded by summer, which, though of no long continuance, is as much upon the extreme, for intolerable heat and close air, as the other is for intense cold. For some months the weather is very uncertain, often changing suddenly from fair and moderate to tempestuous and violent rains; from the latter end of May to the same time in September, they are wrapped up in the gloom of a perpetual fog, during which space the musketa's and other insects are most incessantly tormenting, even by night as well as by day; the autumnal season is of no long duration: and, not-withstanding the great extremes of weather and severity of the winter months, it is an exceeding healthy climate, and agrees as well with strangers as with the natives, who are remarkable here for their longevity.

In all the uplands, I observe the soil is thin and barren; and yet, what is very surprising, they are covered with large timber trees of great length, and generally where there is not even an inch of mold, besides the skin of mossy turf which covers the rock: the lowlands, however, and the marshes, which are very extensive, afford a better prospect, particularly round the Bay of Fundy and on the banks of rivers: and, though at present the grass is everywhere interspersed with a cold spungy moss, yet the soil, if properly cultivated, might in

the space of a few years produce good grain; and this I am inclined
to believe from the excellent culinary and other roots and vegetables
of most kinds raised by the inhabitants in their gardens; particularly
pumpions [pumpkins], which, though much inferior to those raised
in New-England, are nevertheless an excellent succedaneum to cab-
bage in the latter part of the winter. The French have raised corn
in many places, but I am told it was small and shrivelled; I know
maize, or Indian corn, will not arrive to perfection in the neighbourhood of Annapolis; it grows tall and runs to seed, but will not ripen.
I saw some potatoes that were sown, after the Irish manner, from
excellent seed and as good manure; yet they degenerated surprisingly,
though it was a remarkable good season for that vegetable. Upon
the whole, tho' unpromising as this country seems to be, I have been
informed by gentlemen (who have seen more of it, and resided much
longer here than I have done) that it is not uniformly bad, there
being some tracts of land which will not (they say) yield to any of the
best provinces to the southward.

The trees, which are to be met with in the forests of Acadia, are
oak, both red and white; black and white birch; some ash, but these
are not very plentiful; maple and spruce, or spruss, with various
other sorts of fir and pine trees; alder, willow, black and white
thorn; beech, hazel, chestnut, apple, pear, plum and cherry; they
have most kinds of fruit and shrubs, as we have in England and
many of the latter altogether unknown to us; the woods every-
where abound with strawberries, and a great choice of other spontaneous fruits, some of which Europeans are well acquainted with;
others they are strangers to, and such we never presume to meddle
with: their timber trees, particularly the oak, fir and maple, are of a
most gigantic size, seemingly fit for ship and other buildings; the
firing generally used is wood and some coals; but, if ever the country
should be well inhabited and settled, in such manner as not to
apprehend any enemy, they will find excellent coal-pits, with plenty
of peat or turf.

I have seen but few of the various animals which, we are told by
historians, infest the woods of this province; to such as came within
my observation only I shall therefore confine myself: bears are about
the size of a two years old calf (I have heard there are larger, but I
write from my own knowledge, I have seen the skins of some as
large as an ox or cow; but I am inclined to think they came from the
remote northern parts of Canada, from Newfoundland or elsewhere);
they are of a rusty, black colour, and their hair long and thick; they
are seemingly a heavy beast, yet their swiftness, when pursued, is

inconceivable; their food is generally fruit, Indian corn, etc. and sometimes poultry, pigs, mice, etc. Hares are in great plenty, though much smaller than in England, coming nearer to the size of a rabbit; and, when the snow sets in, they change from their natural colour to milk-white; this, however is not peculiar to hares alone, there being, in this and other northern countries, many animals and birds which become white in the winter.

Having mentioned rabbits, I shall only observe, that I never saw or heard of any while I was in America; and this I impute to the great variety of other animals that borough in those northern parts, and which may, perhaps, be noxious to them; they may, for aught I know, have them in the more southern provinces, but these I am a stranger to.

Foxes are of different colours; red or sandy, as in England; grey and black; the first of these are the most common; the last are very scarce. I am told they likewise change to white in winter; but I have seen them at that season, which only varied from those in Europe by having their feet, tips of their ears, muzzle and the extremity of their tail, or brush, of a fine black; this I am very certain of, for we had them chained up as favourites, where I had frequent opportunities of examining them. Squirrels I have seen of various colours and sizes, which are very sweet to eat. The cat-a-mountain, or wild cat, called by the French *enfant de diable*, is an ugly fierce-looking animal, almost as large as a middling sheep, of a greyish colour and very shaggy.

I have frequently seen that species of quadruped called a raccoon, it is about the size of a well grown house-cat, and of the tiger kind, though its head has some resemblance to that of a fox; their fur is of a sandy colour, intermixed with white or grey hairs; their muzzle and paws are black, and, when tormented, they void their excrements, which are of the colour, size and smell of musk; and at the same time they make a hideous screaming noise; these animals are generally caught in the hollowed trunk of an old tree, and are so obstinate when taken, that they cannot be prevailed on to eat any thing, but will live an inconceivable time on the juice of their own paws, which they suck like a bear; their fur is fine and proper for hats, though not of the superfine kind: raccoons, I am told, are frequently eaten, and in great estimation, in New-England, roasted and served up with cranberry or other sweet sauce; but I can in this speak from my own experience, for we had one dressed for our mess with a rich gravy sauce, instead of the other; the flesh of it was white and tender, not unlike kid meat; but it was strong and of a disagreeable fishy flavour.

The musk-rat is of a lead colour, and in all other respects not unlike the large Norway rats in England, except its tail, which is partly round and, at the extremity, like that of a weasel: its fur is short, very fine, and smells as strong as their excrement, which is equal in perfume to the genuine musk; their skins are frequently used (more particularly by the French and those who like to imitate them) for linings of waistcoats; but to this practice I object, as they are too strong, overcoming, and consequently unhealthful. These are all the four-legged animals I have had an opportunity of seeing that deserve notice.

The fowl and birds come next under consideration: the tame poultry bred in this country are much larger than that breed in Great Britain usually are, though their shape, plumage and flavour are in all respects the same; they have two kinds of partridge in great plenty, distinguished by the spruce and the birch partridges, from their making the berries and tender tops of those trees their principal diet; the flesh and feathers of the former are dark, or blackish brown; are fine eating, but have a strong yet agreeable flavour of the tree on which they feed; the flesh of the other is as white as a chicken, its plumage much the same as in England; both kinds are much larger and, I think, the birch partridges are preferable to any I ever met with elsewhere: they are very tame, are killed sitting or running like a hen, and often perched on the branch of a tree.

Authors and travellers mention various kinds of wild ducks as peculiar to this country; I have only seen one sort, which do not differ from those in Europe; snipes they have in great abundance, the same as among us; but I never saw or heard of a woodcock in these parts, the winters here being too severe for them.

There are birds in this province not unlike our blackbird, but of a deeper and more shining colour; they come in small flocks of ten or twelve, and perch upon trees; they make a wild, shrill, chirping noise (not unlike what one hears from a pair of parroquets in a cage); their flesh is so bitter that they are not to be eaten; I have heard several arguments about them; some called them blackbirds, others stares (or starlings) but they differ from both those species of birds in Europe. The robin redbreast is in all respects the same as in England, saving its size, which is somewhat larger than the thrush; but I do not recollect that I ever saw any of them in the winter season, though I am told they have been caged as favourites, and will thrive and sing very melodiously in a warm room.

The owls of this country are a great curiosity, and make a most venerable appearance; they are of different sizes, and some much darker than others: I saw one that had been slightly winged, and lived several weeks after; he was as large as a turkey-cock, his breast, belly and neck as white as snow; his head, body and wings rather greyish, with the finest pair of transparent eyes I ever saw in my life: he seemed to have no dislike to his confinement, feeding heartily upon raw meat. There is a small kind of birds, not larger than larks and exactly of their colour, that, for some months of the summer season, fly in large flocks; after you have fired at them, such as have escaped rise, hover about and, by the time your fusil is again charged, they simply give you another chance, by lighting on the ground very near you: towards autumn they disappear, and return again also in flights when the snow sets in; for we are all agreed in that circumstance of their being the same species; their winter plumage is in general white, interspersed with brown; and they have a streak of that colour from the top of the head along the back down to the tail, two feathers of which in the same line are also brown; in one season we call them snow-birds, and, in the other, small-birds, not knowing their proper appellation: they are fat and delicious to eat at all times, and are termed ortolans by the French; but this is a common epithet among them for all the lesser feathered race that are eatable, and whose real names they are unacquainted with.

The musketa hawk the reader may remember to have seen described under May 1758. I have seen great variety of other two-legged animals in their flight; but, as I had not an opportunity of examining them particularly, I chuse to pass them by in silence.

The last, and least of the feathered race, which remains for me to describe, is the humming-bird; and it may justly be esteemed a miracle of nature, on account of its singular diminutiveness, beauty and plumage: it is said to be peculiar to America, but I am told they are larger, and have more variety of colours, in the southern parts than here; what becomes of them in the winter we know not, except, according to the commonly received notion, they die or sleep, and revive again in the following year: we used to kill them in the gardens about Midsummer, with the heads of pins or sand instead of shot; and generally found them among flowers and sweet herbs; they are about half the size of a wren, and made exactly like a snipe, with a long black bill, which is about the length and thickness of a fine stocking-needle: the head and back are of a dark green, the wings yellow, the breast pearl colour, and below that, towards the tail, of the colour of a lemon; the legs and claws, which support a pair of thighs of pale green, are also black and shining like its bill; they fly exceedingly swift and, by their buzzing or humming noise, are heard before they are seen, from thence called the humming-bird; the males are distinguished from the females by a little tuft of various colours on the top of the head; their eyes I cannot speak of, as all that I have seen were dead; I am told they are remarkable for fine lucid eyes and, in short, I think, in point of beauty and variety, they may justly be called the goldfinch of America.

The only curious insect I have seen in this country is the fire-fly (as it is called); it is about the size of a common hive-bee, though of a brighter colour, and has a double set of wings, of a delightful green, spotted with gold; when they rise in the night (at which time they are mostly seen) they dart such a surprising splendor as to appear, at a distance, like a flash in the pan of a firelock; and this illumination has often been taken for lightning; they are quite inoffensive, having no sting: I have had many of them in my hands, but they never shew to any advantage except when they rise to fly or skip in the grass. The grasshoppers are numerous, large and beautiful, surpassing any I ever saw before. The tormenting musketa, which is not unlike the gnat or midge in Europe, though somewhat larger, carries its sting in its head and not in its tail, as bees, wasps and some other insects do; they are so inexpressibly teasing that I have known many people thrown into fevers by their virulence, and a person's head, face and neck so swelled and inflamed as not to have a feature distinguishable; for this cause we always wore long linen trowsers, with crape or green gauze nets sewed to our hats, which hung down loose before and behind, with a running string at the bottom to gather it round the neck occasionally. There is a very diminutive kind of black fly which also stings most intolerably; it is scarce perceptible to the naked eye, and one would think it was a pupil to the musketa, giving as little quarter wherever he comes.

All the rivers, bays and harbours abound with fish of every genus, exanguious as well as sanguineous, and in the greatest perfection; the latter, that are in most plenty with us, are bass, from eighteen to twenty-six pounds weight; their flesh is firm and white as snow, and in all respects answers the same purposes of good salmon, in pickling, drying, frying or boiling. Mackerel as in Europe, and gasperots, which are between the sizes of a mackerel and a herring, are full of scales and bones; but eat, either fresh or salted, broiled, fried or pickled, as the last-mentioned fish does, and have exactly the same flavour. The finest cod in these seas are taken on the banks and coasts of this country; are even preferable to those of Newfoundland, though not altogether in such great plenty; and ling, also codlings, sardinias, sprats, eels, flukes, small turbots etc but these require no discription.

Oysters we are usually supplied with by the New England traders, fresh and good; they are neither large nor small; many of their upper as well as under shells (which is very uncommon) are concave, but this is not general; and rough or rocky on the outsides; they are well flavoured, and the central part of the inside of the shells, to which the core or firm part of the fish usually adheres, is as black as the rest is white; towards the heel on the inside of each shell are two little rows like teeth; they are not long, but of a fine red colour like coral. Oysters, no doubt, they have upon this coast (with most other kinds of testaceous fish) but I do not recollect that ever I saw any of them, nor indeed were we in the way of it, during our irksome abode in the province.

I cannot dismiss my remarks on Nova Scotia, without observing that the fogs, which are almost perpetual here and farther to the eastward, are certainly to be attributed to the swamps, bogs, lakes, creeks and innumerable rivers, great and small, that intersect the country everywhere; and to which I may add the immense tracts of rude, uncultivated forests. Some people have adopted a different opinion, imputing them rather to the steamy breath of the vast quantities of fish and sea animals wherewith these coasts and waters abound; but, however favourable appearances may be to these last sentiments on account of the remarkable healthiness of the climate, I must take the liberty to differ from them, because I rather ascribe the great salubrity of the air to the myriads of venomous reptiles and insects that absorb the noxious vapours, and purify those misty exhalations, which might otherwise naturally be supposed to be offensive and unwholesome, when arising from swampy grounds or stagnated waters, etc and this, if I am not mistaken, is the prevailing opinion in other countries where they are subject to fogs, and the lands are low and fenny.

The principal fortresses have been already described: the best of them is only calculated against an Indian enemy, and that of Annapolis Royal, I have been lately assured, lies intirely neglected; so that the works, being constructed of a loose, sandy soil, are consequently mouldering away to ruin. However, I am credibly informed the country, since the peace, has assumed a different aspect; that inhabitants increase, and that there are two houses of refreshment upon the road from Fort Edward (thirty-six computed miles from Halifax) to Annapolis, where people may travel with the greatest safety; and the new-comers, who are settled throughout the province, follow their respective occupations without the smallest apprehensions of molestation or danger. This being the case, if the government will continue to persevere in a vigorous support of this tender colony, as they have wisely done within these last twenty years, the next generation, or more likely their descendants, may perhaps consider all that has hitherto been said of Acadia in the same light that ignorant people do, at this day, the records of the primitive state of Great Britain and its then equally barbarous natives, viz. as fabulous, and the mere produce of a fruitful invention!

To conclude, I sincerely wish the views and expectations of the generous mother-country, in their settlement of, and attention to, this (hitherto unpromising) province, may be fully and amply accomplished in every respect, and that the inhabitants may approve themselves, to latest posterity, a loyal, industrious, grateful people: and thus I heartily bid it adieu.

MARQUIS DE MONTCALM

# V

# The Quebec Expedition

*The ordeal of the 43rd in garrison was over. Amherst, appointed Commander-in-Chief in America after Louisbourg, chose to lead the main prong of the British invasion of Canada in 1759 up the line of the lakes from New York to Montreal. Further expeditions were sent west to reduce the French fort at Niagara and regain a foothold on the Great Lakes before turning east. The boldest initiative was to send an army up the St Lawrence in conjunction with the navy. This was commanded by James Wolfe, promoted Major-General, with Brigadiers Monckton, Murray and Townshend. They were accompanied by two exceptionally gifted admirals in Saunders and Holmes, who cooperated in a uniquely successful amphibious operation. The 43rd formed part of Monckton's brigade and set off in high spirits for the rendezvous at Louisbourg.*

AT NOON ON 13 May we sailed with a fair wind and moderate weather; we were saluted by the fort with nineteen guns; also by the *York* sloop and *Monckton* schooner, who discharged eleven guns each; and, by a private agreement among the soldiers of each ship, they gave three cheers expressive of their joy at being released from their tedious and slavish exile, thanking God they were at last going to join the army. This was a surprise upon us, for the officers were not in the secret; and, though it likewise afforded us the highest satisfaction, our pleasure was doubly increased by seeing our poor fellows in such good spirits going on immediate service.

On the 15th, we came to an anchor in Havre le Tems bay; were piloted in here by our mate who, about four years ago, with his ship and crew, were surprised and made prisoners by twenty-four Indians in eight birch canoes; this intelligence set us on the watch, and we therefore mounted a guard in the evening upon deck, consisting of a serjeant, corporal and eighteen men. There are many islands, bays and harbours here, situated on the back of the river St Croix, upon the western side of the Bay of Fundy; this is a very fine harbour and good anchorage; a large fleet might ride here in great safety, the land high all round and covered with dark, thick woods, mostly spruce and pine: the pilot said, as we had troops on board and nothing to apprehend, he would bring us to an anchor in the same place, hoping the enemy would come again, that he might be revenged of them; accordingly we anchored off a point of land which runs into the bason, forming a peninsula, at the distance of about eighty yards, and with a view of decoying the vermin to visit us, we kept our men silent, and none were suffered to be upon deck except the guard, who were obliged to sit down under cover of the ship's waist: the peninsula is covered with pine and under-wood, so dark as to be almost impenetrable; we caught great plenty of fish in this harbour, and we think they are the best we have yet seen in this country.

The officers sat up last night, to oblige the guard to be alert; and gave orders to keep a good look-out upon the water on every side, and not to fire if they saw any canoe approach until they should come within eight or ten yards of the sloop, and then to pour in upon them; in the mean time the corporal was to have apprized us quietly of the first discovery or noise on the water; the rest of our detachment (being two companies) were in readiness below. We were not a little mortified that the savages did not attempt to surprise us, as we hoped to have struck an unexpected *coup d'éclat* upon our quitting this province.

About two o'clock PM on 16 May it was a perfect calm; this seamen looked upon as a prelude to a fair wind, which encouraged us to weigh anchor and work out; for this purpose our boat took us in tow. The entrance to the harbour being narrow (not exceeding sixty or seventy yards) and the channel running close to the peninsula, lest the enemy should give us a fire from the dark cover on that point of land (a scheme which our mate says they meditated against him and his sloop, the day before they surprised and took him), the men were ordered under hatches, except twenty who stayed with the officers upon deck, with their arms presented, in readiness to return the fire instantly; in this situation we were for near half an hour and, though nothing extraordinary happened, the precaution was nevertheless necessary.

Our vessel makes such little way, that we take great plenty of fish: I caught a halibut to-day; it weighed almost one hundred weight, was fifty-six inches long, by twenty in breadth at the broadest part and from fin to fin; I was obliged to have the assistance of two men to pull it up over our sloop's stern; and, I think, I never saw or eat a better or firmer fish.

On the 24th, we came up with several islands and floats of ice, and saw many more to leeward; they resembled low land and ledges covered with snow. At eight AM opened Gabarus Bay; the weather raw and cold; moderate breezes with gloomy air. At ten o'clock, opened the ruins of the late grand Battery; sailed in close by the Light-house Point; a bold shore, entrance narrow. Passed-by most of our capital ships and, about eleven A M, came to an anchor under the walls of Louisbourg, where we had the pleasure to find the remainder of the Bay of Fundy squadron, except the rangers, who are hourly expected. We see troops here reimbarking, who landed for exercise. In the evening a French prize was brought in of two hundred and fifty tons burthen: she was taken by Admiral Durell's squadron, who are gone up the river St Lawrence to intercept succours; was bound to Quebec; had one hundred and twenty soldiers and sailors on board, with a great quantity of ammunition and stores This prize belonged to a fleet of transports under convoy of four frigates, who sailed together from Brest, and had separated off the land.

The following orders, which were published by their excellencies Admiral Saunders and Major-General Wolfe, preparatory to the expedition intended against Quebec, I have, upon our arrival here, obtained authentic copies of, and shall insert them under their respective dates.

'ORDERS by Major-General Wolfe, Halifax, 4 May 1759.
'His Majesty has been pleased to appoint the generals and officers to serve in the army commanded by Major-General Wolfe, the Honourable Brigadier-General Monckton, the Honourable Brigadier-General Townshend, the Honourable Brigadier-General Murray: Colonel Carleton, Quarter-Master-General; Major Barre, Adjutant-General; Captain Guillem, Captain Spittall and the Honourable Captain Maitland, Majors of Brigade; Captain Smith, of the 15th regiment, and Captain Bell to be Aides de Camp; Captain Caldwel and Captain Leslie to be Assistants to the Quarter-Master-General; Major M'Kellar, Sub-director and Chief Engineer, etc etc etc.
'The ten regiments for this service in three Brigades, viz.
*First Brigade*
Brigadier-General Monckton, Major of Brigade Spittall: Amherst's 15th, Kennedy's 43rd, Anstruther's 58th, Fraser's 78th.
*Second Brigade*
Brigadier-General Townshend, Major of Brigade Guillem: Bragg's 28th, Lascelles's 47th, Monckton's 60th.
*Third Brigade*
Brigadier-General Murray, Major of Brigade Maitland: Otway's 35th, Webb's 48th, Lawrence's 60th.
This disposition afterwards underwent an alteration.

'The three companies of grenadiers taken from the garrison of Louisbourg, viz. from the 22nd, 40th and 45th, are commanded by Lieutenant-Colonel Murray; the three companies of light infantry, viz. one from the garrison of Louisbourg, the two others to be formed from the army, and are to be commanded by Major Dalling; the six companies of rangers are to be commanded by Major Scott; these three corps do not incamp in the line. The two companies of light infantry, commanded by Captains Delaune and Cardin, are to be formed from the light infantry of every regiment and battalion, by detachments of well-chosen men, in proportion to the strength of the corps, every regiment furnishing one subaltern officer and one serjeant.

'Order of incampment of the army in one line:

| 28th; 60th; 47th; | 58th; 60th; 35th; | 43rd; 78th; 48th; 15th; |
| --- | --- | --- |
| Second Brigade. | Third Brigade. | First Brigade. |
| Bragg's, Lascelles's, Monckton's. | Otway's, Lawrence's, Anstruther's. | Amherst's, Kennedy's, Webb's, Fraser's. |

Br. Gen. Townshend.—Br. Gen. Murray.—Br. Gen. Monckton.

'Order of battle in two lines, six battalions in the first line, four in the second:

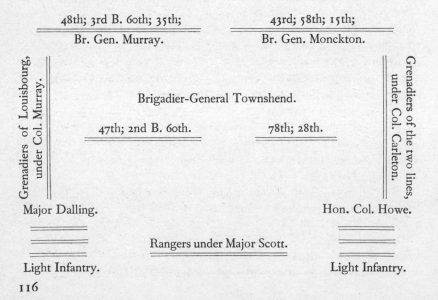

| 48th; 3rd B. 60th; 35th; | 43rd; 58th; 15th; |
| --- | --- |
| Br. Gen. Murray. | Br. Gen. Monckton. |

Grenadiers of Louisbourg, under Col. Murray.

Brigadier-General Townshend.

| 47th; 2nd B. 60th. | 78th; 28th. |
| --- | --- |

Grenadiers of the two lines, under Col. Carleton.

Major Dalling.

Hon. Col. Howe.

Rangers under Major Scott.

Light Infantry.

Light Infantry.

'The detachments of the army will be generally made by battalions, companies of grenadiers, picquets or companies of light
infantry. The picquets of the regiments shall be in proportion to the
strength of the corps, but always to be commanded by a captain. If
the general thinks proper to order intrenchments to be thrown up in
the front or rear of the army, the corps are to fortify their own posts.
   'As the fleet sails from Louisbourg in three divisions,
           The first brigade is the White division;
           The second brigade is the Red division;
           The third brigade is the Blue division.
The grenadiers of Louisbourg and the rangers will be appointed to
one or either of those divisions. If the regiments here have time to
put a quantity of spruce beer into their transports, it would be of
great use to the men. Weak and sickly people are not to embark with
their regiments; measures will be taken to bring those men to the
army as soon as they are properly recovered.'

Weather dark and foggy, with raw, cold air; it was tolerably pleasant
in the morning of 25 May when I went on shore to visit this famous
Dunkirk* of those parts: and observed that, in walking on the parade,
it turned gloomy all on a sudden, and, in the short space of two or
three minutes, there came on so heavy a fog that a person could not
know his most intimate acquaintance at the distance of a very few
yards; this exceeded any thing of the kind I ever saw to the westward
in Nova Scotia. I flattered myself I should have seen the grenadier
companies of this garrison reviewed by General Wolfe, but it was
over before I could get there; I was told they went through all their
manœuvres and evolutions with great exactness and spirit, according
to a new system of discipline; and his excellency was highly pleased
with their performance. Some commanding officers of corps, who
expected to be also reviewed in their turn, told the general, by way of
apology, that, by their regiments having been long cantoned, they
had it not in their power to learn or practise this new exercise: to
which he answered—'Poh! poh!—new exercise—new fiddlestick;
if they are otherwise well disciplined and will fight, that's all I shall
require of them.'
   Every person seems chearfully busy here in preparing for the
expedition. The small vessels being wanted for the rangers and other
light troops, such regiments as arrived here in sloops and schooners
are put on board of large English transports; the vessel in which I
took my passage fell down to the north-east harbour, and our

   * Dunkirk was a notorious haunt of pirates and privateers. Ed.

detachment, with their baggage, were removed on board the *Good-will* transport, being a cat of three hundred and forty tons: this was a most agreeable exchange, being in all respects better accommodated, than we could possibly be in the small craft of New-England; our poor soldiers have also benefitted, as all the articles of provisions in their new quarters are much better than those they have been lately used to, and they are now supplied with excellent ship-beer, to which they have been for a long time strangers.

The fog is so inconceivably thick, and the harbour at the same time so choked up with ice, that it is with the greatest difficulty a boat can put ashore or pass from one ship to another; provisions are immoderately dear in this place; beef and mutton from twelve to fifteen pence per pound. The fleet from Halifax, with the remainder of the troops and rangers from Nova Scotia, are all arrived: they have been off the land for some days past, and could not get in sooner, being obstructed by wind, weather and a surprising quantity of ice in the bay.

Some French and Indians were heard in the woods by some carpenters who were sent out to fell trees; a detachment of light troops was instantly sent in pursuit of them; two prizes were lately taken by Admiral Durell's squadron in the river St Lawrence; they had eighteen hundred barrels of powder, and other warlike stores on board, bound to Quebec.

ORDERS                                                           30 May
'As the cutters and whale-boats are meant for the service of the army, they are not to be given to any of the men-of-war without an order in writing from the admiral; complaints having been made that the transports' boats are often detained by the officers who come ashore, so that the masters cannot get their ships properly watered, the general insists upon the officers paying the strictest obedience to the orders of the admiral on that head. The regiments are to send in returns of all their spare camp-equipage to the brigade-major of the day to-morrow, at orderly time. The following order for the dress of the light infantry, as approved of by his excellency General Amherst: Major-General Wolfe desires the same may be exactly conformed to by the light troops under his command: the sleeves of the coat are put on the waistcoat and, instead of coat-sleeves, he has two wings like the grenadiers, but fuller; and a round slope reaching about half-way down his arm; which makes his coat of no incumbrance to him, but can be slipt off with pleasure; he has no lace, but the lapels remain: besides the usual pockets, he has two, not quite so high as

his breast, made of leather, for ball and flints; and a flap of red cloth on the inside, which secures the ball from rolling out, if he should fall. His knapsack is carried very high between his shoulders, and is fastened with a strap of web over his shoulder, as the Indians carry their pack. His cartouch-box hangs under his arm on the left side, slung with a leathern strap; and his horn under the other arm on the right, hanging by a narrower web than that used for his knapsack; his canteen down his back, under his knapsack and covered with cloth; he has a rough case for his tomahock, with a button; and it hangs in a leathern sling down his side, like a hanger, between his coat and waistcoat. No bayonet; his leggins have leathern straps under his shoes, like spatterdashes; his hat is made into a cap, with a flap and a button, and with as much black cloth added as will come under his chin and keep him warm when he lies down; it hooks in the front, and is made like the old velvet caps in England.'

The first brigade of the army, with the Louisbourg grenadiers, landed to-day for exercise; they performed several manœuvres in presence of the general officers, such as charging in line of battle, forming the line into columns, and reducing them; dispersing, rallying and again forming in columns, and in line of battle alternately, with several other evolutions; which were all so well executed, as to afford the highest satisfaction to the generals. The weather, though cold, favoured our performance; but the ground was swampy and uncomfortable. The troops have been daily engaged in these exercises, whenever the weather permitted.

ORDERS                                                          1 June
'The troops to land no more for exercise: the flat-bottomed boats to be hoisted up, that the ships may be ready to sail on the first signal. When three guns are fired from the saluting battery, all officers are to repair to their ships; the regiments and corps are to send, to-morrow morning at eight o'clock, to the artillery-store for tools, in the following proportions, and receipts to be given for them.' (*See Table overleaf*).

The troops were a-shore again this day for exercise, being the last time while we are to continue here. The rangers scoured the woods to-day, met with some of the enemy, gave them a fire and drove them to some of their inaccessible fastnesses. The harbour is full of ice, insomuch that some foolhardy seamen, who were on shore, went to their ships on the floats, stepping from one to another with

| Regiments | Pickaxes | Spades | Shovels | Billhooks |
|---|---|---|---|---|
| Amherst's | 50 | 20 | 10 | 10 |
| Bragg's | 60 | 30 | 10 | 10 |
| Kennedy's | 80 | 30 | 10 | 10 |
| Lascelles's | 70 | 30 | 10 | 10 |
| Webb's | 80 | 20 | 10 | 10 |
| Anstruther's | 80 | 30 | 10 | 10 |
| Monckton's | 50 | 20 | 10 | 10 |
| Lawrence's | 50 | 20 | 10 | 10 |
| Fraser's | 100 | 40 | 30 | 20 |
| Grenadiers of Louisbourg | 50 | 20 | 10 | 10 |
| In all | 670 | 260 | 120 | 110 |

boat-hooks or setting-poles in their hands; I own I was in some pain while I saw them, for, had their feet slipped from under them, they must have perished. Bragg's regiment, and the three companies of grenadiers (from the three battalions of regulars which are to remain in garrison here), embarked this day.

On the morning of 4 June some of the fleet weighed and worked out: the whole are preparing to sail; the transports have got their anchors a-peek. In the evening some ships of war cleared the harbour, and others put back and came to an anchor, the weather turning foul, with a thick fog: little or no wind. At nine o'clock the next morning the remainder of our fleet, etc weighed and got out; weather wet and foggy. Towards noon the wind came right ahead, which obliged those ships who were not clear of the land to put back into the harbour and come to an anchor. Some fishing-lines, hooks and sinks have been issued out to the troops, in order to use occasionally on the voyage for the preservation of the health of our men; and it is, at the same time, recommended to steep a quantity of ginger in the fresh water which they are to drink on their passage. The remainder of our armament weighed at four o'clock AM on 6 June and cleared the harbour and bay without any accident; at ten came up with the rest of the fleet, who had lain-to in order to wait for us. And, now that we are joined, imagination cannot conceive a more eligible prospect: of which, that the reader may form some idea, I shall here annex a list of our ships of war, frigates, sloops, etc etc independent of an immense fleet of transports, storeships, vituallers, traders and other attendants:

| | Ship's Names | Guns | Commanders |
|---|---|---|---|
| | Neptune | 90 | Admiral Saunders, Commander-in Chief, Captain Hartwell. |
| | Princess Amelia | 80 | Admiral Durell. |
| | Dublin | 74 | Admiral Holmes. |
| | Royal William | 84 | Captain Piggot. |
| | Van-guard | 74 | Captain Swanton. |
| | Terrible | 74 | Captain Collins. |
| | Captain | 70 | Captain Amherst. |
| | Shrewsbury | 74 | Captain Palliser. |
| | Devonshire | 74 | Captain Gordon. |
| | Bedford | 68 | Captain Fowkes. |
| | Alcide | 64 | Captain Douglass. |
| | Somerset | 68 | Captain Hughes. |
| | Prince Frederic | 64 | Captain Booth. |
| | Pembroke | 60 | Captain Wheelock. |
| | Medway | 60 | Captain Proby. |
| | Prince of Orange | 60 | Captain Wallis. |
| | Northumberland | 64 | Captain Lord Colville. |
| | Orford | 64 | Captain Spry. |
| | Stirling Castle | 64 | Captain Everet. |
| | Centurion | 60 | Captain Mantle. |
| | Trident | 54 | Captain Legge. |
| | Sutherland | 50 | Captain Rouse. |
| Frigates: | Diana | 36 | Captain Schomberg. |
| | Leostoffe | 28 | Captain Deane. |
| | Richmond | 32 | Captain Handkerson. |
| | Trent | 28 | Captain Lindsay. |
| | Echo | 24 | Captain Le Forey. |
| Sloops: | Seahorse | 20 | Captain Smith. |
| | Eurus | 22 | Captain Elphinstone. |
| | Nightingale | 20 | Captain Campbell. |
| | Hind | 20 | Captain Bond. |
| | Squirrel | 20 | Captain Hamilton. |
| | Scarborough | 20 | Captain Stott. |
| | Lizard | 28 | Captain Doak. |
| | Scorpion | 14 | Captain Cleland. |
| | Zephir | 12 | Captain Greenwood. |
| | Hunter | 10 | Captain Adams. |
| | Porcupine | 14 | Captain Jarvis. |
| | Baltimore | 10 | Captain Carpenter. |
| | Cormorant | 8 | Captain Mouatt. |
| | Pelican | 8 | Captain Montford. |
| | Racehorse | 8 | Captain Rickards. |
| | Bonetta | 8 | Captain Smith. |

| | Ship's Names | Guns | Commanders |
|---|---|---|---|
| Sloops: | *Vesuvius* | ... | Captain Chads. |
| | *Strombolo* | ... | Captain Smith. |
| | *Rodney* cutter | 2 | Captain Douglass. |

The *Bonetta* and *Rodney*, as also the *Charming Molly*, *Europa*, *Lawrence*, *Peggy* and *Sarah*, *Good Intent* and *Prosperity*, transport cutters, were appointed sounding vessels.

I had the inexpressible pleasure to observe at Louisbourg that our whole armament, naval and military, were in high spirits; and though, by all accounts, we shall have a numerous army and variety of difficulties to cope with, yet, under such admirals and generals, among whom we have the happiness to behold the most cordial unanimity, together with so respectable a fleet and a body of well-appointed regular troops, we have reason to hope for the greatest success.

The prevailing sentimental toast among the officers is—*British colours on every French fort, port and garrison in America.*

We have had neither fog nor hazy weather since we cleared the island of Cape Breton. Gentle breezes, with intermitting showers of rain: the lands on the north and south shores are very high and covered with snow. For several mornings and evenings past, we had periodical calms, breezes, and swells.

A thick fog on the morning of the 16th, which cleared away towards noon; the headlands are remarkably high. An officer on board, being advised by the surgeon to drink sea water for the scurvy, made the experiment, but found the water so fresh as to have no effect on him: an event at which the master of our transport expressed some surprise, as he said it was then about tide of flood. The low as well as high lands are woody on both sides; the water of a blackish colour, 'and the ripple occasioned by the rencounter of the strong currents down, and the tide of flood upwards, is extremely curious'; our wind rather perverse, though the weather is mild and pleasant.

Some of the headmost of our fleet came to an anchor on the morning of the 17th under the north shore to wait for the rear divisions; at nine AM weighed again, sailed till the evening, and then came to an anchor; but, the wind soon after springing up fair, we embraced the opportunity, weighed and made sail.

Early next morning our ship came to an anchor, in sight of the islands of Bic and Barnaby: the former bore W by S at nine leagues, and the other about eight leagues S W and by W of our course; here we met the *Richmond* frigate and a tender of Admiral Durell's squadron. A midshipman was instantly sent on board of us, who gave us the following intelligence:

'That Mr Durell had taken possession of the island of Coudre and had proceeded to Orleans; that he also took three prizes, besides some small craft, laden with flour and other provisions; but that three frigates and ten transports had escaped them and got up to the town, which is about thirty-five leagues from hence: that the enemy have almost finished a large three-decker at Quebec; and, by some packets that were intercepted, the admiral has received information that provisions, and particularly bread, are scarce in the French army.' This gentleman adds that they have got a good number of pilots, which they decoyed, on their passage up the river, by hoisting French colours with the usual signals.

Upon the van of Mr Durell's squadron having appeared under French colours, expresses were sent up to Quebec with the joyful tidings; for the enemy expected some promised succours from France, and the greatest rejoicings imaginable were made throughout the whole country: but they soon changed their note; for when a number of canoes had put off with pilots, and those who remained on shore did not see their friends return, but, on the contrary, saw the *White* colours struck, and *British* flags hoisted in their place, their consternation, rage and grief were inconceivable, and had such an effect on a priest who stood upon the shore with a telescope in his hand, that he dropped down and instantly expired.

The distance between Bic and the south shore is between four and five miles, both lands high and woody; before our ship came within two miles of the island, we found from seven to eight fathoms and an half in our soundings; the N E end of it is rocky, and very long ledges run out from it. Though the river is of an extensive breadth between Bic and the north shore, I observe the channel here is on the south side of the river and of the foregoing island; all our fleet keep that course. We found two other ships of Mr Durell's squadron at anchor here; saw a great number of seals and porpusses to-day, with which this river abounds.

The fleet weighed at four o'clock in the morning of the 19th; wind variable: soon after we had thick weather and a violent storm; we reefed and double-reefed, but at length were obliged to come to an anchor and, finding a strong current to encounter with which drove our ship from her mooring, we were under a necessity of paying out one hundred and forty fathoms of cable; this blowing weather was attended with heavy rain. Towards noon it cleared up and the wind and swell abated: before four PM the wind fair and weather more moderate. A parcel of small birds flew about our ship to-day from the shore; they are very tame and familiar; one of them, having perched on the shrouds, submitted to be made a prisoner: it is about the size of a sparrow, its head and body of a copper colour interspersed with black; its wings and tail are black and white; its beak of ebony, curved-like, though much sharper than those of a hawk or parrot, and with this farther difference, that the extremities of the upper and lower beaks cross each other; we gave it grain to eat, but it preferred feeding on flies and whatever it could find in the crevices of boards.

At seven o'clock PM the *Richmond* frigate passed us, on board of whom was General Wolfe, who politely saluted us, hoping we were all well on board: at eight, came abreast of a small island on the south side of the river, and at nine came to an anchor in twenty fathom water.

We saw an immense number of sea-cows rolling about our ships to-day, which are as white as snow: we diverted ourselves in firing at them, and I observed some of them that were struck on the back with ball did not seem sensible of it, nor did our shot make any impression on their skin or coat, but bounded as it would upon a stone; that part of their body which they expose above the water may be from twelve to fifteen feet in length, but their thickness I cannot be a judge of, having never seen them out of that element.

The inhabitants, of the E and NE parts of Acadia frequently take these sea-cows by the following stratagem: they tie a bull to a stake fixed on the shore in the depth of about two feet of water; they then beat and otherwise torment him, by twisting his tail, until they make him roar; which as soon as these animals hear, they make towards the shore, and, when they get into shallow water, they crawl to the bull, and are then taken with little difficulty: their fore-feet are, in all respects, like those of a cow; the hinder feet are webbed, or joined by a membrane like a goose: they have no hair about them, except on their head, which is generally white or grey; they are covered with a hard scaly substance or shell, which, however, turns to no account; these people, as well as the savages, eat some parts of this animal, and what they dislike they boil, with its fat, to an oily or greasy substance with which they save or cure the skins of other animals for leather.

The master of the *Good-will* transport, who is an elderly man, one of the younger brothers of Trinity-house, a pilot for the river

Thames and an experienced mariner, says he has sailed up most of the principal rivers in Europe, and that he esteems the river St Lawrence to be the finest river, the safest navigation, with the best anchorage in it, of any other within his knowledge; that it is infinitely preferable to the Thames or the Rhone, and that he has not yet met with the least difficulty in working up. He added, 'when we go higher up, if they should put a French pilot on board of me, ye shall see, masters, how I will treat him.'

We have had frequent opportunities of speaking with other ships in this voyage, and, by one of them, we are told that a midshipman of Admiral Durell's ship was surprised on the isle of Coudre, and made prisoner. We also learn that a ship has been intercepted, bound to France, on board of whom was a female relation of the Governor-General of Canada, with several nuns and some families of distinction; all of whom were returned by the admiral to Quebec, under a flag of truce, that they may have ocular proof of the valour of a British armament and, we hope, of the reduction of their boasted capital of Canada.

The reason of our not working up with more dispatch does not proceed from any obstructions in the navigation, but in the necessity there is of sounding as we advance; for which purpose, a number of boats are out ahead. By the situation of this river, of the capital and of the upper country, it is not possible for a fleet to sail up to Quebec, without its governor's having the earliest notice of it; this is apparently of great advantage. We have settlements now on each side of us, the land uncommonly high above the level of the river; and we see large signal-fires every where before us: Mr Durell's squadron, and the island of Coudre are just discernible.

The river is of an immense breadth between the island and the south country, but the channel is on the north side of it. Coudre is large, for the most part cultivated, and, by the number of houses, it seems to have been tolerably well inhabited; churches, crucifixes and images are now to be seen almost every-where. The land on the north side of the island is the highest I ever remember to have seen, and justly deserves the name of a mountain: it is a barren rock, having neither trees or grass on it, and only producing a short kind of heath, with a few shrubs on the lower part of the face of it. At a small distance, north-west of this promontory, stands another, and between the two lies a beautiful vale, in which is situated the pleasant-looking village (with a large parish-church) of St Paul: here we had in our view a number of cattle on shore, particularly horses, and several men and women; I think I never saw a settlement in a more desirable place, and the buildings appear cleanly and decent. Between Coudre and the north shore is a most rapid current; the master of the *Good-will* says it runs ten miles in an hour; here we got foul of another transport, and luckily cleared her again without any accident.

One of our sounding-boats was fired at from the shore, upon which a boat, full of men and officers from the 15th regiment who were astern of us, put off to amuse the enemy until the other should take all the soundings along shore; our people made several feints, as if intending to land at different places, from each of which the enemy directed a heavy fire, but they were not within reach of their shot; these unhappy natives paid dear for this behaviour, as will be seen in the sequel of this work. The man-of-war's boat executed her commission without any farther molestation, and the detachment of the 15th returned to their transport.

At three PM on 25 June a French pilot was put on board of each transport, and the man who fell to the *Good-will*'s lot, gasconaded at a most extravagant rate, and gave us to understand it was much against his inclination that he was become an English pilot. The poor fellow assumed great latitude in his conversation; said, 'he made no doubt that some of the fleet would return to England, but they should have a dismal tale to carry with them; for Canada should be the grave of the whole army, and he expected, in a short time to see the walls of Quebec ornamented with English scalps'. Had it not been in obedience to the admiral, who gave orders that he should not be ill used, he would certainly have been thrown overboard.

At four PM we passed the Traverse, which is reputed a place of the greatest difficulty and danger, between the entrance of St Lawrence and Quebec: it lies between Cape Tourmente (a remarkably high, black-looking promontory) and the east end of Orleans on the starboard side, and Isle de Madame on the larboard. Off Orleans we met some of our ships of war at anchor. Here we are presented with a view of a clear, open country, with villages and churches innumerable; which last, as also their houses, being all white-limed on the outsides, gives them a neat elegant appearance from our ships. At five in the evening we had a violent storm of rain, and at six we anchored in fifteen fathom water.

As soon as the pilot came on board to-day, he gave his directions for the working of the ship, but the master would not permit him to speak; he fixed his mate at the helm, charged him not to take orders from any person except himself, and, going forward with his trumpet to the forecastle, gave the necessary instructions. All that could be said by the commanding officer and the other gentlemen on board was to no purpose; the pilot declared we should be lost, for that no French ship ever presumed to pass there without a pilot 'aye, aye, my dear' (replied our son of Neptune) 'but d——me I'll convince you, that an Englishman shall go where a Frenchman dare not shew his nose'. The *Richmond* frigate being close astern of us, the commanding officer called out to the captain and told him our case; he inquired who the master was—and was answered from the forecastle by the man himself, who told him 'he was old Killick, and that was enough'.

I went forward with this experienced mariner, who pointed out the channel to me as we passed, shewing me, by the ripple and colour of the water, where there was any danger; and distinguishing places where there were ledges of rocks (to me invisible) from banks of sand, mud or gravel. He gave his orders with great unconcern, joked with the sounding boats who lay off on each side, with different-coloured flags for our guidance; and, when any of them called to him and pointed to the deepest water, he answered, 'aye, aye, my dear, chalk it down, a d——d dangerous navigation—eh, if you don't make a sputter about it, you'll get no credit for it in England', etc. After we had cleared this remarkable place, where the channel forms a complete zig-zag, the master called to his mate to give the helm to somebody else, saying, 'D—— me, if there are not a thousand places in the Thames fifty times more hazardous than this; I am ashamed that Englishmen should make such a rout about it'. The Frenchman asked me if the captain had not been here before? I assured him in the negative, upon which he viewed him with great attention, lifting, at the same time, his hands and eyes to heaven with astonishment and fervency.

We had incessant rain, thunder and lightning all night. Our division weighed early next morning: at seven AM came to an anchor off the parish of St Lawrence, on the island of Orleans, in eighteen fathom water: this is the deepest course of the river, the channel on the north side of the island having only a sufficient depth of water for boats and other small craft, as we are told; but of this, I presume, we shall be better informed before many months are elapsed. Here we are entertained with a most agreeable prospect of a delightful country on every side; windmills, water-mills, churches, chapels and compact farm-houses, all built with stone and covered, some with wood and others with straw. The lands appear to be every-where well cultivated, and, with the help of my glass, I can discern that they are sowed with flax, wheat, barley, pease, etc and the grounds are enclosed with wooden pales. The weather to-day is agreeably warm;

a light fog sometimes hangs over the highlands, but in the river we have a fine clear air. Where we now ride, the tide does not run above six knots an hour, and we have good anchorage; the rest of our fleet are working up and, by the situation of affairs, I am inclined to think we are happily arrived at the place that, to all appearance, will be the theatre of our future operations.

In the curve of the river, while we were under sail, we had a transient view of a stupendous natural curiosity called the water-fall of Montmorency, of which I hope, before the close of the campaign, to be able to give a satisfactory relation. A point of land running from the west-end of Orleans, and inclining to the southward, intercepts our prospect of Quebec at present, from which we are now between five and six miles; the country-people, on the south shore, are removing their effects in carts, and conducting them, under escorts of armed men, to a greater distance. At ten o'clock AM a signal was made for the quarter-masters of regiments, by which we conjecture the army will be ordered to prepare to land. At three PM another signal was made for the transports to work up under the commodore's stern, and we soon after anchored again, off the parish church of St Lawrence.

ORDERS

On board the *Richmond* off the island of Orleans, 26 June. 'Captain Deane will range the transports in proper order along the shore of the Isle of Orleans this afternoon, and tomorrow morning, about six o'clock, a signal will be made for landing. The sloops and schooners that have rangers on board are to draw close in shore: the six companies of rangers, and Captain Cardin's company of light infantry, are to be landed first to reconnoitre the country. The flat-bottomed boats only will be employed in landing the men; they are to assemble at the *Leostoffe* at four in the morning, and from thence first to the rangers, etc then to Amherst's regiment, then to the other corps, according to their rank or the conveniency of their situation; the men are to take their knapsacks, tents, camp-equipage and one blanket of the ship-bedding, besides their own blankets: thirty-six rounds of ammunition, all the tools and four days provisions. The rangers and light infantry are not to take their baggage on shore in the morning, two days provisions and a blanket only. As the weather, in the months of July and August, is generally very warm in Canada, there are to be no more than five men in a tent, or, if the commanding officer likes it better and has camp-equipages enough, he may order only four. Otway's, Webb's and

THE FIRE-SHIP ATTACK FROM QUEBEC

the Highland regiments, who are each in number equal to two battalions, are to incamp their companies in double rows of tents, that they may have more air and more room in their incampment, and consequently be healthy. The two pieces of artillery in the *Russel* are to be landed after the troops are on shore, or sooner, if there be occasion. The officers must be contented with very little baggage for a day or two, until it can be conveniently carried to the camp. In each flat-bottomed boat there will be an officer of the men-of-war and twelve seamen; and no more than seventy soldiers are to be landed at a time: these will help to row the boats. The provisions for the troops are to be for the future at full allowance.'

Lieutenant Meech, with forty rangers, landed late that night on the Island of Orleans without opposition; they went soon after on a scout and, in the woods on the north side of the island, they met a body of the inhabitants who were secreting their effects; the rangers, seeing them much superior in numbers, wanted to avoid them, but were pushed so close as to be almost surrounded; which Mr Meech perceiving, resolved upon engaging, as the only resource whereby he and his men had any probability of extricating themselves: they accordingly skirmished for a few minutes, when the Canadians, not relishing such treatment, even on their own ground, retired a little way; which Mr Meech suspecting to be a snare laid for him, instead of pursuing, withdrew to a farm-house and took post there until it was clear day-light: the rangers had one man killed, whom they went in search of, and found him scalped and butchered in a very barbarous manner; whereupon they went in pursuit of the enemy, and traced them, by their blood, to the water's edge on the north side of the island, whence this expert officer supposes they embarked.

The army landed during the morning on the fertile and agreeable Island of Orleans, and under the church of Laurentius (or St Lawrence). The light troops scoured the island and took some cattle and hogs; we marched about a mile north-west of the place of landing, and incamped in one line, with our front to the north-ward. As we halted for some time on the beach after we came on shore, I went with some other officers to take a view of the church, which is a neat building with a steeple and spire: all the ornaments of the altar were removed, a few indifferent paintings only remaining; the rector (or curate) of the parish left a letter behind him, directed *To the Worthy Officers of the British Army*, praying, 'That, from their well known humanity and generosity, they would protect that church and its sacred furniture, as also his house and other tenements adjoining to

I

it; and this, if not for his sake, yet for the love and mercy of God, and in compassion to his wretched and distracted parishioners'; he added, 'that he wished we had arrived a little earlier, that we might have enjoyed the benefit of such vegetables, viz. asparagus, radishes, etc etc as his garden produced, and are now gone to seed'; he concluded his epistle with many frothy compliments and kind wishes, etc consistent with that kind of politeness so peculiar to the French.

An abler pen than mine might find sufficient subject for encomiums on the beauties and situation of this island, which is universally confessed to be a most delightful spot: it lies on a noble river in the heart of a charming country, and surrounded by a great number of natural curiosities and pleasant villages; the north-west end and north side of Orleans are woody, and all the rest of it is laid out in compact farms, and very well cultivated: the soil appears to be fruitful, producing every species of grain and vegetables as the best lands in England. The inhabitants abandoned their houses, after having removed all their effects; and such articles as were of least value they concealed in the woods on the island. General Wolfe took an escort of light troops, accompanied by Major M'Kellar, our chief engineer, to the west end of Orleans, in order to reconnoitre the situation of the enemy, the garrison, the bason and the circumjacent country; he discovered the French army incamped on the north side of the river, their right extending close to Quebec, and their left towards the cataract of Montmorency; the ground which the French general has made choice of is high and strong by nature, with the village of Beauport in the center of their camp, and that of Charlebourg in the rear of their right: to this post they are all employed in adding every kind of work that art can invent to render it impenetrable. In the afternoon we had a dreadful storm of wind and rain, which lasted for some hours; the troops were very fortunate in finding great quantities of wheaten and pease straw that had been lately threshed, with some excellent hay to lie upon. A boat was sent down to view our fleet in the river, and was taken. Some detachments from the army marched this evening towards the west end of the island, by way of amusing the enemy; and returned soon after to camp. Great damage has been sustained in the fleet this afternoon by the storm; it fell mostly on the boats and other small craft; some transports were driven on shore, and others ran foul of each other: many of the flat-bottomed boats suffered much by this hurricane, and several of them are rendered unfit for farther service; the weather is now more moderate towards night.

ORDERS                        28 June

'A cantonment-guard to be mounted immediately by Otway's regiment at the general's quarters, consisting of one captain, three subalterns, four serjeants, four corporals and one hundred men. All detachments of light infantry, and all companies of rangers, when posted on the front, rear or on the flanks of the army, if out of sight are to acquaint the officer commanding the brigade or corps nearest to them of their situation. The detachment that was under Colonel Carleton's command is to return their tools and spare ammunition immediately to the commanding officer of artilley. Whenever the regiments send for straw, or any thing else they want, proper officers must go with their men, to prevent such irregularities as the general saw yesterday, and will be obliged to punish very severely. No detachments, either with or without arms, are to be sent to any distance from the camp, without the knowledge of the brigadier-general of the day. Regiments, or detachments, when cantoned, must always have an alarm-post, or place of assembly. It is ordered once for all, that soldiers are to keep close to their incampment and are not to pass beyond the out posts or guards, nor wander through the country in the disorderly manner that has been perceived here. *The army must hold themselves in readiness always to get under arms, either to march or fight, at the shortest notice . . .*'

# VI

# Montmorency

*Montcalm had been obliged to divide his forces. His second-in-command, the Chevalier de Lévis, was in Montreal to guard the hub of French Canada and counter the growing threat from the west. The second brigadier, de Bourlamacque, was on Lake Champlain to deny passage to Amherst. But with a mixed force of regulars, marine troops, a levée en masse of militia and his Indians, the French looked impregnable in the Quebec basin.*

*The British had established themselves on the Island of Orleans below the town and experienced little difficulty in taking possession of the south shore of the St Lawrence and part of the north shore east of the falls of Montmorency. But from the Montmorency gorge westwards past the Charles river and the town and extending far up-river, the north shore of the St Lawrence consisted of seemingly unscalable cliffs, manned by the entire garrison. For three months, Wolfe sought with increasing frustration to find a way of breaching this natural fortress. His first attempt, below the Montmorency falls, failed completely.*

ON THE NIGHT of the 28th, about twelve o'clock, the enemy sent down five fire-ships and two rafts to destroy our fleet; as they drew near to the west end of the island, some cannon that had been loaded on board the vessels with round and grape shot, played off and rattled about the shore and trees at that extremity; which so disconcerted some small detached parties, and out-sentries, that they quitted their posts and, in retiring towards the camp, fell in upon each other in a confused manner and alarmed the army: the picquets were immediately advanced, with the light troops, to the north side of the island; the line turned out and were ordered to load: the quarter and rear guards remained under arms, until it was clear day-light.

Nothing could be more formidable than these infernal engines were on their first appearance, with the discharge of their guns, which was followed by the bursting of grenado's also placed on board in order to convey terror into our army; the enemy, we are told, formed sanguine expectations from this project, but their hopes were happily defeated; some of these dreadful messengers ran on shore, and the rest were towed away clear of our fleet by the seamen, who exerted themselves with great spirit and alertness on the occasion. They were certainly the grandest fire-works (if I may be allowed to call them so) that can possibly be conceived, every circumstance having contributed to their awful, yet beautiful, appearance; the night was serene and calm, there was no light but what the stars produced, and this was eclipsed by the blaze of the floating fires, issuing from all parts and running almost as quick as thought up the masts and rigging; add to this the solemnity of the sable night, still more obscured by the profuse clouds of smoke, with the firing of the cannon, the bursting of the grenado's and the crackling of the other combustibles; all which reverberated thro' the air and the adjacent woods, together with the sonorous shouts and frequent repetitions of *All's well*, from our gallant seamen on the water, afforded a scene, I think, infinitely superior to any adequate description.

Though this sight was intirely new and unexpected by the soldiery, which, I am credibly informed, was not the case with our commanders (they having been apprised of these matters before they left England), we had the pleasure to observe our men were not at all dismayed, but, on the contrary, were eager to meet the enemy on such open ground as we then occupied, even under the disadvantages of night and our being strangers to the country. But, with due deference to superior judgment, I am of opinion the expectation and design of these fire-stages ought to have been communicated to the troops, that they might have been the better prepared against any surprise from the enemy co-operating therewith; for, had the French general been so circumstanced as to have had it in his power to spare (without any considerable diminution to his army) three or four thousand choice veterans, or perhaps half that number, at so critical a juncture, it is difficult to say what turn our affairs might have taken. Therefore, with all respect, I would recommend that, on every future occasion, all expectant occurrences of this nature may be imparted to and circulated throughout the army.

The enemy's fire-ships and *radeaux à feu* continued burning until five o'clock the next morning; one of them went on shore at the NW point of this island, another on the SSW point, and the rest were towed away and anchored close under the south shore. The officer who had the command of all the advanced parties on the western extremity of Orleans that abandoned their posts and caused an alarm in the army, was put under an arrest, in order to be tried by a general court-martial, whenever it could be conveniently assembled; but, in consideration of his excellent character, both as an officer and a gentleman, and at the generous interposition of Briga-

dier-General Monckton, his excellency General Wolfe was pleased
to forgive him, to the inexpressible joy of every officer of his
acquaintance.

The soldiers have brought in great quantities of plunder, such as
apparel, kitchen and household furniture, etc that they found concealed in pits in the woods. The troops at this time are ill-off for
fresh provisions, which, however, we expect will be remedied in a
few days, when the army are tolerably settled and our affairs put
under some kind of regulation. Weather cold and showery. About
two o'clock this afternoon three regiments, with some rangers and
light infantry, were ordered to strike their tents and be ready to
march at a moment's warning under the command of Brigadier-
General Townshend; and, in a short time after, the first brigade
received the like orders (the other corps, with their commander,
having been countermanded) also to be ready to march down to the
waterside, embark, and cross the river.

The admiral being desirous to work the *Neptune* and some other
ships up into the bason (where he may have a better view of the
operations of the army and, at the same time, be near at hand to
distribute such orders to the fleet as he may see necessary), sent to
the general to order a detachment of the army to take post on Point
Levy, where, he apprehended, the enemy had a battery to defend the
channel. This is the object in view, and is the reason of Brigadier
Monckton's brigade being under orders to embark. At five o'clock
we stood to our arms and, by the time that the light infantry and
rangers, and one regiment, had crossed over and taken possession of
the church of Beaumont on the south side of the river, the tide of ebb
was so far exhausted that the remainder were ordered to lie on our
arms this night, and to make fires to keep us warm; which was
highly necessary, for it was excessively cold, having froze hard with
the wind at north.

The light troops had a successful skirmish early in the morning
with some of the enemy's colony troops, seven of whom were killed
and scalped by our rangers, and five were made prisoners. Our loss
amount to two only, who were slightly wounded. Brigadier
Monckton, with the remaining regiments of his brigade, were ferried
over about seven o'clock, marched up to the church, and we lay on
our arms for some time, until the light troops should return, who
were upon a scout: there was no regular road up the hill, only a
serpentine path with trees and underwood on every side of us,
and upon the top of the precipice. This seems to be the case
everywhere; so that a few men, advantageously posted above,

would probably have defeated the views of those who had crossed over.

While our brigade halted at Beaumont, Brigadier Monckton was pleased to order a manifesto in the French language to be fixed on the door of the church, of which the following is an exact translation:

'By his Excellency James Wolfe, Esq; Colonel of a Regiment of Infantry, Major-General and Commander-in-Chief of his Britannic Majesty's Forces in the River St Lawrence, etc etc. 'The formidable sea and land armament, which the people of Canada now behold in the heart of their country, is intended by the king, my master to check the insolence of France, to revenge the insults offered to the British colonies, and totally to deprive the French of their most valuable settlement in North America. For these purposes is the formidable army under my command intended. The King of Great Britain wages no war with the industrious peasant, the sacred orders of religion, or the defenceless women and children: to these, in their distressful circumstances, his royal clemency offers protection. The people may remain unmolested on their lands, inhabit their houses and enjoy their religion in security; for these inestimable blessings, I expect the Canadians will take no part in the great contest between the two crowns. But, if by a vain obstinacy and misguided valour, they presume to appear in arms, they must expect the most fatal consequences; their habitations destroyed, their sacred temples exposed to an exasperated soldiery, their harvest utterly ruined and the only passage for relief stopped up by a most formidable fleet. In this unhappy situation, and closely attacked by another great army, what can the wretched natives expect from opposition? The unparalleled barbarities exerted by the French against our settlements in America might justify the bitterest revenge in the army under my command. *But Britons breathe higher sentiments of humanity, and listen to the merciful dictates of the Christian religion.* Yet, should you suffer yourselves to be deluded by any imaginary prospect of our want of success, should you refuse those terms and persist in opposition, then surely will the law of nations justify the waste of war, so necessary to crush an ungenerous enemy; and then the miserable Canadians must in the winter have the mortification of seeing the very families, for whom they have been exerting but a fruitless and indiscreet bravery, perish by the most dismal want and famine. In this great dilemma, let the wisdom of the people of Canada shew itself; Britain stretches out a powerful, yet merciful, hand, faithful to her engagements, and ready to secure her in her most valuable rights and possessions: France, unable to support Canada, deserts her cause at this important crisis, and, during the whole war, has assisted her with troops who have been maintained only by making the natives feel all the weight of grievous and lawless oppression. Given at Laurent in the Island of Orleans, this 28th day of June, 1759.

JA. WOLFE.'

After the skirmish was over this morning between our light troops and the enemy, the former, in the pursuit, apprehending that the peasants and colony troops might possibly return with a reinforcement, possessed themselves of a large farm-house, where they found a quantity of provisions and moveables, with a fire in the kitchen-chimney: from hence they intended to waylay the enemy, in case they should return; but, hearing the voices of people talking, they searched the house, without however making any discovery; whereupon they resolved to set fire to it and return to the church. After the flames began to spread with rapidity, they were alarmed with bitter shrieks and cries of women and children, who had foolishly concealed themselves among some lumber in a cellar. Our people very humanely exerted themselves for the relief of those miserable wretches, but their best endeavours were ineffectual; the house was burnt to the ground, and these unhappy people perished in the flames. *Such alas! are the direful effects of war.*

About ten o'clock, the light troops being returned to Beaumont, the brigade stood to their arms and marched immediately, leaving a detachment of one major, two captains, four subalterns and two hundred men, besides a captain, subaltern and about forty light infantry (all of the 43rd regiment) at the church as a rear-guard, with orders to remain there until they should receive directions to follow. About an hour and an half after the brigade had marched off, the brigadier sent back an officer, serjeant and twelve men, with orders to us to move forward, and rejoin our corps. Upon standing to our arms, half a dozen straggling fellows appeared on an eminence to the southward of the church, at the distance of near three hundred yards: they were almost naked, with blankets about them. After viewing us for two or three minutes, they beckoned to us to advance; and we did the same to them with our hats: upon which they fired at us; but their shot was thrown away, having trundled along the ground at our feet: an officer was advanced a little way with a white handkerchief on the point of a fixed bayonet, and waved his hat at them to come in; but, finding they only sought to amuse us (for the rascals were well situated, having a stone-wall close behind them, with an opening in it, though which they could retire, in case we had marched up to them, and a thick coppice on their right), our major gave orders to march. Our light infantry moved forward, and had not proceeded far, before a shot was fired, and was followed by a piteous groan.

We immediately pushed after them, on a supposition that they were attacked; but it proved an unfortunate mistake, for one of them, coming to the door of a house, saw a man climbing into a back window which he believing to be a Canadian, fired at him, and shot him through the body: the unhappy sufferer was one of his corporals. This disaster was attended with great trouble and delay to us, being obliged to take charge of the wounded man, and carry him along with us. We fastened a blanket with skewers to two poles, and had him carried like a corpse by six men, whom we relieved every quarter of an hour: for our poor fellows, by some mistake, were otherwise heavily laden with their own necessaries, camp-equipage, intrenching-tools, provisions, etc.

We marched through a fine cultivated country on a pleasant road, and, between five and six o'clock, joined the troops at Point Levy, where we found the enemy warmly disputing that ground with them; the principal skirmishing was in the skirts of some coppices to the westward of the point, a woody commanding rocky eminence to the southward, the church of St Joseph, and the parsonage-house contiguous to it. The troops and the enemy were alternately in possession of these buildings; but at length the brigadier ordered the Highlanders into the woods on the high ground, and the light troops to get round the hill and surround them, while he in person, at the head of the grenadiers, marched up and gallantly attacked the church and houses, which they once more gained possession of after a stout resistance on the part of the enemy, who, finding themselves not able any longer to withstand our fire and numbers, at length gave way.

This place is by nature very strong, and was exceedingly well defended; for, by all accounts, the enemy did not exceed a thousand men, who were partly inhabitants, six hundred colony troops and about forty Indians; our loss in taking this ground was very inconsiderable, not amounting to more than thirty killed and wounded; what the enemy sustained I never could learn, for they always contrive to carry off their killed and disabled men on these occasions. The brigade occupied the houses and all the eminences round the point; where, I must not omit to observe, we found neither batteries, nor any kind of works, as had at first been apprehended. At ten o'clock this night, Colonel Burton, with a detachment of the regiment under his command, joined us from Orleans.

After the siege we were informed by the late fort-major and some other French gentlemen, that Monsieur Montcalm foresaw the great advantages that would result to us over their capital, in being possessed of Point Levy; and proposed, before we came up the river, that four thousand men should be strongly intrenched here with some ordnance, and that other works should also be constructed higher up the country, at certain distances, for the troops to retire to in case their lines should be carried at the point. But Monsieur Vaudreuil over-ruled this motion in a council of war; and insisted that, though we might demolish a few insignificant houses with shells, we could not bring cannon to bear upon Quebec across the river; and it was his firm opinion that it was their duty to stand upon the defensive with their whole army on the north side of the bason, and not divide their force on any account whatsoever.

At nine o'clock on the morning of 1 July the enemy sent down three floating batteries (one mounted two guns, the others one each) in order to dislodge us; for this purpose, last night, they quietly, and undiscovered by our fleet's boats, anchored a canoe in the bason, at a certain distance, the better to remark our situation and the particular houses and other posts which they saw us occupy. Whereupon, apprehending that a body of troops might rush down the hill and attack us, while under a supposed consternation by their floats, we were ordered to stand to our arms, and an advantageous disposition was made of the brigade, leaving, however, proper detachments in the church and other houses, as also on the skirts of the coppices; and the light troops occupied the top of the eminence which commanded the point, and formed a chain from Nadau's great water-mill on the east, to the priest's and other houses that stood detached from the church, westward. In this situation they cannonaded us near an hour and a half, when the admiral, lamenting our disagreeable circumstances, threw out a signal for the *Trent* frigate, who lost no time in coming to our relief; and, the tide of flood then fortunately favouring us, she soon worked up, gave the enemy a few broadsides, and obliged them to sheer off.

General Wolfe also, with the greatest expedition, came to our assistance and brought a detachment of the train, with some guns and carriages; he immediately ordered out a number of workmen from each regiment, and erected a barbet battery close by the shore to prevent any farther annoyance to us from the river; and, at the same time, the *Trent* and other frigates anchored off the point, and some others of our fleet worked higher up, by which good conduct of our naval friends, we were no longer apprehensive of any insult from the floating batteries of the enemy, whose guns were well served, and by their grape-shot we lost several men; but, had not our brigadier judiciously ordered the troops to lie down after we were formed, our loss would probably have been very considerable.

The general, now seeing the necessity of remaining in possession of this ground, and as if apprised of the good consequences that would thereby result to his future operations, resolved to maintain it; for this purpose, we were ordered to incamp, and immediately set about intrenching ourselves, insomuch that, before night, we were in a tolerable state of security. Some batteries on the north shore, which the enemy opened on our ships (though beyond their reach) when they were turning up to our relief this morning, plainly pointed out to the general the necessity of possessing, in like manner, the west end of the Island of Orleans, as thereby the fleet could be better inabled, with security, to co-operate with the army; and accordingly orders were dispatched to Brigadier Townshend to detach a party for this purpose, which was executed, without loss of time, under the direction of Colonel Carleton: a good battery was instantly marked out there, and redoubts were begun to be thrown up, for the safety of the troops who were to cover it.

Some buccaneer firelocks, of an uncommon length, were found by our men to-day, buried in an orchard adjoining to the great water-mill; upon examining them, they were loaded with two balls each, besides a piece of square iron, four inches long, the edges of which were wickedly filed rough, like the teeth of a saw. From this ground we have a full view of the enemy in their camp, on the opposite side of the bason; their right extends above the town, with the river Charles in their front, where they have got the hulks of two frigates advantageously posted for the defence of that rivulet; and their left is close by the fall of Montmorency. Their situation appears to be very strong by nature; and I can discern, by the help of my telescope, that they are numerous and, as if jealous of an attempt by us on that quarter, they are fortifying themselves in every part; the rear of their left seems to be covered with thick woods, and, throughout their camp, there are a continued chain of houses, the windows of which are logged up for the service of musketry.

At three o'clock in the afternoon, we were alarmed by a smart firing of musketry in the woods, and the troops stood to their arms; this was occasioned by a party of Indians coming down to annoy our camp, for whom Captain Goreham and his rangers laid an ambush, and scalped nine of them. Two twenty-four pounders and two twelves are mounted on our barbet battery. Major Scott, with a large corps of rangers, are arrived this evening from Orleans; by whom we learn that thirty of the enemy have been killed and taken on that island, and that two grenadiers of the Louisbourg division were found scalped in the skirts of the woods. It is expected the enemy will attempt to surprise us this night; nevertheless we are landing heavy artillery and stores with great diligence.

The brigade, alarmed at two o'clock in the morning of the 2nd by some popping shots in the woods above South-hill, stood to their arms until it was broad day-light. We are finishing our intrenchments, and parties are out cutting and making fascines. Colonel Carleton is forwarding his works, on the west of Orleans, with great diligence. At one o'clock we were alarmed again by several floating batteries coming down the river; but, seeing our frigates preparing to engage them, they edged over to the north shore. The 48th regiment, with the grenadiers and light troops of this brigade under the command of Colonel Burton, marched up the country as an escort to General Wolfe, who went to reconnoitre the town from the heights to the southward of it; the light infantry, who preceded their march, were fired upon by some straggling peasants, at a distance; the general made choice of a piece of ground, about one mile and an half from our camp, whereon to erect batteries against Quebec; the garrison fired several guns at the detachment, but their shot either fell short of, or passed over them. In their return to camp, by a different route, they found the bodies of four grenadiers who were killed on the 30th ultimo and were most barbarously butchered; the general ordered them to be interred.

Major Scott, with some companies of rangers, marched up the country this morning as far as the river Chaudiere, to try to take a prisoner and reconnoitre that river, the enemy being supposed to have some vessels there; they were not able to make any discoveries except spying a body of Indians on the opposite side of that river; and the major made several attempts to cross over and rout them, but found it impracticable from the great depth of water and rapidity of the current; at the return of the rangers to camp, the general expressed a disappointment at not getting a prisoner for intelligence. The admiral sent a boat towards the north shore, and another towards the town, to sound; the garrison fired at them, as did some floating batteries under Beauport. Some ships are arrived from Boston, with large boats and provisions for the army. I can perceive in the enemy's camp, at least five coloured coats for one French uniform, whence, it is manifest, their army consists chiefly of the militia of the country, and other peasants. We have now got three redoubts in our incampment; the brigadier's tent is in the center of the largest, where there are four brass six-pounders mounted. Our camp forms an half-moon round the point, and has now assumed a respectable appearance; we are ordered to intrench the eastern flank of it, which is in the rear of the 43rd regiment. The officers were all served this day with fresh provisions for the first time: the weather is gloomy and cold, and inclining to rain.

To-day, 4 July, the officers have not yet been able to get their tents on shore; at present they are obliged to lie in those of the men. We are landing more artillery and stores. The fleet are worked up a little higher, and make a delightful appearance in the river. At noon we had a dreadful thunder-storm, succeeded by violent rain and hail, which lasted near six hours; the lightning exceeded anything I ever saw. In the afternoon a boat went up with a flag of truce from the admiral: when she got within gun-shot, another was sent from the garrison to receive her errand, and she was immediately sent back again. In the evening a French flag came down and, the *Trent* hoisting a white jack on her bow, the officer went on board of her. The enemy appear to be indefatigable at their intrenchments, particularly at the left of their camp above the Pointe à Lessay, whence I conjecture that part to be the most accessible, and am confirmed in this opinion by an observation, viz. when the tide is about half ebb, there are banks and shoals that run out to a great length into the bason, along the front of their camp from the center upwards, which are then visible: but there do not appear any obstructions immediately off the point.

ORDERS                          5 July, Camp at the Island of Orleans.
'The object of the campaign is to complete the conquest of Canada and to finish the war in America. The army under the commander-in-chief will enter the colony on the side of Montreal, while the fleet and army here attack the governor-general and his forces. Great sufficiency of provisions, and a numerous artillery is provided: from the known valour of the troops, the nation expects success. These battalions have acquired reputation in the last campaign, and it is not doubted but they will be careful to preserve it: from this confidence, the general has assured the secretary of state in

his letters, that, whatever may be the event of the campaign, his majesty and the country will have reason to be satisfied with the behaviour of the army under his command. The general means to carry the business through, with as little loss as possible, and with the highest regard to the preservation of the troops; to that end he expects that the men work chearfully and without the least un-soldierlike manner or complaint; and that his few, but necessary orders be strictly obeyed; the general proposes to fortify his camp in such a manner as to put it out of the power of the enemy to attempt any thing by surprise, and that the troops may rest in security after their fatigues.

'As the safety of the army depends, in a great measure, upon the vigilance of the out-guards, *any officer or non-commissioned officer who shall suffer himself to be surprised by the enemy, must not expect to be forgiven*. When any alarm is given, or the enemy perceived to be in motion, and that it may be thought necessary to put the troops under arms, it is to be done without noise or confusion; the brigades are to be ranged in order of battle by their brigadier-generals at the head of the camp, in readiness to obey the orders they shall receive. *False alarms are hurtful in an army, and dishonourable to those that occasion them*: the out-posts are to be sure that the enemy are in motion before they send their intelligence. Soldiers are not to go beyond the out-guards; the advanced sentries will fire at all who attempt to pass beyond the proper bounds. It may be proper to apprise the corps that the general may perhaps think it necessary to order some of the light troops to retire before the enemy at times, so as to draw them nearer to the army, with a view either to engage them to fight at a disadvantage, or to cut off their retreat. The light infantry of the army are to have their bayonets, as the want of ammunition may sometimes be supplied with that weapon: and, because no man should leave his post under pretence that all his cartridges are fired, *in most attacks by night, it must be remembered that bayonets are preferable to fire*. That the service of the campaign may fall as equally as possible upon the whole, the corps will do duty for their real strength; no change shall be made in the first regulation, unless any particular loss should make it necessary.

'All cattle or provisions taken by any detachment of the army are to be delivered into the picquet magazine, for the use and benefit of the whole: Mr Wire, the commissary, will give receipts for them. No churches, houses or buildings of any kind are to be burned or destroyed without orders: *the persons that remain in their habitations, their women and children, are to be treated with humanity; if any*

*violence is offered to a woman, the offender shall be punished with death.*
If any persons are detected robbing the tents of the officers or soldiers, they will be, if condemned, certainly executed. The commanders of regiments are to be answerable that no rum, or spirits of
any kind, be sold in or near the camp. When the soldiers are fatigued
with work, or wet upon duty, the general will order such refreshment as he knows will be of service to them, but is determined to
allow no drunkenness, nor licentiousness, in the army. If any sutler
has the presumption to bring rum on shore, in contempt of the
general's regulations, such sutler shall be sent to the provost's in
irons, and his goods confiscated. The general will make it his
business, as far as he is able, to reward such as shall particularly
distinguish themselves; and, on the other hand, will punish any
misbehaviour in an exemplary manner. The brigadiers-general are
desired to inform themselves if the orders and regulations are
properly made known to the soldiers of their respective brigades.'

We now fire an evening gun from our barbet-battery; the troops on
Orleans do the same, and the enemy are so polite as to follow our
example. The *Leostoffe*'s cutter was taken to-day, when she was
sounding. The enemy seem to vie with us in putting our respective
camps in the best posture of defence. Working parties are diligently
employed in erecting batteries against the town: the eminence, made
choice of for this purpose, projects into the river from sixteen to
eighteen hundred yards distance, which, with Cape Diamond, form
the straits of Quebec. Mortars, guns, shells, shot and all manner of
artillery stores are landing at every tide. A brisk cannonading, at six
o'clock in the evening of 6 July, between our frigates and the
enemy's floating batteries; they continued for an hour and a-half,
but no damage was done on either side: the floats were obliged to put
back to the town; their views were to edge down towards the Pointe
à Lessay, as if jealous of an attempt being made on that quarter.
    The troops at Point Levy are under orders to march on the
shortest notice; those on the Island of Orleans, it is said, will remove
suddenly to some other ground in the neighbourhood of the enemy's
camp, leaving a detachment behind for the protection of the battery,
store-houses and other works on that island. The enemy are making
many marches and countermarches in that part of their camp nearest
to the cataract. Some of our fleet are drawing over towards the
north shore. A deserter, from the French regulars, surrendered to us
on the 7th; it is suspected, by his extravagant intelligence, that he
left the French army by consent, for he was uncommonly communi-

143

cative; he said, 'that General Amherst has been defeated with immense loss, and that the French army on the opposite side of the river amount to eighteen thousand effective men, ten thousand of whom are of the best troops of France'; with many other inconsistent circumstances. This fellow, to his great mortification, was instantly sent on board of the admiral, which will defeat any hopes that he may have formed of returning to his army.

We have converted the church of St Joseph into an hospital, and are now fortifying it for that purpose; a smart cannonading between our frigates and the enemy's floating batteries, under the left of their incampment; our bomb-ketches fired several shells at the same time into their camp, some of which, by bursting in the air over their heads, threw them into confusion and made them run different ways for shelter. The garrison (as if by way of reprisal) vigorously bombarded Burton's Redoubt and cannonaded our workmen at the batteries very briskly, but without any success; General Wolfe was there at the same time, and shewed great attention to the preservation of the men by ordering them to lie down or get under cover as soon as a flash was first perceived: the enemy continued their fire until late in the evening.

The works are now completed on the west of Orleans; storehouses are erected, and hospitals for the use of the fleet and army; that post is rendered very defensible. Brigadier Townshend, with the troops we left on that island, embarked in boats this evening in order to land on the north side, east-ward of Montmorency; our frigates still continue to annoy the floating batteries and detached works on the beach, while our bomb-ketches harrass the enemy in the left of their camp.

In order to facilitate the landing of the forces under General Wolfe on the north side of the river, to the eastward of the waterfall, our brigade struck their camp, between one and two o'clock, in the morning, of the 9th with the greatest quietness, marched a little way up the country and concealed ourselves in the woods; a few detachments only remained in the houses and redoubts, and the working-parties, being out of view of the enemy, were not called in. Between six and seven our frigates and bomb-ketches began to play upon the enemy's camp, which obliged them to strike their tents and retire more to their rear; that ground is not only out of reach of our ship's guns, but, by its elevated situation, bids defiance to any annoyance from the river: by this removal, their left appears to extend nearer to the river of Montmorency than before, whence they may probably be routed again, as soon as our troops are landed and artillery can be brought up. Some rain fell this morning, it cleared up at ten o'clock, and we had fine weather for the remainder of the day, which favoured the general's operations on the north shore.

Captain Stark, of the rangers, sent his lieutenant and twenty men on a scout to the southward, yesterday; they returned to-day, and brought in two prisoners; one of them was a lad of fifteen years of age, the other a man of forty, who was very sullen and would not answer any questions: this officer also took two male children and, as he and his party were returning, they saw themselves closely pursued by a much superior body, some of whom were Indians; he wished to be freed from the children as, by their innocent cries and screeches, they directed the pursuers where to follow. The lieutenant made many signs to them to go away and leave him, but they, not understanding him, still redoubled their lamentations; and, finding himself hard pressed, he gave orders that the infants should be taken aside and killed; which was done, though the officer declared to me that it was with the greatest reluctance that can be conceived. As these prisoners were brought to the post where I was on duty with the ranging-captain, I conversed with the lad for some time; he told me that Monsieur de Montcalm had a large army; but added he, very sensibly, 'I cannot tell you any particulars, being too young to be a judge of these matters: this I know, that we are all in great distress for bread, both army, garrison and country; and Monsieur Bois-hébert, with a good corps of Acadians and savages, are in this neighbourhood, etc.'

About one o'clock in the afternoon, the troops under General Wolfe landed on the north side of the river to the eastward of the cataract, and incamped without opposition; they had six brass six-pounders with them, and some howitzers. When the enemy saw our army thus subdivided and occupying three distinct camps, the chief gentlemen of the country made application to Monsieur Vaudreuil to detach a strong body of Canadians, under experienced officers, over the river, and rout our troops from Point Levy; but the governor-general, from a contemptible opinion he had of their prowess, refused, telling them it was his and their duty to act on the defensive. Monsieur Montcalm was strongly prepossessed with the same sentiments of his Canadian forces.

Being on a working-party at our batteries, I had a most agreeable prospect of the City of Quebec for the first time; it is a very fair object for our artillery, particularly the lower town, whose buildings are closer and more compact than the upper. Some time after we

K                                                                          145 were settled at work, a soldier of the 48th regiment, who had an intention to desert, went to an adjoining wood where an officer and a number of men were detached to make fascines; he told the officer he was sent to desire that he and his party would return to the redoubt where we were employed, and in their absence he took an old canoe that he found on the shore, and crossed the river in our view; a boat put off from the enemy and took him safe to land.

Our carpenters are employed here in making several floating stages, in order, as it is pretended, to ferry over this brigade to attack the enemy at Beauport, whilst General Wolfe, with the other two brigades, are to cross the river of Montmorency and fall upon their rear; in this case, it is added that the marines are to defend our redoubts and batteries here, and detachments will remain in the north camp to maintain that post. Such schemes and reports, however, seem only calculated to amuse the enemy, and confirm them in a belief that nothing will be attempted this campaign by our army, except in that quarter; M. Montcalm has a distinct view of these stages from his camp, and the uses they are said to be intended for may possibly be conveyed to him by prisoners or deserters. Our works in this camp are almost completed, our redoubts are very strong, having a ditch, with a stout pricket-work in the center, and an *abbatis de bois* all round them. On the inside of the church, or general hospital, is also an excellent palisade-work, with loop-holes for musketry; and the west end of it is covered by a half-moon, where an officer's guard mounts every day.

We have intelligence by deserters, that Montcalm's army are fifteen thousand strong; that the other, which is to oppose General Amherst, is very inconsiderable; and that there are five frigates and some floating batteries at Les Trois Rivières, as well to prevent the junction of the two armies (in case the commander-in-chief should be able to advance) as to cut off all communication between them.

General Wolfe has been these two nights past at our batteries, with the grenadiers, light infantry of this brigade, and some companies of marines, being in expectation of a visit from the enemy. On the 9th Monsieur Charrier, lord of the manor of Point Levy (esteemed a good soldier and a bold enterprising man) and Mons. Dumas, the town major, crossed the river with fifteen hundred men, composed of five hundred inhabitants, three hundred students, one hundred savages and six hundred militia: that they reconnoitred our redoubts and batteries, and, finding them more defensible than they expected, they sent over for a reinforcement of three hundred *troupes de colonie*, which they obtained; that they were to have attacked on the night of the 12th, but, seeing we then opened our batteries against the town, they deferred their project until the night following; that they formed their corps into two columns, one of which actually set forward to strike this *coup*, and were to be sustained by the other: that they did not proceed above a quarter of a league from their rendezvous, when, being scared by a noise of a coppice on their march, they turned back; and the second column, seeing them advance towards them so precipitately, took them for a detachment of our troops, and fired upon them; which the others, under the like mistake, and through the excess of their panic, returned. Thus their project was defeated, with the loss of seventy killed and wounded; and was never afterwards renewed or thought of. The general was greatly disappointed at their not putting their menaces in execution, being well prepared to receive them: he had two brass six-pounders at the batteries, and two at the great detached redoubt that covers them.

As General Wolfe never had any opportunity of seeing the forty-third regiment, before they rendezvoused at Louisbourg, he was pleased to order them to be reviewed on 15 July by Brigadier Monckton, and directed that, in the firings, they should expend ammunition cartridges; the brigadier was pleased to say, 'he never saw greater regularity, closer fire, arms better levelled, or less disorder in any other regiment, since he had the honour to be an Officer, etc etc'.

The ground whereon we were reviewed was a field of fine wheat and, for my own part, I never saw grain closer cut down by the reaphook, or scithe, than this was; the method we were ordered to observe did not admit of any confusion, though we fired remarkably quick; our firings were from right and left, to the center, by platoons; and afterwards by subdivisions; taking the word of command from their respective officers. The grenadiers made a-half wheel inwards, as is usual in general firings, by word of command from the front: the performance of the regiment did, indeed, great honour to Lieutenant-Colonel Demetrius James, Major Robert Elliot, and to themselves; which, perhaps, might not have been expected by the general from a corps who had been so long cantoned in the remote fortresses of Nova Scotia.

After the firings, a serjeant from another regiment was ordered into the front to shew our men a new method of pushing bayonets; which, as it afforded a good deal of mirth in the field, I shall here describe, with the greatest regard to truth: 'The left hand under the swell below the lowermost rammer-pipe, and the right hand a-cross the brass at the extremity of the butt'. Thus was the firelock secured, which he poked out before him in like-manner as an indolent hay-maker turns hay with a forked pole. The brigadier did not stay in the field to see this new performance, having returned to camp after the firings; therefore, by whose orders this method was shewed to the regiment for imitation, I never could learn, though I made repeated inquiries, because, I confess, I thought it ludicrous, and was not a little ashamed of it.

Ninety-six shells, and seven carcasses, have been thrown into the town these last twenty-four hours ending 16 July. The bearer of the last flag of truce from the enemy told General Wolfe: 'We do not doubt but you will demolish the town; but we are determined your army shall never get footing within its walls'. To which the general replied: 'I will be master of Quebec, if I stay here until the latter end of November next'. At eleven o'clock a fire broke out in a large building in the upper town, and burned with great fury, by the wind's blowing fresh at north-west: the great cathedral church of Quebec with all its paintings, images and ornaments, were intirely destroyed by this conflagration. The enemy seemed thereby much incensed, and cannonaded our batteries very vigorously for the space of two hours; our batteries in the north camp played briskly into the enemy's camp at the same time, without any return. A party of Canadians and Indians shewed themselves on the high ground to the eastward of our camp; the rangers, supported by the picquets, soon went in pursuit of, and dispersed them. The enemy's fire slackened towards evening, and the building, which was in flames, seems to be either consumed or extinguished.

The town and our batteries were very quiet the night of the 16th; the enemy were endeavouring to finish a battery on the west side of the fall; but General Wolfe gave them such heavy fire from his cannon and howitzers as obliged them to desist. M. de Levis often solicited M. Montcalm to erect batteries and dislodge Mr Wolfe and his troops from the fall; but the other refused—saying, 'Drive them thence, and they will give us more trouble; while they are there, they cannot hurt us; let them amuse themselves'.

Notwithstanding the excessive hot fire on our batteries and redoubts yesterday from the town, there was no damage sustained on our part, either to the works or the troops employed there. The savages are very troublesome in the neighbourhood of the north camp, which obliges the troops to be very alert: the general frequently sends out large detachments to scour the environs of his camp, and to endeavour to draw part of the French army out of their trenches, by often counter-marching in the skirts of the woods in their view, as if intending to cross the river of Montmorency and attack them, four grenadiers were scalped there last night.

Two of our floating stages were sent over to-day to Orleans for trial; they will each contain near three hundred men, and are supported on the water by a parcel of iron-bound pipes, or casks, fastened together with small cables; they are exactly square, with a hand-rail to three faces; and the fourth face is covered by a kind of mantlet, or wooden fence, musket-proof; which, upon the floats being towed towards the shore, lets down and forms a stage for the troops to disembark on. I confess I think they are unwieldly, and not likely to answer the intended purposes, as they cannot be otherwise worked (especially on this rapid river) than by boats taking them in tow.

The garrison has not fired at our batteries since three o'clock in the afternoon yesterday, the 17th: they began this day at noon, and continued cannonading and bombarding incessantly until sun-set, without any loss or accident whatsoever: General Wolfe was there for some time; no man can display greater activity than he does between the different camps of his army.

Between ten and eleven o'clock this night, sailed with a fair wind, and with tide of flood, the *Sutherland*, Captain Rouse, with the *Squirrel*, three cats, and two trading sloops with provisions, and passed the town; the *Diana* frigate was to have accompanied them, but she ran aground under the Little Rock-Guard, and stuck so fast that she could not be got off. The enemy did not fire above twenty-eight guns all night, which makes us conjecture that the sailing of these ships into the upper river was a great surprise to them; General Wolfe, who was then at our batteries, gave the town a most incessant fire while this small fleet were passing.

The enemy erected a gibbet on the grand battery above the lower town and hanged two sentinels, we suppose for not being more alert on their posts, and neglecting to apprise them of the first appearance of our ships advancing, to pass the garrison, into the upper river.

Captain Rouse has taken some of the enemy's small craft, set fire to them and sent them down: there are on board the *Sutherland* and the other ships above, the grenadiers of the 15th, 48th and 78th regiments, together with a battalion of Royal Americans; this detachment is under the command of Colonel Carleton, and his object, it is said, is to destroy a large magazine of provisions which the enemy are reported to have at Point aux Trembles, to procure intelligence, and to endeavour to divide the enemy's force and attention from this quarter: the grenadiers of the 43rd regiment were destined for this service, but, being on board of the *Diana*, they were ordered to disembark.

A serjeant has deserted from the enemy, who says, 'he is of opinion General Amherst will meet with little opposition at Carillon (or Crown Point) to which he is advancing very successfully; that the Canadians begin to be dissatisfied and tired of the siege; that, in consequence of General Wolfe's manifesto's, they would gladly quit the army, return to their respective habitations, and remain neuter; but, when there is the least murmur or discontent among them, M. Montcalm and the governor general threaten them with the savages'. This man adds that the most respectable inhabitants of Quebec are retired, with all their portable effects, to Point aux Trembles.

The enemy's floating batteries had the presumption to come and attack the *Diana* frigate, but were soon beat off by two field-pieces which Brigadier Monckton sent down with all dispatch to that part of the shore for that purpose. There was a smart cannonading, the afternoon of the 19th between a battery on the side of the hill in the north camp, the battery on the Point of Orleans, and some of the enemy's floats: one of the latter was blown up, had five men killed and two blasted, who with difficulty crept to the shore; another float was also drove a-shore, not, however, until she had one man killed and had no other way at that time to retire, the tide being too far spent. Our new batteries are in great forwardness, and will soon be ready to open. The command at Orleans have been reinforced by some of the provincials who lately arrived from New-England.

The light infantry, who have been on a scout, returned on the 20th; they brought in some cattle and plunder, also a man and boy, whom they surprised this morning as they were fishing: the former discharged his piece before he would surrender, whereby we had one man killed; we had near an hour's conversation with this fellow, at Nadau's great water-mill, who seemed to be a subtle old rogue, of seventy years of age (as he told us) and I think was a prodigy for his advanced time of life: he boasted a good deal to us, and said the French army were thirty thousand strong, and the half of them were regulars; we plied him well with port wine, and then his heart was more open, and, seeing that we laughed at his exaggerated accounts, he said, 'he wished the affair was well over, one way or the other; that his countrymen were all discontented, and would either surrender, or disperse and act a neutral part, if it was not for the persuasions of their priests and the fear of being maltreated by the savages, with whom they are threatened on all occasions'. The *Diana* frigate has got off with little or no damage; slack firing at our batteries to-day, the enemy silent.

On the 22nd we received advice that the detachment under Colonel Carleton sailed some leagues up the river, landed on the north side, and made a number of prisoners, among whom there are few persons of fashion. The colonel went in search of magazines, but was not so successful as could have been wished; he met with some opposition at landing from a body of Indians, yet sustained no other loss than having a few men and officers wounded, among whom was Major Prevost of the Royal Americans; the soldiers acquired some plunder, though very insignificant. By the same advices, the enemy shewed the like jealousy and attention everywhere, as below the town, fortifying the most accessible parts of the north shore for many leagues upwards: by letters that fell into our hands, the inhabitants describe their situation as completely wretched and lament much our ships riding above the town, as thereby they conclude they have lost their communication with Montreal and the upper country.

On the 24th Colonel Carleton sent down three French gentlemen prisoners, who were immediately transmitted on board of the admiral: that detachment still remains on board the squadron in the upper river. We have maintained an almost incessant fire of shot and shell against the town these last fourteen hours, which set part of it in flames; the enemy very sparing of their ammunition. Our weather is extremely wet and unfavourable. Our out-parties are ordered to burn and lay waste the country for the future, sparing only churches or houses dedicated to divine worship: it is again repeated that women and children are not to be molested on any account whatsoever.

Major Dalling's light infantry brought in this afternoon, to our camp, two hundred and fifty male and female prisoners: among this number was a very respectable looking-priest and about forty men fit to bear arms: there was almost an equal number of black cattle, with about seventy sheep and lambs, and a few horses. Brigadier Monckton entertained the reverend father and some other fashionable personages in his tent, and most humanely ordered refreshments to all the rest of the captives: which noble example was followed by the soldiery, who generously crowded about those unhappy people, sharing their provisions, rum and tobacco with them: they were sent in the evening on board of transports in the river.

While they were on shore, I had an opportunity of conversing with some of the most intelligent of them, who assured me that Mr Wolfe's placart had such effect upon the people in general that they would actually have conformed to his desire and commands, therein proposed and promised to the Canadians, if it had not been for the arbitrary menaces of Mons. Montcalm, who threatened them with the savages; that, after the first surprise was over upon their being made prisoners, they were overjoyed to see themselves in the hands of the English; for that they had been under apprehensions, for several days past, of having a body of four hundred barbarians sent among them to rifle their parish and habitations. All the letters that have been intercepted, as well as their own personal accounts, agree in the scarcity of bread throughout the province. I saw one of these letters that had been wrote by a person in Quebec to his friend in the country, and was to this effect: 'I herewith send you fourteen biscuits, which are all that I can spare, and, in our present distressful and most deplorable situation, are no small compliment,' etc.

The town-major of Quebec, who came down with the last flag of truce, took upon him to reflect on our conduct in making so many captives among the old men, women and children of the country; and on our politeness in returning them, because we did not know how else to dispose of them, etc etc. Whereupon he was desired to inform his superiors that, since they were pleased to view our lenity and generous behaviour in that unfavourable light, we had ships and provisions enough to accommodate all prisoners that we may happen to make hereafter, and for the future we should not trouble them with any more of them. This gentleman intimated that they were now employed in erecting traverses and other works in all parts of the upper and lower town, thereby insinuating that they would stand the consequences of a storm, rather than forfeit their capital.

Colonel Fraser's detachment returned on the morning of the 27th and presented us with more scenes of distress, and the dismal consequences of war, by a great number of wretched families, whom they brought in prisoners, with some of their effects and near three hundred black cattle, sheep, hogs and horses. Though these acts of hostility may be warrantable by the law of nations and rules of war, yet, as humanity is far from being incompatible with the character of a soldier, any man who is possessed of the least share of it cannot help sympathising with, and being sincerely affected at, the miseries of his fellow-creatures, though even his enemies; making every charitable allowance for their repeated barbarities as the natural result of ignorance and prejudice of education.

Late that night the enemy sent down a most formidable fire-raft, which consisted of a parcel of schooners, shallops and stages chained together; it could not be less than an hundred fathoms in length, and was covered with grenades, old swivels, gun and pistol barrels loaded up to their muzzles, and various other inventions and combustible matters. This seemed to be their *dernière* attempt against our fleet, which happily miscarried as before, for our gallant seamen, with their usual expertness, grappled them before they got down above a third part of the bason, towed them safe to shore, and left them at anchor, continually repeating—*All's well.* A remarkable expression from some of these intrepid souls to their comrades on this occasion I must not omit, on account of its singular uncouthness, viz. *Dam-me, Jack, did'st thee ever take hell in tow before?*

A flag of truce was sent up the next day to the garrison, and it is confidently said to convey the following message to the French generals: 'If the enemy presume to send down any more fire-rafts, they are to be made fast to two particular transports in which are all the Canadian and other prisoners, in order that they may perish by their own base inventions'; and it is pretended, that the masters of these transports have received their orders accordingly. This, however, is only looked upon as a menace, that, in case any of our men should fall into the enemy's hands by desertion or otherwise, they may be able to confirm these political threats.

ORDERS                              29 July, Camp at Montmorency
'The regiments are to be under arms at five o'clock this afternoon at the head of their incampments, and to wait there till sent for to their respective alarm-posts. The rest of the light infantry will return this night, from the Island of Orleans to this camp. Colonel Howe will take his former post. Anstruther's, Otway's, and Lascelles's will incamp on their proper ground. Great care to be taken by the regiments within their respective incampments, and in their neighbourhood, that all offals and filth of every kind that might taint the air be buried deep under ground. The general recommends in the strongest manner to the commanders of corps, to have their camps kept sweet and clean; strict inquiry to be made in this camp, at the Point of Orleans and the Point of Levy, concerning the sutlers and followers of the army, and who are known to sell liquors that intoxicate the men, that they may be forthwith dismissed and

sent on board their ships. The regiments are not to call in their working parties this evening, as they must exert themselves to finish the business of this post, that farther operations may take place.

'Two hundred men of the Royal American battalion, with their blankets and two days' provisions ready dressed, to be in readiness below at the cove, by eight in the morning, to imbark in four flat-bottomed boats; this detachment is intended to reinforce the companies of grenadiers, if there should be occasion; these boats are to row up with the flood (but out of cannon-shot) till they come opposite the upper redoubt, where they must lie upon their oars and wait for farther orders. Anstruther's regiments, the light infantry and rangers are to march, at nine o'clock, under Colonel Howe's command, about a mile into the woods towards the ford where the Canadians and Indians are incamped; this body must shift, just within the wood, from the camp of the light infantry to the road, but so as barely to be seen, from the opposite side of the river, by the enemy. As Major Hussey's corps have been up most part of the night, they are to be left to guard the camp of the light infantry; Colonel Howe will lengthen his line of march, so as to appear numerous.

'The remaining battalions will get under arms, when the water begins to ebb, in readiness to cross the ford if there should be an absolute necessity for so doing; in the mean time they will continue their work with all possible diligence and assiduity. If ships can be brought near enough to operate and the wind is fair, an attack will be made on one of the enemy's most detached works; in aid of which attack, the artillery from hence must be employed. Brigadier-General Townshend will be pleased to give such directions as he thinks most for the service upon this head. In general, the cannon are not to be fired, nor even brought up to fire, till it is visible, by the motions of the ships, that the attack will be made; if the day is very hot and no wind, this operation cannot take place. If the battalions should march, Colonel Howe must return to his camp in the most secret manner; the marines must be thrown into the two redoubts. When Lascelles's regiment takes post, the remaining part of the Americans into the great redoubt; Captain Hazen's company into the fortified house; Anstruther's and the light infantry will be ready to join the army. When Captain Cowart's detachment is not wanted with the artillery, forty of his men are to be put into the little redoubt near his camp, and the rest in the great redoubt on the hill.'

At nine o'clock in the morning of the 30th the regiments at Point Levy were ordered to hold themselves in readiness to march at a moment's warning; a signal was made for all masters of transports to repair on board of their agent: in consequence whereof it is said that all the transports' boats are to be manned in order to make a feint and thereby divide the enemy's attention, while the army are to endeavour to penetrate into the French camp between Beauport and the fall. Every seaman is to be armed with a musket, cartouch-box, pistol and cutlass. Very hot work at our batteries to-day, and about two o'clock the enemy gave them a round from every gun they could bring to bear upon them, after being silent for a long time before: we bombarded the town last night from sun-set until sun-rise this morning. The army are in very high spirits, from the confidence they have in their general officers and the great unanimity which happily prevails among them. Several shells were thrown at the *Centurion* and others of our fleet in the channel, but had no effect: most of them bursted in the air before they made the distance. Sultry weather for several days past, wind variable and scant.

At eight o'clock on the 31st the troops at Point Levy were ordered to be ready to imbark immediately, boats coming from the fleet for this purpose.

Nine o'clock. Ordered that the 15th and 78th regiments with Brigadier-General Monckton be ready to imbark: the 43rd and 48th light infantry, under Major Dalling, and the marines remain here to defend our batteries and redoubts.

Ten o'clock. The Louisbourg grenadiers, with those of the 15th, 43rd, 48th and 78th, a detachment of the Royal Americans, the two regiments before-mentioned, and Brigadier Monckton, imbarked, rendezvoused at the Point of Orleans, put off immediately, and remained half-channel over, waiting for farther orders.

Eleven o'clock. Two armed transport-cats, drawing little water, worked over and grounded abreast of the Pointe à Lessay, westward of the fall of Montmorency. A smart cannonading ensued between those ships (supported by Admiral Saunders in the *Centurion*) and a detached battery which the enemy opposed to defend the fording place at the foot of the water-fall, and lasted near two hours: at the same time our batteries on the eminence to the eastward briskly enfiladed the enemy's works at the left extremity of their camp, and also their detached battery and redoubt on the beach below.

Twelve o'clock. The 43rd regiment ordered to be ready at a moment's warning. Colonel James and Major Elliot agreed and ordered that the regiment should embark, land and fight by com-

panies under their own officers, which afforded the highest satisfaction to the soldiers; this method, on a service of this nature, does
not admit of confusion. Weather extremely hot. The enemy throw
shells at the troops (to little purpose) who are in their boats half
channel over. Two corps of the enemy, one regulars, the other
militia, made a motion towards the rear of their left, as if they
intended to cross the river of Montmorency at the upper ford and
march into General Wolfe's camp; where-upon the 48th regiment
received orders to march immediately up the country some miles to
the westward of our batteries, and then to strike into the woods and
return to their camp as much undiscovered as possible; this had the
desired effect, for the two French battalions also returned from the
upper ford, crossed the river Charles, and marched up towards
Sillery to watch the motions of the 48th regiment.

Three o'clock. Colonel James received an order from General
Wolfe, that the 43rd and 48th regiments, and Major Dalling's light
infantry, do hold themselves in readiness to embark, the moment
boats may arrive for them; that these corps are to leave proper
guards to take care of their camps, who, with the marines, are to
have charge of this important post; and the colonel is desired to
remain in command until farther orders.

Four o'clock. The *Centurion* and the two armed cats renewed
a very brisk fire on the enemy's detached works.

Half past four o'clock. A heavy cannonading now from every
quarter.

Five o'clock. Very gloomy weather; some of the boats, in
attempting to land, struck upon some ledges, which retarded our
operations; and, by the enemy's shot and shells, the boats were a
little confused; the enemy abandoned the right of their camp and,
with their whole army, lined their intrenchments from the center to
the left.

Half past five o'clock. The first division of the troops, consisting
of all the grenadiers of the army, made a second attempt, landed at
the Pointe à Lessay, and obliged the enemy to abandon the detached
battery and redoubt below the precipice: by this time the troops to
the eastward of the fall were in motion to join and support the
attack; but the grenadiers, impatient to acquire glory, would not
wait for any reinforcements, but ran up the hill and made many
efforts, though not with the greatest regularity, to gain the summit,
which they found less practicable than had been expected: in this
situation they received a general discharge of musketry from the
enemy's breastworks, which was continued without any return, our

brave fellows nobly reserving their fire until they could reach the top of the precipice, which was inconceivably steep; to persevere any longer they found now to little purpose; their ardour was checked by the repeated heavy fire of the enemy and, as if conscious of their mistake, the natural consequence of their impetuosity, they retired in disorder (in spite of the most unparalleled valour and good conduct on the part of their officers) and took shelter in the redoubt and battery on the beach, where Brigadier Monckton's corps were now landed and formed; those under Brigadiers Townshend and Murray being also at hand, ready to sustain their friends.

The general, seeing the situation of affairs, night drawing on a-pace and the ammunition of the army damaged with the dreadfullest thunder-storm and fall of rain that can be conceived, sent to stop Brigadier Townshend, and ordered Brigadier Monckton to reimbark his division and the scattered corps of grenadiers in the best manner he could, the flat-bottomed boats being at hand for that purpose. The enemy did not attempt to pursue; their ammunition must undoubtedly have shared the same fate with our own, for the violence of the storm exceeded any description I can attempt to give of it.

A few Indians came down to scalp some of our wounded on the beach. Upon this occasion it was, that Lieutenant Henry Peyton, of the Royal Americans, displayed so much gallantry; for he, being at the same time badly wounded, raised himself up, and with his double-barrelled fusil killed two of those barbarians, one after the other, before they could execute their inhuman practice; and must then have fallen a sacrifice to others, but that Providence, willing to reward so much merit, threw an honest Highlander in his way, who happily took him up and laid him in the bow of one of the boats, then ready to put off.

By the excellent disposition which Brigadier Monckton made on the beach, after he had collected all the troops that were on shore, he reimbarked them without farther loss, bringing away as many of the wounded as he could come at; and the army returned to their respective camps. As the tide had left the armed cats dry, the admiral sent orders to have the officers and men taken out, and the hulks burned lest they should fall into the enemy's hands, to whom they might be servicable on some future occasion. The loss of our forces this day, killed, wounded and missing, including all ranks, amounted to four hundred and forty-three; among whom were two captains and two lieutenants slain on the spot; one colonel, six captains, nineteen lieutenants and three ensigns wounded.

The enemy suffered most from our batteries on the eminences to the eastward, having, as I was afterwards informed, at Quebec, near two hundred men and officers killed and disabled.

The object of this day's operations was to penetrate into the enemy's camp and force them to a battle, in hopes, as their army (though infinitely superior in numbers) consisted mostly of militia and peasants, they would have yielded an easy victory to our regular forces; and notwithstanding the variety of difficulties we had to encounter with, such as intrenchments, traverses, redoubts and fortified houses that were loaded with swivels and other small pieces of field artillery (almost innumerable), it is more than probable we would have carried our point (though with great loss) had it not been for a chain of concurrent circumstances that defeated the general's plan and expectations: to enumerate these may seem necessary.

The obstruction our boats met with in their first attempt to land, by which much time was lost, occasioned by a ledge of rocks extending along the north shore from the right to the left of the front of their camp; the storm of uncommon heavy rain, that not only damaged our powder, but rendered the precipices to the enemy's works so slippery as to become impossible for men to ascend them; these, together with the ill-timed zeal of our grenadiers, who, regardless of discipline and the commands of their officers, were eager to distinguish themselves under a man of whom they, and indeed the soldiery in general, had the highest opinion and confidence—to which I may subjoin the retreat of the tide, then more than half ebb, and the hasty approaching night beginning to expand her dreary wings, with a farther prospect of unfavourable weather.

Besides all these, other circumstances there are not less deserving attention; for, had we succeeded, the river Charles remained afterwards to be crossed before we could invest the garrison; and the French army would probably have occupied the high ground behind it and intrenched there: our army was already greatly diminished, and would have been considerably more so if the general had persevered; all which deterring incidents, critically concurring, prevailed on his excellency to withdraw his troops and give up the project for the present.

# VII

# Amherst on Lake Champlain

*Hundreds of miles to the south, the methodical Amherst was arraying the main British army. He was one of those generals who never moved until the last item of the troops' equipment was in place. First he organised his base on Lake George, assembled his forces, hauled up his artillery, built his batteaux and pontoons and then launched them in regatta formation, with flanking forces marching along the banks. He avenged Abercromby's defeat at Ticonderoga, where Lake George meets Lake Champlain, but his movements had been so ponderous that the momentum of the campaign slackened.*

I SHALL NOW TAKE a view of the operations of the army under the commander-in-chief, where we shall find our friends have their share in the great choice of obstacles, which everywhere appear in the reduction of this province.

The army under Major-General Amherst, commander-in-chief of all his majesty's forces in North America, consisting of the 1st, 17th, 27th, 42nd, 55th and 77th regiments of regulars, and the 80th of light armed infantry; with those of Scuyler, Lyman, Ruggles, Whiting, Worcester, Fitch, Babcock, Lovewell and Willard, provincials; a body of rangers and Indians, with a respectable detachment of the royal train of artillery under Major Ord (the rest of the army being detached, as will be hereafter mentioned, whereof the greatest part are under Brigadier-General Prideaux, including a corps of Indians under Sir William Johnson, who are to proceed up the Mohawk river, thence to Niagara; and the remainder, under Brigadier-General Stanwix, destined to the westward, towards Pittsburg, etc with each a party of artillery and light troops) were as early in motion as the season of the year would admit.

The whole month of May had been necessarily taken up in preparations for the campaign by the lakes; the provincial troops rendezvoused at Albany, and incamped as fast as they joined. General Amherst arrived there on the 12th, and ordered the regular troops forward, to take post on the road leading to Fort Edward, distant fifty-six miles from Albany. There is a good navigation for batteaus, etc for thirty-six miles of the way.

A detachment of the army, composed of regulars, light infantry, provincials and rangers, moved forward and took post a few miles on the lake side of the camp at Fort Edward, and there constructed a small stockaded fort, with two bastions and a moat. This service was performed by Major West of the 55th regiment. The general marched to Fort Edward in the beginning of June, and left Brigadier Gage at Albany to bring up the remainder of the army, who were employed in batteauing up provisions, artillery stores, etc. This work was attended with great difficulty, the river being uncommonly high and the current so rapid that, instead of setting, which is much less laborious, they were obliged to have recourse to rowing. The greatest part of the train being left at Fort Edward at the close of the last campaign, the rest from Albany with the troops arrived there by the 12th of June, and incamped.

This camp at Fort Edward is the grand rendezvous of the army, and, as the provincial troops arrive, great pains are taken to instruct them in their duty by making them acquainted with the use of arms, familiarising them to fire at marks; and they, as well as the regulars, are constantly employed in forming and dispersing in the woods, and in other exercises adapted to the peculiar method of carrying on war in close-covered countries; yesterday a party of them were embarrassed in these dark forests, and it was some time before they could find their way, but several guns being discharged for their guidance, from the fort, they happily recovered themselves, and returned safe.

On 13 June Colonel Grant, with eight companies of his Royal Highlanders, and the detachments ordered yesterday, were advanced seven miles forward and took post there; the colonel instantly threw up a rectangular stockade and mounted three four-pounders in it.

ORDERS                                                          20 June

'The *générale* to beat at half an hour before day-break, on which the army will immediately strike their tents. The *assemblée* to beat half an hour after, on which the regiments will draw up in the front of their incampments, and are to be told off ready to march when ordered, the whole in two columns; the regulars by the left by half files; the provincials by the right two deep, as they have always been accustomed to it. Major Rogers, with the rangers, and Major Gladwin, with Gage's light infantry, will form the advance-guard, and are to take great precautions in keeping out flanking parties to the right, as far as the half-way brook; from thence to the lake they will have advanced and flanking parties to the left as well as the

AMHERST OVERLOOKING THE HEIGHTS OF ABRAHAM

right. These corps will draw up at day-break, in the road beyond the front of the camp, on the left of the light infantry. The detachment at present under Major Gladwin's command will join their corps at day-break. The light infantry of the regiments need not strike their tents till the army is near marched by; the grenadiers will march by the left, and halt on the road, in the rear of Gage's, till Forbes's and the Inniskilling regiments join them; which two regiments must march in the front of the first line, the left of the 27th joining the right of the 17th, till they join the grenadiers. Whiting's will march by the right, along their own front, to the front of Worcester's; Worcester's will follow Whiting's in the same order of march, and Fitch's will follow Worcester's; the whole marching along the front of the Rhode island regiment, which will follow Worcester's and march up the hill along the left-hand road, till the left of Whiting's is opposite to the left of the grenadiers; the second battalion of Ruggles's will likewise march from the right along their own front, falling in upon the rear of the Rhode Island regiment; when that is passed, the artillery-waggons will follow; then the tents and baggage are to follow in the following order: first, the general's with his guard, then Brigadier-General Gage's; that of the rangers, light infantry of Gage's; the grenadiers, Forbes's, Inniskilling's, Whiting's, Worcester's, Fitch's, Babcock's, and the second battalion of Ruggles's; the baggage of the light infantry: the light corps under Major Holmes will form the rear-guard of the whole. The 77th, the New Hampshire, and Willard's are not to march, but to remain under the command of Colonel Montgomery; they will strike their tents to change their camp as that colonel will order them.

'The general expects the flanking platoons shall be ready to turn out at a moment's notice; that the whole army have their arms in order, ready loaded; and that the men are, at all times, ready to receive the enemy; on all halts, the column to the right will face to the right, the column on the left to the left; and, in case any attack should happen, the left column shall not face a man to the right, or offer to fire a shot, on pain of the severest punishment. When the regiments are drawn up on their ground, the regulars will wheel their platoons to the left, and the provincial to the right, then as they were, that the officers and men may know the platoons they belong to, before they march off. Every platoon is to be attentive to the officer that commands it. The officer's attention must be intirely to his platoon, obeying the orders of his superiors: and the general expects that, though the officers have fusils, none of them will be so

L

inconsiderate as to amuse themselves in firing at the enemy, by which they would inevitably neglect the much more essential part of service—the care of their platoons; and he absolutely forbids the officers' firing, unless on emergent occasions. Whatsoever post an officer may be sent to take, the general expects he will first visit the ground round him, and post his sentinels as he judges best to make it impossible for the enemy to surprise him; sentinels must not be out of sight or hearing of the guard, or of each other; the officer will throw up logs, or strengthen his post by the best means he can, so that the enemy shall not force it, as the general intends never to take any post that shall be abandoned, but shall be defended and sustained on all occasions, unless he himself, on some extraordinary event, shall give the officer who commands at the post particular orders to the contrary.'

The stockade at the seven-mile post was finished on the 21st; the general with Brigadier Gage and the army, pursuant to the orders of yesterday, marched from Fort Edward, and took post at Lake George; they were joined by the Royal Highlanders from Colonel Grant's post, Lieutenant-Colonel Payson remaining there in command with one thousand provincials, seven field-pieces and an officer and twelve artillery-men; the general took six twelve-pounders, two six-pounders, and two howitzers with him, under the conduct of the officer commanding the artillery, together with a large quantity of every kind of ammunition for cannon and musketry; one hundred carriages with batteaus; and a great many others with provision and other stores. Provisions, batteaus and whaleboats continue to be forwarded from Fort Edward to the seven-mile post. Very hot weather for some days past.

The general is busy in redoubting his camp at Lake George, and repairing the roads; the most prudent precautions are taken to prevent a surprise, and his sentries are all doubled at night-fall. Colonel Payson's post was alarmed, two days ago, by a report of some Indians being seen lurking between his camp and Fort Edward; he detached a company of provincials to scour that part of the country, but they did not make any discoveries. The colonel is very alert in forwarding provisions and stores to the lake as fast as they arrive at his post; he has contracted the works that were thrown up by Colonel Grant, and takes great pains to secure his post from a surprise; to which end frequent scouting parties are detached to South Bay and the neighbourhood of his camp; and, though seldom a day passes without an alarm, he is very diligent in causing his men to be instructed in the exercise of the firelock, and rendering them expert marksmen. The weather is so intolerably hot, that the teams can scarce perform their duty; and on this account provisions only have been forwarded to Colonel Payson's post from Fort Edward for several days; the army at Lake George are well supplied with greens and spruce-beer, and parties are every-where detached to secure the communications between the camp and the dependent posts, by which the waggons can travel in safety.

Several batteaus of the enemy have lately appeared on the lake; they attempted to surprise two officers and a few men, who were fishing off Diamond Island, distant fourteen miles from the army; the officers instantly put a-shore and made the best of their way to the camp, with the enemy close to their heels, insomuch that they had barely time to save themselves; whereupon the general sent a fishing party on the following day to the same place, under Captain Stark; and at the same time a covering party was detached, consisting of two companies of grenadiers, two of light infantry, some rangers and Indians, the whole under Major Campbell, with an intent to form an ambuscade: the fishing party were directed to keep within call of each other, and were to be ready to follow Captain Stark, whose boat was distinguished with a red flag, and he had orders, upon the appearance of an enemy, to row in shore where the ambush lay, and in so seemingly fearful a manner as to decoy the enemy after them. This scheme was exceedingly well concerted, but was not attended with the wished for success; if it had been necessary, Major Campbell was to have been sustained by a larger detachment of grenadiers and light troops, under Colonel Haviland, who were posted for that purpose.

Sixteen men of the New-Jersey regiment went out without leave on the morning of the 30th to cut spruce about a small mile from the left of our camp; they did not take their arms with them; about eleven o'clock they were fired upon by a party of Canadians and Indians, who killed and wounded eleven of them; the others who escaped (with such of the wounded as were able) retired to a redoubt which covers our left flank at the distance of about five hundred yards; the rabble pursued them with great insolence, close to that intrenchment and would have taken and killed every man of them, had not the detachment who are posted there repulsed them with a brisk fire; the picquets of the line, with our Indians and rangers, were instantly sent in pursuit of these blood-hounds; but, before they could come up with them, they scalped all that fell into their hands, retired to their boats, and rowed off: by the time our people got to the lake, the scoundrels were out of musket-shot, and insolently lay some time on their oars, shouting at them.

The most of the articles, which we buried last campaign, remained undiscovered by the enemy; they found a floating-battery that was sunk in the lake, which mounted eight heavy pieces of ordnance; and this was the only thing of any importance. This morning Colonel Montgomery's regiment with two of the provincials (Willard's and Lovel's) and some rangers, marched from Fort Edward and joined the army; they had all our heavy artillery and a great number of covered waggons, with the batteaus on carriages, under their convoy; at Colonel Payson's post they took up a detachment of an officer and twelve artillery-men, with seven field-pieces, and arrived late in the evening; the general, with a small escort, went to meet them, and the weather favoured their march, being fair, and less sultry than of late. The army continue to be well supplied with fresh provisions and spruce-beer.

The French savages are daily sculking in the vicinity of our camp having the advantage of the adjoining eminences, whence they have a distinct view of all our transactions: they lately pursued two of our Indians for almost two days together; but, by our picquets and light troops scouring these hills every day, they are in some measure awed from giving us any considerable annoyance; all our advanced guards are ordered to light fires at night-fall and continue them until morning. The troops are permitted to bathe at stated hours in the lake, which conduces much to the health of the soldiery. A number of men are employed in making brick and lime; others in works of various kinds relating to the farther operations of the campaign, particularly at the new fort, the sloop, batteaus, etc and proper covering parties every-where attend them, by which they work in great safety; the provincial regiments that arrived last with Colonel Montgomery are out at exercise, practising the firing motions and firing by platoons.

On 10 July, ten waggoners of the provincials were tried for stealing his majesty's arms and working-tools; one was sentenced to receive four hundred lashes, the others three hundred each: the general made a public example of the principal, by ordering him first to be punished at the head of every regiment, and then to be turned out of camp and deemed unworthy to serve in the army; the other delinquents his excellency was pleased to pardon, but ordered that they should be marched prisoners to see the punishment inflicted on the chief transgressor; from thence they proceeded to Saratoga for the tools and arms that were stolen. Two others of these provincial teamsters, with three negroes, were also tried as parties concerned, and were acquitted.

Batteaus are delivered to the troops, in the following proportions: the Royal, 42nd and 77th, thirty-five batteaus each; the 17th, 27th, 55th and 2nd battalion of Ruggles's, Willard, Lovewell, Babcock, Whiting, Fitch, Worcester and Lyman, twenty-six each, with their oars and all other appurtenances; a whale-boat per regiment for each commanding officer is also delivered, with orders that proper persons may be appointed to water them to prevent their leaking; and small guards from each corps to take care of their own. Officers commanding regiments are ordered to mark and number their batteaus. In the regulations of this day, it is said that each batteau will carry twelve barrels of flour, or nine of pork, when ordered to load; and it is supposed will have about twenty men, or a few more or less, in each, etc. The proportions for the grenadiers and light troops are: rangers, forty-three whale-boats, one batteau; Gage's light infantry, forty-one whale-boats, four batteaus and the flat-bottomed boat; light infantry of regiments, forty-three whale-boats, five batteaus; and the grenadiers the same; two batteaus will be allowed for the sutlers of regiments, but they must provide boatmen for themselves. The whale-boats are ordered to be marked and numbered in like manner as the batteaus. One batteau per brigade is allowed for the surgeons of the regulars, and two for the surgeons of the provincials; the artillery will be supplied with whatever number they may require.

The embarkation of the army and artillery, etc has proved a work of incredible difficulty, insomuch that though the working parties were employed all the night of 20 July, the whole were not on board until five o'clock, at which time the *assemblée* was beat, and about six the van was in motion; this embarrassment chiefly proceeded from the faulty condition of many batteaus, for, as fast as they were loaded, we had them to unload; one of them, with an hundred barrels of powder, sunk immediately, as did likewise a raft with two ten-inch mortars, which the general thought proper to leave behind, rather than subject the army to farther delay.

Our artillery consisted of six twenty-pounders, four eighteen-pounders, ten twelve-pounders, seven six-pounders, with three three-pounders; six eight-inch howitzers, two of five and an half; eight royal mortars, four ten-inch ditto, and one of thirteen. The army put off in four columns, with two boats only a-breast; the first consisted of rangers, regiments of light infantry, grenadiers and two provincial regiments; the second, of two brigades of regulars; the third, of the detachment of Royal Artillery, twelve rafts with cannon, and the *invincible radeau* in front, with two provincial regiments; and the fourth column consisted of the remainder of the provincials, under Colonel Lyman, who had a boat with an eighteen-pounder on their right, while the rangers in the first division had another with a twelve-pounder on their left; Gage's light infantry, in forty whale-boats, formed the van, rowing in a line a-breast, preceded by a flat-bottomed boat mounting a three-pounder; and the *Halifax* sloop cruised in the rear of the whole. Whenever the wind favoured us, the troops converted their blankets to the use of sails; the ordnance were not dismounted, but carried on their carriages and beds, upon floating stages or rafts, for the sake of expedition at landing; and the radeau (mounting twelve pounders) threw out signals, which were repeated by the sloop in the rear. Thus did the army proceed until we made the first narrows, which was about ten o'clock, when we had a signal to halt and dress our columns; we soon after set sail again, the wind blew fresh, and the weather grew hazy.

A little before night, we had another signal to bring to, which was instantly observed with the greatest order, each corps and division forming in their proper stations, and the rafts were moored to the radeau: in this situation we remained this night, not without considerable apprehensions of danger, as our wind and weather were very rough, with a disagreeable tumbling sea.

As soon as it was clear day-light on the 22nd, a signal was made for the army to proceed, and in a few hours we happily reached the second narrows, where the troops disembarked near to the former landing-place, leaving sufficient force to protect our stores, with proper guards to take care of the boats and baggage; and, in order that the men should be as light as possible, they left their coats and necessaries in the batteaus. Our van, composed of the light troops, soon after fell in with an advanced guard of the enemy, consisting of four hundred regulars and Indians, under Monsieur *Capitaine Bournie*, whom they routed, the enemy's savages not waiting for a second fire; two of Berry's regiment were made prisoners and four of them were scalped; their wounded they carried off with them in their flight.

This rencounter happened near the saw-mills (about two miles from Ticonderoga), a place so immensely strong by nature that an inferior force of veteran troops, if vigorously determined, would probably defeat the utmost efforts of five times their numbers. The army immediately advanced in good order and possessed themselves of this advantageous ground, an event at which the general expressed great satisfaction. The distance between the artillery landing-place and the saw-mills was near an English mile, and the road was every-where obstructed with large trees, which the enemy had cut down for that purpose; these our provincials soon cleared, being very expert ax-men; and an officer, with two six-pounders, were instantly forwarded to this post, where the troops threw up some intrenchments without loss of time, their tools being sent ashore, with several field-pieces, immediately after their landing.

The general, having secured his post at the saw-mills, and de-tached a sufficient force to the place of debarkation, marched for-ward with the main of his army towards the enemy's intrenchments without meeting with the least annoyance; but the field artillery could not follow, pursuant to his orders, on account of the many uncommon difficulties in the roads; so that we were obliged to send them round by water on rafts, and landed them within four or five hundred yards of the lines. The enemy's Indians attacked some of our advanced sentries; but, finding our troops are no longer to be surprised or terrified, they retired after exchanging a few shots. Parties from each regiment and corps were sent for the men's coats, tents and other necessaries. One of the prisoners taken today, acquaints us, 'that Monsieur Bourlamaque commands here, and that his forces amount to near three thousand men, consisting of the regiments of Berry (of two battalions), La Reine, a large body of Canadians, and about four hundred Indians'; he adds that they had been informed for a certainty of the arrival of a fleet and army before Quebec. The other prisoner reports the army in the lines to exceed four thousand men, but, as he is most shamefully intoxicated, no regard is paid to what he advances.

The troops lay on their arms all night; and, on the morning, of the 23rd, the enemy, observing that the general was drawing up his artillery and preparing to attack them in a regular formal manner, spared him the trouble by abandoning their intrenchments, of which his excellency immediately took possession with all the grenadiers of his army; and the troops were incamped behind the lines, the ground being instantly marked out for that purpose: the enemy fired warmly on the trenches from the fort [of Ticonderoga]; but the un-common height of their breast-works were now become extremely useful in covering our people from their shot and shells. Some out-houses and sheds on the point, contiguous to the fort, were set on fire by the French Indians. We are erecting a redoubt to defend the landing-place, and throwing up a breast-work of trees, from thence to the saw-mills, to protect the road. Several boats and canoes are seen on Lake Champlain, and an armed sloop, mounting eight guns, was also discovered; in the afternoon we got up two twelve-pounders and two howitzers attended by a captain and a detachment of the artillery; in the evening some batteaus and planks were drawn to the saw-mills, to make rafts for the heavy cannon.

During the night the enemy attacked our advanced guard of the trenches, by which we had a lieutenant and four men killed, and eleven wounded: it is suspected that our people, in the first confusion, fired upon each other. We got our flat-bottomed boat, with two twenty-four pounders and two ten-inch mortars, up to the saw-mills; the boat was drawn on a carriage, with her brass three-pounder mounted on her bow, as before. A captain, with a party, are gone to make a diversion on Lake Champlain; by the number of movements there, we are inclined to think the enemy are concerting a retreat; heavy firing from the fort to-day. At night-fall a party of rangers got a batteau into the lake, to endeavour to intercept the enemy's canoes, and to watch their motions; the general is very anxious to have the battering-cannon and mortars brought up, being resolved not to open on the fort until he can do it effectually.

Two twenty-four pounders and a thirteen-inch mortar, with their ammunition, were brought up on the morning of the 25th, conducted by the commanding officer of the artillery; the enemy have kept an incessant fire on the trenches these last twenty-four hours; they have now got the distance to the camp, and gall us considerably, four being killed by a shell, and several wounded; notwithstanding these annoyances, we have carried our approaches within six hundred yards of the fort, and Major Rogers, with his Indians, are advanced, endeavouring to amuse the besieged from our works by popping into theirs. The Honourable Colonel Townshend was picked off to-day in the trenches by a cannon-shot; he is very deservedly lamented by the general and the army. The enemy have got a bridge across the lake, with works to cover it, intending thereby to secure their retreat. The flat-bottomed boat, with fifty whale-boats, now on Lake Champlain, are ordered to proceed with a body of light troops to destroy such works as the enemy may have thrown up to obstruct the navigation, as well as to amuse them on that side.

About ten o'clock on the night of the 26th some deserters came into the trenches, to apprise us of the enemy's having abandoned the fort; and, before they could be conducted to the general, their magazine blew up, whereby the wooden works of the place were set on fire; before they went off, they loaded all their shells, guns and musketry up to their muzzles, with port-fuse's to the vents; and the flames, communicating to them, rendered the place for some time inaccessible with any degree of safety. The general, being ascertained of this great event, detached Colonel Haviland with the light infantry of regiments and the rangers on the lake with the flat-bottomed boat and whale-boats to follow and harrass their rear; who came up with some batteaus laden with powder, which they took, and made sixteen men prisoners, one of whom was a cadet.

Early the next morning a serjeant of regulars requested the general's permission to go into the fort and strike the French flag which they left flying; his excellency having consented, this bold volunteer lost no time in executing his resolution, and soon after brought it safe to camp, for which he was genteelly rewarded.

A detachment was sent into the fort to endeavour to extinguish the flames, and some gunners to draw the guns, etc which they are in hopes to accomplish; the enemy's principal mortar was burst yesterday, as we had conjectured by the slackness of their fire. The main of our army, incamped within the lines, began to level our own works and to fill up the road we have made from Lake Champlain, to the saw-mills, for the carrying on the siege; four battalions of provincials are incamped nearer to the fort for repairing the works. Five hundred men are detached back to Lake George for provisions and stores; a number of French batteaus that were sunk in the lake are ordered to be weighed, and a brig with some boats, which Captain Loring had directions to build, are to be finished with all possible dispatch, in order to render us superior to the naval force of the enemy on the lake.

On the morning of the 22nd, when we landed, Mons. Bourla-maque's forces amounted to two thousand eight hundred men (regulars and Canadians) with about three hundred savages, who all immediately retired, except a detachment of four hundred men that were left for the defence of the fort and its dependencies; this information we received from deserters, and it is confirmed by the prisoners, who add that their army are retired to the narrows, about three leagues up the lake; and are resolved to make a stand there, being strongly intrenched with every advantage of situation.

Our loss, in the reduction of the fort and lines of Ticonderoga, amounted to 'one colonel' (Townshend, whose remains are transmitted to Albany for interment), 'one lieutenant and fifteen privates killed, and about fifty wounded'. The army are employed in drawing artillery, stores and provisions to the side of Lake Champlain, also launching batteaus and whale-boats with all expedition, as the general seems anxious to be in possession of Crown Point; the troops are in high spirits. By our last accounts from the south side of Lake George, Colonel Montresor had got the new fort in a respectable posture of defence, which is now called Fort George.

The fort of Ticonderoga is small, though respectably situated, being a square with four bastions raised with large timbers (in like manner as its late formidable intrenchments); there are two ravelins of masonry that cover the front next the lines, to which only approaches can be made; it has a ditch of a moderate depth and breadth, with a glacis and covered way in good condition; the counterscarp of the ditch and glacis are of masonry; there are casemates in the fort which have not suffered by the late revolutions, and eleven excellent ovens that prove very serviceable to the army. The barracks for the garrison, with most of their store-houses, are burned down, but the walls do not appear to be damaged: one bastion and a part of two curtains are demolished by the explosion of the magazine. This famous fortress is built upon a rock and, in order to level the foundation, its surface is covered with masonry: Colonel Eyre has got directions to repair it with all expedition, upon the same plan as the enemy had erected it.

Thus has our commander-in-chief curbed the insolence of the French in this part of the country and, by his incomparable measures and steady perseverance, compelled the enemy, with very little loss on our side, to abandon a pass which has proved, for several years back, a desperate thorn to his majesty's subjects of New-England, New-York, etc and frustrated all our endeavours since the commencement of this war.

Great feats are and have been often achieved by musketry alone, but such daring undertakings should only be reserved for, and attempted in, merely necessitous, desperate cases; and artillery, as in this instance now before us, be employed where it can be rendered truly serviceable; for a general will thereby not only prevent a great effusion of human blood, but prudently preserve the lives of his valiant troops (his fellow-creatures) for farther enterprises, acquire to himself the reputation of an able commander, and discharge his duty more effectually to his maker, his king, and his country.

Having now deduced the operation of the campaign on the lakes to the same period with the army below Quebec, it is time to turn our eyes to that quarter, and observe the measures that have been taken to reduce the capital of Canada to our obedience.

# VIII

## Wolfe Seeks a Way

*Before Quebec, Wolfe was in a despairing mood. His frail health began to give way. He was increasingly at odds with his brigadiers, of whom Townshend, who had powerful political connections in London, was a sore trial, and Montcalm countered his every move. The season was advancing and the time for active campaigning was beginning to run very short. He finally decided, partly at the prompting of his near-mutinous brigadiers, to attempt a landing up the steep cliffs west of Quebec, using the navy with the admirable Saunders and Holmes to decoy the French with the movements of their ships and so divide their forces, leaving the chosen landing point vulnerable. The expeditions to Niagara and the Great Lakes found better fortune and the French perimeter began to shrink.*

THE READER WILL be pleased to remember I ended the operations of the army before Quebec on the 31st of July, upon their being repulsed in the attempt that was made on the enemy's intrenchments; in consequence of which the general was pleased to issue out the following orders:

ORDERS                      1 August, Camp at Montmorency.
'The check, which the grenadiers met with yesterday, will, it is hoped, be a lesson to them for the time to come; such *impetuous, irregular* and *unsoldierlike* proceedings destroy all order, make it impossible for their commanders to form any disposition for an attack, and put it out of the general's power to execute his plan. The grenadiers could not suppose that they alone could beat the French army, and therefore it was necessary that the corps under Brigadier Monckton and Brigadier Townshend should have time to join, that the attack might be general; the very first fire of the enemy was sufficient to repulse men who had lost all sense of order and military discipline; Amherst's and the Highland regiments alone, by the soldierlike and cool manner they were formed in, would undoubtedly have beat back the whole Canadian army if they had ventured to attack them. The loss, however, is inconsiderable, and may be easily repaired, when a favourable opportunity offers, if the men will shew a proper attention to their officers . . .'

The enemy appear much elated at our miscarriage on the 31st, and have these two days hoisted several white flags on their intrenchments; they are now very assiduously employed, endeavouring to render their works still more inaccessible. We bombarded the town with great spirit last night. Brigadier Murray, with a strong detachment, are under orders to proceed on board of Admiral Holmes's division, to make a diversion above the town, with a view to divide the enemy's attention; we are inclined to hope the general's schemes may still be productive of some great event; the harvest must be reaped, or a famine is inevitable: and, if the Canadians should disperse for that purpose, and General Amherst should be inabled to advance farther into the province and thereby compel Monsieur Montcalm to draw off some of his forces hence to the side of Montreal, we may yet have it in our power to give a satisfactory account of the capital of Canada.

Twenty of our flat-bottomed boats went up on the night of 5 August with the tide of flood, rowed by the enemy's batteries and passed the town: the garrison did not discover them until they got almost clear, and then they discharged three guns and one mortar, which we think was a signal of alarm; for their drummers in the town and camp instantly beat to arms, and continued to do so near an hour and an half; by this we are inclined to believe they apprehended a storm. Our batteries, who have now an unlimited credit for every species of ammunition, fired so quick and so regular, while the boats were passing, as to resemble platoons; the weather being wet, and the night dark, favoured our intentions: the boats are for the service of the troops under Brigadier Murray, whose object is to destroy a large magazine of flour, corn and stores which the enemy are said to have a few leagues above the town: also to endeavour, in concert with Admiral Holmes, to destroy the French ships, if they can get at them, and thereby open a communication with General Amherst. A farther object of the brigadier's is to draw such parties of the enemy as he may meet with to action, and thereby divide the attention of their army below the town.

I was an eye-witness to the ceremony of burying a sailor alive, *mirabile dictu*, for the cure of the sea scurvy. To explain this matter it must be observed that a pit was made in the ground and the patient stood in it, with his head only above the level of the earth; then the mold was thrown in loose about him, and there he remained for some hours: this I am told is to be repeated every day until his recovery is perfected; the poor fellow seemed to be in good spirits, laughed and conversed with the spectators who were about him.

Some sailors and marines strayed to-day into the country, contrary to repeated orders, to seek for vegetables: they were fired upon by a party of the enemy, and three were killed and scalped; the remainder, being ten in number, made their escape; two of them, however, were slightly wounded. Three Indians shewed themselves to the westward of our batteries, and set up a war-shout; whereupon an officer and thirty rangers, being detached to that quarter, scoured the environs for several miles without making any discovery. We esteem ourselves very happy in this country, having no fogs as in Nova Scotia, nor are we tormented with musketa's: we have myriads of the common black window fly, which, though they have no sting, are nevertheless troublesome in tainting our victuals. We are now tolerably well provided with the conveniencies of life; at times butchers' meat is scarce, but that is supplied by young horse-flesh; a loin of a colt eats well roasted, and there are many other parts of the carcase, which, if disguised in the same manner that one meets with other victuals at table, may deceive the nicest palate.

About one o'clock in the morning of 10 August a fire broke out in the lower town and, by the wind's freshening, the flames spread with great rapidity and continued burning until ten, by which the greatest part of that quarter was destroyed: it communicated to one of their batteries, blew up a small magazine or powder-chest, burned their platforms and carriages, and discharged some of their guns. The low town, in the center of which stood l'Eglise de la Sainte Victoire, was completely destroyed by this conflagration: it was occasioned by one of our shells, which forced its way into a vaulted cellar, hitherto deemed bomb-proof, wherein were twenty pipes of brandy and several smaller casks of other spirituous liquors; this was the richest and best inhabited part of the whole city, and contained the most magnificent houses, churches and public buildings excepted. Another fire was perceived to burst forth in the upper town at the same time, which was extinguished in less than an hour. Our artillery officers observe that they can now reach the north suburbs, where the intendant's superb palace is situated; and this quarter they hope they shall soon put on the same romantic footing with the rest.

A great smoke is perceived this morning on the north side, at a distance below Orleans: this is supposed to be occasioned by Captain Goreham's detachment, who are burning the settlements abreast of the Isle of Coudre. When the lower town was in flames early this morning, Mr Wolfe ordered the picquets and grenadiers to march down to the beach and make a feint to cross the ford leading

173

to the Pointe de Lest; which the enemy perceiving, beat instantly to arms and lined their works; whereupon the general gave them a spirited discharge from all his cannon and howitzers, and did great execution among them. The batteries of the town have re-assumed a little vigour to-day in dealing their shot and shells with great profusion, and to as little purpose as heretofore. When the last flag of truce came from the enemy, the bearer of it was told that we were surprised at their silence, and that we took unkind our not hearing from their batteries as often of late as usual. To which Monsieur replied—'They had intelligence from our deserters that they did no execution, and would therefore reserve their ammunition for an-other occasion'. He then demanded why we did not fire as briskly on the garrison for some time past as before? And was answered to this effect: 'We have sufficiently damaged your town already, and we do not chuse to destroy all its buildings, as we hope soon to be in possession of it'.

During the night of the 13th a great firing of cannon and small arms was heard up the country at a distance above the town; the enemy were thereby alarmed, and their drums in the garrison and camp beat to arms for a considerable time: this is supposed to have been occasioned by Admiral Holmes and Brigadier Murray in the upper river. The general bombarded the enemy's camp warmly this morning, by which one of their houses took fire, and, while they were endeavouring to extinguish it, he gave them a vigorous dis-charge from all his artillery, and maintained it above an hour. The detachment of the forty-third disembarked, and were ordered to dress three day's provisions. Upwards of a thousand cannon-shot and twenty thirteen-inch shells, which came from the enemy at different times, have been collected in the precincts of our batteries, and were sent on board an ordnance-ship to be transmitted, as it is said, to Louisbourg; the soldiers are allowed two pence for a shot, two shillings and six pence for a ten-inch, and five shillings for thirteen-inch shells. Two marines deserted to-day. Nothing extra-ordinary at our batteries; moderate firing between them and the town: our weather gloomy; wind right a-head and, by the deluges of rain we have had of late, the air is rendered cool and our camp uncomfortable.

A midshipman has made several efforts to go up the river with a packet to Brigadier Murray, but cannot succeed: when he was sent down express from Admiral Holmes's squadron to General Wolfe, he spied the enemy's floating batteries at the Foulon; whereupon he unshipped his oars and helm, directed his men to lie down in the boat, and let her drive, knowing it was tide of ebb, with the current; by this means he passed the town, if not unobserved at least unmolested; it is probable, if the enemy did discern the boat, they supposed it might be, as the night was dark, an old tree or piece of timber floating up and down with the tide; a circumstance not uncommon in this river.

The detachment under Captain Goreham, that went down the river on 6 August, returned on the afternoon of the 19th: at setting out, they crossed over to Orleans in boats and embarked at the lower end of that island in small trading sloops. After they passed l'Isle de Madame, they bore down upon the *Zephir* sloop of war, who was cruising in the river, Captain Goreham being charged with a particular message for the commander of her; but, as it was late in the evening and there being many creeks and bays yet unknown to us, where it is not improbable but the enemy might have small craft concealed, the *Zephir* fired upon them and continued to do so for a considerable time, not chusing to know them in the dark. At length, Mr Goreham, ordering his vessels to lie to, took to his boat and rowed up within hailing of the *Zephir*; and, telling who he was, and that he brought some commands from the admiral and general, he was taken on board; luckily there was no mischief done in this blundering rencounter. The sloop of war then taking the detachment under convoy, they came to an anchor off the Island of Coudre, and next morning, at day-break, they got into their boats, and rowed to Paul's Bay; when they came within reach of the shore, they were saluted with a shower of musketry, by which one man was killed, and eight were wounded; among the latter was a midshipman (dangerously) and two sailors; before the villagers could load again, the boats were grounded, and the troops instantly pushed on shore, charged and routed the wretched inhabitants.

Captain Goreham, finding the houses abandoned, set fire to the village and destroyed every building therein, except the church; on the door of which he fixed up an advertisement of the general's, informing the Canadians, 'that the rigorous measures he now pursued, and should certainly persevere in, were occasioned by the contempt they shewed to the manifesto he published in June, and to the gracious offers he therein proposed to them; moreover, that they made such ungrateful returns, in practising the most unchristian-like barbarities against his troops on all occasions, that he could no longer refrain, with justice to himself and his army, chastising them as they deserved, etc.' This detachment took twenty head of black cattle, forty sheep and hogs, a great quantity of poultry, and an immense deal of plunder, consisting of books, apparel and house-hold-stuff of various kinds.

They had a Swiss for their guide, who had been a captain of militia, also a resident for several years in the township of St Paul, and deserted from the enemy some time before. Monsieur de Vaudreuil had much confidence in this fellow, and gave him the command of all the men in that district who were able to bear arms, with orders to harass us, as often as opportunity should offer, by landing small parties on the east end of Orleans, the Island of Coudre, etc 'and, if he should make two or more British officers prisoners, to reserve one only for intelligence and scalp the others; all sailors and private soldiers were to have no quarters granted them'. Among the priest's papers there was a letter from the governor-general to him, with positive commands, if he could possibly discover the Swiss captain (alluding to that deserter), to hang him instantly, without a moment's hesitation or ceremony.

It is with the greatest concern to the whole army that we are now informed of our amiable general's being very ill of a slow fever: the soldiers lament him exceedingly, and seemed apprehensive of this event before we were ascertained of it by his not visiting this camp for several days past. The general was lately heard to say in con-versation, 'that he would chearfully sacrifice a leg or an arm to be in possession of Quebec'.

I crossed the river on the 24th to wait on the general and receive his orders for this brigade; this is the first and only opportunity I had of being in that camp, where no pains have been spared to render it impregnable: a tolerable house stood convenient here for Mr Wolfe's quarters, but he was so ill above stairs as not to be able to come to dinner. There being no particular commands for me, and as I had some spare time on my hands, I ventured to take a walk to the west-ward, and view more distinctly the Leap (as the French term it) of Montmorency and the enemy's intrenchments: this natural curiosity appears, from the south shore, to be much higher than it is in reality; I believe it does not exceed fifty feet, if so much, though others think differently, from its level of the beach, where it falls in a per-pendicular line; and the rivulet which supplies it is so inconsiderable, not surpassing thirty feet in breadth (though it contracts gradually towards the bottom, like an artificial ditch in an intrenchment, but not altogether so regular), that it is amazing to see so stupendous a cataract from such an insignificant brook; this I can no otherwise take upon me to account for, than upon a supposition that this body of water is considerable towards its source, and its being reduced at

A VIEW OF THE LANDING ABOVE QUEBEC

the south end to the narrow limits of a stream, causes it to rush down the cliff with a strength and rapidity not to be conceived.

I had very nigh paid dear for my inquisitiveness; for, while I stood upon the eminence with a paper and pencil in my hand, making some observations on this cascade, the advantageous situation of the enemy on the opposite side of it, with the superiority of this ground over the left of theirs in point of height; and the natural strength of the country all round me, I was hastily called to by one of our sentinels, when, throwing my eyes about, I saw a Frenchman creeping under the eastern extremity of their breast-work, next the main river, to fire at me; this obliged me to retire as fast as I could out of his reach, and, making up to the sentry to thank him for his attention, he told me the fellow had snapped his piece twice, and the second time it flashed in the pan at the instant when I turned away from the fall. Having satisfied my curiosity, and not finding myself disposed to give monsieur another chance at this time, on so trivial an occasion, I returned to the head quarters.

At nine o'clock on the night of the 25th Brigadier Murray returned from the upper river: he destroyed a magazine at Chambaud, consisting of provisions, ammunition, spare cloathing, with other stores and baggage of the French army, took several prisoners and obliged the enemy to burn a brigantine of two hundred tons; this however was not effected without some loss, Mr Murray having made two different attempts to land, before he could carry his point.

By sundry letters that were found, and are confirmed by some fashionable prisoners, we have agreeable accounts of General Amherst's success at Ticonderoga and Crown Point, the enemy being obliged to abandon those important posts, upon the approach of his artillery; and Monsieur Bourlamaque is retired to a strong pass at Isle au Noix, on the Lake Champlain, with his forces amounting to near three thousand men; where they are fortified with a resolution to defend it, as they give out, to the last extremity. Through the same channel we have the happy news of the reduction of Niagara by a detachment of Mr Amherst's army commanded by Brigadier-General Prideaux consisting of three regiments of regulars, some provincials, and a large body of Indians under Sir William Johnson; but that unfortunately the brigadier and another officer of distinction were killed. We are likewise assured that the whole number of men in arms throughout this province do not exceed twenty-five thousand, including regulars, Indians and Canadians from the age of sixteen to seventy: that the latter are very discontented, and would

M

chearfully surrender their capital if they had people of resolution among them to excite and encourage a revolt, rather than see their country thus groaning and bleeding under the calamities of war.

His Excellency General Wolfe is on the recovery, to the inconceivable joy of the whole army.

Some French letters have been intercepted by our rangers; in one of them we learn that Monsieur Montcalm has hanged two Canadians, and whipped several others, for quitting the army without his permission; and that he has promised to discharge them all by the 25th of September, at which time he pretends that our fleet and army will sail down the river. Monsieur Vaudreuil, in his letters to the priests in the several parishes of the lower country, expresses his surprise at their disobedience to his orders in not concealing their cattle within the more interior woods of their districts to prevent their falling into our hands; his excellency reprimands them for this neglect with great *hauteur*, and injoins them to pay more respect to his commands for the time to come, on pain of incurring his highest displeasure. In a letter to one of those spiritual guides at a place called the South River, a considerable way to the eastward of this camp, he commands him to pay the strictest attention to the care of Monsieur Boishébert's batteaus and shallops, to inable that officer, with his partisans, to return to his government of Acadia after our departure, which, he pretends, 'will soon take place'; he likewise orders the priest to save and barrel up a large quantity of eels against the winter. It is privately rumoured, with some confidence, that the main body of our army is shortly to be conveyed above the town, to endeavour to force a landing on the north side of the river, between Cape Rouge and Cape Diamond.

General Wolfe is preparing to withdraw his troops from the ground eastward of the cataract; for this purpose he has sent over all his artillery, stores, baggage, tents, etc. Some of the regiments will incamp here, and others are to remain on the Island of Orleans until farther orders: the settlements on that agreeable spot have, for the most part, shared the same fate with the rest of the country, wherever our light troops have been detached. General Wolfe is endeavouring to draw the flower of the French army from their strong intrenched camp to an engagement on his own ground, before he abandons it.

Being now come to that period at which the general drew up a summary of the various transactions of this armament, since our arrival before Quebec, I take the liberty, to annex here a transcript of that review comprehended in his excellency's letter to the Ministry, as it is not only the best and most lively recapitulation that can

be made of our sundry proceedings to this day, but also demonstrates, in a great measure, the authenticity of my labours:

'The obstacles we have met with in the operations of the campaign
are much greater than we had reason to expect or could foresee; not
so much from the number of the enemy (though superior to us) as
from the natural strength of the country, which the Marquis de
Montcalm seems wisely to depend upon. When I learned that
succours of all kinds had been thrown into Quebec, that five battalions of regular troops, completed from the best of the inhabitants
of the country, some of the troops of the colony and every Canadian
that was able to bear arms, besides several nations of savages, had
taken the field in a very advantageous situation, I could not flatter
myself that I should be able to reduce the place. I sought, however,
an occasion to attack their army, knowing well that with these
troops I was able to fight, and hoping that a victory might disperse
them. We found them incamped along the shore of Beauport, from
the river St Charles to the fall of Montmorency, and intrenched in
every accessible part.

'The 27th of June we landed upon the Island of Orleans; but,
receiving a message from the admiral that there was reason to think
the enemy had artillery and a force upon Point Levy, I detached
Brigadier Monckton with four battalions to drive them from thence.
He passed the river the 29th at night, and marched the next day to
the point; he obliged the enemy's irregulars to retire, and possessed
himself of that post: the advanced parties, upon this occasion, had
two or three skirmishes with the Canadians and Indians, with little
loss on either side. Colonel Carleton marched with a detachment to
the westermost point of Orleans, whence our operations were likely
to begin. It was absolutely necessary to possess these two points and
fortify them; because from either the one or the other the enemy
make it impossible for any ship to lie in the bason of Quebec, or
even within two miles of it.

'Batteries of cannon and mortars were erected with great dispatch
on Point Levy to bombard the town and magazines, and to injure
the works and batteries: the enemy, perceiving these works in some
forwardness, passed the river with sixteen hundred men to attack
and destroy them. Unluckily they fell into confusion, fired upon one
another, and went back again; by which we lost an opportunity of
defeating this large detachment. The effect of this artillery has been
so great, though across the river, that the upper town is considerably
damaged, and the lower town intirely destroyed. The works, for the

179

security of our hospitals and stores upon the Isle of Orleans, being finished, on the 9th of July, at night, we passed the north channel and incamped near the enemy's left, the river Montmorency between us. The next morning Captain Danks's company of rangers, posted in a wood to cover some workmen, were attacked and defeated by a body of Indians, and had so many killed and wounded as to be almost disabled for the rest of the campaign: the enemy also suffered in this affair, and were, in their turn, driven off by the nearest troops.

'The ground to the eastward of the fall seemed to be, as it really is, higher than that on the enemy's side, and to command it in a manner that might be made useful to us. There is besides a ford below the fall, which may be passed for some hours in the latter part of the ebb and beginning of the flood tide; and I had hopes that possibly means might be found of passing the river above, so as to fight the Marquis de Montcalm upon terms of less disadvantage than directly attacking his intrenchments. In reconnoitring the river Montmorency, we found it fordable at a place about three miles up; but the opposite bank was intrenched, and so steep and woody that it was to no purpose to attempt a passage there. The escort was twice attacked by the Indians, who were as often repulsed; but in these rencounters we had forty officers and men killed and wounded.

'The 18th of July two men of war, two armed sloops and two transports, with some troops on board, passed by the town without any loss, and got into the upper river. This inabled me to reconnoitre the country above, where I found the same attention on the enemy's side, and great difficulties on our's, arising from the nature of the ground and the obstacles to our communication with the fleet. But what I feared most was that, if we should land between the town and the river Cape Rouge, the body first landed could not be reinforced before they were attacked by the enemy's whole army. Notwithstanding these difficulties, I thought once of attempting it at St Michael's, about three miles above the town: but, perceiving that the enemy, jealous of the design, were preparing against it and had actually brought artillery and a mortar—which, being so near to Quebec, they could increase as they please—to play upon the shipping, and as it must have been many hours before we could attack them, even supposing a favourable night for the boats to pass by the town unhurt, it seemed so hazardous that I thought it best to desist.

'However, to divide the enemy's force and to draw their attention as high up the river as possible, and to procure some intelligence, I sent a detachment, under the command of Colonel Carleton, to land at the Point aux Trembles to attack whatever he might find there, bring off some prisoners and all the useful papers he could get. I had been informed that a number of the inhabitants of Quebec had retired to that place, and that probably we should find a magazine of provisions there. The colonel was fired upon by a body of Indians the moment he landed; but they were soon dispersed and driven into the woods: he searched for magazines, but to no purpose; brought off some prisoners, and returned with little loss. After this business I came back to Montmorency, where I found that Brigadier Townshend had, by a superior fire, prevented the French from erecting a battery on the bank of the river, whence they intended to cannonade our camp. I now resolved to take the first opportunity which presented itself of attacking the enemy, though posted to great advantage and every-where prepared to receive us.

'As the men-of-war cannot, for want of sufficient depth of water, come near enough to the enemy's intrenchments to annoy them in the least, the admiral had prepared two transports, drawing but little water, which, upon occasion, could be run a-ground to favour a descent. With the help of these vessels, which I understood would be carried by the tide close in shore, I proposed to make myself master of a detached redoubt near to the water's edge, and whose situation appeared to be out of musket-shot of the intrenchment upon the hill: if the enemy supported this detached piece, it would necessarily bring on an engagement, what we most wished for; and, if not, I should have it in my power to examine their situation, so as to be able to determine where we could best attack them. Preparations were accordingly made for an engagement.

'The 31st of July, in the forenoon, the boats of the fleet were filled with grenadiers and a part of Brigadier Monckton's brigade from Point Levy: the two brigades under the Brigadiers Townshend and Murray were ordered to be in readiness to pass the ford, when it should be thought necessary. To facilitate the passage of this corps, the admiral had placed the *Centurion* in the channel, so that she might check the fire of the lower battery which commanded the ford: this ship was of great use, as her fire was very judiciously directed. A great quantity of artillery stores was placed upon the eminence so as to batter and enfilade the left of their intrenchments. From the vessel which ran a-ground, nearest in, I observed that the redoubt was too much commanded to be kept without very great loss; and the more, as the two armed ships could not be brought near enough to cover both with their artillery and musketry, which I at first conceived they might. But, as the enemy seemed in some confusion and we

were prepared for an action, I thought it a proper time to make an
attempt upon their intrenchment.

'Orders were sent to the brigadiers-general to be ready, with the
corps under their command; Brigadier Monckton to land, and
Brigadiers Townshend and Murray to pass the ford. At a proper
time of the tide, the signal was made; but in rowing towards the
shore many of the boats were grounded upon a ledge that runs off a
considerable distance. This accident put us into some disorder, lost
a great deal of time, and obliged me to send an officer to stop
Brigadier Townshend's march, whom I then observed to be in
motion. While the seamen were getting the boats off, the enemy
fired a number of shot and shells, but did no considerable damage.
As soon as this disorder could be set a little to rights, and the boats
were ranged in a proper manner, some of the officers of the navy
went in with me to find a better place to land. We took one flat-
bottomed boat with us to make the experiment; and, as soon as we
had found a fit part of the shore, the troops were ordered to disembark, thinking it not yet too late for the attempt.

'The thirteen companies of grenadiers, and two hundred of the
second Royal American battalion, got first on shore. The grenadiers
were ordered to form themselves into four distinct bodies and to
begin the attack, supported by Brigadier Monckton's corps, as soon
as the troops had passed the ford and were at hand to assist. But,
whether from the noise and hurry at landing, or from some other
cause, the grenadiers, instead of forming themselves as they were
directed, ran on impetuously towards the enemy's intrenchments, in
the utmost disorder and confusion, without waiting for the corps
that was to sustain them and join in the attack. Brigadier Monckton
was not landed, and Brigadier Townshend was still at a considerable
distance, though upon his march to join us in very great order. The
grenadiers were checked by the enemy's first fire, and obliged to
shelter themselves in or about the redoubt, which the French abandoned upon their approach. In this situation they continued for some
time, unable to form under so hot a fire, and having many gallant
officers wounded, who, careless of their persons, had been solely
intent upon their duty.

'I saw the absolute necessity of calling them off, that they might
form themselves behind Brigadier Monckton's corps, which was now
landed and drawn up on the beach in extreme good order. By this
new accident, and this second delay, it was near night, and a sudden
storm came on, and the tide began to make; so that I thought it most
advisable not to persevere in so difficult an attack, lest, in case of a

repulse, the retreat of Brigadier Townshend's corps might be hazardous and uncertain. Our artillery had a great effect upon the enemy's left, where Brigadiers Townshend and Murray were to have attacked; and it is probable that if those accidents I have spoken of had not happened, we should have penetrated there, whilst our left and center, more remote from our artillery, must have borne all the violence of their musketry. The French did not attempt to interrupt our march. Some of their savages came down to murder such wounded as could not be brought off, and to scalp the dead, as their custom is.

'The place where the attack was intended has these advantages over all others hereabout: our artillery could be brought into use, the greatest part, or even the whole of the troops, might act at once, and the retreat, in case of a repulse, was secure, at least for a certain time of the tide; neither one or other of these advantages can any-where else be found. The enemy were indeed posted upon a commanding eminence; the beach upon which the troops were drawn up was of deep mud, with holes, and cut by several gullies; the hill to be ascended very steep, and not every-where practicable; the enemy numerous in their intrenchments, and their fire hot. If the attack had succeeded, our loss must certainly have been great, and theirs inconsiderable, from the shelter which the neighbouring woods afforded them. The river St Charles remained still to be passed, before the town was invested. All these circumstances I considered; but the desire to act in conformity to the king's intentions induced me to make this trial, *persuaded that a victorious army finds no difficulties.* The enemy have been fortifying ever since with care, so as to make a second attempt still more dangerous.

'Immediately after this check, I sent Brigadier Murray above the town with twelve hundred men, directing him to assist Rear-Admiral Holmes in the destruction of the French ships, if they could be got at, in order to open a communication with General Amherst. The brigadier was to seek every favourable opportunity of fighting some of the enemy's detachments, provided he could do it upon tolerable terms; and to use all the means in his power to provoke them to attack him. He made two different attempts to land upon the north shore, without success; but in a third was more fortunate. He landed unexpectedly at de Chambaud [Deschambault] and burned a magazine there, in which were some provisions, some ammunition and all the spare stores, cloathing, arms and baggage of their army. Finding that their ships were not to be got at, and little prospect of bringing the enemy to a battle, he reported his situation to me, and

I ordered him to join the army. The prisoners he took informed him of the surrender of the fort of Niagara; and we discovered, by intercepted letters, that the enemy, having abandoned Carillon and Crown-Point, were retired to the Isle au Noix; and that General Amherst was making preparations to pass the Lake Champlain, to fall upon Monsieur de Bourlamaque's corps, which consists of three battalions of foot and as many Canadians as make the whole amount to three thousand men.

'The admiral's dispatches and mine would have gone eight or ten days sooner, if I had not been prevented from writing by a fever. I found myself so ill, and am still so weak, that I begged the general officers to consult together for the public utility. *They are all of opinion* that, as more ships and provisions are now got above the town, they should try, by conveying up a corps of four or five thousand men, which is nearly the whole strength of the army, after the Points of Levy and Orleans are left in a proper state of defence, to draw the enemy from their present situation and bring them to an action. *I have acquiesced in their proposal*, and we are preparing to put it in execution.

'The admiral and I have examined the town with a view to a general assault; but, after consulting with the chief engineer, who is well acquainted with the interior parts of it, and after viewing it with the utmost attention, we found that, though the batteries of the lower town might be easily silenced by the men-of-war, yet the business of an assault would be little advanced by that, since the few passages leading from the lower to the upper town are carefully intrenched, and the upper batteries cannot be affected by the ships, which must receive considerable damage from them and from the mortars. The admiral would readily join in this, or in any other measure for the public service; but I could not propose to him an undertaking of so dangerous a nature, and promising so little success. To the uncommon strength of the country, the enemy have added, for the defence of the river, a great number of floating batteries and boats; by the vigilance of these, and the Indians round our different posts, it has been impossible to execute any thing by surprise.

'We have had almost daily skirmishes with these savages, in which they are generally defeated, but not without loss on our side. By the list of disabled officers (many of whom are of rank) you may perceive that the army is much weakened. By the nature of the river, the most formidable part of this armament is deprived of the power of acting, yet we have almost the whole force of Canada to oppose.

In this situation *there is such a choice of difficulties* that I own myself
at a loss how to determine. The affairs of Great Britain, I know,
require the most vigorous measures; but then the courage of a
handful of brave troops should be exerted only where there is some
hope of a favourable event; however, you may be assured that the
small part of the campaign which remains shall be employed (as far
as I am able) for the honour of his majesty and the interest of the
nation; in which I am sure of being well seconded by the admiral
and by the generals, happy if our efforts here can contribute to the
success of his majesty's arms in any other parts of America.'

On the morning of 5 September, at six o'clock, the enemy marched
two columns into the woods, northward of the left of their camp, as
if they intended to cross the river of Montmorency at the upper ford
and fall upon General Wolfe's rear, on his quitting that ground;
which Brigadier Monckton perceiving, immediately ordered his
brigade under arms: at eight o'clock a number of long-boats, being
assembled, were sent to us by the admiral, and instantly the forty-
third and seventy-eighth regiments embarked and rowed off,
covered by sloops and frigates half-channel over, in order to favour
the general's motions; we remained near four hours on the water,
and made several feints, as if intending to land and attack the enemy
in the center of their camp at Beauport. This finesse had the desired
effect, for the columns were directly ordered back to their camp, and
lined their breast-works to oppose our imaginary descent, whereby
General Wolfe and his troops embarked perfectly unmolested.
After they had put off, a few straggling French and Indians appeared
in the abandoned camp; but the motive of their coming seemed
rather to proceed from curiosity than from an hostile intention. As
the boats crossed the river, they were warmly saluted from the
battery westward of the fall, without any accident; the forty-third
and seventy-eighth regiments were ordered back to the camp.

The General's markee, etc were pitched in the interval between
the forty-third and seventy-eighth regiments, and his excellency
dined in our camp. The general was heard to say that he received a
letter from General Amherst, wherein he informed him, 'that
Monsieur de Bourlamaque gave him some trouble, first at Ticonderoga and afterwards at Crown Point, until he drew up his artillery
and broke ground in order to attack him in form, which as soon as
the enemy perceived, they abandoned those two important places
and retired'. Mr Wolfe added, 'that he did not yet despair of seeing
the commander-in-chief here before the end of the campaign'.

An expedition is on foot to the upper river, in which the greatest part of the army, with our three brigadiers, are to assist; the general will command in person, if his health will permit. Two ranging officers and four privates arrived express from the commander-in-chief, whom they left at Crown Point: this great journey was performed in twenty-seven days, and the route they took was first to Boston, thence up Kennebec river, whence they directed their course to the Chaudiere, which discharges itself into the river St Lawrence about five leagues above Quebec; they met a few straggling peasants in different places, but did not molest them lest they should alarm the country: one of these Canadians informed them that our fleet and army were fallen down the river. All the intelligence which we have lately received by letters that were intercepted, deserters and other authorities of the success of our arms at Ticonderoga, Crown Point and Niagara, is confirmed by these expresses.

ORDERS                                                    5 September
'The light infantry, twenty-eighth, thirty-fifth, forty-seventh, fifty-eighth, and the grenadiers of Louisbourg, with those of Monckton's regiment, are to march to-morrow at two in the afternoon; they are to receive their orders from Brigadier Murray: the parts of those corps which are to remain are to incamp on the ground now occupied by the Louisbourg grenadiers. The whole to be drawn up two deep; the Louisbourg grenadiers on the right, Bragg's on the left, and so on by seniority to the center: the brigadier proposes marching from the center. Colonel Howe's own division of light infantry will form the van-guard, and cover the head of the column; that of Major Dalling the rear-guard. Two files will be detached from each platoon, in order to cover their own flanks; when the woods are out of musket-shot, they are to keep near to the battalion; when they are within musket-shot, they are to march within the skirts in the woods.'

Fair wind and weather to-day: the boats passed the town last night undiscovered: the troops under orders, commanded by Brigadier Murray, marched this afternoon to Goreham's post, where the flat-bottomed boats are to meet them to convey them on board the ships in the upper river. The houses and fascine works in the abandoned camp by the fall of Montmorency still continue burning. General Wolfe was much indisposed last night; he is better to-day; but the army are, nevertheless, very apprehensive lest his ill state of health should not permit him to command this grand enterprise in person. The other regiments destined to go up the river are to move off to-morrow.

We had an uncommon storm of rain last night; on the 6th showery weather and wind variable. We fired warmly on the town these last eighteen hours, without a single gun or shell in return. At three o'clock this afternoon the fifteenth, forty-third and seventy-eighth regiments, with the Brigadiers Monckton and Townshend, marched to Goreham's post; at the same time a schooner of a most diminutive size, whimsically called the *Terror of France*, weighed and passed the town, the enemy foolishly expended a number of shot at her, but she nevertheless got safe up with her colours flying; and, coming to an anchor in the upper river, she triumphantly saluted Admiral Holmes with a discharge from all her swivels; there was no other accident that happened, except one man's being slightly wounded on board, and our batteries fired briskly on the town, to favour her as she passed.

The officers and gunners at the enemy's batteries were provoked at this small vessel's presumption in open day-light, which they captiously looked upon as a contemptuous affront upon their formidable batteries, many of our ships having passed them at different times without any considerable damage; but they paid dear for their resentment; for, at the same instant, a shot from our batteries rendered one of their guns useless, overset and discharged a number of loaded firelocks that were rested against an adjoining wall, by which two of their officers and seven men were killed on the spot, and four were wounded. The more generous officers in the French camp politely expressed concern (as they afterwards told us) at the schooner's being fired upon, as they imagined her passing was the result of a frolicsome wager, and therefore would have disregarded her.

In the evening we arrived at Goreham's post, where we lay on our arms until boats should arrive. At night-fall we forded the river Etchemin, about fifty yards over, a stony and uneven bottom, and very slippery, with a rapid current; fortunately the waters were fallen, for we were not above mid-thigh; the troops, who passed yesterday, found it much deeper, and our situation in fording was rendered disagreeable by a battery which the enemy have at Sillery, opposite to the mouth of this rivulet, whence they cannonaded us as we passed; but, luckily, their shot was either over or short of us: on the west side stood a straggling village, which terminated in a point and formed a cove, where boats were ready to receive us and conduct the regiments to their respective ships. The forty-third regiment was particularly fortunate, being put on board the *Seahorse* frigate, where Captain Smith and his officers entertained us in a most princely manner, and very obligingly made it their principal care to render our crouded situation as agreeable as possible. The general joined the army and upper fleet this night.

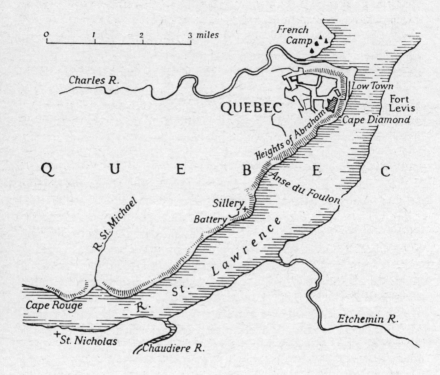

# IX

## Anse du Foulon

*The second week in September 1759 saw Wolfe's plan come to fruition.*
*He succeeded in landing enough of his army at the cove called Anse du*
*Foulon, just west of Quebec. They held their ground unmolested until*
*the rest of his army poured over from the south bank. The battle that*
*followed lasted little more than ten minutes. Both Wolfe and Montcalm*
*were mortally wounded. The French defeat was sudden and total and a*
*great breach had been forced in the central redoubt of Canada. It was*
*one of the determining battles of history, in spite of the small numbers*
*engaged.*

ADMIRAL HOLMES'S SQUADRON weighed early on the morning
of 7 September; at six o'clock we doubled the mouth of the
Chaudiere, which is near half a mile over; and at eight we came to an
anchor off Cape Rouge; here is a spacious cove into which the river
St Michael disembogues, and within the mouth of it are the enemy's
floating batteries; a large body of the enemy are well intrenched
round the cove (which is of a circular form) as if jealous of a descent
in those parts; they appear very numerous, and may amount to about
one thousand six hundred men, besides their cavalry, who are
cloathed in blue and mounted on neat light horses of different colours;
they seem very alert, parading and counter-marching between the
woods on the heights in their rear and their breast-works, in order to
make their numbers shew to greater advantage. The lands all round
us are high and commanding, which gave the enemy an opportunity
of popping at our ships this morning, as we tacked in working up: I
did not hear of any damage sustained, though they were a little
troublesome.

Upon our coming to an anchor, they turned out their floats and
ranged them in great order; their cavalry then dismounted, formed
on the right of the infantry, and their whole detachment ran down
the precipice with a ridiculous shout and manned their works. I have
often reflected upon the absurdity of this practice in the French, who
entertain a high opinion of their own discipline and knowledge in
the art of war; there is nothing that can be more absurd than such
noises in engaging an enemy; I think it expressive of the greatest
diffidence, and must tend to defeat all regularity and good order

189

among themselves, because their men are thereby confused and are rendered incapable of paying attention to their officers or their duty; it is a false courage. How different, how nobly awful and expressive of true valour is the custom of the British troops! They do not expend their ammunition at an immense distance; and, if they advance to engage or stand to receive the charge, they are steady, profoundly silent and attentive, reserving their fire until they have received that of their adversaries, over whom they have a tenfold advantage; there are cases where huzzaing may be neccssary, but those are very rare; the practice is unmilitary in an army or body of regulars; and experience plainly shows us that the troops who, in perfect silence, engage an enemy, waiting for their first fire, will always preserve a superiority.

This afternoon, at two o'clock, the *Seahorse*, *Leostoffe*, and two floating batteries that were lately taken, were ordered to edge into the cove and attack the enemy's armed floats; at the same time the troops put into their boats and rowed up and down, as if intending to land at different places, to amuse the enemy; the brigadiers, no doubt, knew this was intended only as a *finesse*, but the corps thought they were, in reality, going ashore; and such was their zeal that they were much disappointed when, after parading some time in this manner, they were ordered back to their ships; this seems calculated to fix the attention of the enemy on that particular part, while a descent is meditated elsewhere, perhaps lower down. Our frigates, etc exchanged a number of shot, but at so great distance that nothing extraordinary could happen; after this, the general officers went up the river in the *Hunter* sloop to take a farther view of the country, and to reconnoitre the coast: they returned in their barge at night, leaving the sloop above at anchor. The enemy are very industrious in adding to their works to render them more impregnable; and they have an incredible number of fires at their post in our view, as well as in the cover of the eminence behind them.

Wet weather, wind up the river: on the morning of the 8th, at day-break, a transport cat, two sloops and a schooner passed the town with provisions, etc and were followed soon after by two other small vessels; they were all warmly cannonaded in their passage and sustained some damage. Orders are issued out this evening for the troops to land and make a diversion to-morrow morning at daylight; the corps to be in the boats at two o'clock; Colonel Young, with part of the army, are to work up as if intending to land elsewhere; and the like feint is to be made by others at Cape Rouge Bay, in order to favour Brigadier Monckton's brigade, who are to land, if possible.

The extreme wetness of the weather prevented the operations. At eight o'clock the forty-third regiment was removed from the frigate on board the *Employment* transport, that the *Seahorse* may fall down to preserve the communication between Admiral Holmes's fleet and Goreham's post: this was ordered in consequence of the adjutant-general's being chased by some canoes as he came up in a boat this morning. The detachments under the Brigadiers Monckton and Murray put off in their boats this afternoon and rowed to the cove, as if intending to land; whereupon the enemy stood to their arms and lined their works; after thus menacing them, in different places, the troops stretched over to the south side and landed in the evening under the church of St Nicholas without any opposition; the French floating batteries attempted to pursue the boats, but the *Leostoffe* slipped her cable, exchanged several shot with them, and obliged them to sheer off; late in the evening the wind shifted, and the weather cleared up.

On the 10th a small party of Indians crossed the river to the neighbourhood of St Nicholas to endeavour to take a prisoner or two for intelligence; of which Brigadier Monckton being informed, he gave immediate notice to the troops under his command, and has taken every salutary measure to prevent his men being picked off or surprised. A parcel of canoes were discovered paddling along the north shore, as if intending to cross the river above our fleet in order to annoy our people on the south side and watch their motions; our two floating batteries and some armed boats were immediately dispatched against them, and drove them ashore; they then took to the bushes and fired at our men; but our batteries plied them so well with grape-shot that the rascals were forced to scramble up the precipice, where there was a breast-work of corded fire-wood; they seemed to be fifty in number, and had an officer of regulars with them. By the time they had gained the summit and got under cover, they were reinforced and discharged several vollies at our boats, who still edged towards the shore, as if intending to land; and it is not improbable but they expected we should made a descent there; for in a short space of time their numbers increased, and we could observe from our ships several officers on horse-back, who seemed to be employed in forming and animating their men. A signal being made from the *Sutherland* for our boats to come off, the enemy gave a heavy fire, and set up a hideous shout after it.

General Wolfe sent for an officer and thirty men of the forty-third regiment to escort him on a reconnoitre, with Brigadier Townshend, the chief engineer, Colonel Carleton, etc. For this purpose six of our grenadiers' coats were also sent by his excellency's orders. Some deserters crossed over from Montmorency to Orleans, by whom we are informed that Monsieur Vaudreuil and part of the French army are come up the river to watch our motions; that the Sieur de Montcalm remains below to defend the town; and that Monsieur de Lévis, the second in command, is detached to Montreal, with a large corps of chosen men from the army. The general, with his reconnoitring party, returned late in the evening from Goreham's point, where they had been with their glasses viewing the cove to the eastward of Sillery, and the eminences above it.

ORDERS                                                  11 September
'The troops on shore, except the light infantry and Americans, are to be upon the beach to-morrow morning at five o'clock, in readiness to embark; the light infantry and Americans will reimbark at, or about, eight o'clock; the detachment of artillery to be put on board the armed sloop this day. *The army to hold themselves in readiness to land and attack the enemy.* As the *Leostoffe* and *Squirrel* frigates are ordered to follow the flat-bottomed boats, the troops belonging to those ships are to remain in them, and the boats intended for these corps are to take in others, according to the following distribution.

| | | |
|---|---|---|
| *Stirling Castle* | 1 | To take fifty into each boat of Bragg's regiment, out of the *Ann and Elizabeth* transport, instead of Amherst's. |
| *Dublin* | 2 | |
| *Alcide* | 3 | |
| *Pembroke* | 4 | To take in Kennedy's regiment out of the *Employment* transport. |
| *Van-guard* | 4 | To take in Colonel Howe's corps of light infantry out of the *Jane and Mary* transport. |
| *Trident* | 4 | |
| *Centurion* | 2 | To take in Anstruther's out of the *George* transport. |
| *Shrewsbury* | 4 | |
| *Medway* | 2 | To take Lascelles's regiment, in five boats, out of the *Ward* transport; and fifty of the Royal American grenadiers out the *Sutherland*, in the sixth boat. |
| *Captain* | 4 | |

'There remain to be taken into the boats of the fleet two hundred Highlanders, of which the *Terror of France* schooner takes fifty from the *Ann and Elizabeth*; the remaining one hundred and fifty High-

REPRESENTATION OF THE BATTLE OF THE PLAINS OF ABRAHAM

landers, in the *Ward* transport, will be taken by the following boats: *Sutherland*'s long-boat, forty; *Alcide* and *Medway*, forty each; admiral's flat-bottomed boat, fifteen; *Sutherland* cutter, fifteen. Ships that carry troops immediately after the flat-bottomed boats:— *Leostoffe* frigate, three hundred of Amherst's; *Squirrel*, two hundred and forty of Louisbourg grenadiers; *Seahorse*, two hundred and fifty Highlanders; *Hunter* sloop, one hundred and twenty Highlanders; three armed vessels, two hundred light infantry; *Laurel* transport, four hundred Royal Americans; *Adventure* transport, four hundred of Otways. Ordnance vessels, with tools and artillery men: the *George* transport to be evacuated, and the Highlanders, being one hundred and fifty, to be removed into the *Seahorse* frigate; and one hundred of the same corps, from the *Ann and Elizabeth*, to be removed also on board the *Seahorse* to-morrow morning, after the reimbarkation of the first body of troops from Brigadier Monckton's corps at St Nicholas.

'Order of troops in the line of boats.

| Number of Boats | | |
|---|---|---|
| 8 | 1st | Light infantry leads. |
| 6 | 2nd | Bragg's regiment. |
| 4 | 3rd | Kennedy's regiment. |
| 5 | 4th | Lascelles's ditto. |
| 6 | 5th | Anstruther's ditto. |
| 1 | 6th | { Detachments of Highlanders and American grenadiers. |

'Captain Chads, of the navy, has received the general's directions in respect to the order in which the troops move and are to land; and no officer must attempt to make the least alteration, or interfere with Captain Chads' particular province, lest, as the boats move in the night, there may be disorder and confusion among them. The troops must go into the boats about nine to-morrow night, or when it is pretty near high water; but the naval officers commanding the different divisions of boats will apprize them of the fittest time; and, as there will be a necessity for remaining some part of the night in the boats, the officers will provide accordingly; and the soldiers will have a jill of rum extraordinary to mix with their water; arms and ammunition, two days' provisions, with rum and water, are all that the soldiers are to take into the boats; their ships, with their blankets, tents, etc will soon be brought up.'

An officer of the forty-third regiment was sent ashore to St

N

Nicholas to endeavour to procure some fresh provisions, but could not succeed, the troops not having sufficient for themselves; the party that went in search of cattle found only seven cows and two sheep, guarded by a few Indian men and women, upon whom our advanced-guard too eagerly fired before they were within reach, by which the rabble made their escape, shouting and yelling in their flight, intending thereby to alarm the country. Great preparations are making, throughout the fleet and army, to surprise the enemy and compel them to decide the fate of Quebec by a battle: all the long-boats below the town are to be filled with seamen, marines, and such detachments as can be spared from Points Levy and Orleans, in order to make a feint off Beauport and the Point de Lest, and endeavour to engross the attention of the Sieur de Montcalm, while the army are to force a descent on this side of the town. The officer of our regiment, who commanded the escort yesterday on the reconnoitring party, being asked, in the general's hearing, after the health of one of the gentlemen who was reported to be ill, replied— 'he was in a very low indifferent state'; which the other lamented, saying, 'he has but a puny, delicate constitution'. This struck his excellency, it being his own case, who interrupted: 'Don't tell me of constitution, that officer has good spirits, and good spirits will carry a man through every thing'.

ORDERS                              12 September, On board the *Sutherland*. 'The enemy's force is now divided, great scarcity of provisions now in their camp, and universal discontent among the Canadians; the second officer in command is gone to Montreal or St John's, which gives reason to think that General Amherst is advancing into the colony: *a vigorous blow struck by the army at this juncture may determine the fate of Canada.* Our troops below are in readiness to join us; all the light artillery and tools are embarked at Point Levy, and the troops will land where the French seem least to expect it. The first body that gets on shore is to march directly to the enemy and drive them from any little post they may occupy; the officers must be careful that the succeeding bodies do not, by any mistake, fire upon those who go on before them. The battalions must form on the upper ground with expedition, and be ready to charge whatever presents itself. When the artillery and troops are landed, a corps will be left to secure the landing-place, while the rest march on and endeavour to bring the French and Canadians to a battle. *The officers and men will remember what their country expects from them, and what a determined body of soldiers, inured to war, is capable of doing, against five weak French battalions mingled with a disorderly peasantry.* The soldiers must be attentive and obedient to their officers, and resolute in the execution of their duty.'

The Brigadiers Monckton and Murray, with the troops under their command, reimbarked this day from the parish of St Nicholas and returned to their ships. This evening all the boats of the fleet below the town were filled with marines, etc etc covered by frigates and sloops of war, worked up and lay half-channel over, opposite to Beauport, as if intending to land in the morning and thereby fix the enemy's whole attention to that quarter, the ships attending them are to edge over, at break of day, as near as possible without grounding, and cannonade the French intrenchments. At nine o'clock this night, our army in high spirits, the first division of them put into the flat-bottomed boats and, in a short time after, the whole squadron moved up the river with the tide of flood and, about an hour before day-light next morning, we fell down with the ebb. Weather favourable, a star-light night.

Before day-break on the 13th we made a descent upon the north shore, about half a quarter of a mile to the eastward of Sillery; and the light troops were fortunately, by the rapidity of the current, carried lower down, between us and Cape Diamond; we had, in this debarkation, thirty flat-bottomed boats containing about sixteen hundred men. This was a great surprise on the enemy, who, from the natural strength of the place, did not suspect, and consequently were not prepared against, so bold an attempt. The chain of sentries, which they had posted along the summit of the heights, galled us a little and picked off several men and some officers before our light infantry got up to dislodge them.

Captain Donald M'Donald, a very gallant officer, of Fraser's Highlanders, commanded the advanced-guard of the light infantry and was, consequently, among the foremost on shore; as soon as he and his men gained the height, he was challenged by a sentry and, with great presence of mind, from his knowledge of the French service, answered him according to their manner: it being yet dark, he came up to him, told him he was sent there with a large command to take post, and desired him to go with all speed to his guard and to call off all the other men of his party who were ranged along the hill, for that he would take care to give a good account of the B——Anglois, if they should persist; this *finesse* had the desired effect, and saved us many lives.

This grand enterprise was conducted and executed with great

good order and discretion; as fast as we landed, the boats put off for reinforcements, and the troops formed with much regularity: the general, with Brigadiers Monckton and Murray, were ashore with the first division. We lost no time here, but clambered up one of the steepest precipices that can be conceived being almost a perpendicular and of an incredible height. As soon as we gained the summit, all was quiet, and not a shot was heard, owing to the excellent conduct of the light infantry under Colonel Howe; it was by this time clear day-light. Here we formed again, the river and the south country in our rear, our right extending to the town, our left to Sillery, and halted a few minutes.

The general then detached the light troops to our left to rout the enemy from their battery and to disable their guns, except they could be rendered serviceable to the party who were to remain there; and this service was soon performed. We then faced to the right, and marched towards the town by files, till we came to the Plains of Abraham; an even piece of ground which Mr Wolfe had made choice of while we stood forming upon the hill. Weather showery: about six o'clock the enemy first made their appearance upon the heights, between us and the town; whereupon we halted, and wheeled to the right, thereby forming the line of battle.

Quebec was then to the eastward of us in front, with the enemy under its walls. Our right was flanked by the declivity and the main river to the southward, and what is called the lower road leading (westward) from the town, with the river Charles and the north country, were on our left. If the reader will attend to this description, observing the cardinal points, he may thereby form as lively an idea of the field of battle as if a plan were laid before him; and, though our first disposition was afterwards altered, yet our situation, with that of the enemy and the scene of action, could not vary.

The first disposition then was: 'grenadiers of Louisbourg on the right, forty-seventh regiment on the left, twenty-eighth on the right, and the forty-third on the left'; part of the light infantry took post in the houses at Sillery, and the remainder occupied a chain of houses which were opportunely situated for that purpose, and covered our left flank, inclining towards our rear; the general then advanced some platoons from the grenadiers and twenty-eighth regiment below the height on our right, to annoy the enemy and prevent their getting round the declivity between us and the main river, which they had attempted. By the time the fifteenth and thirty-fifth regiments joined us, who formed a second line, and were soon after followed by the forty-eighth and fifty-eighth, two battalions of the sixtieth and seventy-eighth regiments (Highlanders), by which a new disposition was made of the whole; viz. 'first line, thirty-fifth to the right, in a circular form on the slope of the hill; fifty-eighth, left; grenadiers, right; seventy-eighth, left; twenty-eighth, right; forty-seventh, left; forty-third, in the center'. General Wolfe, Brigadiers Monckton and Murray, to our front line; and the second was composed of the fifteenth, and two battalions of the sixtieth regiment, under Brigadier Townshend, with a reserve of the forty-eighth regiment, under Colonel Burton, drawn up in four grand divisions with large intervals.

The enemy had now likewise formed the line of battle, and got some cannon to play on us with round and canister-shot; but what galled us most was a body of Indians and other marksmen they had concealed in the corn opposite to the front of our right wing, and a coppice that stood opposite to our center, inclining towards our left; but Colonel Hale, by Brigadier Monckton's orders, advanced some platoons, alternately, from the forty-seventh regiment, which, after a few rounds, obliged these sculkers to retire: we were now ordered to lie down, and remained some time in this position. About eight o'clock we had two pieces of short brass six-pounders playing on the enemy, which threw them into some confusion and obliged them to alter their disposition, and Montcalm formed them into three large columns; about nine the two armies moved a little nearer each other. The light cavalry made a faint attempt upon our parties at the battery of Sillery, but were soon beat off, and Monsieur de Bougainville, with his troops from Cape Rouge, came down to attack the flank of our second line, hoping to penetrate there, but, by a masterly disposition of Brigadier Townshend, they were forced to desist, and the third battalion of Royal Americans was then detached to the first ground we had formed on after we gained the heights, to preserve the communication with the beach and our boats.

About ten o'clock the enemy began to advance briskly in three columns, with loud shouts and recovered arms, two of them inclining to the left of our army, and the third towards our right, firing obliquely at the two extremities of our line, from the distance of one hundred and thirty, until they came within forty yards; which our troops withstood with the greatest intrepidity and firmness, still reserving their fire and paying the strictest obedience to their officers: this uncommon steadiness, together with the havoc which the grape-shot from our field-pieces made among them, threw them into some disorder, and was most critically maintained by a well-timed, regular and heavy discharge of our small arms, such as they could no longer oppose.

When the general formed the line of battle, he ordered the regiments to load with an additional ball. The forty-third and forty-seventh regiments, in the center, being little affected by the oblique fire of the enemy, gave them, with great calmness, as remarkable a close and heavy discharge as I ever saw performed at a private field of exercise, insomuch that better troops than we encountered could not possibly withstand it: and, indeed, well might the French officers say that they never opposed such a shock as they received from the center of our line, for that they believed every ball took place, and such regularity and discipline they had not experienced before; our troops in general, and particularly the central corps, having levelled and fired—*comme un coup de canon.*

Hereupon they gave way, and fled with precipitation, so that, by the time the cloud of smoke was vanished, our men were again loaded and, profiting by the advantage we had over them, pursued them almost to the gates of the town and the bridge over the little river, redoubling our fire with great eagerness, making many officers and men prisoners. The weather cleared up, with a comfortably warm sun-shine: the Highlanders chased them vigorously towards Charles's river, and the fifty-eighth to the suburb close to John's gate, until they were checked by the cannon from the two hulks; at the same time a gun, which the town had brought to bear upon us with grape-shot, galled the progress of the regiments to the right, who were likewise pursuing with equal ardour, while Colonel Hunt Walsh, by a very judicious movement, wheeled the battalions of Bragg and Kennedy to the left, and flanked the coppice where a body of the enemy made a stand, as if willing to renew the action; but a few platoons from these corps completed our victory. Then it was that Brigadier Townshend came up, called off the pursuers, ordered the whole line to dress and recover their former ground.

Our joy at this success in inexpressibly damped by the loss we sustained of one of the greatest heroes which this or any other age can boast of—GENERAL JAMES WOLFE, who received his mortal wound as he was exerting himself at the head of the grenadiers of Louisbourg; and Brigadier Monckton was unfortunately wounded upon the left of the forty-third and right of the forty-seventh regiment at much the same time; whereby the command devolved on Brigadier Townshend, who, with Brigadier Murray, went to the head of every regiment and returned thanks for their extraordinary good behaviour, congratulating the officers on our success.

There is one incident very remarkable, and which I can affirm from my own personal knowledge, that the enemy were extremely apprehensive of being rigorously treated; for, conscious of their inhuman behaviour to our troops upon a former occasion, the officers who fell into our hands most piteously (with hats off) sued for quarter, repeatedly declaring they were not at Fort William-Henry (called by them Fort George) in the year 1757.

While the two armies were engaged this morning, there was an incessant firing between the town and our south batteries. By the time that our troops had taken a little refreshment, a quantity of intrenching tools were brought a shore, and the regiments were employed in redoubting our ground and landing some cannon and ammunition. The officers who are prisoners say that Quebec will surrender in a few days: some deserters, who came out to us in the evening, agree in that opinion, and inform us that the Sieur de Montcalm is dying, in great agony, of a wound he received to-day in their retreat.

Thus has our late renowned commander, by his superior eminence in the art of war, and a most judicous *coup d'etat*, made a conquest of this fertile, healthy and hitherto formidable country with a handful of troops only, in spite of the political schemes and most vigorous efforts of the famous Montcalm and many other officers of rank and experience, at the head of an army considerably more numerous. My pen is too feeble to draw the character of this *British Achilles*; but the same may, with justice, be said of him as was said of Henry IV of France: *He was possessed of courage, humanity, clemency, generosity, affability and politeness.* And, though the former of these happy ingredients, how essential soever it may be in the composition of a soldier, is not alone sufficient to distinguish an expert officer, yet I may, with strict truth, advance that Major-General James Wolfe, by his great talents and martial disposition, which he discovered early in life, was greatly superior to his experience in generalship, and was by no means inferior to a Frederick, a Henry, or a Ferdinand.

> *When the matter match'd his mighty mind,*
> *Up rose the Hero: on his piercing eye*
> *Sat observation, on each glance of thought*
> *Decision follow'd, as the thunderbolt*
> *Pursues the flash.*

Deserters, who are come over to us since the action, inform us that it was very difficult to persuade Monsieur de Montcalm and the other commanders that the flower of our army were behind the town; and, after the marquis had marched his troops over the river Charles and taken a view of us, he said—'They have at last got to the weak side of this miserable garrison, therefore we must endeavour to crush them with our numbers, *and scalp them all before twelve o'clock*'. Every coppice, bush or other cover that stood on our ground this morning, were cut down before night and applied to the use of our new works; the houses were all fortified, and several redoubts thrown up round our camp, which is about one thousand yards from the garrison, before ten o'clock.

ORDERS      14 September. Parole, Wolfe; countersign, England. 'The remaining general officers, fit to act, take the earliest opportunity to express the praise which is due to the conduct and bravery of the troops; and the victory, which attended it, sufficiently proves the superiority which this army has over any number of such troops as they engaged yesterday; *they wish that the person who lately commanded them had survived so glorious a day, and had this day been able to give the troops these just encomiums*. The fatigues which the troops will be obliged to undergo, to reap the advantage of this victory, will be supported with a true spirit, as this seems to be the period which will determine, in all probability, our American labours; the troops are to receive a jill of rum per day, and will receive fresh provisions the day after to-morrow. The regiments and corps to give returns of their killed and wounded yesterday, and the strength of their corps. The pioneers of the different regiments to bury the dead: the corps are to send all their tools not immediately in use to the artillery park. All French papers, or letters found, are desired to be sent to the head-quarters. No soldier to presume to strole beyond the out-posts. Arms that cannot be drawn are to be fired into the swamp near the head quarters. The admiral has promised the continuance of all the assistance which the naval service can spare, to ease the troops of the fatigues which the farther operations will require of us. General Townshend has the satisfaction to acquaint the troops that General Monckton's wound is not dangerous; the commanding officers of the corps will order the rolls to be called every half-hour, to prevent marauding, etc etc.'

The garrison appear to be at work upon their ramparts, as if resolved to prolong the siege. Some deserters, who came out to us this day, inform us, that Monsieur de Lévis, who has rejoined and collected their shattered forces, had intended to surprise the rear of our camp at day-break this morning, but, upon reconnoitring our situation and finding that we had made such excellent use of our time in erecting redoubts and other works, prudently declined the undertaking. The Sieur de Montcalm died late last night; when his wound was dressed, and he settled in bed, the surgeons who attended him were desired to acquaint him ingenuously with their sentiments of him, and, being answered that his wound was mortal, he calmly replied, 'he was glad of it': his excellency then demanded, 'whether he could survive it long, and how long?' He was told, 'about a dozen hours, perhaps more, peradventure less'. 'So much the better,' rejoined this eminent warrior; 'I am happy I shall not live to see the surrender of Quebec.'

He then ordered his secretary into the room to adjust his private affairs, which as soon as they were dispatched, he was visited by Monsieur de Ramsay, the French king's lieutenant, and by other principal officers who desired to receive his excellency's commands, with the farther measures to be pursued for the defence of Quebec, the capital of Canada. To this the marquis made the following answer—'I'll neither give orders, nor interfere any farther; I have much business that must be attended to, of greater moment than your ruined garrison and this wretched country: my time is very short—therefore pray leave me—I wish you all comfort, and to be happily extricated from your present perplexities.' He then called for his chaplain, who, with the bishop of the colony, remained with him till he expired. Some time before this great man departed, we are assured he paid us this compliment—'Since it was my misfortune to be discomfited and mortally wounded, it is a great consolation to me to be vanquished by so brave and generous an enemy. If I could survive this wound, I would engage to beat three times the number of such forces as I commanded this morning, with a third of their number of British troops.'

We are drawing artillery and ammunition ashore with all expedition; in which we are much favoured, at present, by the weather, and have found a convenient road for the purpose, leading directly from the cove to the camp; this is the place that had been intended for our descent, but, the morning being dark and the tide of ebb very rapid, we were imperceptibly carried a little lower down, which proved a favourable circumstance; for there was a strong intrenchment that covered the road, lined by a detachment of one hundred and fifty men. It is still much more fortunate that the general had not deferred the execution of his project to another day; for two French regiments, with a corps of savages, were actually under orders of readiness to march at six o'clock on the morning of the 13th and intrench themselves immediately along the heights; but happily our troops were in possession of that ground before the enemy had any thoughts of stirring.

After our late worthy general, of renowned memory, was carried off wounded to the rear of the front line, he desired those who were about him to lay him down; being asked if he would have a surgeon, he replied, 'it is needless; it is all over with me'. One of them then cried out, 'they run, see how they run'. 'Who runs?' demanded our hero, with great earnestness, like a person roused from sleep. The officer answered, 'the enemy, Sir; egad they give way everywhere'. Thereupon the general rejoined, '*Go one of you, my lads, to Colonel Burton; tell him to march Webb's regiment with all speed down to Charles's river, to cut off the retreat of the fugitives from the bridge*'. Then, turning on his side, he added, '*Now, God be praised, I will die in peace*': and thus expired.

Various accounts have been circulated of General Wolfe's manner of dying, his last words, and the officers into whose hands he fell: and many, from a vanity of talking, claimed the honour of being his supporters after he was wounded; but the foregoing circumstances were ascertained to me by Lieutenant Brown, of the grenadiers of Louisbourg and the twenty-second regiment, who, with Mr Henderson, a volunteer in the same company, and a private man, were the three persons who carried his excellency to the rear; which an artillery officer seeing, immediately flew to his assistance; and these were all that attended him in his dying moments. *I do not recollect the artillery officer's name or it should be chearfully recorded here.*

Wet weather on the 15th: more deserters coming out to us; they inform us that Monsieur de Ramsay, who commands in the town, and the principal officers of the garrison are settling the preliminaries for a capitulation; that the Indians have robbed one of their best store-houses and are gone off to their respective districts; that the citizens and Canadians in general are much dissatisfied and impatient to have the town delivered up to us. We are landing more battering cannon and stores, which the sailors and marines are drawing up to our camp. We are considerably annoyed by shot and shells from the town, nevertheless we are spiritedly rendering our works more defensible: two thousand men are employed in making fascines and gabions to inable us to carry on approaches. A parcel of sailors, going to some houses on the beach under Cape Diamond in search of plunder, were fired upon and made prisoners. The enemy have brought up a mortar to their south-west bastion to bombard our ships above the town, and have thrown several shells for that purpose, without any effect. The wind shifted to the NW this evening, and the weather cleared up.

The enemy acknowledge to have had near fifteen hundred, killed, wounded and prisoners on the 13th instant; among the latter, which amounted to almost three hundred, are included one lieutenant-colonel, nine captains, five first and second lieutenants and two cadets. Besides Monsieur de Montcalm, the two next in command were also killed, viz. Monsieur de Sennezergue and Monsieur de St Ours, brigadiers. This great loss fell mostly on their regular troops.

About ten o'clock at night on the 15th the enemy beat a chamade, and an officer was sent to the general; we flattered ourselves they were about to capitulate, but it was only to request permission to send their women and children, over Charles's river, into the country; which was generously granted. We profited by this cessation, having advanced a large detachment with a covering party nearer and opposite to Port St Louis, to clear the ground of brush, take post and throw up a spacious redoubt, it being intended to erect a battery there: these parties were augmented to-day, and the enemy are endeavouring, by a very hot fire, to rout them thence. The second in command of the marine department, with a priest and thirty Canadians, were brought in prisoners by a party of Highlanders on the 16th. The enemy seem to be more lavish of their ammunition than heretofore, neither sparing our camp nor the south batteries. We are drawing up more artillery, and large parties are employed in cutting fascines, etc; the most effectual preparations are making to hasten the reduction of this capital, and, in a day or two, we hope to open a formidable fire upon the upper town and the works on this side of it; which, however, do not seem calculated to bear much battering.

On the 17th the admiral moved the fleet up into the bason, and is preparing to attack the lower town: the artillery which we have now in this camp consists of twelve heavy twenty-four pounders of brass, four light ditto, sixteen of twenty-two pounders, and eight of iron; four thirteen-inch brass mortars, and one of iron; four brass ten-inch mortars, and eight of eight inches; four brass twelve-pounders, and sixteen ditto six-pounders; eleven royal howitzers of five inches and an half, and thirty of four inches and three quarters; in all, sixty pieces of cannon and fifty-eight mortars, etc. The enemy fire now, almost incessantly, into our advanced works, our camp and our batteries on the south side of the river; an officer of the twenty-eighth regiment, sitting at the door of his tent, had one of his legs so shattered by a shot from the town, that he was compelled to undergo immediate amputation. A new battery is to be erected this afternoon, contiguous to the advanced redoubt, for cannon and mortars.

Between the hours of two and three an officer came out to our camp with proposals to capitulate, upon which the admiral was instantly sent for. At four the working party for the advanced works and battery were paraded, and we lay some time on our arms to wait the event; between five and six we were ordered to the left of the line, to cut down all the underwood and cover that stood within half a mile of our flank and rear; which employed us until almost nine. The army are ordered to be very alert this night, the town having agreed to capitulate, upon condition that it is not relieved, before to-morrow morning, by the troops under Messieurs de Lévis and de Bougainville, who have signified their intentions to the Sieur de Ramsay of endeavouring to dispossess us of this ground with all the force of Canada.

The garrison capitulated on the 18th, and the articles were duly ratified and exchanged. The fleet and army are to take possession of the upper and lower towns this afternoon. The keys of the ports were given up this evening to General Townshend, and safe-guards were sent into the town, pursuant to the treaty: the Louisbourg grenadiers marched in, preceded by a detachment of the artillery and one gun with the British colours hoisted on its carriage: the Union flag was displayed on the citadel. And Captain Palliser, with a large body of seamen and inferior officers, at the same time took possession of the lower town and hoisted colours on the summit of the declivity leading from the high to the low town, in view of the bason and the north and south countries below Quebec. Deserters are coming in from Monsieur de Lévis's army every hour, and the Canadians are surrendering by whole families, to submit to the general's mercy.

A body of the enemy took post in an intrenchment on the north side of Charles's river, and have got some cannon there; they had the presumption to fire at our men passing through the environs of the town and the limits of our camp, pretending that they were not included in the capitulation; however, a spirited message was sent to Monsieur de Ramsay, in which it was threatened 'to disannul the capitulation, prosecute the siege with the utmost rigour and storm the town, if he, or any of his troops by his connivance, should persevere in that, or in any other ungenerous act or procedure; and insisting that all such parts of the country, north and south, as are and have been reputed in the district of Quebec, shall be comprehended in the treaty'. This vigorous menace had the desired effect, and an officer was immediately sent to that quarter to command them to desist from all farther acts of hostility: Major Elliot, with a detachment of five hundred men, were instantly sent to take possession of the enemy's late intrenched camp, and to disarm the inhabitants of the village of Beauport. A noted rebel, by name Long, by birth a Briton, and formerly a pilot in our service, is made a prisoner and has been sent in irons on board one of our ships of war; this fellow was a great partisan among the French banditti in Nova Scotia, where he has frequently proved a desperate thorn in the sides of his countrymen.

Having now brought our labours to a glorious determination, I shall only observe that, if any fleet and army ever exceeded their predecessors in valour, perseverance and unanimity, that merit may justly be claimed by this armament before Quebec and by its commanders respectively. This harmony and concord, particularly among our general officers, shine conspicuously in the successful event, notwithstanding many groundless insinuations and reports to the contrary; and, if the reader is still desirous to be farther ascertained of it, let him pay proper attention to Mr Wolfe's incomparable letter of the 2nd instant, and to the orders that were published after his death by his successors; which must sufficiently obviate every illiberal suggestion, artfully circulated by unthinking or designing men from a motive of endeavouring to appear *of consequence*.

The army had, indeed, uncommon obstacles to contend with; the enemy exceedingly superior in number, the country every-where strong, and its shores almost inaccessible. The ardour and activity of our fleet, from their first entrance into the river St Lawrence, and particularly against the numerous floating batteries and formidable rafts and fireships of the enemy, diffused such an emulation among the troops as inabled them to discharge their duty in contempt of the greatest fatigues and dangers; and, at length, to overcome every difficulty which at first appeared to them. The admirable service performed by the artillery, under that experienced master of his profession, Colonel, now Major-General, Williamson, exceeds every thing that can possibly be said in their behalf: and, for the honour of that corps, it may, with the strictest justice, be alledged that not any other country can boast of greater proficients in the art of gunnery than those produced by that excellent academy at Woolwich. I am happy in an opportunity of thus declaring my sentiments of the gentlemen educated in that royal seminary, and at the same time to confute a variety of pompous vauntings which one frequently hears advanced in favour of our enemies, by giving them the preference, in that science, to the rest of Europe: for, how great soever the merit of the French may be in the art of war in other respects, I must confess their eminence, in this particular branch, was not conspicuous at any time in the course of this campaign. Upon the whole, our seamen, marines and soldiers of every rank and station, employed upon this important enterprise, have respectively, with the greatest chearfulness and intrepidity, discharged their duty in such a manner as to reflect the most illustrious honour on themselves, on the British arms, and on their country.

Our late much lamented general has been embalmed, and on the 19th his remains were sent from Point Levy on board a ship to be carried to England: the detachments in that quarter, under Colonel James, attended the corpse to the waterside, and the officers and men most sensibly expressed their grief on this melancholy occasion.

Being, on the 20th, detached to the camp at Point Levy on regimental affairs, I passed through the garrison and took a boat from the lower town, by which I had an opportunity of viewing more distinctly the great effect our artillery had upon it from the south side of the river; and indeed the havoc is not to be conceived. Such houses as are standing are perforated by our shot, more or less; and the low town is so great a ruin that its streets are almost impassable; the parts least damaged are the streets leading to Port Louis, Port St John, and the Palace-Gate; and yet these, though more remote from our batteries, have had some share in the almost general destruction.

The army is now incamped, in two lines, nearer to Quebec; and large detachments are employed in levelling our redoubts, clearing the streets and houses in the town, landing stores and forming magazines of provisions, ammunition, etc etc. Brigadier Murray is to remain here in command, and Colonel Burton, of the forty-eighth regiment, is to act as lieutenant-governor. An express is sailed for England with an account of the success of our arms.

The country-people are now returning to their habitations with their cattle and effects, and are beginning to reap their harvest; it is with the utmost satisfaction that I have daily ocular experience of the most distinguished humanity and generosity in our worthy soldiers; they not only share their provision with the distressed

Canadians, but even their small allowance of rum: to-day I saw above twenty of our men assisting those poor people in cutting and binding their sheaves of corn; they being within the district of the post where I was on duty, I went towards them, and, asking the soldiers what they were to get for their labour, they replied, 'They sought not any thing; what they did was out of good-will to the poor creatures, who had little enough for themselves'. One of them added, 'It would be rank murder to take any thing from the poor devils, for they have lost enough already'.

While I stood reflecting on the matchless goodness of our honest Britons, with the oddity of the fore-going speech, I saw a peasant take from his pocket a sealskin pouch, with a pipe, and offer his tobacco to the soldiers, which they all refused: one of them instantly produced a rusty iron box that was also filled with tobacco, and tendered it to the Canadian, saying, 'When it is out, I know where to get more; perhaps that is not your case, poor man!' Charmed with such benevolence and nobleness of heart, I approached the poor American in order to explain to him what had been said; whereupon he dropped his reaping-hook and raised his hands and eyes, with seeming fervency, to Heaven; astonished no doubt, at so much un-expected, nay undeserved, goodness.

This instance furnished me with a spacious field for agreeable reflections; well, thought I, here our soldiers have manifested the suitableness and justness of those incomparable ideas so elegantly expressed by the inimitable Mr Wolfe in his placart to the Canadians: *Britons, breathe higher sentiments of humanity, and listen to the merciful dictates of the Christian religion.* My pleasing meditations were now interrupted by the arrival of an express to advertise me of the approach of a relief; so, after I had commended the soldiers for their admirable display of generosity to a conquered enemy, I retired to my post.

The troops marched into winter quarters on the 29th, except the forty-eighth regiment, who keep the field by choice until the inten-dant's palace, which is assigned to that corps, is completely fitted up for their reception. For some time our men are likely to be very indifferently lodged, by the inconceivably ruinous condition of the houses in almost every corner of the garrison; but those dwellings particularly that are situated along the summit of the cliff between the high and low town, extending from the bishop's palace to Cape Diamond (which fell to the lot of the royal artillery, thirty-fifth and forty-third corps), having been mostly exposed to our batteries, are considerably the greatest sufferers, and must, indeed, undergo incredible repairs, to render them in any degree habitable.

The inhabitants of town and country are apprehensive of starving this winter; in the years 1757 and 1758 their harvests failed them; and though their crops promised well this year, yet the calamities of war (say they) have frustrated all their prospects and expectations. The citizens inform us that, if it had not been for the arrival of the succours which they received from France last spring, and narrowly escaped the English squadron then in the river, the garrison would have surrendered to us, after exchanging a few shot and shells with our batteries for form's sake, in order to prevent the ruin of their town, warehouses, magazines, and particularly their religious houses.

It has been already observed, that part of our troops took possession of the upper, and a detachment from the navy, in like manner, of the lower town, on the 18th instant; from that time to the 30th, we have been landing provisions, ammunition and stores of all kinds from the fleet; taking the submission of the inhabitants within the government of Quebec and disarming them; levelling our redoubts; forming a large magazine of fascines, etc; procuring firewood for present use; clearing the garrison and repairing houses for the reception of the troops; we also evacuated the posts at Point Levy and the Isle of Orleans; removed our camp nearer to the town, and afterwards marched into quarters for the winter; we embarked the French troops for Europe, with such of our sick and wounded men as were recoverable; the latter to be transmitted to the southward, for the speedier re-establishment of their health; and such as were rendered unfit for service were discharged and put on board a ship, in order to be conveyed to England and provided for at their ease for the remainder of their lives.

Add to this the securing the avenues from the country to the town, strengthening our defences as much as possible for the present, and making such farther provision for the comfort and safety of the army who are to remain here as the season and our present circumstances will admit of. Thus have our forces nobly surmounted a great variety of the most inconceivable difficulties, and, with a truly British spirit, perfected as irksome and laborious a campaign as ever was heretofore conducted. It is now time to take a view of the transactions of the armies upon the lakes, where we shall find they have been exerting, with equal valour, their utmost efforts in the prosecution of the war in that quarter.

THE DEATH OF WOLFE

MONTCALM MORTALLY WOUNDED

# X

# The British Consolidate

*To the south, Amherst was consolidating his gains, but winter overtook the second intended part of his campaign, and the French survived to fight another year. Nevertheless, the pressure of the British armies in the south and west had prevented any reinforcement of Montcalm and on the Great Lakes their forces were routed.*

Camp before Ticonderoga, 1 August, 1759.

A PARTY WHO HAD been on a scout from our camp before Ticonderoga, returned on 1 August at noon, and reported that the enemy have abandoned Crown Point; upon this intelligence the second battalion of Royal Highlanders were detached to Oswego, to reinforce, if necessary, the army before Niagara. We have set the saw-mill to work, and have got a new radeau nearly completed; the army are employed in removing provisions, artillery and stores, for the convenience of embarking them as soon as batteaus and whale-boats can be launched in the Lake Champlain, in which we are using all expedition.

The army embarked very early on the morning of 4 August but could not put off immediately for want of batteaus for one of the regular regiments, which, however, were soon obtained; and we proceeded in four columns as before, and arrived at Crown Point about four in the afternoon; the troops were instantly landed, and disposed of in such manner as to prevent any surprise: part of the army remained all night on their arms, and the rest were incamped. Now that we have got into the habit of chasing the enemy from post to post, our only apprehensions are lest the season will not permit us to take up our winter quarters at Montreal (to which we repute this place half-way from Albany) and thereby assist more effectually the forces before Quebec. The reduction of Crown Point is, indeed, a great acquisition to his majesty's arms, as it secures the whole country hence to New-York and about Lake Champlain, at the head of which it is situated, on a small point of land that is surrounded on all sides by branches of this lake; the country hereabout appears to be extremely fruitful, and regales the eyes with the most agreeable prospects imaginable; immense quantities of sugar-trees grow here; and a root that I have heard is in high repute with the natives of

China, called ginseng, is also in great abundance; which is a fine aromatic, and is much esteemed by the Indians of these parts for its medicinal virtues; between this fortress and those of Ticonderoga, considerable quantities of artillery stores of all kinds, with intrenching tools, several pieces of cannon, mortars, howitzers (all of iron) and some small arms, have fallen into our hands: their largest guns are eighteen pounders, and from that down to four-pounders, besides swivels.

An officer arrived express from Niagara with the agreeable news of the surrender of that important place; the terms on which it capitulated, with a transcript of Sir William Johnson's letter to his excellency the commander-in-chief, I shall present to the reader, being the most authentic accounts of this glorious event:

'I have the honour to acquaint you, by Lieutenant Moncrief, that Niagara surrendered to his majesty's arms on the 25th July. A detachment of twelve hundred men, with a number of Indians, under the command of Messieurs Aubry and des Ligneries, collected from Detroit, Venango and Presqu'isle, made an attempt to re-inforce the garrison, the 24th in the morning; but, as I had intelligence of them, I made a disposition to intercept them. The evening before, I ordered the light infantry and piquets to take post on the road upon our left, leading from Niagara-falls to the fort; in the morning, I reinforced these with two companies of grenadiers and part of the forty-sixth regiment. The action began about half an hour after nine; but they were so well received by the troops in front, and the Indians on their flank, that, in an hour's time, the whole was completely ruined, and all their officers made prisoners, among whom are M. Aubry, des Ligneries, Marin, Repentigny, to the number of seventeen. I cannot ascertain the number of the killed, they are so dispersed among the woods; but their loss is great.

'As this happened under the eyes of the garrison, I thought proper to send my last summons to the commanding officer for his surrendering, which he listened to. I inclose you the capitulation: Mr Moncrief will inform you of the state of our ammunition and provisions; I hope care will be taken to forward an immediate supply of both to Oswego. As the troops that were defeated yesterday were drawn from those posts which lie in General Stanwix's route, I am in hopes it will be of the utmost consequence to the success of his expedition. The public stores of the garrison that can be saved from the Indians, I shall order the assistant quarter-master-general and the clerk of the stores to take an account of as soon as possible. As all my attention at present is taken up with the Indians, that the capitulation I have agreed to may be observed, your excellency will excuse my not being more particular. Permit me to assure you, in the whole progress of the siege, which was severe and painful, the officers and men behaved with the utmost chearfulness and bravery. I have only to regret the loss of General Prideaux and Colonel Johnson. I endeavoured to pursue the late general's vigorous measures, the good effects of which he deserved to enjoy.'

Nothing could be more fortunate and critical than M. Aubry's attempting to relieve the place, and the entire defeat of his detachment; for I am assured that Sir William Johnson was much streightened for provisions and ammunition, occasioned by some unforeseen delay in the expected convoys that were forwarded to his army; but, as the success of that action brought on the immediate surrender of the garrison, his troops thereby happily procured a most seasonable supply of both these articles.

It was on the 23rd of July that Sir William received intelligence, by some of his scouts, of the approach of the enemy to relieve the fort, and instantly made a disposition to defeat their intentions. The guard of the trenches was commanded by Major Beckwith; and, lest the garrison should sally out and either attempt to surprise or overpower that guard and thereby hem in our troops between two fires, Sir William very judiciously posted the forty-fourth regiment, under Lieutenant-Colonel Farquhar, in such manner as to be able to sustain the major, upon the first alarm. The road on the left of the line, which leads from the cataract to the fort, was occupied by the light infantry and piquets of the army on the evening of the 23rd; and, early next morning, these were reinforced by the grenadiers and part of the forty-sixth regiment, the whole commanded by Lieutenant-Colonel Eyre Massey, to whose good conduct in the distribution of the troops, and the steadiness with which he received the enemy in front while our Indians attacked them on the flanks, the honour of the day is in a great measure, attributed. Our savages endeavoured, before the engagement began, to hold a *talk* with those in alliance with the French, hoping, as their affairs were growing desperate, to be able to induce them to take part with us, at least, to observe a neutrality; but the enemy's Indians declined the interview, whereupon the usual signal of yelling and shouting was given, for the action to begin, by the barbarians on both sides. Among the prisoners were seven captains; the first and second in command were both wounded, as was the officer who had the direction of the Indians.

Sir William Johnson merits the highest applause from his king and country, and his inclination to put a stop to the farther effusion of human blood was truly laudable; to this end he detached Major Harvey to the governor, with a detail of what had happened and a list of the captives in his possession, recommending it to him to surrender, lest, by forcing him to extremities, he should not have it in his power to restrain his Indians, who would, doubtless, by an obstinate fruitless resistance, become too much inraged to be withheld. The governor thought proper to listen to these proposals; but, in order to be ascertained of the reality of the discomfit, he sent an officer out to take a view of the prisoners, who were immediately produced to him. In consequence of this ocular demonstration, the garrison capitulated; the troops consisted of above six hundred men, besides several females and a great many officers. The place was well provided with a considerable quantity of provisions, ammunition, and stores of every kind; above forty pieces of cannon, from two to fourteen pounders, nineteen of which were twelve-pounders; several mortars, and an immense number of hand-grenado's.

The importance of this conquest is immense, and reflects the highest honour on the commander-in-chief who, sensible of its vast consequence, wisely planned this expedition; and the executing officers, with their troops, justly claim a large share of merit, for so gallantly and effectually seconding his excellency's views and intentions. Niagara is situated in the heart of the Iroquois country, surrounded by all the great lakes; particularly by Ontario on the north, Erie on the south, by Huron and others on the north and north-west sides, and by the Appalachian mountains, running serpentine through the Carolinas, part of Virginia, Maryland and Pennsylvania, terminating abruptly in the heart of this country on the south-east; it has the whole continent open to it on the west, and our colonies on the south and south-east: this post and that of Crown Point were the passes by which the French and Canadians had access to, and invaded, our settlements, exercised the most wanton barbarities on our people and, in a great measure, engrossed the whole fur trade to themselves, thereby gaining the confidence and friendship of numbers of Indian tribes and their confederates, our allies, who inhabit the borders of these lakes, for several hundreds of miles.

The fort of Niagara was erected by the French so late as the year 1751; and it was by them looked upon as the key to all these inland seas which communicate with each other, and afford a navigation that extends almost over the whole continent of North-America; the country immediately about this place is mountainous and barren; but, at some distance on the borders of Ontario and Lake Erie, the soil is rich and good, producing vegetables, Indian corn and other grain in great perfection and abundance. To conclude, our colonies settled on the sea-coast, being surrounded by almost impassable mountains, were hitherto precluded, by the French being possessed of Niagara, from the lakes, our communication with the numerous natives residing on their banks, and from the profitable fur trade carried on in those parts.

At Brigadier Gage's departure to take the command of the army under Sir William Johnson, he received orders, as soon as Niagara should be reduced, to proceed, with the principal of those forces, by Lake Ontario up the river Cataraqui, and possess himself of a very important post which the enemy have got on the west side of it, called La Galette; and the general, perceiving the vast advantage that would result from our securing that place, whereby we should become intire masters of the lake before-mentioned, and our settlers on the Mohawk river would benefit considerably, as they would be no longer apprehensive of the barbarous incursions of the enemy, was pleased this day to inforce these orders, in a letter sent by Major Christie, appointed quarter-master-general in that enterprise.

Captain Loring being left at Ticonderoga to build a brigantine, the main of our army have been employed here, since the 5th, in erecting the new fort, fortifying our camp, and preparing, with all expedition, to pass Lake Champlain.

By deserters, who came in on the 16th, we received intelligence of the enemy being retired to the lower end of the lake, and incamped on Isle au Noix; that they consist of eight battalions of regulars, some detachments or piquets from other corps, colony troops and Canadians, amounting to three thousand five hundred men, with an hundred pieces of cannon; that they have four armed vessels under the direction of several sea officers from the royal navy of France, with reserves from the regiments of Languedoc, Bearn and La Sarre on board; one of these vessels carries ten guns, six and four-pounders; the second, two brass twelves and six iron six-pounders; the third, eight guns, six and four-pounders; and the fourth, of the same number and weight; besides swivels almost innumerable throughout this little squadron.

Captain Loring arrived on 17 August, in consequence of a summons; and, being informed of the naval force of the enemy, he is of opinion the brigantine he is constructing will still be insufficient, and therefore determined upon building a radeau to carry six twenty-four-pounders, in such manner as to render them serviceable on the water, besides barely transporting them over the lake.

We received farther intelligence on 1 September that the enemy are endeavouring to have a superior naval force, and, for this purpose, have actually launched a new vessel pierced for sixteen guns, whereupon the commodore was again sent for; the general, being resolved not to leave any thing to mere chance, has agreed upon building a second vessel, if it may be done without retarding the radeau.

Captain Loring returned on 3 September to Crown Point, and concluded with his excellency upon building a sloop to carry sixteen guns; this causes a great delay in our operations, to the unspeakable mortification of the general and the army; but still it is unavoidable. The repairs of the forts at Ticonderoga are in great forwardness; and the new fortress we are constructing here has all the advantages of situation and strength of ground that can be desired.

An express arrived on the 19th from Brigadier Gage, with a letter to the general of the 11th instant; wherein he acquaints him that, from the various difficulties that present themselves, he finds it will be utterly impracticable to establish a post at La Galette before the winter; this is no small disappointment to his excellency, as he has, for some time, been very intent upon that important object, and is now under the necessity of resigning all thoughts of it for this campaign, the season being so far advanced, or at least will be, before his farther commands can reach the brigadier.

We are using the utmost diligence in augmenting our naval force, and on 29 September this day the new radeau was launched; she is eighty-four feet in length by twenty. The brigantine arrived on 10 October from Ticonderoga, and mounts six six-pounders, twelve four-pounders and twenty swivels; she has seventy seamen on board, besides a detachment from the troops of sixty men, with officers in proportion, to serve as marines. The new sloop of sixteen guns came down the next day, commanded by Lieutenant Grant of Montgomery's Highlanders; her weight of metal consists of four six-pounders, twelve four-pounders and twenty-two swivels, with sixty seamen and fifty soldiers. The army immediately got into their batteaus; the sloop and brigantine sailed about four in the afternoon, and the troops followed in four divisions; at night, a light was hoisted for their guidance on board the brigantine, and another, on board the radeau.

Some guns were heard early on the morning of the 12th, and a message was sent to the general, acquainting him that our vessels with those of the enemy were come to an action; but this proved a mistake, and proceeded from some batteaus of the forty-second regiment, under Major Reid, having followed the light of the brigantine, which, in the night, he took for the radeau, and thereby fell in with the enemy's sloops, who fired several guns at them; but they all fortunately made their escape, except one batteau with a lieutenant and twenty men, which were made prisoners. Some time after, we perceived the enemy's sloops crowding sail; towards the evening we had very rough, blowing weather; the batteaus were ordered into a commodious bay on the western shore for shelter; the troops were landed for exercise, after such long sitting, and to boil their kettles, covered by Gage's light infantry, who were advanced for that purpose; and the rangers were put ashore on a contiguous island.

The perverse wind, with an angry agitated sea, which renders the lake impassable for boats, has obliged us to remain here. The two whale-boats, that were sent express to Captain Loring on the 13th, returned on the evening of the 17th, being forced back, after the crews had, in vain, exerted all the efforts in their power to get down the lake; they say the waves ran so high that they were under the greatest apprehensions of being lost.

The weather being more moderate, and the wind having veered to the southward, we proceeded on our voyage on the 18th, as low down as the bay where the French sloops are; one of them has been so far repaired that she sailed immediately with the brigantine and our own sloop; two hundred men are detached in whale-boats to assist Captain Loring in his researches for the enemy's schooner.

The general, forseeing, by an appearance of winter setting in, that the season will be too far advanced, by the time he can reach Isle au Noix, to rout the enemy thence and make any farther progress in the campaign with safety to the army, has resolved to lose no farther time on the lake, but to return to Crown Point and complete the works as fast as possible, before the troops are distributed into quarters for the winter. Accordingly, his excellency having intimated his intentions and given the necessary orders, we returned to the bay, where we were so many days unluckily wind-bound.

The army proceeded up the lake, and got within four leagues of Crown Point, whither the light infantry and grenadiers are detached in whale-boats; as the radeau and boats that are heavily laden cannot make such dispatch, they are to continue this night with the rest of the troops, under the particular care of the rangers. The general, with the remainder of the forces, happily arrived at

Crown Point on the 21st, where I shall just leave them, to contemplate the transactions of another quarter.

When his excellency concerted the reduction of Niagara, he also formed a plan to co-operate therewith, by detaching Brigadier-General Stanwix to the westward, as well to secure our conquests on that side, and overawe the numerous tribes of barbarians inhabiting that vast country between the delightful river Ohio and Lake Erie, as to cut out work for the enemy, in that district, by attacking their chain of forts, viz. Venango, to the northward of Pittsburgh, and about half-way to Presqu'isle; another fortress his excellency had in view, together with Pont Chartrain, a fort established under the direction of a French officer of that name, at a streight of a river which communicates with the Lakes Erie and Huron, commonly called Detroit, thereby to command the intire navigation of the former of these waters, and either prevent the enemy from sending reinforcements tnence to Niagara, or, in case of an attempt of that kind, to deprive them of those important posts on that lake.

For these several purposes it was that Brigadier Stanwix was detached with a battalion of Royal Americans, commanded by Colonel Bouquet; another of Virginians, three battalions of Pennsylvanians, commanded respectively by Colonels Byrd, Armstrong, Mercer and James Burd, with three companies of Delawares under Captain Battel; amounting, in all, to about four thousand men. It has already appeared that a corps of the enemy, as was suspected, not less than twelve hundred, besides Indians, collected from the different forts above-mentioned, were drawn off towards Niagara by Messieurs Aubry and des Ligneries, with a view to surprise the forces lately under Brigadier Prideaux, and thereby compel them to raise the siege: in consequence of which procedure, we find, by dispatches received some time after our arrival here, at Crown Point, that Mr Stanwix has possessed himself of Venango and Presqu'isle without much trouble, put those places into an excellent posture of defence, and garrisoned them; he has also completed the works of Pittsburgh and Fort Ligonier, together with our other posts on the frontiers of Pennsylvania; and closed his expedition by taking the submission of various tribes of Indians, with whom he has renewed treaties of alliance; Detroit, however, still remains to the enemy, whose garrison are so infeebled and, in other respects, miserably circumstanced, being destitute of every kind of succour or relief from Canada, that it is no longer in their power to give us the least disturbance. Thus has the commander-in-chief the extreme satisfaction to behold the glorious effects of his incomparable measures.

It is certainly a most agreeable contrast to draw a comparison between the situation of our affairs in this boundless territory, at the conclusion of this memorable campaign, with the state in which they stood at the commencement of the year 1757. Upon the return of the army to Crown Point, we found the new fortress in such forwardness as to be almost finished; whereupon the general gave immediate orders for constructing three additional forts, without loss of time, for the grenadiers and two corps of light infantry, the better to strengthen this important post and protect the country to the southward of it, now farther secured by the completion of the works at Ticonderoga.

The abilities displayed by his excellency, in the whole progress of this year's very difficult and severe service, must be universally admitted to exceed all imagination; the obstacles he had to encounter, in a country so different from all others, are not to be enumerated; the precautions taken to secure the army, as we advanced, with our chain of detached posts, from insult or surprise; the expedition used in constructing several vessels to render us superior to the naval force of the enemy on the lakes; the judicious manner in which the troops were embarked, and our order of rowing or sailing was directed; the provident regulations that were made, whereby the army never wanted provisions or refreshments; the unwearied pains taken to train up the raw provincial troops, with the exact discipline supported throughout, and the constant attention paid to preserve the health of the men; the admirable diligence, spirit and patience exerted in dragging artillery, rafts, boats and other craft over the carrying-places; and, finally, the general's pursuing our advantages no farther than is consistent with the utmost good policy—these, together with the steadiness and precaution displayed in conducting the different operations of the campaign, and the effectual manner in which he now employs the remainder of it in securing our conquests, are all such eminent excellencies in the art of war as must excite the astonishment and admiration of all mankind.

# XI

# Winter in Quebec

*The victorious British army at Quebec had a hard winter's trial aheaa of them. The Navy had to scurry down the St Lawrence before the ice formed. The town had been shattered by the British bombardment and accommodation for the troops was makeshift. Supplies were adequate, but the lack of fresh food caused an outbreak of scurvy and half the garrison went through the hospitals. They were marooned in a hostile land. No other British forces were within hundreds of miles of them and the wreckage of the French forces which had lost Quebec were thrashed into shape by Lévis at Montreal with the intention of recapturing the capital of French Canada in the Spring. Brigadier Murray, who had been left in command of the British forces, organised them as best he could and constructed such defences as the ferocious winter allowed.*

I MUST NOW RETURN to our famous garrison of Quebec, of which I shall present the reader with a description at the time of its surrender; and then proceed with the occurrences of a very severe winter campaign.

The City of Quebec consists of two towns, distinguished by the high and low town: they are separated from each other by a steep cliff of rock which is a natural fortification to near two thirds of the upper town, at the same time that it serves as a shelter to the low town from the keen, penetrating, north-west winds; the buildings were, in general, very good, until destroyed by our artillery during the siege, and consisted, besides dwelling-houses, of a number of churches, colleges, convents and other public edifices which, in the city as well as the country throughout, are built of a durable kind of greyish stone, whereof they have great plenty in this province.

There is a large parcel of vacant ground within the walls of the upper town, which, however, does not furnish them with many gardens, the land being so barren and rocky as not to bear cultivation; and the few that they have within the city, being naturally of a shallow soil, are indebted to borrowed mold from other places. The streets of the high town are broad but uneven, running upon a declivity from the south, where they are highest, to the north. Those of the low town are narrow, standing on a confined spot of ground which was formerly overflowed by the tide to the foot of the precipice and, by the retiring of the waters, pointed out a place, at the head of a spacious and most delightful bason, commodious in all respects for merchants to build and inhabit for the convenience of *trade*.

Their principal public buildings were the cathedral, of which only the walls remain: the bishop's palace, the colleges of the Jesuits and Recollects, the convents of the Ursulines and Hôtel de Dieu, with their churches, a seminary for the education of youth, almost beat to pieces, with a neat chapel adjoining; a stately, but unfinished, house

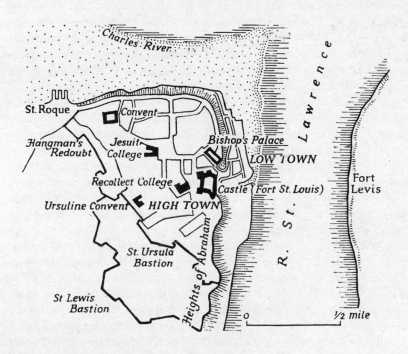

for the Knights-Hospitallers, the intendant's magnificent palace in the suburbs of St Rocque, and the church of Madame la Victoire in the low town, of which the walls only are standing. I am credibly informed they had a fine painting in that church, representing a town in flames, with an inscription setting forth that, in the year 1711, when this capital was threatened with a siege by Walker and Hill, one of their pious women, pretending to be inspired, prognosticated, 'that this church and lower town would be destroyed by the British, perhaps heretics, in a conflagration, before the year of our Lord 1760'. Which made so great an impression on all ranks of people that they dedicated two days, every year, to fasting and worship, and implored the intercession of their patroness with the Almighty to protect that church and city from fire and sword, etc. In the corner-houses of the streets are niches in the walls, with statues as large as the life of St Joseph, St Ursula, St Augustine, St Dennis and many others; with the like figures in the fronts of their churches and other religious houses, which have an agreeable effect to the eyes of passengers.

The castle, or citadel, and residence of the late governor-general, fronting the Recollects' college and church, and situated on the grand parade, which is a spacious place surrounded with fair buildings, is curiously erected on the top of a precipice south of the episcopal house, and overlooks the low town and bason: whence you have a most extensive and delightful prospect of the river downwards, and the country on both sides, for a very considerable distance. This palace, called Fort St Louis, was the rendezvous of the grand council of the colony. There is, besides, another citadel on the summit of the eminence of Cape Diamond, with a few guns mounted in it; but, excepting its commanding view of the circumjacent country for a great extent, and of the upper as well as lower river for many leagues, it is otherwise mean and contemptible.

Most of the other public buildings carry a striking appearance, particularly the Jesuit's college, Ursuline and Hôtel de Dieu convents with their churches; the bishop's palace and chapel of ease adjoining and, above all, the superb palace of the late French intendant, with its out-offices and spacious area, would be ornaments to any city in Europe: but the residence of the bishop, by its situation on the top of the precipice between the high and low town, suffered very considerably from our batteries, as did that of the governor-general before-mentioned, which are both built of brick, they being conspicuously exposed to our view from the south side of the river. The custom-house is also in the low town, where the collector is splendidly lodged; and this is almost the only house in that quarter, which by its particular situation, escaped the flames and ravages made by our merciless messengers of destruction in the siege.

The general hospital stands near a mile from the town on the WNW side of it, and is a very stately building: it is situated on the south side of the river Charles, which meanders agreeably under its walls, and consists of a spacious dome, looking to the east, with two great wings, one fronting the north and the other the south; in this house is a convent of nuns of the Augustine order, who have lands particularly appropriated for their maintenance; and the sisters, from religious motives, have assigned the principal parts of this habitation

for the reception of sick and wounded officers and soldiers, to whom
they are excedingly humane and tender; the French king has hitherto
endowed this hospital with a bounteous salary for the support of a
physician, surgeons, directors, clerks, stewards, inspector, etc for
whom there is a very decent table, as likewise for such officers of the
troops as happened to labour under any infirmity. These women are
subject to the direction of a mother-abbess, who is sister to M. de
Ramsay, the late governor; and, according to their monastic custom,
assumes the name of 'Sainte Claude'.

Every soldier pays a weekly stipend while he is here, besides his
allowance of salt provisions; and then he is not at any farther expence. They eat and drink well of such things only as are fit for
them, in the soup and spoon-meat way; whatever beverage the
surgeons think proper to direct is provided for them, and no men
can lie more clean or comfortable than they do. Our soldiers were
taken equally as good care of; for the nuns make it a point of conscience, and perform every menial office about the sick as uncon-
cerned and with the same indifference that one man would attend
another; when our poor fellows were ill and ordered to be removed
from their own odious regimental hospitals to this general receptacle,
they were indeed rendered inexpressibly happy; each patient has his
bed with curtains allotted to him, and a nurse to attend him; sometimes she will take two, three or more under her care, according to
the number of sick or wounded in the house. The beds are ranged in
galleries on each side, with a sufficient space between each for a
person to pass through; these galleries are scraped and swept every
morning, and afterwards sprinkled with vinegar, so that a stranger
is not sensible of any unsavoury scent whatsoever; in summer, the
windows are generally open, and the patients are allowed a kind of
fan, either to cool them in close sultry weather, or to keep off the
flies which, at that season, by reason of the vicinity of some marshes,
together with the river Charles, are numerous and troublesome.

Every officer has an apartment to himself, and is attended by one
of those religious sisters who, in general, are young, handsome and
fair; courteous, rigidly reserved and very respectful; their dress consists of a black, sometimes a white, gown, with a bib and apron, a
close cap on their head, with a forehead-cloth down to their brows;
their breasts and neck intirely covered; the sleeves are made long, so
that not above half the arm from the elbow is in sight: their cloaths
sweep the ground; on the top of the head is pinned a square piece of
black shalloon which serves as a cloak, flowing carelessly over their
shoulders, a little below their waist. Every woman wears a silver

crucifix, about three inches in length, which hangs by a black rib-band from the neck to the girdle or apron-string; and, in this dress, they make a very decent, grave and modest appearance: they are not under the same restraint as in other Popish countries; their office of nursing the sick furnishes them with opportunities of taking great latitudes, if they are so disposed; but I never heard any of them charged with the least levity.

On this occasion, I shall recite a circumstance thought to be a little extraordinary: Lieutenant-Colonel John Young, of the Royal Americans, having, when made a prisoner in August 1757 at Fort William-Henry, been shamefully stripped and plundered among the rest of his fellow-sufferers, lost, with several other things, a pair of silver-mounted, screw-barrelled pistols: Monsieur Bellecombe, a very agreeable French officer, was particularly polite to the colonel in his captivity; this gentleman is now, in his turn, a prisoner to us, and thereby had an opportunity of renewing his acquaintance with Mr Young. Yesterday he took a merchant of his own nation, and his intimate friend, to wait upon the colonel and to request a favour, which the other chearfully promised to grant if in his power: there-upon the officer produced a pair of pistols, now the property of the merchant; and intreated he would take them into his possession in trust for this citizen until the fate of Quebec should be determined by a peace, lest, upon a general search being made for arms, the pistols should be taken from him, especially being of English workmanship.

The colonel, no doubt, agreeably surprised to meet with his old companions, of whom he had been master above twenty years, interrogated the Frenchman how and where he obtained them, and how long he had been possessed of them? To these questions he at first received evasive replies, till acquainting Monsieur Bellecombe and his friend that they were formerly his property, taken from him by the Indians, as before mentioned; producing, at the same time, a seal, some spoons and other articles in plate, all equally alike en-graved with the colonel's own crest; and comparing them with the pistols, put it beyond a doubt. At length the merchant politely restored them, upon Colonel Young's paying him five *louis d'or*, the sum for which he affirmed he bought them from an Indian Sachem, some time after the demolition of Fort William-Henry.

On 5 October I removed to the tenement assigned me for my quarters, which is a cart-house and a stable, called by the inhabitants *Un Hangar*; within it is a spacious, but unfinished, apartment, with a closet; it has no ceiling, save a parcel of boards laid loose; and it thereby forms a loft, or place for hay; a rack and manger stood at the other end for horses, from which however I was separated by a stone partition. I have troubled the reader with this trifling circumstance, to give him some idea of our winter cantonment; several officers, it is true, were better lodged, particularly those of superior rank; yet I was far from being singular: there were a great many who, though they had a more decent entrance to their houses, were much more indifferently lodged; for, with the assistance of a good stove and some carpentry-work, my habitation was rendered tolerably comfortable.

On 11 October I was sent on a week's command to the convent of the Augustines, or general hospital; my orders were 'to prevent soldiers and others from plundering or marauding in that neighbourhood; to protect the house, with all its inhabitants, gardens and inclosures from insult; to examine all persons that arrive from the country; to give immediate notice to the garrison if any number of men should appear in arms, either by detaching a serjeant or firing three distinct muskets; and, if not instantly answered, must be repeated; not to suffer any luggage, horse or cart loaded, to depart the hospital without a positive order or passport; to seize all firearms, ammunition, or whatever may be useful to the enemy, which may happen to be in the environs of the guard; and, finally, to grant permits to surgeons, mates or domestics belonging to the convent, etc when they are necessitated to pass towards the town on their lawful occasions.'

I lived here, at the French king's table, with an agreeable polite society of officers, directors and commissaries; some of the gentlemen were married, and their ladies honoured us with their company; they were generally chearful, except when we discoursed upon the late revolution and the affairs of the campaign; then they seemingly gave way to grief uttered by profound sighs, and followed by an *O mon Dieu*. The officers soon perceived that, though I did not express myself with great facility in their language, I perfectly understood them, and therefore they agreed to converse in Latin; which, though far from being consistent with their boasted *politesse*, did not affect me so as to be offended; for I was more upon an equality with them in that tongue, especially as they spoke it with less fluency, than their own. They generally concluded with some rapturous sentences, delivered theatrically, such as

*Per varios casus per tot discrimina rerum*
*Tendimus in Latium, sedes ubi fata quietas ostendunt.*

[Through various misfortunes, through so many crises we make for Latium, where the Fates promise a restful home.]
and

*Nos patria fines et dulcia linquimus arva*
*Nos patriam fugimus.*
[We are leaving our country's borders and its beloved fields, we are fleeing from our native land.]

—at length, after racking my memory for a distich, or line applicable to the times, I interrupted them with this citation from Virgil, *O Meliboee, Deus nobis hæc otia fecit!* [O Meliboeus, God has granted us these pleasures!] which so surprised them that, having stared at each other for some moments, one of them approached me and asked if I could speak Latin? I then, with seeming diffidence, answered in the affirmative, affecting their accent with tolerable exactness; this discovery put a period to all farther conversations in that language; for they neither attempted to spout or utter a word of Latin while I continued among them.

We dined every day between eleven and twelve, and afterwards were respectively served with a cup of *laced* coffee; our dinners were generally indifferent, but our suppers (what they call their *grand repas*, or best meal) were plentiful and elegant. I was at a loss, the first day, as every person was obliged to use his own knife and wine, there being only a spoon and a four-pronged fork laid with each napkin and plate; however, in the evening, my servant attended me with some excellent port, a goblet, knife and fork; the latter, being different from theirs, particularly the knife's being round and not sharp-pointed, together with the superior strength of my wine (which they by no means disliked) to their poor sour stuff, afforded us a copious subject for agreeable conversion, with variety of opinions and remarks upon the different customs of countries. Each person here produces an ordinary clasped knife from his pocket, which serves him for every use; and, when they have dined or supped, they wipe and return it: the one I had, before I was provided with my own, was lent me by the Frenchman who stood at my chair, and it gave my meat a strong flavour of tobacco, which, though it might have supplied the want of garlick to the owner or his countrymen, was so exceedingly disgustful to me that I was obliged to change my plate, and it was with difficulty I could eat any more: the hour for supper was between six and seven in the evening.

As we dined so early, I gave myself no trouble about breakfast; but, after being there two or three days, one of the nuns delivered me a polite billet from Madame St Claude, the mother-abbess, requesting my company to partake of an English breakfast, as she called it; to which the bearer added, 'If you are ready, Sir, I will do myself the honour to shew you the way'. I instantly followed my conductress to a spacious apartment, where I found the lady with several of the sisters employed at needle-work. A table was placed in the middle of the room, on which stood two large silver coffee-pots, one quart and one pint mug, a plentiful loaf of bread, a plate of butter and a knife; on another plate lay five or six slices of bread, not less than an inch thick each and half the circumference of the loaf, covered with a profusion of butter. Upon my entering, I paid my compliments to the oldest of the ladies (in which I happened to be right, she being the governante) and then to the others; two chairs were immediately set to the table and, Madame St Claude desiring I would take may place, we both sat down.

She then pointed to the coffee-pots, telling me one contained tea, the other milk; but, perceiving it was not to my taste, for the tea was black as ink, she assured me there was half a pint of it in the pot, and it had been well boiled with the water; I told her it was rather too good for me, and that I should make a good repast of bread and milk. Hereupon, I was not a little incommoded with apologies; and I remember she observed, 'that they are not accustomed to such diet, for that they never drink tea except, in cases of indisposition, to work off an emetic, when it is always boiled in water, to render it as strong as possible'. Madame, with some concern, politely proposed to order in a pot of coffee, which I did not consent to; and she assured me it should have been prepared at first, but she had heard the English always preferred tea for breakfast. However, I fared exceedingly well upon the other provision that was made for me, and passed near two hours most agreeably, in the society of this ancient lady and her virginal sisters.

ORDERS                                                  23 October
'The honourable Brigadier-General Murray, being to remain in command of the corps, is appointed to act as governor, and Colonel Burton as lieutenant-governor, of the town of Quebec and its dependencies. The five following regiments to be ready on their alarm-posts to be reviewed to-morrow at eleven o'clock if weather permits, viz. the forty-seventh, forty-eighth, fifty-eighth, third battalion of Royal Americans, and seventy-eighth. The adjutants are desired to apply to the assistant quarter-master-general for a proportion of thread, which was found in the French stores, to be

P                                                                 225 distributed to the respective companies of the several corps, in order to repair and keep their cloaths whole.'

On the 26th General Monckton went down the river and embarked to proceed to New-York for the re-establishment of his health; he was saluted by the garrison. Major Irving, of the fifteenth regiment, is appointed to act as quarter-master-general in the room of Colonel Carleton: and the honourable Captain Maitland, of the forty-third regiment, to act as adjutant-general in the room of Major Barré, both having retired to the southward for the recovery of their wounds.

A barrier is erected on the outside of the strong angle near the hangman's redoubt, which covers the lower road leading from Palace-gate through the suburb of St Rocque to the general hospital, the river Charles and the adjacent country; a house, conveniently situated without this barrier, is fortified to contain a detachment; as is also a smaller habitation on the inside for a serjeant's guard; the former is on the north side of the road, and the other on the south. From these posts, intirely round that quarter, we have extended a line of picquets with loop-holes for musketry, which are strengthened, at the extremities of the point, by block-houses; a chain of these timber fortresses are to be constructed on the heights, round the outside of the ramparts, at six or seven hundred yards distance, across the isthmus: these will effectually prevent any attempts of the enemy by surprise; yet, after all the additions we can make in this way, it will still be an indifferent fortification, and tenable only against light field artillery and musketry.

The effective strength of the army in this garrison will appear from the return opposite:

We are likely to be much distressed for fire-wood this winter, being at present obliged to shift with what can be procured from old fences and demolished houses; but, the soldiers having abused this indulgence, we are forbidden to collect any more from the ruined habitations; so that it is not improbable but we shall be driven to the necessity of providing ourselves here, in the same manner as when we wintered in Nova Scotia.

Doctor Russell having represented to the governor that our men are kept exceedingly warm in the conventual hospitals by stoves, his excellency has therefore desired the commanding officers of corps to keep the soldiers a fortnight from duty, after being discharged from those places, lest their being early exposed to the cold should occasion relapses; these men are not to be reported fit for duty in the weekly returns, that they may not be included in the detail of the

29 October, 1769.

| Regiments | Colonels | Majors | Captains | Lieutenants | Ensigns | Chaplains | Adjutants | Surgeons | Mates | Quarter Masters | Serjeants | Drummers | Fifers | Rank and File |
|---|---|---|---|---|---|---|---|---|---|---|---|---|---|---|
| 15th | 1 | 1 | 3 | 16 | 8 | 1 | 1 | 1 | 1 | 1 | 33 | 14 | 2 | 455 |
| 28th | 1 | 1 | 4 | 9 | 8 | 0 | 1 | 1 | 1 | 1 | 25 | 18 | ▪ | 536 |
| 35th | 0 | 1 | 7 | 15 | 8 | 0 | 1 | 1 | 1 | 1 | 39 | 16 | 2 | 728 |
| 43rd | 1 | 1 | 7 | 10 | 7 | 1 | 1 | 1 | 1 | 1 | 29 | 18 | 2 | 585 |
| 47th | 0 | 1 | 2 | 15 | 8 | 1 | 1 | 1 | 1 | 1 | 38 | 17 | 2 | 538 |
| 48th | 1 | 0 | 5 | 10 | 7 | 1 | 1 | 1 | 2 | 0 | 28 | 16 | 2 | 802 |
| 58th | 0 | 1 | 3 | 9 | 8 | 0 | 0 | 1 | 1 | 1 | 26 | 16 | 2 | 508 |
| 2nd Battal. R. Amer. | 0 | 0 | 4 | 12 | 6 | 0 | 1 | 1 | 1 | 1 | 31 | 14 | 2 | 465 |
| 3rd Ditto | 1 | 0 | 6 | 16 | 7 | 0 | 1 | 1 | 2 | 1 | 34 | 16 | 2 | 540 |
| 78th | 1 | 0 | 7 | 24 | 12 | 1 | 1 | 1 | 2 | 1 | 50 | 25 | 4 | 978 |
| Rangers | 0 | 0 | 1 | 2 | 0 | 0 | 0 | 0 | 0 | 0 | 4 | ? | 0 | 100 |
| Royal Artillery | 0 | 1 | 2 | 9 | 0 | 0 | 1 | 1 | 0 | 1 | 6 | 6 | 0 | 195 |
| Total | 6 | 7 | 51 | 147 | 79 | 5 | 10 | 11 | 14 | 10 | 343 | 178 | 22 | 6430 |

Total of all Ranks 7313

garrison. Lamps are to be forthwith made and fixed up at the corners of streets, and at other convenient places: which is an excellent procedure to prevent confusion in case of alarms; for this purpose the quarter-masters of corps are ordered to pick out all the tinmen they can find in the different regiments. The regiments are desired to send in a return, of the number of chimnies they will be obliged to occupy in their respective quarters. Six hatchet-men per regiment are ordered to parade, three with axes and the like number with handsaws, all in good order; these men are to be employed in ripping up a French ship of war on the stocks, and are to be under the direction of Captain Wettestroom, of the Royal Americans, who is appointed for that service, and be excused all other duties.

By this state of our duty, the reader may form some idea *of the manner in which we earn our daily bread in this inhospitable winter climate,* where we have indifferent quarters and vile bedding for our poor soldiers, who are ill cloathed, without regular pay or any kind of fresh provisions; in all those difficulties, the officers bear a proportionable share; but such hardships cannot, with justice, be imputed to any other cause than our critical situation in the heart of an enemy's country, remote and excluded from the sea, and consequently from every kind of commerce with the rest of the world, at this severe season of the year.

The commanding officers of corps are now permitted to cut up the blankets that were found in the French magazines, and delivered to them, to be applied to such uses as they shall think proper; these are a great acquisition to the soldiers, as they serve them for socks and gloves, etc. Neither officer nor soldier, except the sick and those who are to conduct them, are permitted to go to the general hospital without a passport from the governor. The officers have hitherto received rum from the stores, in proportion to their rank; as have likewise the women who were on the victualling roll, but, by an order of early November, they are all struck off; the women are, for the future, to be victualled at two thirds' allowance only; for this purpose they are to be mustered to-morrow by the town-major: such as from sickness cannot appear are to be certified for by their commanding officers. Provisions are issued to the women upon a presumption that they are useful to the soldiers, either by attending hospitals or by washing for them and the officers; but henceforth those who suttle are not to be enrolled, nor will any be issued to those who do not reside in the men's quarters. Various articles are issuing out of the French stores to our soldiers gratis; viz. uniform coats and waistcoats, coarse hats with copper laces, powder-horns, moggosans, some remnants of flannel, coarse and damaged linens.

The French ships, which have been for some time expected, are at length fallen down, and are at anchor off Sillery: one of them ran a-ground at a point a little higher up, whereupon an officer, with a small sculking party, were sent out secretly to listen to their conversation, watch their motions, and to annoy any of their people that may attempt to land; two twelve-pounders were intended to have been sent out to attack this frigate, but that project seems to be postponed for the present: their boats ply frequently from ship to ship and, by the continual noise and chattering on board, our party are of opinion they are much crowded, though we are informed that many principal families are gone down the country, with their effects, in order to embark for France after the ships shall have passed the town.

Two pieces of cannon, twelve-pounders, with a detachment, were in readiness to march to the late battery at Sillery, opposite to the river Etchemin, in hopes of frustrating their intended voyage, or at least of making prize of the frigate that was a-ground; but the enemy found means to lighten her before our scheme could be executed, whereby she got off with the flood, and joined the rest of her fleet above. Our weather is again changed to frost and snow, and seems to be setting in for the winter; yet the atmosphere is perfectly serene, with sun-shine, and very agreeable.

On the night of 24 November, between the hours of eleven and twelve, the French ships passed the town with the tide of ebb, except one which, by the weight of our fire, we drove a-shore on the south side of the river; there are various reports of their numbers; but it is certain they were not more than eight, or fewer than five, they had a fine breeze of wind in their favour, which, luckily for them, freshened as they got abreast of Cape Diamond; our batteries were prepared for them, and gave them an hundred shot, besides a vast number of shells: the night being extremely dark, likewise, propitiated their escape, our gunners having fired almost at random.

A most unlucky disaster happened on the morning of the 25th; when the enemy abandoned their ship that lies stranded on the south-shore, they left a train of powder from the powder-room to the fire-place of the great cabin, with a slow match, and then betook them-selves, in their boats, to a schooner we had at anchor in the channel to watch their motions, of which they possessed themselves; Captain Miller, of his majesty's sloop the *Racehorse*, with his lieutenant and a number of men (it is said above forty) went and boarded her; the match being extinguished, Mr Miller, not suspecting the horrid snare, gave orders to strike a light to inable them to rummage the ship: when, unfortunately, some of the sparks, falling on the loose powder, caught immediately and blew up the vessel, so that most of the party were killed almost instantaneously, and the few survivors are in as deplorable a condition as can be imagined.

A Canadian peasant, venturing to go aboard soon after the ex-plosion, in search of plunder as he confessed, to his great astonish-ment (for he knew not of any living creatures being in the ship) discovered the captain, lieutenant and two seamen lying in the greatest agony, and dreadfully scorched; finding they were still alive, he went and alarmed the neighbourhood, and, having pro-cured assistance, he brought the unhappy sufferers, with six or seven others whom they afterwards found, to his own house, where he had them rubbed with bear's grease, and otherwise manifested to them every act of humanity in his power: in the afternoon this man crossed the river to make his melancholy report to the governor (for as yet we were intirely ignorant of the matter); and his excellency was pleased to reward the Canadian for his attachment and Christian-like behaviour with twenty dollars and a quantity of salt provisions. Proper conveyances were immediately sent over for these distressed officers and their men, who were removed, without loss of time, into the hospital of the Ursuline convent, where they will have the best attendance and relief that can be desired.

Our brave soldiers are growing sickly; their disorders are chiefly scorbutic, with fevers and dysenteries; this is far from being surprising, when we consider the severe fatigues and hardships they have hitherto, and still unavoidably undergo, which, with indifferent cloathing, uncomfortable barracks, worse bedding, and their being intirely confined to a salt provision diet, are sufficient to reduce or emaciate the most robust constitutions in this extremely frigid climate. Fire-wood is now, and hereafter, to be issued regularly to the troops, pursuant to the orders for that purpose: hitherto we have been obliged to shift for it by tearing down decayed fences and damaged houses; these, with some habitations that were situated in the suburbs of St Louis and St John, which it was thought advisable to demolish on account of their proximity to the works of the place, have hitherto supplied us, though very sparingly, with that necessary article.

ORDERS                                        3 December
'. . . As the sentries on their posts, and the soldiers otherwise employed on the duty of the garrison, may, from the severity of the weather at this season of the year, be exposed to be frost-bitten, Doctor Russell recommends that every person to whom this accident may happen should be particularly careful to avoid going near a fire, and to have the part frost-bitten rubbed with snow by one who has a warm hand, and, as soon as can be, afterwards put into a blanket, or something of that kind, that will restore heat to the part. *This order to be read at the head of every company for six days following by an officer.*'

Though there is little wind, and the firmament is perfectly serene, with sun-shine, yet the bitterness of the season is not to be conceived; several of the men, who were clearing the snow that was lodged under the scarp of the town-wall, were frost-bitten, and some even swooned away with the excessive cold. Our artificers are now completing a chain of block-houses, which are to be erected upon the heights of Abraham, extending from Cape Diamond down to the suburbs of St John. Captain Leslie's detachment is detained at Point Levy church to watch the motions of some sculking parties of the enemy in that neighbourhood. Three soldiers of the command at St Foy were surprised and made prisoners by a body of French regulars, who came down to reconnoitre that post.

The governor being under a necessity of borrowing money for the use of the government, some of the troops have assisted his excellency in this loan. The privates, as well as the officers, of Colonel Fraser's regiment of Highlanders, by their remarkable frugality and sobriety, have been inabled to distinguish themselves: the creditors are to receive legal interest until they are repaid. Our garrison now undergo incredible fatigues, not only within but also without the walls, being obliged to load and sleigh home fire-wood from the forest of St Foy, which is near four miles distant, and through snow of a surprising depth; eight men are allowed to each sleigh, who are yoked to it in couples by a set of regular harness, besides one man who guides it behind with a long stout pole to keep it clear of ruts and other obstructions.

The sickness among the troops does not at present increase—this we impute to their more temperate manner of living—yet it is surprising to see them bear up so well under their inconceivable fatigues, which they undergo with wonderful alacrity, from a just sense of the necessity there is for them: it is, now-a-days, a consolation to a soldier when he is ordered for guard, notwithstanding what he even suffers upon that duty, between standing sentry, going frequent patroles, receiving different rounds, and several other contingent services in this rigorous season, well known to the experienced officer; hence we may form an idea of the hardships they are, at other times, incessantly exposed to, and that this must continue all the winter they are well convinced of; but their daily allowance of rum contributes not a little to exhilarate them under their present harrassing circumstances. A parcel of creepers are now issuing out of the stores for the use of the soldiers, for which they pay five pence per pair.

A body of two hundred Indians are sculking about the country, between the garrison and our most advanced post at Lorette; which is the cause of the governor's precautions respecting the woodsleighers, who have a party of light infantry to cover them; and, in case of our being attacked, the eldest field-officer of the day is to sally out, at the head of the main-guard, to reinforce, and command the whole.

Lamps are now set up throughout the high and low town for the convenience of the troops. Two of the inhabitants have been whipped through the streets for appearing abroad at an unseasonable time of night without a lanthorn, contrary to repeated orders. The British and French merchants and shop-keepers have waited on Colonel Young, as justice of the police, pursuant to directions for that purpose, in order to fix a price on all sorts of commodities, liquors and provisions; notice whereof is given to the citizens and country-people. This, it is hoped, will prevent monopolies and other gross impositions upon the troops and inhabitants. At present we are tolerably well supplied with fresh provisions (I mean the officers); which, however, except the articles of beavers, hares, partridges and other game, are very indifferent in their kinds. The weather is now become inconceivably severe, and our soldiers grow numerous in the hospitals; some, who died within these few days, are laid in the snow until the spring, the ground being, at this time, impenetrably bound up with frost. Our several duties, and all other affairs, have been so admirably well adjusted that every thing is now conducted and executed with great order and regularity, and as much ease to the troops as the nature of the service in this inclement season will permit.

Our guards, on the grand parade, make a most grotesque appearance in their different dresses; and our inventions to guard us against the extreme rigour of this climate are various beyond imagination: the uniformity, as well as nicety, of the clean, methodical soldier, is buried in the rough fur-wrought garb of the frozen Laplander; and we rather resemble a masquerade than a body of regular troops; insomuch that I have frequently been accosted by my acquaintances who, though familiar their voices were to me, I could not discover or conceive who they were; besides, every man seems to be in a continual hurry; for, instead of walking soberly through the streets, we are obliged to observe a running or trotting pace. Yet, notwithstanding all our precautions, several men and officers have suffered by the intenseness of the cold, being frost-bitten in their faces, hands, feet and other parts least to be suspected.

Beacons are now erected along the road from the garrison to the forest of St Foy, which were extremely necessary as the whole country is covered to the depth of several feet with snow; the soldiers and Canadians are ordered not to remove those marks, on pain of severe punishment. The guard-houses are all provided with stoves, which are a most incomparable invention, particularly well calculated for this northern climate, and far exceeding those used in the

Netherlands: the chimnies in those places are ordered to be shut up, whereby the heat, being close confined in the apartment, renders it much more comfortable to its inhabitants.

The manner by which the people supply themselves with fish, at this season, is deserving of notice. A hole or well is made in the ice, about eight or ten inches diameter; there the fish gather in great numbers, for air as some conceive; and others are of opinion it is for light. The person then amuses them by throwing down crumbs of bread, entrails of fowl, etc and, while the fish are greedily employed in feeding, he slips down a black hair gin tied to a short stick; and, guiding it round one at a time, he draws it out of its element with a sudden jirk, and thus repeats it as long as his frigid situation will permit him to continue on the ice; before his departure, he lays a broad stone over the well to render the air or light less familiar to the inhabitants of these aqueous regions, of which there are an inconceivable variety, of different sizes, from that of a sprat to a herring, of divers colours, and most delicious to eat, fried or stewed.

Our soldiers make great progress in walking on snow-shoes, but men not accustomed to them find them very fatiguing. These inventions are made of hoops of hickery, or other tough wood, bended to a particular form, round before; and the two extremities of the hoop terminate in a point behind, secured well together with strong twine; the inward space is worked, like close netting, with cat-gut or the dried entrails of other animals. Each racket is from three quarters to one yard in length. At the broadest part, which is about the center, where it is fastened by thongs and straps to the person's foot, it is about fourteen, fifteen or sixteen inches; a light lively man does not require them so large as he who is more corpulent and less active; the hard-soled shoe is not at all suitable to them; they must be used under moggosans, as well for the sake of the wearer's feet, to keep them warm and preserve them from the snow, as that they will not bind on so well, nor be so soon worn out. The uncouth attitude in which men are obliged to walk is what renders them laborious; the body must incline forward, the knees bend, ancles and instep remain stiff as if the joints in those parts were completely ossified, and the feet at a great distance asunder; by this description, which is the best I can give, the reader may form to himself a lively idea of the snow-shoes, or snow-rackets, and the use of them; the boys in Canada have them suited to their own size, and walk on them for exercise and as one of their winter sports; the heaviest man whatever, with a pair of them, may walk on snow that would take him to his neck, and shall not sink above an inch and an half or two inches: light men, who are accustomed to them, leave barely their impression behind them.

This invention, which I have delineated, seems to be a great improvement upon the kind used by the Russians and Calmuc Tartars in Siberia; one of their travellers thus describes them: 'They are made of a very thin piece of light wood, about five feet long and five or six inches broad, inclining to a point before and square behind; in the middle is fixed a thong, through which the feet are put: on these shoes a person may walk over the deepest snow; for a man's weight will not sink him above an inch; these, however, can only be used on plains. They have a different sort for ascending hills, with the skins of seals glued to their boards, having the hair inclined backwards, which prevents the sliding of the shoes so that they can ascend a hill very easily; and, in descending, they slide downwards at a great rate.'

In America they have only one kind of snow-shoe, both for hill and dale, and, by their central part being worked, as I have observed before, racket-fashion, they cannot slip backward or forward, in going up or down a precipice; besides, a board seems to be a rude discovery; for, when the snow clots to the under parts, it must render them heavy and troublesome; and I am inclined to think the tightness that seems requisite in fastening on a boarded shoe of such an unwieldy length, must incommode the foot considerably; whereas the rackets are secured with such freedom and ease to the feet that the muscles and sinews are not confined, neither is the circulation of the blood interrupted; a circumstance deserving of the highest attention in all frozen climates.

We have variety of weather in January; some days it is mild and pleasant, at others cold and windy, with drifts of snow, and frequent showers of hail, liquid and freezing rain: we have had forty-eight hours so inconceivably severe that, notwithstanding our distress for fuel, the sleighing parties could not stir out; the town, just now, is one intire sheet of ice, insomuch that, being to mount guard in the lower town, I found it impossible to get down the precipice with safety, and we were therefore obliged to sit down on the summit and slide to the bottom, one after the other to prevent accidents, the mens' arms being loaded.

A magazine of wood is now forming on the heights of Abraham, and is supplied by horse-sleighs: in a few days the garrison will be inabled to draw from thence, which being so near, and the soldiers being excused taking their arms, they will be able to make two turns per day, a circumstance that affords general satisfaction. The men grow more unhealthy as the winter advances, and scarce a day passes without two or three funerals; though several do recover, yet the hospitals still continue full: it is, indeed, melancholy to see such havock among our brave fellows, and their daily sufferings distress the officers beyond expression. The detachment of six hundred, with the officers and engineers, are employed in clearing the defences on the outside and within, opening communications and throwing up parapets in the different avenues: these new works are composed of spare dry casks filled with snow well rammed down, and are supposed to be an excellent cover against musketry.

M. de Lévis has postponed his design of retaking Quebec from Christmas to the 20th instant, when he is to come down with a parcel of mortars, first to bombard the town and endeavour to burn the Jesuits' college, knowing we have made it our grand repository of provisions; after which he supposes he shall find little difficulty in storming the place; and, for this purpose, he will only conduct the flower of his army against us, consisting of seven thousand regulars, including select bodies of *grenadiers de France,* and other superfine fellows, chosen from the most experienced and approved Canadians.

It is whimsical enough to see what servitude is exacted even from the dogs in this country; in the winter, one of these animals, seemingly of the Newfoundland breed, naturally strong and nearly in size to a well-grown sheep, is yoked by a regular set of harness to a sleigh suitable to his bulk and strength, on which they draw wood, water, etc and, when employed in this manner, may be said to resemble horses in miniature: I have seen one of these creatures draw a cask of water from fifteen to twenty gallons, of an equal weight of wood, from one extremity of the lower town to the upper, which is a constant ascent; when he is tired, he casts a piteous significant look towards the driver, who understands the signal; and, if it is on the pinch of a hill, the man places his foot, or something else, behind the sleigh to prevent its running backward; which the dog immediately perceiving, and not before, lies down in his harness for a few minutes to rest; at other times, he will whimper under his load when he wants to be refreshed, particularly if his driver is not attentive to him; and then he is sure to be indulged. In passing through the streets yesterday, as our soldiers were drawing, in like manner, their loaded sleighs from the magazine of wood, they met two dogs also under their drudgery; some of the men commiserated the poor animals, and others merrily called them by the epithets of comrade, yoke-mate, brother hack, etc asking them what allowance of pork and rum they got per day, with many other pleasantries, which they concluded by inviting the peasant and his dogs to dine with them, telling the man where their barrack was and the number of their mess.

I was in company when these circumstances were mentioned in the presence of the governor who, though he expressed himself like a tender parent towards his brave soldiers for their immense, yet unavoidable, hardships, could not forbear laughing at their humour, and admiring the alacrity and steadiness displayed by the poor fellows in this rigorous climate, and their very laborious situation; it must indeed be confessed they have an uncommon share of merit, for, instead of grumblings and discontents at their repeated toils, the harassed life they lead, the want of pay, from which they might derive many comforts and refreshments under their present exigensies, they contentedly and chearfully submit to the necessity of the times, exerting *all the man*, and the good soldier, upon every occasion; which excites still greater admiration in us, when we reflect upon the many different dispositions and multifarious humours of such a body of men as generally compose the privates of an army.

A subaltern, serjeant, corporal and fifty privates, provided with thirty rounds of ammunition, three flints and eight days' provisions per man, marched out, on 22 January to reinforce the post at Lorette: a twelve-pounder, with a quantity of artillery-stores and some gunners, were also sent out; upon a double discharge whereof, which is to be the signal for the approach of an enemy, the detachment at St Foy are to throw up rockets until answered by the guard at the citadel on Cape Diamond. This procedure is in consequence of intelligence being brought that a large body of the enemy are come down to Cape Rouge; the sentries round the line, and the patroles, are ordered to keep a good look-out, on this, and every succeeding night, for the rockets.

It may seem extraordinary that the enemy have never attempted to molest the wood-cutters in the forest of St Foy and the men continually employed in drawing it to the garrison; to this I must observe it has been frequently reported, but I cannot take upon me to affirm it as matter of fact, that, if we meet with any annoyance or interruption in this business during the course of the winter, every house in the town not actually occupied by troops and British merchants shall be dilapidated, not sparing convents or other public buildings; their timber cut up for the use of the garrison, and the inhabitants driven into the country. Moreover, that, in consequence of a letter or message to this purpose to M. de Lévis, he has promised that our detachments, cutting and drawing wood for fuel, shall not be molested; and that immediate orders to this effect have been circulated throughout the country, and among the regular Canadian and Indian forces. All that I shall offer upon this subject is that, though confidently and repeatedly this has been spoken of, it was not universally believed; nor did it ever gain credit with me: for, I am persuaded, the judicious precautions that hitherto have been, and still continue to be taken, are the principal causes of our not being interrupted or attacked through the whole progress of this indispensable service.

A deserter, from one of the enemy's advanced posts, informs us that the French troops are so inconceivably distressed, for all kinds of provisions and liquors, that their perseverance is astonishing; he adds that their numbers may amount to about twelve thousand, including savages, etc. who are all so dispersed and at their liberty to shift for themselves that they scarcely deserve the name of an army. When this fellow was brought before the governor, there was a French officer present who is a prisoner on his parole: he seemed disconcerted at the admission of the deserter, and swaggered about the apartment in great wrath; after the governor had examined him, he gave him a dollar and, as soon as he got it into his hand, looking attentively on it, he cried out, '*ça, ça, l'argent blanc!*—This is no French money! Indeed, please your excellency, it is a long, long time since I was master of so many livres; a few of these, properly applied, would induce even the officers, as well as soldiers of the miserable French army, to follow my example.' This speech enraged the officer to such a degree, that he exceeded all bounds of decorum, till at length being told, in a very peremptory tone of voice, 'that if he did not behave himself as he ought to do, he should be confined under the same roof with this deserter, but not in such good company', monsieur thought it advisable to alter his haughty deportment and apologise for his indiscretion. This garrison, it is now pretended, is to be stormed in three different places by three divisions of five thousand men each, who are to be sustained by a corps of six thousand chosen men, including five hundred Indians.

We received accounts on 6 February, that a strong body of the enemy are assembled near the church at Point Levy, and have the modesty to declare they are now resolved to attack Quebec, and are in daily expectation of being reinforced with a more powerful corps, who are upon their march, escorting a formidable detachment of artillery. The night before they made a chain of fires upon the hills opposite to the garrison, by way of amusing us; and, lest it should be their design to make an attempt upon the contrary side of the town, the guards at the fortified house and the other posts in the suburbs of St Rocque received orders to be as alert and vigilant as possible.

On the 13th, a little before day, the light infantry crossed the river and, upon gaining *terra firma*, Major Dalling caused a rocket to be thrown up as a signal for the cannon to follow; a detachment of two hundred men marched at the same time, and inclined downwards, in order to divide the enemy's attention, while the major was to gain the church and eminences of Point Levy: the enemy, alarmed at the rocket, began immediately to fire and yell, according to custom; but perceiving, as the day dawned, that we had got possession and were marching towards the church, they made a disposition as if they intended to maintain their ground, hoping their snow-shoes would give them a great superiority over us.

The field-pieces being by this time arrived, the major drew up one of them in front, which was so briskly served that a few discharges of round and grape shot threw them into confusion and dispersed them: our people then advanced, and, approaching the church and the priest's house on the other side of the road, they received a furious fire which, as usual, only served to animate our men, who instantly surrounded those buildings, and pelted them through the windows until they dispossessed them; (for the light infantry, having their snow-rackets, were inabled, by means of the snow, to command the windows of the church, which were otherwise too high for them); the enemy then betook themselves to the heights, whence they were soon routed and, at length, retired to a post we formerly had there, called the lesser rock-guard: here they hoped to make a stand, as that place, by its singular situation, overlooks all the circumjacent ground where our forces were last year incamped; but, perceiving, by some excellent movements made by our troops, that they were in danger of being surrounded, after first firing a few irregular shots they retired with precipitation, leaving us in possession of the church and its environs; our intrepid soldiers pursued them for several miles with great eagerness, killing and wounding them in their flight: of the latter we think there must be many among them, as great quantities of blood everywhere appeared on the snow in their rear.

In this morning's rencounter a lieutenant and fifteen men were made prisoners, seven were found dead in the church and the priest's house, and five on the road to the westward of them; we also recovered a great stock of provisions they had collected, consisting of beef, mutton, bread, flour and pease. On our side, a serjeant was killed, an officer and twenty men wounded; which was our whole loss. We cannot ascertain the number of the enemy that were engaged, for they had detached several parties down the river to lay the country under contributions; but we compute them at about six hundred: one of the savages was killed at the first discharge made by the six-pounder, which so discouraged the rest of his painted fraternity that they thought it advisable to keep at a greater distance and wait the issue of the day; for they have an invincible dread of artillery. Carpenters were immediately sent over to barricade the windows of the church and the priest's house, and a detachment will relieve the light infantry there to-morrow, being now resolved to keep that post, in like manner as the others at St Foy and Lorette.

A flag of truce came to the church of Lorette on the 28 February at night, with proposals for an exchange of prisoners; a complimentary letter was also sent to the governor, with others on business to merchants of this city inclosed in the same packet for his excellency's inspection. The French army are arrived at Jacques Cartier; it is pretended that Monsieur de Lévis will form his forces into three divisions and make a rapid attack on our detached posts, *tout d'un coup*, which is to be executed by a signal of three rockets; and, after cutting off such a number of healthy and effective men, they flatter themselves, from the weakness of our garrison by sickness and mortality, we shall be reduced to the necessity of surrendering to their superior army. Captain McDonell, of the seventy-eighth regiment, was sent out with an answer to the French general; and, as the enemy expected it, they detached a serjeant's party to a certain distance from their most advanced post to meet our flag, that we might not gain any intelligence of their strength or situation; but McDonell, instead of delivering his dispatches to the serjeant, told him he was a captain, and spiritedly ordered him back to his commander with this message, 'that, if he would not send out an officer of equal rank by a certain time limited, he would return to Quebec without imparting the purport of his errand'; monsieur was too polite to be refractory on this occasion, a captain and drummer being immediately sent out to receive his express. I am credibly informed that the proposal, on the part of the enemy, for an exchange of prisoners, was only *finesse* to procure an opportunity of reconnoitring our post at Lorette.

The duty of this garrison is now so severe, by reason of our immense numbers of sick and weak men, that the general has been pleased to ease the corps of their regimental guards; in this case, all prisoners are to be sent to the guards most contiguous to each regiment's district, together with their crimes specified in writing, signed by an officer; and must be immediately reported to the commander of that battalion to which such delinquents may belong.

Ginger being esteemed a most specific corrective in scorbutic cases, a quantity of that spice is issued out to the troops, for which, as is mentioned in the orders, 'they will pay the government's price'.

The effective strength of our garrison, on the 29th of October last, was seven thousand three hundred and thirteen, all ranks included: at this period I am concerned to observe, comprehending every degree, we are reduced to four thousand eight hundred fighting men; fevers, dysenteries and most obstinate scorbutic disorders have been the cause of this great decrease; and our various hospitals are, at this instant, overcrowded with patients.

On the night of 18 March, two hundred light infantry were detached with three days' provisions, and, at the same time, on the 19th, the remainder of that corps, with a company of grenadiers, marched to Lorette church, being the place of rendezvous; and the whole proceeded the next morning at break of day, guided by a French deserter in a British uniform. In their route they surprised an advanced post of the enemy, and made the party prisoners, consisting of a corporal and nine privates; having secured these, they pushed forward with the greatest speed, fearing lest a straggling peasant, whom they met, should mar their farther views by alarming the country: the light infantry having reached the wished for object, which was a strong camp or intrenchment of logs and timbers, with a house detached at a small distance from it, situated between our people and that post; they first surrounded, attacked and carried the dwelling with their accustomed bravery, killed four, and took the rest, being twenty in number; nine of whom were wounded.

The main body of the enemy had, by this time, manned their works, which were breast-high and environed with an *abbatis de bois* to the distance of about three hundred yards, whence they fired a few random shots, and shouted as usual. Captain McDonell, who commanded this detachment, seeing the enemy advantageously situated, and perceiving the French officers very active in encouraging their men, expected a warmer dispute than we have lately been habituated to, and therefore made a disposition of his men to attack them in form; as soon as our light troops advanced to the charge, and poured in a brisk fire upon them, the enemy threw down their arms and took to flight; but our grenadiers, who were not able to keep pace with the hunters in marching, critically came up at that instant and cut off the retreat of near four-score who were made prisoners; and, what is very remarkable, there is not an officer among them. Monsieur

Herbin commanded this detachment, whose watch, hat and feather, *fille de joie*, with a cask of wine and a small trunk *de liqueurs*, fell into our hands; these two last articles were a most seasonable acquisition to the conquerors, who were so benumbed with the severity of the cold that they could scarcely draw their triggers. In this attack of the intrenchment, five were killed and thirteen wounded on the part of the enemy: on our side six only were wounded in the whole; but unluckily we had near an hundred so disabled by the frost that they were obliged to be brought back to the garrison on sleighs.

ORDERS                                                    10 April
'The visible effects of the spruce, or hemlock-spruce, which has been given for some time to the scorbutic men in the hospitals, put it beyond doubt that it must also be the best preservative against the scurvy; and, as the lives of brave soldiers are ever to be regarded with the utmost attention, it is ordered that the regiments be provided with a sufficient quantity of that particular spruce, which each corps must send for occasionally; and it is to be made into a liquor, according to the method with which the surgeons are already acquainted; and commanding officers must be answerable that their men drink of this liquor, at least twice every day, mixed with their allowance of rum.'

We have the happiness to see our men on the recovery, though they as yet gain ground very slowly. This is attributed to the virtues of the hemlock-spruce, which is a particular species and an excellent antiscorbutic; it has been recommended and drank in the hospitals for some time past, and was discovered by an old Canadian empiric, for which he was suitably rewarded. The tops of this spruce are ordered 'to be well bruised and put into a large tub, with as much boiling water poured on as will cover them; they must remain twenty-four hours before used, in which time they must be frequently stirred up': of this infusion, when strained off, the men in the hospitals were injoined to drink at least three pints per day, and bathe such parts of their limbs as were affected by the scurvy with some of the liquor made warm; the duty-men, and those who get rum, are obliged to drink it in such manner as is mentioned in the foregoing orders. This spruce is very different from that of which our common beverage is made, called by us spruce-beer; the leaves of it are exceeding small, dark-coloured and crisp to the touch, not much unlike the juniper-tree; and it is more dwarfish than any other species of spruce: I tasted some of the infusion, which had a compound flavour (I could not tell what to compare it to) and was a very strong bitter; it is esteemed one of the greatest purifiers of the blood, and I am much prepossessed in favour of it for gouty constitutions.

M. de Lévis, at the head of an army of twelve thousand men, with a fleet of seven frigates and sloops under M. Vauquelin, Chef d'Escadre, are actually preparing, with all expedition, to execute the impending stroke with which this garrison has been menaced these six months past and upwards; we are told they have preserved sixty days' full allowance of provisions for the regulars of this army in support of their important enterprise. At the same time it is pretended that the Canadians have refused to serve until they see what assistance France will send them, or which of the two fleets will first enter the river St Lawrence; this, however, does not gain credit. If it should appear requisite, some of the most insignificant houses in the lower town and suburb of St Rocque are to be demolished after the departure of the citizens, and the timber applied to the use of the troops for fuel. Two large field-pieces, with a quantity of ammunition, are ordered to be drawn out to Lorette; the roads being at this time rendered impassable for horses by the mass of dissolving snow that covers them, the soldiers are under the necessity of performing that service.

At ten o'clock on 21 April, a proclamation was fixed up at all public places, acquainting the inhabitants that the enemy are preparing to besiege us; that they must therefore quit the town with their families and effects; and not presume to re-enter until farther orders; for this purpose three times twenty-four hours are allowed them to remove. This has caused immense confusion and discomfort among these poor people, who are, notwithstanding the urgent necessity of this procedure, greatly to be commiserated for all their sufferings. A lieutenant of the thirty-fifth regiment, who was formerly in the sea-service, is appointed to the command of a schooner which has this day fallen down to Orleans to undergo some repairs and be fitted out for an express; a master and six sailors, from one of our sloops of war, with twenty sea-bred soldiers, two pieces of cannon and a number of swivels, etc etc are taken on board; this vessel is ordered to reconnoitre the river and proceed to Halifax to hasten up our fleet, in case they have not yet sailed, by acquainting the admiral or commodore of our precarious situation, together with the strength of the enemy's squadron in the upper river.

The wretched citizens evacuated the town by the 24th: it is

impossible to avoid sympathising with them in their distress. The men prudently restrained their sentiments on this occasion, but the women were not so discreet; they charged us with a breach of the capitulation; said 'they had often heard *que les Anglois sont des gens sans foi*; and that we have now convinced them of the propriety of that character'. They pretend that there is not the smallest room to apprehend any disturbance on the part of M. de Lévis, and that, if the governor would rely on them, he should have the earliest intelligence of the motions of the enemy; and would submit to any restrictions whatever, if he would permit them to remain in their habitations; moreover, if they, or any among them, shall presume to betray us, they would answer it with the forfeiture, not only of all their effects, but also of their lives. Overtures to this purpose, we are informed, have been made to the general; but his excellency is not to be imposed upon by any such *bagatelles* arguments or *Gallic* rhethoric.

We have demolished the bridges over the river St Michael, near Cape Rouge; our light infantry continue in that neighbourhood to watch the motions of the enemy. We have also razed our post at Lorette, and the detachment that kept it are fallen back to St Foy. A number of caulkers are demanded from the regiments to repair our sloops of war and small craft, for which the order says, 'they shall be well paid'. All the different fatiguing parties are to work from nine o'clock until noon, and from two till six in the evening.

About two o'clock in the morning of the 27th the watch on board the *Racehorse* sloop of war in the dock, hearing a distressful noise on the river, acquainted Captain M'Cartney therewith, who instantly ordered out his boat, which shortly after returned with a man whom they found almost famished on a float of ice; notwithstanding all imaginable care was taken of him, it was above two hours before he was able to give an account of himself; when the terrors of his mind had subsided and he could speak, he gave his deliverer the following intelligence: 'That he is a serjeant of the French artillery, who, with six other men, were put into a floating battery of one eighteen-pounder; that his batteau overset in a great storm, and his companions he supposes are drowned; that he swam and scrambled alternately through numberless floats of ice, until he fortunately met with a large one, on which, though with great difficulty, he fixed himself; that he lay on it for several hours; passed the town with the tide of ebb, which carried him near to St Lawrence's church on the island of Orleans; and was driving up again with the tide of flood, at the time that our boat happily came to his relief.'

He added, 'that the French squadron, consisting of several frigates, armed sloops and other craft, such as *galiotes*, floating batteries and batteaus innumerable, laden with ammunition, artillery, provisions, intrenching-tools and stores of all kinds, were coming down to the Foulon, at Sillery; where they were to meet the army under M. de Lévis and M. Bourlamaque, amounting to twelve thousand men at least, though many people computed them at fifteen. That their fleet, particularly the small craft, were separated by the storm, and he believes many of them are lost, by the number of different articles which he saw floating down with him, and several guns he heard and supposes may be signals of distress from their larger vessels.' He says farther, 'that they are made to believe they will be reinforced by a powerful fleet and army from France, before an English ship can enter the river; and they are in daily expectation of a frigate laden with ammunition and stores, that has wintered at Gaspée.'

His story told, Captain M'Cartney immediately conducted him in a sailor's hammock up to the governor, to whom he recounted all the foregoing particulars; whereupon his excellency gave the command in the town to Colonel Fraser, and he, with the lieutenant-governor, marched out at the head of the grenadiers of the army, the five regiments under orders of readiness for the field and the picquets for the garrison to sustain the light infantry and rangers, who are already advanced. This large detachment, which composed the greatest part of our forces, took ten six-pounders and a proportionable quantity of ammunition with them. The remainder of the troops were instantly paraded and marched down to St John's Gate, prepared to push out in case circumstances should require it.

Moderate weather, with a thick and cold misting rain. The light troops exchanged several shot with the enemy, but they kept at so great a distance that it availed nothing: the governor formed the line of battle on an advantageous piece of ground beyond St Foy, and endeavoured to invite them to action; in which they seemed as if inclined to indulge him, and afterwards retired to the woods behind them, hoping, by various stratagems, to decoy our troops to follow them. Their cavalry and savages made frequent ostentatious displays by repeated countermarches.

Within the skirts of their cover, sometimes in large and at other times in small divisions to appear more numerous, yet they would not advance, though within the distance of our artillery, which galled them immensely; for they were frequently thrown into confusion, and seen to drag off many killed and disabled men. At length the governor, perceiving they were only trifling and protracting time, gave order for the demolition of our post at the church and, after the performance thereof, marched back his forces to the garrison without any other accident, in the course of the day, than having two men slightly wounded; the enemy affected to pursue them in their march, but our field-pieces obliged them to keep aloof; and the flanks of the line were so well covered by the light troops that they could not make the least impression: so that they contented themselves with firing and shouting at a great distance.

The army, being extremely harrassed and wet with a constant soaking rain, were allowed an extraordinary jill of rum per man; and some old houses at St Rocque were pulled down to provide them with fire-wood in order to dry their clothes. We have also withdrawn our posts from Point Levy and burned the two blockhouses that had been erected there. All the British merchants were reviewed and, at their own request, formed into an independent company of volunteers, to be commanded by Lieutenant Grant, of the fifty-eighth regiment; this gentleman they particularly made choice of, and they, including their servants, are about one hundred in number. The sick and wounded of our garrison, who are capable of using their arms, are to have their firelocks, bayonets and ammunition near them in readiness, and all the troops are to be quite alert and prepared to turn out, or march out, at a moment's warning. The naval armament of the enemy are fallen down to Cape Rouge; and they pretend that there are four French topsail vessels below at the Traverse.

# XII

# The French Siege

*By April 1760, the French under de Lévis were ready. Leaving holding forces at the head of Lake Champlain and west of Montreal, he concentrated all his strength in men and artillery for the march on Quebec. The British garrison was enfeebled and emaciated. The town walls were incapable of withstanding heavy bombardment, so Brigadier Murray took the hazardous step of leading his fit men out on the glacis where the September battle had been fought, in order to check the French as far from the town as possible. The British line could not hold, and the survivors tumbled back into the town. In the artillery duel that followed, they more than matched their besiegers. Frantic messages were sent down the St Lawrence to discover who held the river and whether reinforcements were on their way. On 14 May, two ships of war entered the Quebec basin. To the unspeakable relief of the garrison, they were British. De Lévis and his army broke camp and retired to Montreal.*

MONSIEUR DE LÉVIS and his army occupied the village and neighbourhood of St Foy on the night of 27 April, and his advanced posts possessed the coppice contiguous to the general hospital; early the next morning our light troops pushed out, and, with little difficulty, drove them to a greater distance:

> *'Tis not in mortals to command success,*
> *But we'll do more—we'll deserve it.*

About seven o'clock our army marched out to the heights of Abraham with a respectable artillery consisting of eighteen pieces of cannon, viz. two twelve-pounders with sixteen six-pounders and two howitzers; we also carried out our tools, as if intending to intrench ourselves and cover the town; which seemed to be the sole resolution taken by the governors previous to our march. Upon coming to our ground, we descried the enemy's van on the eminences of the woods of Sillery, and the bulk of their army to the right marching along the road of St Foy, inclining, as they advanced, in order to conceal themselves. Upon this discovery, and our line being already formed, the troops were ordered to throw down their intrenching-tools and march forward, this being deemed the decisive moment to attack them, in hopes of reaping every advantage that could be expected over an army not yet thoroughly arranged.

In consequence of this resolution, our forces advanced with great alacrity; the forty-eighth regiment, the fifteenth and second battalion of the sixtieth forming the right brigade, under Colonel Burton; the twenty-eighth, seventy-eighth and forty-seventh, the left under Colonel Fraser; the fifty-eighth was the right center corps, and the forty-third the left center, commanded by Colonel James. The second line was composed of the thirty-fifth and the third battalion of Royal Americans, drawn up, to appear more numerous, two deep. Our right flank was covered by Major Dalling's corps of light infantry, and our left by the company of volunteers and rangers, under their respective commandants, Captains McDonell and Hazen. The artillery were placed occasionally in front, in the intervals, or on the flanks, as circumstances might require, commanded by Major Godwin and assisted by Major M'Kellar, our chief engineer. Thus did our little army advance, weak in point of numbers when compared with that of the French, but powerful in every other respect; and having an enemy to encounter who, by frequent experience and repeated trials, were unaccustomed to stand long before us. Our field-pieces were exceedingly well served, and did amazing execution; as soon as we came within the range of musketry, the light infantry attacked the French grenadiers on the left of their army, and routed them: at the same instant the volunteers and rangers engaged their right, repulsed them in like manner, and possessed themselves of a redoubt occupied before by the enemy; the center posts, seeing their right and left give way, fled without firing a shot.

Whilst we gained this small advantage over their van, the main body of their army advanced with great expedition, completely formed in columns, in spite of the utmost efforts exerted on our part to prevent them; one of these columns came without loss of time to sustain their flying grenadiers, now pursued by our light infantry, who, being overpowered with great loss, retired to the rear and were of little service afterwards; the enemy, profiting thereby, instantly wheeled round some rising grounds, and charged our right wing vigorously in flank, while M. de Lévis, with another division, made the like movement on our left, and then the action became obstinate on both sides. The general immediately ordered the thirty-fifth from the second line to support our right wing; and the third battalion of the sixtieth the left, who acquitted themselves with great honour. Quebec being the grand object, the enemy seemed regardless of our center, hoping, if they could out-flank us, they could be able to get between us and our garrison; and this it was that attracted their greatest attention. They sustained their right and left wings with

247

fresh reinforcements; and Fortune, who appeared for some time undetermined on whom to confer her laurel, at length inclined to the more numerous army.

The enemy possessed themselves of two redoubts upon our left, which gave them a great advantage; but, by an excellent movement of the forty-third regiment, ordered by Colonel James from the center to support the third battalion of Americans on the left, both these corps made a vigorous effort to recover those works, and succeeded; they maintained them for some time with admirable firmness, but, at length being reduced to a handful, they were compelled to yield to superior numbers. In the course of the action we were insensibly drawn from our advantageous situation into low swampy ground, where our troops fought almost knee-deep in dissolving wreaths of snow and water, whence it was utterly impracticable to draw off our artillery under those unhappy circumstances, after this infeebled army had performed prodigies of valour exceeding all description; having the whole force of the country to contend with, and our communication with the town in danger of being intercepted, we were obliged to give up the contest.

The troops being ordered to fall back, a command they were hitherto unacquainted with, as if sensible of the critical posture of our affairs, they drew a natural conclusion; and, growing impatient, some of them cried out, *Damn it, what is falling back but retreating?* The inference was immediately communicated to the whole, and accordingly put in execution. This discomfit was however so regularly conducted that the enemy did not pursue with that spirit which the vast importance of their victory required; the truth was they were very roughly handled; and from their losses, which fell mostly upon the flower of their army, they were heartily sick of it.

The action was immensely warm for near two hours, and we had eleven hundred of all ranks killed, wounded and prisoners; the enemy, by their own acknowledgement, lost considerably above that number; and I am induced to think, if the invalids of our garrison had been able, or one thousand fresh men only could have been brought up to sustain us, we should not have quartered within the town this night, nor permitted our antagonists to incamp so near us; for they lost no time in intrenching themselves within nine hundred yards of our walls. The strength of our army in the morning was three thousand one hundred and forty; and that of the enemy amounted to fifteen thousand, as we have been informed [by] prisoners and deserters; though by a state which I saw, and was copied from a return of the possession of M. Vauquelin, the French commodore, they made eighteen thousand, viz. *troupes de France*, five thousand; *de la colonie*, three thousand; *milice*, eight thousand five hundred; Acadians and savages, thirteen hundred; cannoniers, etc two hundred.

The enemy's fleet have fallen down to the Foulon by Sillery, and their boats are continually employed in landing their stores, artillery and provisions. The army have thrown up a line of countervallation, their right extending to the Foulon and their left towards St Charles's river beyond our chain of blockhouses; by their attention to one particular spot, opposite to St Louis's bastion, we suspect they are erecting a battery, having provided a quantity of fascines and gabions for that purpose. We are opening embrasures in the curtains for cannon, revesting the parapet wall with fascine-work, and our carpenters are employed in preparing and laying platforms for guns. The enemy have brought up a piece of ordnance to bear upon our large advanced blockhouse, being much annoyed at their work by the fire of its artillery. Soft, open weather, with little wind and variable.

The women are all ordered to cook for, and attend, the men at work with their victuals; also to nurse the sick and wounded. The officers are desired to be very circumspect in keeping the men sober; their rum to be continually mixed with water in the presence of an officer. The men for duty are directed to parade with their canteens of rumbo, and always twenty-four hours' provisions ready dressed. In case the enemy should beat a parley, the officer commanding the nearest guard is injoined to send out an officer, with a drum, to meet him as far as possible from the place. Two hundred men are appointed to do duty with the artillery. The officers of guards are ordered to be very attentive and send the general early notice when they observe any of the enemy approaching, or any thing else extraordinary that may happen. The regiments are desired to remove their sick from the convents, and settle them in houses appointed for them by the quarter-master-general. Smart firing between the blockhouse and the enemy.

Ensign Maw, of the forty-third regiment, with two non-commissioned and twenty volunteers, sallied out during the night of the 29th, hoping to get a prisoner for intelligence; but unfortunately, his sight not being equal in goodness to his spirit and ability, he fell into the enemy's hands, and six of his men were killed and wounded. The French are forwarding their works with great diligence, notwithstanding the warm salutations they receive from our cannon and mortars; we shall shortly be able to open a continual line of fire from Cape Diamond down to the hangman's redoubt. The advanced blockhouse blew up this morning, by a spark falling on some loose powder which communicated with their magazine: the officers and men suffered considerably, but no lives were lost. The troops fit for duty, by the returns made to the head quarters, amount to two thousand and one hundred, and no more: they incamped this evening at the alarm-posts. Frequent flags of truce pass and repass between us and the enemy, for necessaries for our officers who are prisoners; they are treated with great politeness, and are to be sent to Montreal for their better accommodation. Immense irregularities are hourly committed by the soldiery in breaking open store and dwelling houses to get at liquor: this is seemingly the result of panic and despair, heightened by drunkenness; one man was hanged this evening *in terrorem*, without any trial, which it is hoped will effectually prevent farther disorders and influence the soldiers to a lively sense of their duty.

The *Racehorse* frigate sailed on the morning of 1 May with a fair wind and pleasant weather for Louisbourg and Halifax, in order to hasten up a fleet and succours to our relief. A soldier, who was made prisoner last campaign, escaped from Montreal and came into town this night; he says that country is left almost desolate, the whole force of Canada being engaged in this enterprise; and he has been informed that the enemy lost some of their best artillery, with a great quantity of ammunition and other stores, by the late storm; which dispersed their fleet, overset some of their store-vessels and staved others to pieces. (This is a most remarkable instance of the kind interposition of Providence in behalf of the troops of this garrison and the British arms in America.) It being of the utmost consequence at present, the governor injoins all officers to attend the men on every kind of fatigue, and keep them close to their work.

Any officers who chuse to go volunteers upon *sorties*, are desired to give in their names at the head quarters, and his excellency promises to recommend them to his majesty; any serjeant who chuses to go volunteer upon the like service, and can find twelve men, also volunteers, will be well rewarded. In consequence of this intimation, two or three serjeants only, and a few privates, did offer themselves; but not one commissioned officer shewed any inclination to go out of his own proper turn: the sense of the gentlemen upon the publication of this order was that, if the general should think proper to command a corps, large detachment, or a small party from any particular regiment to sally out, they were ready and willing chearfully to execute his excellency's orders to the utmost of their power, in their regular tour of duty. We maintain a brisk fire on the enemy's works, which are nevertheless in great forwardness.

We are exerting our most strenuous efforts towards a vigorous defence both in the high and low town; and our men are thoroughly recovered from their late irregularities and despondent state of mind. If the enemy have, or do still entertain, thoughts of storming the place, it seems now too late, and they have let slip a golden opportunity: had they followed their blow on the 28th, 29th or 30th, before the soldiers recollected themselves, I am strongly inclined to think, notwithstanding the active zeal and spirit of the governors and officers in general, Quebec would have reverted to its old masters. We no longer harbour a thought of visiting France or England, or of falling a sacrifice to a merciless scalping knife. We are roused from our lethargy; we have recovered our good humour, our sentiments for glory; and we seem, one and all, determined to defend our dearly purchased garrison to the last extremity. Batteries are erecting to enfilade the road leading to the lower town; two noble cavaliers are begun upon the commanding rocky eminence between the citadel of Cape Diamond and Port St Louis, which is a work of labour, the earth being borrowed from other places; and we are throwing up traverses in different parts of the city. The general and lieutenant-governor visit the guards and working parties frequently, to encourage the men and influence them to diligence and alertness.

Some of my readers, especially those who are unacquainted with military affairs, may be desirous to know the necessity for the troops incamping within the walls of a town when besieged; for their information, therefore, I shall only offer what naturally occurs to me upon this occasion: it is impossible to have troops altogether so alert in quarters as in tents; for soldiers cannot take those indulgences in camp which they may be too much induced to do in their barracks, where their bedding, etc lie convenient for them. In the next place, by the extensiveness of the garrison, men could not be so soon assembled upon any sudden emergency, as in a compact incampment contiguous to their alarm-posts, which will not admit of the least confusion or delay in turning out for service; and, moreover, (a consideration not unworthy of the greatest general, and deserved particular attention in our circumstances) the troops are less exposed to accidents and danger in tents than in houses of stone, brick or wood, as it is well known that soldiers are subject to a greater number of casualties from splinters than from shot or shell. Lastly, the practice is neither unprecedented nor uncommon where there is vacant ground and the town is extensive enough to admit of in-camping; though there were some among us who affected to be of a different opinion, and that has partly induced me to offer my sentiments and to express my approbation of this procedure.

The fortified house was accidently fired on 5 May by a wad from one of our own guns, which, communicating by the freshness of the wind with the stockades and adjoining houses, swept away almost that whole quarter of the town; luckily the intendant's palace escaped the fury of the flames, though all his out-offices, with one of our blockhouses which stood opposite to the *jettée*, the picquet-work contiguous thereto, together with some of our boats and naval stores, were destroyed; all the guards immediately turned out and beat to arms, the troops manned their alarm-posts and remained there for some hours. As it was apprehended the enemy might seize this opportunity to storm the place, and the sentries seeing some motions in their camp, our batteries played incessantly upon them, obliging them to abandon their works and retire from the range of our guns; at length two boats came down under a flag of truce, and the French, taking the advantage of the cessation, returned to their trenches, as did our troops, in like manner, to their respective occupations.

A French sloop from Sillery passed our batteries during the night of the 4th undiscovered, until she was almost out of reach of our artillery, and sailed down the river. An unlucky accident happened at one of our batteries, by some sparks of fire having reached one of the chests of ammunition, which instantly blew up and, communicating with the men's arms, discharged some of them, whereby three soldiers received shot wounds; a lieutenant and several others of the forty-third regiment were most severely scorched; very fortunately the fire did not reach to another chest adjoining, which lay also open and was full of loaded shells ready for embassy; had the flash reached these infernal messengers, we should probably have had a large breach made in the rampart, and lost many lives. The enemy have got another frigate at the Foulon, and their approaches were advanced this night within seven hundred yards of the Ursuline bastion, under cover of a small coppice opposite to that quarter; they are drawing cannon to-day from their camp to the trenches, so that we may soon expect to hear from them.

We shall very soon have a most formidable line of fire against the enemy of near one hundred and forty pieces of cannon: for this purpose we are stripping all our batteries next the river of their guns, planks and platforms. The parapet wall, surrounding the country side of the town, is now strengthened considerably, being re-dressed with fascines, and a quantity of earth rammed down between the lining and masonry work; this has been executed with astonishing diligence and perseverance, by day and night, from Cape Diamond to the hangman's redoubt. We have likewise added to the miserable defences eastward of Palace-gate, and round that quarter which over-looks the *jettée* and river St Charles; the enemy are also very very diligent, yet perfectly quiet.

Two soldiers, who deserted from this army last campaign, returned to us early on the 7th: by them we are informed that the enemy say they will not fire a gun at us until they open a battery of forty pieces of cannon together; but where they will procure them, these men say, they cannot conceive; for, after having stripped their ships of their best and heaviest metal, they did not see above twenty-six pieces of different dimensions in their park. That they are in the greatest distress for provisions, each man having only one quarter of a pound of fresh meat and half a pound of bread per day; that a detachment of five thousand men are thrown into the trenches every night, each of whom is served with a jill of brandy, but the rest of their army do not receive any; and that their savages, who amount to three hundred and fifty, are very clamorous for liquor.

These deserters add that, on 28 April, we repulsed the French army at two different times with immense loss, and that, if M. Bourlamaque, who is the life and spirit of the troops, had been wounded earlier in the day, we should have gained a complete victory. The enemy, say they, compute their loss in the action at eighteen hundred killed and wounded, and near five hundred since that day by our shot and shells; but that they heard an aide-major, or adjutant, acquaint some of their officers that they had considerably above two thousand killed and disabled in the engagement. The deserters assure us moreover, that there is a fleet in the river, but whether English or French is yet uncertain.

Our troops are in great spirits, and work with the utmost diligence: we are drawing up heavy cannon to our new batteries from those next the river; as these guns are dragged up a continual ascent, it renders this work immensely laborious to our brave fellows, and the officers generously assist them as much as in their power when they meet with any difficulty. It is recommended to the officers to send all their useless linen to Dr Russell for the service of the hospitals. The officers are injoined not to interfere with the gunners, except those who are appointed for that service. As there is no wine to be had at present even for money, the general has very seasonably ordered two gallons of brandy to be delivered out to every officer, which the quarter-masters of regiments are ordered to receive immediately from the commissary; nothing can be more acceptable to us in our present situation, except a supply of fresh provisions, those issued from the stores being so inconceivably hard and salt as to become disgustful.

M. de Lévis has agreeably disappointed us; we never ceased firing all the night of 8 May; our line must have appeared immensely tremendous to the enemy, and such as perhaps the most experienced among them never beheld before, for we have not a mortar or gun mounted that was not employed, and without the smallest intermission; one half of the garrison stood to arms at our alarm-posts from sun-set in the evening until one o'clock this morning, when they were relieved by the other half, who continued until five, prepared to give the enemy a warm reception if they had been disposed to strike their *coup*; from which we are inclined to think they were deterred by the uncommon weight of our numerous artillery. The French sloop that whisked by the town on the 4th instant, returned about midnight and worked up to the Foulon: by this we flatter ourselves that a fleet is at hand; we hailed the sloop without firing at her; but she took no notice of us, and an officer, from the citadel of Cape Diamond, inquired, *why she did not stay below to pilot up the French armada?* It blows fresh, with a delightful gale at east-south-east.

About eleven o'clock in the forenoon of the 9th we had the inconceivable satisfaction to behold the *Leostoffe* frigate sail up into the bason and come to an anchor; for a little time we were in suspence, and all our perspectives were employed in viewing her; but we were soon convinced of her being British, though some among us, who had found means to enrich themselves by the American war and were afraid of losing their acquisitions, were cunningly wise; they endeavoured to allay the joy of the troops, thinking it too premature; and strenuously insisted she was a French ship: at length, Captain Deane, having saluted the garrison with twenty-one guns and put off in his barge to come ashore, dissipated all apprehensions. The gladness of the troops is not to be expressed: both officers and soldiers mounted the parapets in the face of the enemy and huzzaed, with their hats in the air, for almost an hour; the garrison, the enemy's camp, the bay and circumjacent country for several miles, resounded with our shouts and the thunder of our artillery; for the gunners were so elated that they did nothing but fire and load for a considerable time: in short, the general satisfaction is not to be conceived, and to form a lively idea of it is impossible, except by a person who had suffered the extremities of a siege and been destined, with his brave friends and valiant countrymen, to the scalping knives of a faithless conqueror and his barbarous allies.

I believe I may venture to advance, that the garrison of Vienna, when closely besieged and hard pressed above fourscore years ago by the Turks, were not more rejoiced on sight of the Christian army, under the famous Sobieski, marching to their relief, than we of Quebec were upon the arrival of the *Leostoffe*, with the agreeable intelligence of a British fleet being masters of the river St Lawrence and nigh at hand to sustain us. Captain Deane left England in March last, with some ships of the line and other frigates under the command of Commodore Swanton, from whom he parted at sea and, not being able to rejoin them, he kept his course, knowing his ship to be a good sailor, and made the best of his way hither; he spoke with Lord Colville's fleet from Halifax, who were cruising off Newfoundland seven days ago; and was told they received orders to rendezvous at the island of Bic. The London news papers, fraught with the defeat of Conflans, Thurot and many other interesting events, were sent to the French generals, early in the evening, by a flag of truce.

The situation of affairs and the circumstances of the enemy, now grown desperate, render it necessary to take every precaution that human prudence and foresight can dictate to prevent a surprise. Repeated assurances have been received that the French generals are meditating a *dernier effort* for the recovery of this fortress; but herein they have verified the old adage, *l'occasion perdue ne se retrouve pas toujours*: for our forces, instead of slackening or growing supine at the prospect of being soon relieved by a fleet, exert themselves to the utmost of their power for the defence of the garrison and the honour of his majesty's arms. The convalescents are under orders to be ready to turn at their alarm-posts on the shortest notice, with their firelocks and accoutrements.

On the morning of the 11th the enemy opened their batteries; one was opposed to Cape Diamond, a second against the citadel, and the third the Ursuline bastion; their shot are twenty-four, eighteen and twelve-pounders. They likewise bombarded us with three nine-inch mortars, and we returned this salute with great vigour; a few of our men were wounded by their shot, but their shells have not as yet done any execution. As four officers of the forty-third regiment were sitting on the ground in a soldier's tent, eating a dish of pease-porridge, a shell pitched within a yard of the door of the tent, and they had barely time to stretch themselves at their length, when the shell burst; but, by being extented flat on the ground, they happily received no other damage than losing their mess, which was overset in the bustle.

We have got near an hundred and fifty pieces of cannon on the ramparts between Cape Diamond and the hangman's redoubt. We now take it alternately to stand to our arms, both day and night, at our alarm-posts, one half relieving the other. A sloop sailed on the morning of the 12th in quest of the fleet. One of our guns burst on the line, without any disaster happening. The garrison have received the same orders, with respect to their remaining alert, as before; with this difference that, as the general will have no man exposed to the enemy's fire but when necessity requires it, he directs that, instead of being drawn up on the ramparts, they are to keep under cover below, leaving a sufficient number of sentinels to give them intelligence of the enemy's approach; the regiments are then instantly, as well the resting men as the others, to be disposed of upon the ramparts according to the former directions they have received on this head: every soldier, not on duty, is commanded to have his arms and ammunition close by him in his tent; but they are not to load until called upon to man their alarm-posts. Brisk firing between us and the enemy this evening; by their shells flying over the town, they seem to be intended against the *Leostoffe* riding at anchor in the channel off Cape Diamond: they have nearly got her direction.

All the guns bearing on the enemy's batteries are ordered to be chalked, that they may be distinguished from the rest; and the gunners are desired to regulate their fire by that of the French, taking care that the guns are well pointed and rammed home; which will prevent the like accidents that have already happened by the bursting of cannon. A French shot will not fit British guns; the governor recommends it to the artillery officers to be very attentive to that particular, and to fire slow and sure. The additional gunners' arms are to be inspected, that we may be certain they are in good order; and care must be taken to lay them and their ammunition in such places on the ramparts where they will be secured from wet or other accidents. We have had fierce cannonading and bombarding between the town and the enemy for these last thirty-six hours; but with little loss on our side, except a few men being wounded; and we perceive this evening that we have dismounted some of their guns, though they are still extremely lavish of their shells. The troops have continued under arms both day and night, one half relieving the other as before; and the soldiers, seeing there is a necessity for our being thus harrassed, are amazingly alert, and take pleasure in doing their duty.

We did not molest our neighbours much during the night of the 12th, but we renewed our fire the next morning, and continue it with our usual vigour; they amused us, about midnight, with two rockets, one from their fleet and the other from Point Levy; which obliged us to beat to arms, man our defences and remain there until it was clear day-light: as these are the customary signals for military achievements, we expected, every moment, to see the enemy's columns advance to the charge; the troops were well prepared, and the soldiers orderly and in good spirits: about five o'clock half of the garrison returned to their tents. We are now distributing our powder and provisions in different places for safety, the enemy having directed their shells at our magazines and particularly at the Jesuit's college, knowing the use we have converted it to. The *Porcupine* sloop of war is thoroughly repaired, and has taken her guns on board. Wind easterly until the evening, when it became variable and died away; (the safety of this garrison depending on the arrival of a British fleet induces me to be thus particular with respect to the winds).

That our men may be as little exposed as possible to the enemy's fire, they are ordered, in passing to or from camp to the batteries, to go along St Louis street, and under cover of the ramparts. Moderate weather on the 14th, with a dropping rain and wind westerly: at noon it was variable, but in the evening it sprang up easterly and blew a steady gale. The troops on the watch, both day and night as before. The enemy have been very sparing of their ammunition these last twenty-four hours, in which time we have had only two shells from them: we seem to regulate our fire by theirs, being at present equally quiet.

At night-fall came to an anchor in the bason, to the unspeakable joy of this harrassed garrison, the *Van-guard* ship of war, Commodore Swanton, with the *Diana* frigate, Captain Schomberg, and the armed schooner which was sent down the river on the 23rd ultimo; our gunners immediately gave the enemy a general discharge of all our artillery, three times repeated, without any return; and Captain Deane repaired instantly on board the commodore to acquaint him with our situation and to concert measures for our relief.

We had an officer and twelve men advanced during the night of the 15th, under cover of a rising ground, beyond the blockhouse

Number two; fifty French grenadiers, with a captain and two officers, crept upon them unperceived, and gave them a brisk fire; which our little party spiritedly returned, and then fell back to the blockhouse, lest they should be surrounded: our officer lost three men, two of whom were scalped and otherwise barbarously butchered; the third was wounded and made prisoner, as we suppose. This affair caused an alarm through-out the garrison; our drums beat to arms, and the troops stood upon their defence until it was clear day-light. This act of cruelty, perpetrated by men who are the flower and boast of the French armies (*les grenadiers de France*) and under the eyes of their officers, obliges me to digress a little in this place.

That the natural troops of France, namely the regulars, did give quarter, on 28 April, to several of our officers, *I confess*; but that they did refuse protection to others *is equally certain*. Four of my particular acquaintance, one of whom was slightly wounded, were among the prisoners and, being conducted to some officers of the regiment *de la Sarre*, their uniforms faced with scarlet, they, one and all, waved their hands, and cried aloud—*Allez vous en*—*Allez vous en*; but, the fellows having already got some booty from their captives, and being promised more if they would escort them to the general hospital, they accordingly took them there, and delivered them up safe; for which they were better rewarded than they knew they could expect to have been, in the present situation of affairs, for their scalps.

It is no less true that, when our army began to give way, several officers who, by slight wounds, were rendered incapable of retreating with the rest, were never more heard of; though, as I observed before, others were more humanely treated, for which they may thank their own money, the avarice of their captors and the sinking state of the French finances, now no longer able to reward scalping as heretofore; moreover, it has been always the practice of the French to preserve some prisoners, to save their own credit and keep up an appearance of generosity and christianity. As a farther proof of this charge, I have to add that, of the immense number of wounded men who were unavoidably left on the field of battle, twenty-eight only were sent to the hospital, the rest being given up as victims to glut the rage of their savage allies, and to prevent their forsaking them.

But to return to the occurrences of the memorable 16th of May: a ranging officer and twelve men, being advanced last night close by the river St Charles, not far from the general hospital, surprised a courier, who swam that river with his horse, and was returning with dispatches for M. de Lévis from the lower country, where he was detached for intelligence; by him we learn that there are some straggling ships in the river, and that he saw a fleet enter the gulph, which we suppose to be Lord Colville's. The wind continues easterly.

Early this morning the *Van-guard* and frigates worked up with the tide of flood, and attacked the French squadron; at first M. Vauquelin shewed an appearance of engaging, but soon made off: our ships forced the *Pomona* ashore and burned her; then pursued the others; drove the *Atalanta* also ashore near Point aux Trembles and set her on fire; took and destroyed all the rest, except *La Marie*, a small sloop of war who, to avoid being taken, threw her guns overboard and escaped to St Peter's lake, above the Three Rivers: After the commodore, *eminent for his valour, great abilities in naval affairs, faithful services and long experience,* had performed this morning's notable business, he fell down to the channel off Sillery, laid his broadside to the right flank of the enemy's trenches, and infiladed them for several hours so warmly that, between his fire and that of the garrison, they were intirely driven from their works. M. de Lévis sent two field-pieces to play upon the *Van-guard*, but without any effect; for, by the ship's sheering in the current, she brought some of her guns to bear upon those of the enemy, and obliged them to retire.

We have the pleasure to see several large bodies of Canadians filing off towards Charlebourg and Beauport, and others down the south country, that have found means to get a-cross the river; hence we flatter ourselves, that M. de Lévis is going to raise the siege. Some deserters, who are just arrived, confirm us in our conjecture, by assuring us that the militia are ordered to return to their respective parishes, and the regular and colony troops to march back to Jacques Cartier; they add, that our artillery has done amazing execution in the enemy's camp; that the regiment de Guienne lost five hundred men in the late engagement, and near three hundred since that day by our shot and shells; this corps consisted of two battalions.

Other deserters are coming in to us, who inform us that the enemy have abandoned their camp and works, except the grenadiers and picquets who are intrenched up to their necks to cover the retreat of the army. In consequence of this intelligence, the governor has sent an order to the batteries to fire a *ricochet*, hoping our shot may overtake them in their flight, and scour the circumjacent country to a great extent by elevating their guns at least ten degrees above the level, that the shot may bounce and roll after they strike. Mortars and howitzers are likewise frequently served in this manner with great success, their shells doing the execution of shot and shell. The surprising effect our artillery had upon this fortress, when we cannonaded and bombarded it a-cross the river, is to be imputed to this method of firing; and shot will extend considerably farther than when discharged *point blank*. It is a very advantageous invention, and is ascribed to the celebrated Marshal de Vauban; for guns are loaded with a smaller quantity of powder than usual, and are consequently less damaged.

After the gunners had prepared to execute these directions, I believe I may venture to advance that there never was such tremendous firing heard (even at Bergen op Zoom, when it was besieged, or elsewhere) as our artillery displayed this evening for near two hours. The light infantry are ordered to be immediately completed to five hundred rank and file, and they, with the grenadiers, are injoined to hold themselves in readiness to march at a moment's warning. This favourable prospect makes no alteration in the usual fatigues and duty of the garrison. Half the troops are to take the watch this night, and the remainder are likewise under orders of readiness to march at the shortest notice.

On the 17th the enemy discharged a volley of musketry from their intrenchments towards the garrison, which, as we supposed, was *prendre leur dernier congé*; for a lieutenant, with a small reconnoitring party, being sent out, found the trenches abandoned, marched into them, and immediately transmitted notice thereof to the governor; whereupon the light infantry and grenadiers instantly pushed out, and early this morning his excellency followed with a detachment from the ten regiments, and the whole proceeded to Lorette, eagerly hoping to come up with the cream of the French army and pay them off for all our suffering since the 27th ultimo. Unfortunately they had crossed the river at Cape Rouge before we reached Lorette: some stragglers however fell into our hands, and we had nearly surprised a body of Indians in the hamlet of St Foy, who, upon sight of our van, threw down their arms and packs, set up a hideous shout, dispersed themselves, and got instantaneously clear of us.

All the sick and wounded of the enemy, among whom were many officers who had been distributed among the neighbouring houses and parishes, were made prisoners: and the general, perceiving it to no purpose to continue the pursuit any farther, refreshed his troops, and marched back to his garrison, where he found a polite billet from

M. de Lévis, recommending the prisoners and the wounded in the general hospital to his excellency's care, and assuring him he was so tender of the people who had taken the oath to his Britannic majesty that he did not insist on their taking up arms, though he had compelled them to work for his army, which, he said, he had a right to do in this or any other country by the rules of war.

Our loss, during the siege, by every accident, men and officers included, did not exceed thirty, killed and wounded; and, now that our affairs have re-assumed their former successful complexion, to take a retrospective view of the different works performed here within these twenty days by a handful of men, who have been continually harrassed with labour and watching, both day and night, is indeed stupendous, beyond conception; however they at length find themselves well recompensed for all their toils, and are so happy and in such high spirits that it is impossible, even at this time, to express their ardent desire for new enterprises, to which they are encouraged by their confidence in our two governors, the greatest dependence on the officers their fellow-labourers, and their own strength, far surpassing till now their most sanguine ideas.

The enemy certainly abandoned their camp and retired in the most precipitate manner, leaving their tents, cannon, mortars, *pétards*, scaling-ladders and intrenching-tools almost innumerable, fire-arms in great abundance, ammunition, baggage and some provisions behind them; we are at a loss to what cause to impute this shameful flight of an army so superior in numbers, so well provided beyond what we could have expected, and, in short, with so many other advantages over us, except to a suspicion, as we surmised and were afterwards confirmed in by the prisoners and deserters, of our frigates landing some fresh troops above to charge them in the rear, while the garrison should sally out and thereby take them between two fires; this wise conjecture struck them with such a panic that they instantly forsook every other consideration, except their safety, by a hasty and inglorious retreat. The loss of the enemy, from 27 April inclusive, has fallen mostly on their regular and colony troops, having one hundred and fifty-two officers killed and wounded; of the latter, twenty-two are since dead. The Indians committed great disorders in their camp by getting drunk, plundering the officers' baggage and cutting up tents: to this end they fell upon a small guard of grenadiers, who had the charge of the officers' effects, and scalped every man, except one who made his escape. All the deserters agree that our artillery did immense execution in their trenches which is partly evident from the handles of the wheel-barrows and other tools being tinged with the blood of their late masters.

The troops decamped on the 18th, and returned to their quarters. Lord Colville's fleet are at length arrived in the bay, and were saluted by the garrison. We have now in the bason six ships of the line, with seven frigates and sloops of war: a most grateful prospect to the remains of our shattered army, and the British traders who wintered here with us. It is amazing to see the effect of our artillery

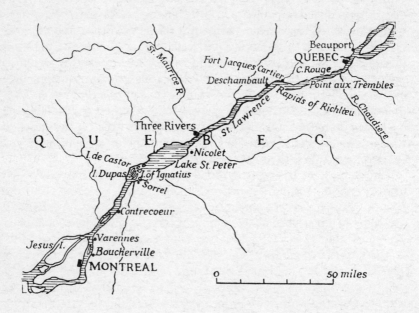

in the environs of the late French camp and circumjacent country, for the extent of almost two miles, the ground being ploughed up by our *richochet* firing. The enemy did not bury our dead, but suffered them to be scalped and mangled in an unheard of manner, drew them away clear of their camp, and left them for ravenous birds and beasts to prey upon.

It remains now to be observed that we buried a thousand men since we marched into this garrison, and had almost double that number alternately in the hospitals; so that it will appear, by recapitulating the various occurrences and operations of the winter, that about four thousand men have accomplished this great work and sustained incredible fatigues continually for the space of eight months; and this at a season of the year usually reserved in other countries for the relief and refreshment of troops. I have only to subjoin that the active example and abilities of our governors, together with the most exact discipline observed and supported throughout by the officers of every rank, the great harmony and unanimity which has subsisted among the several corps, even to the private men, and between them and their superiors as one family, the unparalleled humanity to the sick and wounded and the invariable attention displayed on every occasion to the preservation of the health of the soldiery, all these circumstances concurring inabled the army, with alacrity, to surmount every difficulty and to conduct their affairs to the prosperous issue wherein we now behold them; whilst the enemy, by the desperate situation of theirs, are incapacitated from giving us any considerable trouble, or exerting any efforts of consequence against the commander-in-chief in completing the reduction of upper Canada.

The troops are ordered to be in readiness to take the field, or proceed upon immediate service, on the shortest notice; some armed vessels are fitting out, and the army are to be conveyed up the river to perfect a junction with the commander-in-chief: we are to be attended by all the flat-bottomed boats, with detachments of officers and sailors from the fleet. The Canadians have levelled the late works of the enemy, pursuant to the governor's commands; and the duty of the garrison is reduced for the ease of the forces.

# XIII

# Advance on Montreal

*Reinforced from Halifax and Louisbourg, the Quebec garrison re-
formed the third prong of the advance on Montreal. Murray and the
admiral had only the vaguest idea of the progress of the other two
British armies, but calculated rightly that the French were in increasing
disarray and that speed was essential. They took the bold decision to
reach Montreal by water, by-passing any forts and strong points and
leaving them to be mopped up by the forces following them. Knox's
lively narrative shows that the campaign was something of a pleasure
cruise.*

THE TROOPS INTENDED for the expedition marched out on 5
July, and incamped about a quarter of a mile from the town; and,
on the 7th, a great number of men arrived from Orleans, surprisingly
recovered and fit for duty. Captain Deane's squadron worked up
from the bason and anchored off the left of our incampment. The
remainder of the forces, left for the defence of Quebec, are ordered
to incamp separately without the town. A number of recovered men
and officers of this army have rejoined us from New-York and other
places. All soldiers unfit for farther service are to be sent to England,
and recommended to Chelsea hospital; their discharges and clearances
are to be left with Colonel Fraser, who will forward those men by the
earliest opportunity. We are informed that the enemy are cantoned
between Jacques Cartier and les Trois Rivières.

The baggage of the troops, going on the expedition, was imbarked on 11 July; the general reviewed them on the 12th and, on
the 13th, they went on board their transports: the right brigade at
five in the morning, and the left at the same hour in the afternoon.
These embarkations were extremely well conducted by our two
brigadiers, notwithstanding some few irregularities committed by
our poor fellows, in consequence of their being at this juncture
indulged with a small advance of money in part of their respective
balances.

After we had passed Jacques Cartier, the river narrowed until we
opened the church and village of Chambaud, at the distance of three
leagues, where it widened considerably: here we came to an anchor
about nine oclock AM on the 15th in ten fathom water. The north

and south inhabitants are all in arms, terrified, no doubt, at their approaching fate; it is not probable they ever saw so numerous a fleet in this part of their country; we amount to about thirty-two sail, besides nine floating batteries, with a number of flat-bottomed boats and batteaus. In the evening some boats went, at low water, to sound the channel through what are called the Rapids of Richelieu; they found from six feet to six fathom, irregular soundings, and the navigation difficult by reason of the different turnings; a detachment of the enemy, incamped at Chambaud, fired a gun and some musketry at our boats, but without effect. From the channel, which is nearly central to the north and south shores, the river is shallow and full of rocks, whose heads appear above the surface like steppingstones in a ford: at high water the tide rises here about nine feet.

The battalion-detachments disimbarked, and the general went, with the rangers and a company of light infantry, several miles up the country: fifty-five men of St Croix, and seventy-nine of the parish de Lobiniere, took the oath of neutrality. Some of his excellency's arguments to these people were to this effect: 'Who can carry on or support the war without ships, artillery, ammunition, or provisions? At whose mercy are your habitations, and that harvest which you expect to reap this summer, together with all you are possessed of in this world? Therefore consider your own interest, and provoke us no more.' Then, turning to a priest, he subjoined— 'The clergy are the source of all the mischiefs that have befallen the poor Canadians, whom they keep in ignorance, and excite to wickedness and their own ruin. No doubt you have heard that I hanged a captain of militia; that I have a priest and some Jesuits on board a ship of war, to be transmitted to Great Britain: beware of the snare they have fallen into; *preach the Gospel*, which alone is your province; adhere to your duty, and do not presume, directly or indirectly, to intermeddle with military matters, or the quarrel between the two *Crowns*.' The troops reimbarked in the evening. It was this day ordered, 'when the wind is fair, to pass Chambaud; the men are not to be allowed to expose themselves upon deck, but to be kept below'.

The general, having received intelligence that a body of Indians are sent to the south side of the river to annoy and pick off our men, has dispatched a flag of truce to M. Dumas, commanding officer at Chambaud, to assure him, 'that, if these savages are not instantly recalled, or any barbarities should be committed upon our troops, they shall have orders to give no quarter either to regulars, or others, that may fall into our hands; and that the country shall undergo military execution, wherever we land'. The battalion corps and grenadiers are to land alternately, without farther orders; and a market is established under proper regulations, for the benefit of this armament. The tide, or current, runs here between four and five miles in an hour. The parish of St Antoine have this day delivered up their arms and taken the oath of neutrality; as the form of swearing is solemn, it may not be improper to particularise it. The men stand in a circle, hold up their right hands, repeat each his own name, and then say:

'Do severally swear, in the presence of Almighty God, that we will not take up arms against George the Second, King of Great Britain, etc etc or against his troops or subjects; nor give any intelligence to his enemies, directly or indirectly:

So help me God.'

A serjeant of the French regulars, disguised in the habit of a Canadian peasant, was sent by the enemy to the south side of the river, in the capacity of a spy, hoping, through him, to get an exact account of our numbers and our intended plan of operations: this fellow was discovered by some of our men who had been in the French service, and brought to the general; being examined, he produced a forged letter in his vindication from a captain of militia who, being immediately summoned, made oath that the man was an intire stranger to him, and the letter was not his hand-writing. After the serjeant had undergone a strict examination, and the men who had detected him having sworn to his serving in the character of a spy last year, he was condemned to be hanged, except he would make some important discoveries; and was accordingly reconducted ashore for execution: however, being brought to the fatal tree, and disdaining so ignoble an exit, he stepped up to the commanding officer and requested he would remand him to the frigate, and he would satisfy the general in every particular he wished to be informed of.

This being complied with, he says, 'that the whole force of the enemy, between les Trois Rivières and Quebec, consists of seven picquets and one company of grenadiers, amounting to four hundred men; that two battalions of regulars, with a body of Canadians and Indians, are posted at l'Isle Royale, Isle au Noix, Isle Galot, etc etc and that the remainder of the French army are cantoned between the Three Rivers and Montreal, who, upon the first signal, are to repair, without loss of time, to the island of Montreal, and defend it to the last extremity'; he adds, 'that their capital is a place of no strength; that they have no artillery there, except the brass field-pieces taken from us on 28 April; and, at the Three Rivers, are six pieces of cannon, one mortar and about thirty men. Moreover, that our armament strikes the greatest terror imaginable, as the enemy are apprehensive lest General Murray should attempt to complete the conquest of Canada before the arrival of the other two armies, our forces being calculated at four thousand regulars, besides a body of marines and rangers.' A deserter came in this morning from Montreal, who acquaints us that the French army are greatly dissatisfied and mutinous; that the Canadians are abandoning their posts and concealing their effects; and, finally, that one quarter of a pound of meat, with a pound of indifferent black bread, to each man per day, is their only allowance, having no other kind of provisions, nor brandy nor wine.

Two armed boats went up to the Three Rivers to sound and, contrary to their expectations, discovered a channel along the south shore, and so close in with the land that they expected to have been fired upon, a body of Canadians having drawn up with their arms on the heights above them; but they were not molested: a person called out in our language, 'What water have you, Englishmen?' And being answered, 'Sufficient to bring up our ships and knock you and your houses to pieces; if you dare molest us, we will land our troops, burn your habitations and destroy your country'; whereupon an officer, as is supposed, starting up, replied, 'Let us alone, and you shall not meet with any annoyance; if your officers chuse to come ashore and refresh themselves, I will be answerable for their being at liberty to return when they please.' This invitation was not accepted, yet, as a mark of these people's (compulsive) sincerity, two canoes put off to our boats, with a quantity of greens and salading.

On 4 August both divisions unmoored and worked up abreast of Les Trois Rivières, where we came to an anchor close to the south shore, in seven fathom water. This government derives its name from one single river, which is about two leagues and an half to the northward of St Lawrence, where it discharges itself, branches out into three streams or rivulets, not fordable except for horses, and are intersected by two islands or uninhabited strips of land producing only rushes and under-wood; the capital, which is situated at a small distance higher up, is but an open straggling village, with batteries close to the banks of this river; it lies very low, and is a fair object for a bombardment: the French have always hitherto dignified it with the appellation of a garrison town of great consequence.

The inhabitants of the south coast come on board our ships without reserve, supplying us with vegetables, poultry, eggs and whatsoever else they can spare, in exchange for salt, pork and beef; on the former of these three articles they set the highest value, on account of the eels and other fish, which they are desirous to preserve against the winter. The Canadians say, if our fleet should remain here a week to intercept the communication between the garrison and the south country, they, being in such distress for provisions, would be compelled to disperse and abandon their works at the village; but a delay here on this account would be absurd, as that wretched place must share the fate of Montreal and the remainder of the country upon our junction with the other armies acting by the lakes. The enemy appear jealous of our landing at Trois Rivières, and are therefore very diligent in throwing up retrenchments to cover the most accessible places.

Our fleet sailed on the morning of the 8th; upon the signal being made to get under sail, the armed vessels and floating-batteries ranged themselves half channel over, opposite to the enemy's batteries, and remained in that situation until the whole of our convoy had passed the village: the troops, apparently about two thousand, lined their different works, and were in general cloathed as regulars, except a very few Canadians and about fifty naked Picts or savages, their bodies being painted of a reddish colour, their faces of different colours, which I plainly discerned with my glass; and otherwise whimsically disfigured, to strike terror into their enemies: their light cavalry, who paraded along shore, seemed to be well appointed, cloathed in blue, faced with scarlet; but their officers had white uniforms; in fine, their troops, batteries, fair-looking houses, their situation on the banks of a delightful river, our fleet sailing triumphantly before them, with our floats drawn up in line of battle, the country on both sides interspersed with neat settlements, together with the verdure of the fields and trees, afforded, with the addition of clear pleasant weather, as agreeable a prospect as the most lively imagination can conceive.

The ground round the E and NE parts of the village is high, with a steep sandy bank to the river, and a breast-work on the summit of it, terminating, or rather communicating with, two small redoubts thrown up on two points of land: the upper part is low, almost level with the water; but they have been at much pains to intrench it to a windmill about a quarter of a mile above the place, where they have erected a strong redoubt, communicating again to a larger one, on an eminence about three hundred yards NW of the mill where I could perceive they had some guns mounted: and, between the village, the intrenchments along shore and these two redoubts, were various traverses and other works indicating an intention to have disputed every inch of ground with us if we had made a descent there; which it may be presumed they expected. Their houses are built of wood, except the churches and convents, which are of stone and very magnificent; yet, upon the whole, the village of Trois Rivières has all the appearance of an infant settlement situated in a barren part of the country; immediately opposite to it is the parish of the Recollects, who have a college at the Three Rivers: the land there is well cultivated, seemingly fertile, and abounding in every thing.

I think nothing could equal the beauties of our navigation, with which I was exceedingly charmed: the meandring course of the channel, so narrow that an active person might have stepped ashore from our transports either to the right or left; the awfulness and solemnity of the dark forests with which these islands are covered, together with the fragrancy of the spontaneous fruits, shrubs and flowers; the verdure of the water by the reflection of the neighbouring woods, the wild chirping notes of the feathered inhabitants, the masts and sails of ships appearing as if among the trees, both ahead and astern; heightened by the promiscuous noise of the seamen and the confused chatter of the rapturous troops on their decks; formed, all together, such an inchanting diversity as would be far superior to the highest and most laboured description; in short, the novelist and the painter could here find copious entertainment in their respective professions exhibited in the rural and romantic and in the greatest perfection.

The people of this country have not so much the appearance of poverty as those immediately in the neighbourhood of Quebec and the lower country; I have been in a great many farm-houses since I embarked on this expedition, and I may venture to advance that in every one of them I have seen a good loaf—[or] two or three, according to the number of the family—of excellent wheaten bread; and such of the inhabitants as came on board our ships from time to time in order to traffick, disdained our biscuits upon being offered refreshments, and drew some good bread from their own pockets to eat with the victuals that were presented to them; in short, notwithstanding all that has been said of the immense distress and starving conditions of the Canadians, I do not find that there is any real want, except for luxuries, viz. pickled pork or beef, sugar, salt, pepper, ginger, soap, tobacco, spirituous liquors and wine; the meaner sort of people drink water, but the beverage of their betters is spruce-beer, sweetened with maple-sugar instead of molasses; while their superiors drink brandy and a small French red wine, which however they have not in great abundance.

All the troops went ashore on the Island of Ignatius that their transports may be cleaned out and aired: several detachments were employed in making fascines and picquets; the inhabitants returned to their settlements, as did those of Isle Dupas and Isle de Castor, who all delivered up their arms and took the oath of neutrality: five Indians were sent to these people by M. de Lévis to desire them to continue to defend their country, and they should have a sufficient reinforcement to compel us to keep on board our ships. The Canadians inform us that they have heard a heavy firing of cannon for several days together, which ceased on Sunday morning, the 10th instant. We are told that M. de Lévis and M. Dumas are intrenched, with four thousand men, at a place called Bartré, between two and three leagues to the southward, and abreast of our fleet; the troops at Sorrel, under M. Bourlamaque, are indefatigable in adding to the strength of their works, and we are informed the priest of the parish is their principal engineer. The Louisbourg division made their appearance far astern of us on the morning of the 16th, and in the evening some boats came up from them to the general.

The enemy still continue to honour us with their attendance; the Louisbourg division joined us this morning and, at seven o'clock, the whole fleet weighed together; but, the current being strong and the wind failing us, we were obliged to come to an anchor about noon, in seven fathom: in our soundings we had not less than five and a half. The division under Lord Rollo did not steer our course in passing through Lake St Peter, but kept to the southward of those islands, where the redoubts were thrown up to cover the boom laid across the channel. When his lordship lay off St Francis, an Englishman went on board his ship to demand protection for himself, nineteen of his countrymen, and ten women who had been carried off at different times from our back settlements; being asked why did they not surrender to General Murray, he answered that it was their intention, but they were told by the priests if ever they came among us, they would be instantly hanged; however, tired of their captivity, they cast lots, upon the appearance of the succours from Louisbourg, to see which of them should venture on board to make application for their enlargement and protection; this being accordingly granted, a signal was made to his fellow-captives who were waiting on the shore, and they all came off, with their effects, in batteaus.

The garrison at Quebec being augmented by the recovery of our sick and wounded, the general has transmitted orders to Colonel

Fraser to form a detachment from the troops under his command, and proceed to reduce the fortress of Jacques Cartier. A descent being meditated against Sorrel, the Louisbourg brigade fell down to the Island of Ignatius, under pretence of procuring fire-wood; on the 21st, in the morning, the floating-batteries were detached and, late at night, a division of flat-bottomed boats followed them. On the 22nd, at one o'clock in the morning, Lord Rollo and the regiments under his command, with the rangers, got into their boats and rowed off: about two they landed near a mile below Sorrel, burned many houses and laid waste the greatest part of the parish; this disagreeable procedure affected the general extremely, but the obstinate perseverance of the inhabitants in arms made it necessary, as well for their chastisement as *in terrorem* to others.

His excellency, in his letter to Mr Secretary Pitt, expresses himself very pathetically on this occasion: 'I found the inhabitants of the parish of Sorrel had deserted their habitations and were in arms; I was therefore under the cruel necessity of burning the greatest part of these poor unhappy people's houses; I pray God this example may suffice, for my nature revolts when this becomes a necessary part of my duty.' After this service was performed, his lordship marched up within view of the enemy's works, formed the line of battle, and endeavoured, by small parties, to draw them out of their intrenchments, but they did not think proper to indulge him; so that, having called in all his scouts, he reimbarked his troops and returned to their ships without any accident. The country, hence to Montreal, appears to be well inhabited and very populous; the navigation is exremely agreeable to the eye, the river being interspersed with a multiplicity of beautiful islands, some rude, but the greatest part of them are cultivated.

On the 23rd, the fleet weighed and, after a run of three hours, we came to an anchor off Contrecœur in ten fathom, the enemy politely attending us, as we advanced: this is about nine leagues from the object of our wishes; we have various accounts from prisoners and deserters of the armies under General Amherst and Brigadier Haviland, but they are too vague and contradictory to deserve any attention. I am inclined to think, if the artillery and ammunition, which the enemy lost and expended before Quebec last spring, had been carefully reserved for the defence of the upper country, they might have been rendered much more serviceable against this armament by the narrowness of the river in many places; for, if they did not intirely frustrate our measures, they might annoy our ships and forces very sensibly, and retard our operations.

The troops are ordered to be completed to thirty-six rounds of good cartridges, with three flints per man, and to be in readiness to land at the shortest notice. A soldier of the seventeenth regiment, who says he was made prisoner last year and has now made his escape, was brought off from an island ahead by one of our guard-boats; he relates that General Amherst has interrupted the communication between l'Isle Royale and Montreal, where the bulk of the French army, consisting of·five thousand men composed of regulars and chosen Canadians, are now assembled; that the Indians have abandoned them, notwithstanding the greatest arguments were used to prevail on them to continue; and that many of the militia, who had been draughted to complete their French battalions, deserted in such numbers that three have been lately hanged for examples to others.

A great firing of artillery has been heard, for several days and nights, by the people of the country. By the various reports of prisoners, deserters and those who are now become neutrals, Monsieur de Lévis's intire aim seems to incline to an action with this army before the arrival of the commander-in-chief and the corps expected by the Isle au Noix. The enemy have lately made many efforts to get a prisoner from the main army, in which they succeeded; but, being closely pursued, they butchered him with their war-hatchets to prevent his being retaken alive. We are told that all the British deserters in the French troops are actually gone off to Louisiana, and that M. Vaudreuil did once entertain thoughts of abandoning Canada and flying to that country; but had been prevailed on to alter his system, and share the fate of this colony: the deserters are commanded by one Johnston, a proscribed rebel, who is a lieutenant in the French service. We hear of great discontents, as well among the regulars as the Canadians, who, taking the advantage of the times, affect great indifference to good order and discipline, insomuch that the French officers are obliged to substitute intreaties in place of authority.

We have received intelligence, by a letter found ashore without any date, that Isle au Noix was abandoned, and that Fort Lévis, on l'Isle Royale, after a few days' siege, had surrendered to General Amherst; this letter also mentioned, that a spy was taken at Sorrel, *et que l'on a lui cassé sa tête d'une hache*: however, he was no spy, for, by better authority, the affair was as follows: a soldier deserted lately from the forty-third regiment, and another soon followed from the Royal Americans; the enemy, persuaded that men in their senses would not desert a plentiful and victorious army to share their miser-

CHEVALIER DE LÉVIS

able fate, concluded they must be spies, and therefore gave one of them up to the Indians, and killed the other with a hatchet, as before-mentioned.

M. Colonel de Bougainville commands the troops opposed to Brigadier Haviland, and M. Bourlamaque has a corps of observation consisting of five thousand men at a parish to the southward of Varenne, where it is pretended he will unite with the colonel in case of being compelled to retire, and fall upon the Brigadier as soon as he shall advance: M. Bourlamaque likewise threatens to destroy Mr Murray's forces if we should attempt a junction with Mr Haviland; fifteen hundred men are intrenched on the island of St Helen, opposite to Montreal, and the Chevalier de Lévis commands on the north side of the river; such, we are told, is the present disposition of the French army.

Late on the night of 3 September an officer of the Royal Americans in disguise, with four rangers, arrived from Brigadier Haviland's corps, who they say will actually be at La Prairie in two or three days at farthest. Several French grenadiers deserted to us early this morning; they inform us that M. Bourlamaque is advantageously posted, with twelve hundred men and four pieces of cannon, to oppose the brigadier: that his command did amount to seventeen hundred men, but five hundred of them have abandoned him, and it is not improbable the rest may follow their example. The regulars now desert to us in great numbers, and the Canadian militia are surrendering by hundreds. The detachments at Varenne lay off last night in their boats, as on the preceding night; and returned to the church this morning.

General Murray has dispersed manifestoes from thence to all the neighbouring parishes, acquainting the inhabitants, 'that if they will surrender and deliver up their arms, he will forgive them; if not, they know what they may expect, from the examples which he has hitherto reluctantly given them; and, as for such Canadians as have been 'incorporated in the battalions of regulars, if they will surrender by a day limited, his excellency will not only reinstate them in their settlements and lands, but likewise enlarge and protect them; but if, after all, they shall still persist, they must expect to share the fate of the French troops, and be transported with them to Europe, etc.' This had a happy effect on these brave unfortunate people; for this evening four hundred of them, belonging to the parish of Boucherville, came to Varenne and delivered up their arms: after taking the customary oaths, they requested the general would give them safe-guards for their parish, which was granted, and a serjeant's party were immediately sent off with them to protect them from our savages, who, they say, are within a day's march of them. M. Bourlamaque is retired to the island of St Helen, being totally abandoned by the Canadians.

The remainder of the troops disembarked, and incamped on the north side of the fertile, pleasant and well cultivated island of St Teresa. Crowds of Canadians are surrendering to us every minute, and the regulars, worn out with hunger and despair, desert to us in great numbers.

On the morning of the 5th the General and Colonel Burton, with the grenadiers, light infantry and rangers of this army, crossed the river and marched to Longville, or Longueuil, to reinforce Brigadier Haviland and protect the country from our Indian allies as they advance; at the same time a captain, three subalterns and one hundred men passed over to take post in the church of Varenne. M. de Lévis, with the remainder of his principal officers and regulars, have retired to the capital. Lord Rollo commands at present on the Island of Teresa. I was assured by some deserters to-day that the commander-in-chief's army were arrived at Perrot Island, within less than four leagues of the city of Montreal; in this case his most Christian majesty is in a fair way of being speedily *checkmated* in Canada.

Brigadier Haviland has reduced Fort Chambly, where he found some of our brass field-pieces; the van of his corps arrived yesterday at Longueuil, and they report that Sir William Johnson, with a large body of Indians computed at fourteen hundred, will be there this day from General Amherst's army. Eight Sachems, of different nations, lately in alliance with the enemy, have surrendered, for themselves and their tribes to General Murray: these fellows, after conferring with his excellency, and that all matters had been adjusted to their satisfaction, stepped out to the beach opposite to Montreal, flourished their knives and hatchets, and set up the war-shout; intimating to the French that they are now become our allies and their enemies.

While these chieftains were negociating a peace, two of our Mohawks entered the apartment where they were with the general and Colonel Burton: after viewing the others with great earnestness, they made a set at that side of the room, in order to seize upon them; but the general and colonel interposed, and exacted a promise from the Mohawks that they would not molest the others, who had been put out for a few minutes and were again called in; upon their re-entering, they looked eagerly at each other, uttering *heh! heh! heh!* with great vehemence; after which one of the Mohawks expressed himself, in disjointed sentences, to the following effect: 'It is well for you that you have surrendered—and that these generals are here—it is they that protect you—or we two Mohawks would scalp every man of you.' Hereupon one of the French warriors took a small stick with his knife, and notched it: the other then re-assumed —'Do you remember when you treacherously killed one of our brothers at such a time?—Ye shall one day pay dearly for it, ye cowardly dogs—let the treaty be as it will—I tell you, we will destroy you and your settlement—root and branch—ye are all cowards—our squaws are better than you—they will stand and fight like men—but ye sculk like dogs, etc etc.' Between every pause the French chief uttered *heh! heh!* and repeated his notches on the stick, till at length, being reproached with cowardice and equalled to the squaws, he could no longer contain himself, but set up a horrid yell and, with a tenfold emotion, cut a long sliver off the stick, which seemed to be a signal for his companions to fall on; but the general and colonel exerted themselves in keeping the peace, put the Mohawks out of the room, and laid both parties under the strongest injunctions not to molest each other, on pain of being most severely chastised by the commander-in-chief.

General Murray and Colonel Burton, with the grenadiers, light troops and detachment, returned from the south coast early this morning: the latter were relieved by a body of rangers under Major Rogers. Soon after the following orders were issued out to the army on the Island of Teresa.

ORDERS                                                              7 September
'The army will get to cross the river as soon as possible; the tents to be struck, and the baggage to be carefully packed up and left in care of a guard, which will consist of one serjeant and six men from each corps, and a subaltern from each brigade. The first landing will consist of grenadiers, light infantry, with the first brigade, and as many of the third as the boats will contain; the boats will immediately return for the remainder of the troops. Should the enemy oppose the debarkation, the troops will quickly form under the bank, and instantly march up, charge them with their bayonets, and give them one discharge; the light infantry and rangers will endeavour to gain the nearest the enemy's flanks, and pursue them spiritedly when they fly; in which they must be supported by the grenadiers with vigour and vivacity. The boats of the light infantry will be upon the left flank; those of the grenadiers between them and the battalions; and the rangers upon the right.

'When the enemy has been routed, or should we land without opposition, the brigadiers will form the line, with a reserve agreeable to their former orders. The army will march from the left in two columns; Colonel Burton will lead the right column, and Brigadier Howe the left: Lord Rollo of course, in his place, will be at the head of that part of his brigade which will be of the right column. The vanguard of the army will consist of three companies of light infantry, supported by three companies of grenadiers, two from the first and one from the third brigade, commanded by Lieutenant-Colonel Agnew; the fourth company of light infantry will cover the flank of the right column. The rear-guard will consist of the rangers and Major Scott's battalion. Should the enemy attempt the flanks of the right column, Brigadier Howe will form the line, with their front to the woods if a considerable body of the enemy should be in front; but, if there should not, he will form his brigade only to the front, in order to oppose them: in either of these cases the general will dispose of the reserve; and the light infantry will do their utmost to cover the forming of the army, by skirmishing to check the enemy: but, when the army is formed, they will give *overflanks*, viz. the Louisbourg companies on that of the right, and those of Quebec on that of the left. The pioneers, with the quarter-masters, will march with the van-guard, and must be completed with tools from the train. The regulars and light troops of General Amherst's army wear green boughs to distinguish them from the different corps of the enemy; our army will do the same; and the soldiers will be very careful they do not fire upon our friends, as the commander-in-chief's army are actually landed on the Island of Montreal. The two field-pieces will march at the head of Brigadier Howe's brigade; and, upon the assembly-beating, the army will get under arms.'

This morning, at eight o'clock, our army were ordered to accoutre and prepare to march: at ten our camp was struck, tents and baggage packed up, boughs mounted in our hats, and all were in readiness; between one and two we embarked, and soon after landed, without opposition, at the lower end of the parish of Point aux Trembles, on the Island of Montreal. The place where we disembarked is about three leagues and an half from the city. The country-people brought horses to draw our artillery, and others saddled for the officers to ride, besides carts for our baggage. We marched through a delightful country and a pleasant village bearing the name of the parish, where there is a convent of nuns, whose inhabitants, with their curate, or rector as among us, came to the door and saluted us as we passed, and told us we were welcome; at the same time the roads were lined with men and women who brought pitchers and pails of milk and water for the refreshment of the soldiers, with many courteous expressions of concern that they had not better liquor for the officers.

We met with frequent interruptions in our march, the enemy having destroyed all the bridges before us, which retarded our motions insomuch that, by nine o'clock, we got no farther than the parish of Longue Pointe, where, the night being dark, we received orders to take up our quarters in the houses and barns along the road, which are numerous, resembling a long straggling village; before we were thus cantoned, a few Mohawk Indians, from the south side of the river, passed us on the march, who were going express to General Amherst with the news of Brigadier Haviland and the forces under his command, being actually arrived within a day's march of the meadows and parish of Longueuil, opposite to Montreal.

At day-break, on the 8th, our advanced-guard, with the quarter-masters and pioneers, moved forward to repair the roads and bridges; about nine the army marched, but it was noon before we reached our ground on the north-east side of the city, where we immediately incamped, with the high cape or mount, whence this island derives its name, in the rear of the right of our line; and General Murray took up his quarters in the suburbs.

Before I resume the operations of the forces under the commander-in-chief, with the concerting and effecting this glorious junction of the three armies and the completion of the conquest of Canada, I cannot pass over in silence an event that has happened in the vicinity and government of Quebec; which, though inconsiderable, redounds to the honour of his majesty's arms in this country.

On this day Colonel Fraser, pursuant to orders transmitted for that purpose by General Murray, with the Majors Prevost and M'Pherson, a detachment of eleven captains, twenty-eight subalterns, forty serjeants, nineteen drummers and about nine hundred rank and file, with a suitable train of artillery, embarked and sailed from Quebec to reduce the fortress of Jacques Cartier; it was late on the evening of the 9th when they landed above the fort without opposition and instantly possessed themselves of an advantageous piece of ground which, by its unevenness, saved the colonel the trouble of erecting any cover, either for his guns or his men. As it was customary for ships to pass up and down since the departure of

the forces under the general, the enemy were not alarmed at the
movement of this little armament, neither did they suspect any
design against their post, from a belief that the garrison at Quebec
were too weak to undertake such an enterprise, or that it did not
deserve our attention, and well knowing that all would depend on
the fate of Montreal and the upper country; this being the case, an

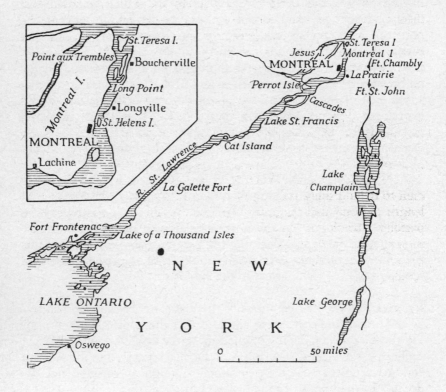

attack upon Jacques Cartier was not expected, particularly as the
general, in coasting upwards, had not discovered any design to
molest the enemy there, or at the Three Rivers. Colonel Fraser
having secured all the avenues leading from the fort to the country,
the detachment lay on their arms until the morning of the 10th,
when, a small party being advanced to reconnoitre the works of the
place, and the ships having by this time fallen lower down, the
garrison was alarmed and the drums beat to arms.

　　M. le Marquis d'Albergatti, the commanding officer, was then
summoned in form to surrender; but he refused, with great parade,
farcically returning the usual answer—*that he would defend that post*

*to the last extremity*; which was seconded by a discharge of a few guns. The colonel then ordered up two field-pieces and as many howitzers, under cover of a rising ground, to play upon the fort, and, at the same time, formed his corps into three divisions, being determined to storm the place without loss of time; all things being prepared, the assailants boldly advanced to the attack, which the marquis perceiving, instantly beat a *chamade* and surrendered at discretion. The garrison consisted of two lieutenants and fifty of the regulars, with one hundred and fifty militia, two gunners, and few indifferent guns, with a very trifling proportion of ammunition, but no provisions, except a few calves, pigs and poultry. After the garrison were disarmed, and the usual oath tendered to the Canadians, they were permitted to disperse and return to their respective habitations. The colonel then left a captain, two subalterns and fifty men at Jacques Cartier, and returned, with the remainder of his detachment and prisoners, by land to Quebec. The works of the place are in good condition, and very tenable against musketry, but are so extensive that they would require a garrison of fifteen hundred men to defend them properly: thus has this mighty fortress been at length reduced without any bloodshed, which was reputed so respectable a barrier on the side of the enemy, while, at the same time, it served as a rendezvous for all their detachments who, in the course of the winter, were such troublesome neighbours to our army at the capital.

# XIV

## French Canada Falls

*New France had no strength left. The final stages of the war were almost
a formality. Amherst had decided to take over the advance from the
Great Lakes as providing the most difficult line of approach. In the
event, apart from the hair-raising descent of his army in rowboats down
the upper St Lawrence rapids, the advance was militarily uneventful
once an enterprising army officer had mounted artillery on rafts and
destroyed the miniature French navy on Lake Ontario. Brigadier
Haviland had taken over the army on Lake Champlain and brushed
aside French opposition competently. With the vast distances involved
and the extreme difficulties in communication, which relied on occasional
colonial rangers slipping through the French lines and trackless forest,
co-ordination between the three British armies was remarkable.*

*Faced by overwhelming forces, the French in Montreal surrendered
without a final battle. Most of North America came under the British
flag. In spite of Knox's exultant postscript, it was a hollow victory.
The French cordon round the British colonies had been broken for ever.
But victory was also liberation for the American subjects of King George.
Fifteen years later they filled the vacuum and entered into their own
destiny.*

I COME NOW TO take a view of the proceedings of the army upon
the lakes, under the commander-in-chief.

Although M. de Lévis had made a vigorous effort for the recovery
of Quebec, and exerted his whole force and abilities to that important end, yet his endeavours, as I have already shewn, were by no
means propitious to his cause. On the contrary they contributed to
the success of our future operations in facilitating the final reduction
of Canada, the object of the campaign and the ultimate of the
general's wishes in America. With this view, three armies were proposed to rendezvous at Montreal: one to penetrate by Lake Champlain, to consist of regulars, rangers, provincials, etc commanded
by Brigadier-General Haviland; a second corps under Governor
Murray, with a suitable fleet, to work up from Quebec, composed of
the flower of the remainder of his garrison, reinforced by two intire
battalions from Louisbourg, amounting to between three and
four thousand men; while the commander-in-chief, reserving the

most difficult department for himself, proposed to enter the colony by the Lake Ontario which, with that of St Francis, communicates with the river St Lawrence a few leagues above the Island of Montreal.

How this arduous undertaking has been effected by the Brigadiers Murray and Haviland, the reader has already, in some measure, seen: it remains, however, to be noticed, that the latter sailed from Crown Point on the 11th of August, leaving Lieutenant-Colonel Foster, of the Royal, with a sufficient force to garrison and defend that post with its dependencies; that the enemy made no preparations to oppose this armament, except at the Isle au Noix, where, after giving the brigadier the trouble to break ground and erect batteries, they abandoned the island, and afterwards every other post in like manner, according as he advanced, until he reached Longueuil.

The greatest embarrassments now lay in the route of the main army, whence the enemy formed the highest expectations of being able to protract the intire reduction of the colony for some time longer, flattering themselves that the news of a peace might arrive, whereby the colony would be restored to the state in which we found it last year, and all the British troops be withdrawn. This, however, was mere delusion: a steady resolution and perseverance on the part of the commander-in-chief surmounted every difficulty and, by the most approved discipline and zeal of the troops, his excellency had the happiness to reap the fruit of his labours, to the accomplishment of which, every preparation was made. The regiments were completed, both Europeans and Provincials, as fast as they arrived at Albany, the place of their first rendezvous, and incamped: there they were instructed in the regular and irregular, if I may so express it, method of fighting, and exercised in firing ball; in fine, they were trained up in every particular that prudence, with experience, could dictate to render the troops expert in an open or covered country; thus were the general and army employed, until the season approached for opening the campaign.

It has already appeared that there was little or no preparation made to oppose Brigadier Haviland until he was well advanced; and then, if we may believe the country-people, they would have struck a blow, had they not been over-awed by the critical arrival of the forces from Quebec, with their frequent descents on the north and south coasts, which infused such terror in the Canadians that, to prevent military execution on their parishes, they dispersed: and this conduct had so great an effect upon the French regulars, who deserted their cause in such numbers, that those who remained were incapacitated from making any attempt on the brigadier's corps; moreover, having experienced that Governor Murray acted cautiously and did not appear disposed to undertake any thing of consequence, they turned their principal attention towards the commander-in-chief's army; reinforced such of their remaining frontier-posts in his route as time and circumstances permitted; detached scouting parties to watch his excellency's motions, or harass his troops in case of landing; and their armed vessels were in motion on Lake Ontario early in the month of June.

The general, with part of the troops, arrived on 9 July at Oswego. The French armed vessels appeared off the harbour, and, as our two snows [square-riggers], the *Onondaga* and *Mohawk*, were hourly expected, some batteaus were detached that way, hoping the enemy's vessels would endeavour to intercept them; but they disregarded them, and bore away for the Bay of Cataraqui. A fort is marked out to be constructed here, in which we are well seconded by the provincial troops, who furnish us with artificers of all professions; gallies are likewise building to proceed with the army; they are to mount cannon and to be worked with oars.

Several men, both of the regulars and provincials, who had inlisted to serve for a limited time, having applied for discharges, were refused: the general having issued orders that, as the service required it, no man should be discharged until the end of the campaign; but, in consequence of their being thus compelled to continue, a suitable gratification is directed to be paid to them respectively, which has prevented any discontents, many of them having desired to be re-inlisted.

All our advanced posts are ordered to intrench, to prevent a surprise; quarter and rear-guards are faced outwards, with the same directions to strengthen their ground. The army continues healthy, being supplied with fresh and salt provisions almost alternately; a market is established in the center of the line; spruce-beer is brewed, and issued to the men at three coppers, or English halfpence, per gallon; and fresh bread is baked for them according to the following regulation:

ORDERS                                                  23 July
'No baker, in this army, will be allowed to take more than one penny sterling for baking seven pounds of flour, which makes a loaf nine pounds weight; if the provincials pay the bakers in kind, they are not to take seven pounds of bread for seven pounds of flour, which is a shameful deduction from the portion allowed to the

soldier, and too exorbitant a profit to the baker; any of the corps are
at liberty to get it baked cheaper, if they can.'

The works at the fort are carrying on with great diligence; above
four hundred labouring men, with officers in proportion, are daily
employed there, besides artificers of every occupation; and a number
of ship-carpenters, etc are engaged in the navy-yard on the row-
gallies and repairing other vessels. The regiments are out alternately,
exercising and firing balls; for this purpose, stuffed gabions are fixed
up for them, that the shot may be recovered when ordered to be
sought for.

The troops were ordered to embark early on the morning of 10
August, but this business being unavoidably attended with great
delay, where such prodigious numbers of batteaus and other craft
are necessary, the general went forward with the remainder of the
regulars, leaving the provincials and rear-guard of the army to
follow with all convenient speed under Brigadier Gage. At night we
had a violent storm, which continued, whereby several batteaus and
boats were staved and lost, but very fortunately we had only one
man drowned. By the number of men left to garrison the different
posts behind us, and a variety of other casualties, the embarkation
return of the army does not exceed ten thousand one hundred and
forty-two: and, notwithstanding our strong muster of Indian warriors on the 5th instant, they are now, by desertion, reduced to seven
hundred and six.

The General having received intelligence by an Indian that one of
the enemy's vessels lies off La Galette, that the other is aground and
so much damaged that she cannot sail from the fort, his excellency
has determined not to wait for the snows, but to push forward with
all expedition, and rout the enemy from their advanced post at l'Isle
Royale, the only obstruction, we are told, we may expect in the
river, the navigation excepted. The General advanced on the 16th
with the five row-gallies, after first fixing an eight-inch howitzer on
board one of them, attended by the van of the army commanded by
Colonel Francis Grant, consisting of the grenadiers, light infantry
corps, and rangers: but, as it was late in the afternoon before we
reached the Point de Barille, an express was sent back to Brigadier
Gage, with orders, in case he cannot make that point, to land the
army on the north shore. Some time after, we got a view of the
enemy's brig, who, upon discovering us, fired signal-guns; upon
which, the weather being mild and favourable, we endeavoured to
push on and attack her, but, sable night interposing, we are obliged

to postpone it, and therefore have taken shelter in the south shore; the remainder of the army arrived very late at the Point de Barille.

The *Outawa* brig attempted to escape up the river very early on the 17th, but was interrupted by our row-gallies, commanded by Colonel Williamson, who attacked her vigorously, when, after an obstinate engagement of two hours and upwards, wherein she had fifteen men killed and wounded, her commander, M. Labroquerie, thought proper to strike; it has been observed before that four of these gallies carried each a brass twelve-pounder, and the fifth an howitzer. This is a remarkable action, and does great honour to the colonel, who was a volunteer on this occasion; for the brig mounted one eighteen-pounder, seven twelve-pounders, two eights, with four swivels, and had one hundred men on board, being a topsail, of near one hundred and sixty tons: she discharged seventy-two rounds; and the gallies, who had five officers and twenty-five artillery-men only exclusive of provincial rowers, fired one hundred and eighteen: the general was highly pleased at this capture, which he testified by his acknowledgements to the colonel and officers, with a generous reward to the gunners. Such was the service performed by four guns and one howitzer, with the sole loss of one man killed and two wounded; and such the prowess displayed in this fight by a land-officer in the Lake Ontario, that it deserves to be transmitted to the latest posterity, and registered among the most memorable naval engagements that are recorded in the British annals. Two engineers, with covering parties, were, immediately after the action, detached down the river to reconnoitre l'Isle Royale, with the adjoining coasts and islands. Brigadier Gage, with the main of the army, joined, from the Point de Barille; and the general having possessed himself of Oswegatchie, the whole incamped there.

The weather is exceedingly unfavourable to our operations, yet the general, intent on a vigorous prosecution of his measures, resolves to lose no time: the morning of the 13th was taken up with the repairs of the row-gallies and prize-vessel, and at ten o'clock the engineers, with the covering party, returned and made their report; but his excellency was predetermined, and the army are in readiness. The first division, consisting of the grenadiers, two battalions of light infantry, the right brigade of regulars, Scuyler's regiment, the greatest part of the Indians with Sir William Johnson, three row-gallies and some field artillery, are to proceed down by the north shore, commanded by the general in person; pass the fort, and take possession of the islands and coasts below it; at the same time the second division, composed of the left brigade of regulars, Lyman's regiment, two ranging companies, the remainder of the Indians and two row-gallies, under the command of Colonel Haldimand, to row down to the south coast and take post opposite to the fort, where they will not be exposed to the fire of the place, whilst the prize, now deservedly called the *Williamson* brig, under Lieutenant Sinclair, will sail down the center of the river, between the two divisions, with directions to moor at random shot from the fort; Brigadier-General Gage, with the rest of the army and the heavy artillery, to remain at Oswegatchie.

Such is the disposition his excellency made before the return of the engineers, and it was spiritedly executed accordingly, under a brisk and continued cannonade directed against the brig and the general's column, whereby one galley was sunk, ten men were killed and wounded, one of whom lost a thigh, and many batteaus and oars were grazed with shot; as the north division rowed in single files, it was eleven at night before the sternmost boat joined, and then the blockade of the fort was completely formed. Our Indians landed on the islands Gallop and Picquet, which the enemy abandoned with the greatest precipitation, having left a number of scalps, two swivel-guns, some barrels of pitch, a quantity of tools and utensils, with some iron, behind them; our Indians were so exasperated at finding the scalps, that they fired all their houses, not sparing even the chapel. Late in the night an attempt was made to weigh up the galley that was sunk, but we could not succeed.

The general, with Colonel Williamson and Lieutenant-Colonel Eyre, reconnoitred the fort on the 10th and the islands nearest to it, on two of which ground is made choice of for batteries, about six hundred yards from the fort, as also for a third on an advantageous point of land on the south shore; and detachments are immediately ordered to break ground, cut and make fascines, with every other preparation for carrying on the siege. Orders are sent to Oswegatchie for the heavy artillery, which are expected down this night.

The batteries were opened on the morning of the 23rd, and had such effect that the enemy drew in their guns and endeavoured to serve them *à couvert*. After some hours' firing, a disposition was made to storm the fort with the grenadiers of the army, in which the three vessels were to have assisted; for this purpose a number of marksmen were judiciously placed on board each ship, with a view of compelling the enemy to abandon their guns; and they were ordered to fall down on the fort, within the range of small arms; but whether the vessels were confused with the weight of the enemy's fire, or that the miscarriage may be imputed to the navigation or the wind, is difficult to determine; for the general, not approving of their manner of working down, sent orders to them to return to their former station, and desisted from his project for the present. The garrison expended a great deal of ammunition to little purpose; and our artillery were so well served that the enemy were rather shy of standing to their guns.

We have had warm cannonading on both sides, but their guns being at length dismounted by our superior fire, M. Pouchot, the governor, after displaying as much gallantry as could be expected in his situation, beat a *chamade* on the 25th, and, in the afternoon, capitulated for his garrison, who are become prisoners of war; they consist of two captains, six subalterns and two hundred and ninety-one men, all ranks included; they had a lieutenant of artillery, with twelve men, killed, and thirty-five wounded; our loss, in this siege, are, twenty-one men killed, and twenty-three wounded.

From the reduction of l'Isle Royale to the 30th inclusive, the army have been employed in repairing the fort, with our batteaus and other vessels, landing stores and provisions for the new garrison, which consists of two hundred men, with officers in proportion, under the command of Captain Osborne; as also for the sick and wounded, who are left in hospitals here to the number of two hundred and fifteen.

All things being prepared, the army proceeded down the river; we passed the rapids Galot and Plat, through a most terrifying navigation, without any accident; reached Cat Island where we incamped, about forty-four miles from Ontario. The country on both sides is seemingly fruitful, the ground level, some cleared, and some producing extensive veins of excellent timber of various kinds. The Indians exceedingly disappointed at not being permitted to butcher and scalp the late garrison of Fort Lévis, twenty whale-boats of them have deserted Sir William Johnson since the reduction of that fortress: this is quite uniform with their conduct on all occasions, whenever opportunity seems to offer for their being serviceable to us.

The army re-imbarked very early on the morning of 4 September, and put off; but the navigation was inconceivably dangerous, insomuch that the loss of the greatest part of the troops seemed inevitable: we encountered the rapids, *cotau du lac, battures des Cedres, Buisson, trou et le Cascade,* of which the two last are the most dreadful that can be imagined. The general, apprehensive lest the enemy, whose greatest dependence was placed in what might happen in working through those rifts, had provided a parcel of gallies and armed boats, with troops, to surprise the army, upon a supposition that it would be no difficult matter to rout or destroy them in this dismal passage, pushed through, regardless of his own safety, with all expedition, at the head of the grenadiers, light infantry battalions, rangers, row-gallies and a detachment of artillery, leaving Brigadier Gage, with the remainder of the forces, to follow more leisurely, one boat after another, hoping, by his own presence, to prevent a total discomfit in case of an enemy being immediately before him: his excellency most happily effected this passage with the loss only of forty-six batteaus, seventeen whale-boats and one row-galley, whereby eighty-four men were unfortunately drowned, a few pieces of ordnance, and some stores and provisions lost: trifling, indeed, to what otherwise might have happened if the enemy had been more attentive to this place, which it was extremely natural to suppose they would; and why they disregarded a project of this kind is amazingly unaccountable. The greatest part of the army worked through without any farther accident and reached l'Isle Perrot, about two miles from the river St Lawrence; but, it being too late for the remainder to join, they were obliged to put ashore, and incamp by themselves.

The troops halted to repair their whale-boats and batteaus, which afforded time for the rest to come up, who joined us next day; there are several settlements on this island, but the inhabitants abandoned them and concealed themselves in the woods; some of them were afterwards taken, and others, seeing there was no violence offered to their houses, came in and took the oath of neutrality. The poor creatures rejoiced that they have now so fair a prospect of peace and quietness, and expressed the greatest astonishment at the excellent discipline kept up in this army, particularly among the Indians, of whom they were under the greatest apprehensions.

The army reimbarked at day-break on the 6th, rowed along the south coast in four divisions and, having no farther obstructions in the river, happily arrived in a few hours at Lachine, on the south-west end of the Island of Montreal, the period of our labours, without any material opposition. The enemy were more complaisant to General Amherst than to their old acquaintances from Quebec, his excellency having only one bridge to repair as he advanced: the greatest part of the army marched on directly towards Montreal, about two leagues and a half from the place of landing, where five battalions of provincials remained in charge of the batteaus, etc etc. The general formed the troops at a small distance from the city on the north-west side of it, got up ten field-pieces from three to twelve-pounders, detached the picquets of the line to cover his ground, and doubled all his advanced sentries; the same steady precautions were taken at Lachine, and the whole army lay on their arms this night.

Two French officers came to one of the advanced-posts on the morning of the 7th, and, desiring to be conducted to the commander-in-chief, presented him with the following billet, dated from Montreal:

'SIR,
'I send to your excellency M. de Bougainville, Colonel of Infantry, accompanied by M. de Laas, a Captain of the Queen's regiment; you may rely on all that the said colonel shall say to your excellency in my name, etc etc.

VAUDREUIL.'

The conversation, that ensued between the general and the colonel terminated in a cessation of hostilities until noon, at which time proposals for capitulating were sent out and returned by the general, along with his own and the annexed letter:

'SIR,                                       Camp before Montreal
'I am to thank your excellency for the letter you honoured me with this morning by Colonel Bougainville; since which, the terms of capitulation which you demand have been delivered to me. I send them back to your excellency with those I have resolved to grant you; and there only remains for me to desire, that your excellency will take a determination as soon as possible, as I shall make no alteration in them. If your excellency accepts of these conditions, you may be assured that I will take care they shall be duly executed, and that I will take a particular pleasure to alleviate your fate, as much as possible, by procuring to you, and to your retinue, all the conveniences that depend on me.

JEFFREY AMHERST.'

This was followed by an exchange of letters here subjoined:

The Marquis de Vaudreuil to General Amherst.
'I have received the letter your excellency has honoured me with this day, as well as the answer to the articles which I had caused to be proposed to you by M. de Bougainville. I send the said colonel back to your excellency; and I persuade myself that you will allow him to make, by word of mouth, a representation to your excellency which I cannot dispense with myself from making.'

AN EAST VIEW OF MONTREAL

The general, being determined upon the surrender of the colony on his own terms, declined an interview with M. de Bougainville by sending Major Abercromby to receive the foregoing letter, to which his excellency returned the following answer:

'Major Abercromby has, this moment, delivered to me the letter with which your excellency has honoured me, in answer to that which I had addressed to you, with the conditions on which I expect that Canada shall surrender: I have already had the honour to inform your excellency that I should not make any alteration in them; I cannot deviate from this resolution. Your excellency will therefore be pleased to take a determination immediately, and acquaint me in your answer whether you will accept them or not.'

The general then received a letter from the Chevalier de Lévis, which, with his answer, came next in succession:

'I send to your excellency M. de la Pause, assistant quarter-master general to the army, on the subject of the too rigorous article which you impose on the troops by the capitulation, and to which it would not be possible for us to subscribe; be pleased to consider the severity of that article. I flatter myself that you will be pleased to give ear to the representations that officer will make to you on my part, and have regard to them, etc etc.'

When the bearer of this billet saw that the general had perused its contents, he attempted to support the chevalier's complaint respecting the article alluded to: but his excellency commanded him to silence, and told him, 'he was fully resolved, for the infamous part the troops of France had acted in exciting the savages to perpetrate the most horrid and unheard of barbarities in the whole progress of the war, and for other open treacheries, as well as flagrant breaches of faith, to manifest to all the world, by this capitulation, his detestation of such ungenerous practices, and disapprobation of their conduct; therefore insisted he might decline any remonstrances on this subject.' When the General had thus nobly expressed his sentiments to M. de la Pause, he dismissed him with the following answer to the letter adressed him by the Chevalier:

'The letter which you have sent me by M. de la Pause has this instant been delivered to me: all I have to say in answer to it is that I cannot alter, in the least, the conditions which I have offered to the Marquis de Vaudreuil; and I expect his definitive answer by the bearer on his return; on every other occasion I shall be glad to convince you of the consideration with which I am, etc.'

T

Brigadier Murray, who was now on the eastern extremity of the island, having received certain information of General Amherst's army being actually arrived before the city, and concluding, from the apparently peaceable disposition of the islanders, a choice of authentic intelligence, and many other circumstances conformable to the present crisis, that the governor-general might be in treaty with our commander-in-chief, advanced in great order with the forces under his command, and two twelve-pounders in front, towards the city, to add weight to the general's measures and to be nearer at hand to co-operate with his excellency in case any event might happen to make it necessary. By the time we had reached Long Point, the brigadier received an express from the general, by which he acquainted him that a cessation of hostilities had taken place, that proposals for capitulating were sent out to him, and that the enemy were deliberating on those he was resolved to grant and had transmitted to them in return; to which he demanded, and was in hourly expectation of, a final determination and answer: the general desiring an expert officer from our troops might be instantly transmitted to him, from whom he could get certain information of such matters as he wished to know respecting our armament, the navigation up the river, the face of the country, and the posture of affairs at Quebec. Captain Malone, of the forty-seventh regiment, was immediately detached for this purpose; at the same time, the night being very dark, the roads indifferent and in some places rendered impassable by a number of bridges broken up, the brigadier thought proper to canton his forces, except the van and rear guards, who lay on their arms until morning; as did likewise the commander-in-chief's army, as on the preceding night.

Early on the morning of the 8th, the general received the following letter from the Marquis de Vaudreuil, dated from the city, as before:

'I have determined to accept the conditions which your excellency proposes: in consequence whereof I desire you will come to a determination with regard to the measures to be taken relative to the signing of the said articles.'

The general then returned this answer by Major Abercromby, who was charged to bring back the articles of capitulation, signed by the Marquis de Vaudreuil: 'In order to fulfil so much the sooner, on my part, the execution of the conditions which your excellency has just determined to accept, I would propose that you should sign the articles which I sent yesterday to your excellency, and that you would send them back to me by Major Abercromby, that a duplicate may be made of them immediately, which I shall sign and transmit to your excellency. I repeat here the assurances of the desire I have to procure to your excellency, and to the officers and troops under your command, all possible conveniencies and protection: for which purpose I reckon that you will judge it proper that I should cause possession to be taken of the gates and place guards immediately after the reciprocal signature of the capitulation: however, I shall leave this to your own convenience, since I propose it only with a view of maintaining good order, and to prevent, with the greater certainty, any thing being attempted against the good faith and terms of capitulation; in order to which I shall give the command of those troops to Colonel Haldimand, who, I am persuaded, will be agreeable to you.'

M. Vaudreuil having immediately signed the capitulation, and thereby surrendered Canada to his majesty's arms, the general lost no time in returning him a counterpart thereof also signed, together with the following letter to the marquis:

'I have just sent to your excellency, by Major Abercromby, a duplicate of the capitulation which you have signed this morning; and, in conformity thereto and to the letters which have passed between us, I likewise send Colonel Haldimand to take possession of one of the gates of the town, in order to inforce the observation of good order, and prevent differences on both sides. I flatter myself that you will have room to be fully satisfied with my choice of the said colonel on this occasion.'

While these important affairs were in agitation this morning, Brigadier-General Murray and his troops were in motion: and having received intimation from Captain Malone that, in proceeding last night towards General Amherst's camp, he fell in with the enemy's advanced post, where he was detained a prisoner, notwithstanding the strongest remonstrances, without effect, to M. Bourlamaque of the injustice of such a detention; whereupon the brigadier, justly exasperated at so inconsistent and ungenteel a procedure, pushed forward with grenadiers and light troops, leaving orders that the main body, with the artillery, should follow as fast as possible: several expresses were sent out to request the brigadier would not advance, for the enemy were very apprehensive of our resenting the insult offered to Mr Murray and his forces in the person of Mr Malone, but it was to no purpose; we marched on until we got within a little way of an advanced redoubt, where we halted and made a disposition for an attack; which the enemy perceiving, immediately presented a flag of truce, and M. Bourlamaque advanced singly under another flag and desired to have the honour of a conference with Governor Murray, who instantly stepped up to him.

However, all the rhetoric that the former could urge had no weight; for his excellency assured him, if Captain Malone was not sent out to him in the space of five minutes, he would commence hostilities and not leave one stone upon another in Montreal. The brigadier, having thus declared his intentions, in order to inforce them, drew out his watch, and subjoined: 'Sir, go back to your post; I now allow you five minutes; if my officer is not returned to me before the expiration of that time, you must take the consequences.' Happily, however, before that short period was elapsed, an officer from General Amherst, accompanied by a French officer, came out to us on a full gallop, and acquainted the brigadier, 'that the articles of capitulation were ratified on both sides, whereby the French troops had consented to lay down their arms, and the colony had surrendered to his majesty'. Our project being thus frustrated, we marched on to our ground; and, the like notice being transmitted to Brigadier Haviland, now arrived with all his corps at Longueuil, the three armies incamped.

Upon Colonel Haldimand's taking possession of Montreal, he demanded the colours of the French regiments, as well as those of ours which had fallen into their hands in the course of the war: the former they refused, declaring, 'that, although each regiment had brought their colours with them from France, they found them troublesome, of little use in this woody country, and had therefore destroyed them'. If we may rely on their word, this must be since the memorable 13th of September, upon the adverse turn of their affairs; because it is notorious they had their colours that day in the field; and, if the cloud of smoke after the general fire had vanished half a minute sooner, I would actually have possessed myself of one stand, for the officer who carried them was wounded, and ill able to drag them off; they were a white silk flag, with three *fleurs de lys* within a wreath or circlet in the center part, and two tassels at the spear-end, all of gold.

This answer being transmitted to the general at camp, his excellency immediately insisted that the Marquis de Vaudreuil and the Chevalier de Lévis should affirm it on their *parole d'honneur*, which they instantly complied with, and then restored two stands of British colours that were taken from the late regiments of Pepperell and Shirley at Oswego, in the infancy of the war.

The critical and happy junction of our three armies at this place, effected in the space of forty-eight hours with so inconsiderable a loss, must appear extremely providential to the reader, when he reflects on the immense difficulties they had every-where to encounter, from a numerous and wary enemy, still infinitely heightened by the singular nature of the country and the dangers of an uncommon navigation, the most formidable and hazardous that can possibly be conceived: such an instance can scarcely be paralleled in any history, and will remain an everlasting monument of the conduct and intrepidity of the general and other officers who commanded on this particularly intricate service.

Having now deduced the French war in America to a glorious period, reflecting the highest honour on his majesty's arms, and extended the British empire in the new world, a final review of the most remarkable events that happened there, since the commencement of this work, cannot fail to be acceptable to every reader.

In the year 1757 we were said to be masters of the province of Nova Scotia, or Acadia, which, however, was only an imaginary possession; it is true, we had a settlement in Chebucto harbour, namely Halifax; a garrison at Annapolis Royal, one at Chiquecto, called Fort Cumberland; and three other insignificant stockaded intrenchments, Fort Sackville, Lunenburg, and Fort Edward, all in the southern peninsula; but the troops and inhabitants of those several places could not be reputed in any other light than as prisoners, the French being possessed of the north and north-east, with all the interior parts of it, considerably above three fourths of the whole; together with its islands, of which the principal are Cape Breton and St John. The condition of our provinces, west and south of Acadia, was truly alarming, the enemy having drawn a line from Cape Canseau, on the east side of the peninsula opposite to Cape Breton, across the Bay of Fundy to the river Penobscot in the province of Maine, through New Hampshire, New-England, and along the frontiers of Albany, through New-York and Pennsylvania, excluding also the greatest part of Virginia, by the Allegheny mountains, down through the Carolina's and Georgia, as far south as Cape Escondide, in the gulph of Mexico, claiming all the countries, lakes and rivers north and west of this line: which immense extent of territory they secured by a chain of forts, thereby depriving us of the greatest part of our most valuable settlements, and the benefit of the fur-trade with our Indian allies on the Lakes Champlain, Erie, and Ontario. Moreover, by frequent *sorties* and excursions from these numerous posts, which they could reinforce at pleasure, they continually struck terror into the unfortunate inhabitants of those countries by scalping and otherwise barbarously butchering our people of both sexes, of all ages; and dragging some, whose lives they chose to spare, into a horrible captivity. Such was the un-bounded power of France in the new world, and such the state of British America in the year 1757.

A respectable armament, under the Earl of Loudoun and Admiral Holburne, was sent out this year to reduce the islands of Cape Breton and St John, hoping thereby to curb the unparalleled in-solence of these restless and, I may add, faithless invaders; those isles, by their situation in the gulph of St Lawrence, being deemed barriers to Canada and the keys of the eastern navigation into the bowels of their country; at the same time General Webb was left at Albany to assemble a body of provincial troops to cover Fort William-Henry on Lake George, garrisoned by a body of regulars under Colonel Monroe. How the expedition to the eastward mis-carried, and what befel the brave but unfortunate colonel and his abandoned forces, would, I am of opinion, be unacceptable in the recital, especially as these events are still recent in all men's remem-brance: suffice it to say, the one did not take place, and the other was wrested from us and demolished, its garrison, after a gallant defence, being obliged to capitulate; and fell afterwards a prey, by the con-nivance of the French, contrary to that good faith which should subsist between Christian nations, to the fury of a merciless savage enemy, and this in the presence of the Marquis de Montcalm and his whole army. The enemy, farther encouraged by these successes, continued their depredations, spreading terror throughout our back settlements, and threatening destruction to our fortresses in Nova Scotia, which they flattered themselves they should be able to effect by surprise, with strong detachments from Louisbourg; but, by the disposition made of the forces by the Earl of Loudoun, their inten-tions were defeated: his lordship having reinforced the garrisons at Halifax, Annapolis, Fort Cumberland etc, assigning the command of the troops in that province to Major-General Hopson, while he, with the remainder of the army, proceeded to the southward to stop the enemy's career in that quarter.

In the year 1757 our affairs assumed a better aspect; for, though the army led by General Abercromby, then commander-in-chief, towards Crown Point, were roughly handled in storming the lines at Ticonderoga, with very considerable loss, yet the success of the armament against Cape Breton, under Admiral Boscawen and Major-General Amherst, and the happy consequences thereof, in a great measure, compensated for that fatal blow, and paved the way to our future conquests.

After the reduction of this important island, with that of St John, the general detached Brigadier Monckton up the Bay of Fundy, and Brigadier Wolfe up the River St Lawrence, to the bays of Chaleur and Gaspée, who respectively executed their orders in so masterly a manner, that the British forts and settlements in the province of Acadia were completely secured against any attempts from the enemy, the Indians of those countries, and the other barbarous inhabitants, being routed from almost every corner, with the loss of many lives, houses and effects, *the just punishment of all traitors*; besides, numbers of them, who fell into our hands, were transmitted, in captivity to Europe: in these expeditions Brigadier Monckton re established a fortress on the north side of Fundy Bay, at the entrance of the river St John; dignified it with the name of Frederic, and reinforced all the garrisons throughout the province, wherein he himself commanded the following winter.

General Abercromby, after his undeserved discomfit at Ticonderoga, took post at Lake George, with the remainder of his army, to cover the frontiers of New-York, Albany and New-England: thence he detached a corps of three thousand men to Lake Ontario, where he reduced Fort Frontenac, the object of the enterprise; and destroyed an immense quantity of stores, provisions and artillery, which proved a severe stroke to the enemy on that side, as there was their grand magazine whence the numerous chain of forts they had established to defend their encroachments were to have been supplied. The colonel made many prisoners, took nine armed vessels, from eight to eighteen guns, being the whole of their naval force on the lake, with a prodigious collection of furs, to an incredible amount; and this service was executed without any loss. Another fortunate circumstance derived, in a great measure, from the success of that enterprise, was that it facilitated the conquest of Fort Duquesne, now Pittsburgh, by which we recovered an extensive tract of fertile country, on the river Ohio; which expedition was admirably conducted, amidst innumerable difficulties, in this same year, by Brigadier-General Forbes; so that, upon the whole, we gained considerable advantages over the enemy in the course of this campaign.

In 1759 we were still more prosperous: General Amherst was now

(happy for his country and the honour of the British arms) commander-in-chief of all his majesty's troops and forces in America;
his excellency proceeded, with the greatest part of the army, by
Lake George and, upon his arrival before the once fatal lines of
Ticonderoga, he wisely erected batteries, drew up his artillery, and
besieged them in form: the enemy, perceiving the old inconsiderate
farce was no longer to be acted of attempting to surmount impossi-
bilities by a mere *coup de mousqueterie*, abandoned their trenches and
contiguous fort; and, shortly after, the fortress of Fort Frederic, or
Crown Point, in like manner. The general also detached some
troops, under Brigadier Prideaux and Sir William Johnson, to
Oswego, thence to Niagara, which was presently reduced after an
action with a respectable corps of the enemy, who advanced in full
expectations of relieving the place, but were defeated by Sir William,
the brigadier being unfortunately killed by an accident in the trenches
some time before. These several strong-holds being thus subdued,
the commander-in-chief ordered them to be repaired, and others to
be erected, more effectually to secure the countries bordering on the
lakes, for the safety of our Indian allies inhabiting thereon, and to
protect our frontiers.

Upon the general's receipt of the news respecting the death of
Brigadier Prideaux, Brigadier Gage was dispatched to take the command of those troops, with orders to proceed, after the reduction of
Niagara, and dispossess the enemy of another important post they
had on the west side of Cataraqui river, to the northward of Frontenac and Ontario, called La Galette; but the season being far advanced, and many other concurrent difficulties intervening, rendered
it impossible that time; so that the project was postponed to a more
favourable opportunity. Another corps was detached to the westward, under Brigadier Stanwix, to overawe the numerous tribes of
Indians inhabiting the borders of the Ohio, to complete the fortifications of Pittsburgh and Fort Ligonier, likewise to reduce the fortress
of Venango and Presqu'isle, in order to add greater weight to our
influence on the Lake Erie, in all which we succeeded to our wishes;
but the most important conquest, in the course of this campaign, was
that of Quebec and a great part of lower Canada: an armament was
sent up the river St Lawrence for this purpose and to co-operate
with the commander-in-chief in the reduction of the colony, under
Admiral Saunders and Major-General Wolfe, wherein the admirals
and general officers greatly distinguished themselves; the French
army, under the Marquis de Montcalm, being amused by Mr Wolfe
and lulled into a state of security, were, by the sole discerning judge-

ment of that eminent young general, allured from their strong retrenched camp and defeated; the able commanders of the land-forces were slain on both sides, and the loss of the enemy was considerable; ours trifling in comparison, all things considered, except in the death of our amiable and justly lamented general. In consequence of this perfect defeat, the capital of New France surrendered to Brigadier-General Townshend on very advantageous terms, General Monckton, his superior on that expedition, being then ill of a dangerous wound he received in the action.

The winter setting in early preventing General Amherst's advancing farther into the upper country, he therefore contented himself with securing his new acquisitions, garrisoned them with part of his army, and the remainder were quartered in such manner as to be able, not only to succour them in case of necessity, but to be earlier in readiness, by the next year, to penetrate effectually into the heart of the colony, and thereby complete the conquest of Canada. The forces under Brigadier-General Monckton, now in a fair way of recovery, remained in garrison at Quebec, under the command of Brigadier Murray, as governor, and Colonel Burton, as lieutenant-governor; Admiral Saunders, having furnished the place with artillery, ammunition and stores of all kinds, with every other necessary that could be required, a twelvemonth's provisions, with a considerable quantity of spirituous liquors, vinegar, etc etc sailed with his fleet for Europe, to receive the thanks of his sovereign, and acknowledgements of his country, for his steady and spirited conduct throughout the whole progress of this expedition.

The troops had no sooner taken possession of the garrison than they were menaced by M. de Lévis, who publicly declared his intentions of making a vigorous effort for the recovery of Quebec, as soon as the most severe part of the winter should set in. I shall not trespass on the reader by recapitulating all the *petites guerres* that happened in the course of this, or the preceding winter and summer campaigns; it is sufficient to observe that, though in some, and these in times past, we were worsted, yet, in general, we were successful, particularly in Canada proper, where they always redounded to the honour of his majesty's arms; but, passing these by, I shall enter immediately on 1760, a year remarkable in the annals of Great Britain, not only for the constancy and prowess of her troops, but the conspicuous abilities and faithful conduct of their several commanders, together with the total extirpation of the French dominions in North America.

After a winter's campaign, the most irksome and rigorous that can possibly be conceived, the Chevalier de Lévis, with the whole force of the colony, took the field and, in the latter end of April, appeared before Quebec, to put his long premeditated threats in execution, flattering himself with an easy conquest, especially as he was well acquainted with the sufferings of the garrison and their weakly condition by sickness and mortality, having buried a thousand men since they took possession of the place, and had double that number still in the hospitals; but, notwithstanding all these circumstances, and the great superiority of the chevalier's army, as to numbers, he found himself grossly mistaken. Brigadier-General Murray, in a great measure, surprised him by marching out with the gallant remains of his hitherto victorious forces, who, to use his excellency's significant and agreeable expressions on this occasion, *were in the habit of beating that enemy*, and gave them battle: the contest was obstinate, and well maintained on both sides; but the British troops, now more considerably reduced, were compelled to retire within their walls. The enemy however reaped no sort of advantage from our discomfiture, which, on their part, was dearly purchased: on the contrary, they were then in a worse condition than ever, for their loss fell mostly on their regulars; and, after besieging us for near three weeks, in which time the garrison were inconceivably harrassed, and performed prodigies, such as posterity will hardly give credit to, for the defence of their conquest, the enemy raised the siege, upon the arrival of a British squadron under Commodore Swanton, with the most unaccountable precipitation; leaving all their artillery, implements, stores, provisions, behind them: but they had first the mortification of being eye-witnesses to the destruction of their fleet, which were all burned and destroyed by our ships.

After the governor had indulged his troops with a few weeks' refreshment, he embarked the flower of his garrison, who were soon after reinforced by two regiments from Louisbourg, the fortifications of that famous city being ordered to be demolished; and sailed up the river to join General Amherst's army upon their arrival at Montreal. In this inland voyage, the brigadier made frequent descents on the north and south coasts, disarmed a number of parishes on both sides, dispersed manifestoes throughout the country, and compelled the greatest part of the inhabitants to submit, swearing them to an exact neutrality. In the execution of all these affairs, his excellency paid the most stedfast attention to the preservation of the conquest already made, and, sensible of its importance at that juncture, he wisely declined, though contrary to his own natural disposition and thirst for glory, to engage in any measures that could possibly put the success of the campaign to the least hazard; and, by this invariable conduct, he apparently defeated the hopes of the French generals, who not only attended him as his ships advanced, but lay *perdue* for him at different places, with the principal force of the country.

Upon the arrival of this armament at the Island of Teresa, near to that of Montreal, the brigadier landed and incamped his troops there to await the movements of the commander-in-chief; the first intelligence of moment his excellency then received, was the advance of a corps under Brigadier Haviland, who had been detached from the main army towards Crown Point, thence to penetrate by the Lake Champlain and the river Sorrel, with orders to rendezvous, in like manner, at or near Montreal. This service was also extremely well executed, for the enemy, having perceived by the precautions of that commander and the uniform steady conduct in all his proceedings that any resistance would be entirely fruitless, *fell back*, as he advanced: boasting at the same time of a resolution they had taken to make a firm stand at the Isle au Noix; which, however, upon the nearer approach of these forces, was abandoned, and the enemy continued to retire before the brigadier, until he reached the meadows opposite to the City of Montreal.

The army under General Amherst was early in motion, but the completing a numerous chain of forts, building sloops, gallies, rafts and other floats for this particular navigation; providing an incredible number of batteaus and whale-boats for transporting so great a force, with all its provisions, artillery, stores of every kind, and intrenching-tools, etc etc retarded his excellency's operations so long, that it was 10 August before the first division embarked at Oswego, and the remainder followed the next day, under Brigadier Gage. It is a matter of much greater difficulty than can possibly be conceived, to convey so considerable an army through the lakes and rivers of this uncommon country: such an undertaking required exquisite judgment, great deliberation and the most exact order to prevent, if possible, the various accidents to which a fleet of this nature were exposed in traversing the vast expanse of Ontario, besides a number of dangerous rapids between that inland sea and the Island of Montreal; which, notwithstanding the utmost circumspecion to prevent it, proved fatal to many men, upwards of fourscore of them being drowned, and several boats, with artillery, stores and provisions, staved to pieces. The general met with some opposition and farther delay at l'Isle Royale, the last effort of ex-

piring Canada: but this, with all other difficulties, were nobly surmounted by the activity and valour of the troops, and the incomparable conduct of their leaders; it must be universally confessed
there never was an expedition so admirably concerted, or executed
in so masterly a manner and with so inconsiderable a loss.

How well pleased the general was at the manner in which he was
seconded by the other principal officers, and at the behaviour of the
three armies, are best expressed in his own words: 'I should not do
justice to Governor Murray and Colonel Haviland if I did not
assure you they have executed the orders I gave them to the utmost
of my wishes. I must likewise beg leave to say I am obliged to
Brigadier-General Gage for the assistance he has given me; and I
have taken the liberty to give, in public orders, my assurances to the
three armies that I would take the first opportunity of acquainting
the king with the zeal and bravery which has always been exerted by
the officers and soldiers of the regular and provincial troops, as also
by his majesty's faithful Indian allies. Sir William Johnson has taken
unwearied pains in keeping the Indians in humane bounds; and I
have the pleasure to assure you that not a peasant, woman or child
has been hurt by them, or a house burned, since I entered what was
the enemy's country.'

Upon the whole, the mild, yet determined, method of negociating
with the Marquis de Vaudreuil does great honour to General
Amherst, while his moderation and humanity, which have so conspicuously appeared in the whole course of his command in America
and now more superlatively to a conquered ungenerous enemy, not
only reflects the greatest reproach on them for past cruelties and
repeated breaches of faith, which have at length provoked the
Almighty to confound all their devices, councils and measures, and
finally to deliver themselves and their country into our hands; but
likewise, adds a tenfold lustre to the general's conquest, denominat-
ing him the *hero* and the *Christian*; whilst it demonstrates to the
whole world the justice of our cause, and the authenticity of what
was so sensibly advanced by the immortal Wolfe in his first manifesto: 'The unparalleled barbarities exerted by the French against
our settlements in America might justify the bitterest revenge in the
army under my command: but Britons breathe higher sentiments
of humanity, and listen to the merciful dictates of *the Christian
religion.*'

On 14 September I had an opportunity of viewing the interior
parts of Montreal; and, for delightfulness of situation, I think I never
saw any town to equal it; besides the advantages of a less rigorous

climate, it is infinitely preferable to Quebec. It stands on the side of a hill sloping down to the river with the south country, and many gentlemen's seats thereon, together with the Island of St Helen, all in front: which form a most agreeable landscape, the river here being about three miles a-cross, I mean from the south side of Montreal to the south coast. Though the town is not of a considerable breadth from north to south, it covers a great length of ground from east to west, and is nearly as large and populous as Quebec; the streets are regular, the houses well constructed, and particularly the public buildings, far exceeding those of the capital of Canada in beauty and commodiousness; that of the Knights Hospitallers being extremely magnificent.

There are several pleasant gardens within the walls, in which however the owners have consulted profit and convenience more than elegance; among these are the sisters of the congregations, the nunnery-hospital, Recollects, Jesuits, seminary, and a sixth which, if I am not mistaken, is the property of the governor; besides these, there are many other gardens and beautiful plantations without the gates, such as the general hospital and the improvements of M. Linière, which exceed all the rest and are at an agreeable distance, on the north side of the town. I have been informed that the fathers of the order of St Sulpicius, at Paris, were proprietors of the island, which they held by grant or charter from the crown and produced them a considerable revenue. I saw no paintings or any thing remarkably curious in their churches or other religious houses; every thing carried an air of neatness, simplicity and plainness; how they may be on festival days I cannot take upon me to say.

There are six or seven gates, large and small, to this famous place, but its fortifications are mean and inconsiderable; it is surrounded by a slight wall of masonry, solely calculated to awe the numerous tribes of Indians, who resort here at all times from the most distant parts for the sake of traffic; particularly at the fair, a kind of carnival held every year and continues near three months from the beginning of June till the latter end of August; I have heard various accounts of this fair from the inhabitants of Quebec and Montreal, and the trade on with these barbarians; but they are so confused, contradictory and, withal, so marvellously romantic, that I shall pass them by in silence, my residence in the country after the conquest not affording me an opportunity of being an eye-witness to those scenes. The inhabitants are gay and sprightly, much more attached to dress and finery than those of Quebec, between whom there seems to be an emulation in this respect; and, from the number of silk robes, laced coats and powdered heads of both sexes, and almost of all ages, that are perambulating the streets from morning to night, a stranger would be induced to believe Montreal is intirely inhabited by people of independent and plentiful fortunes.

Having obtained General Amherst's permission to return to Europe for the re-establishment of my health, and Governor Murray's indulgence to repair to Quebec in order to settle some affairs preparatory to my departure from America, I set out, on the evening of the 15th, in a batteau, attended by a serjeant and six men, and provided with a quantity of sugar, salt, tobacco and pork, to inable me to traffic with the Canadians, in my passage, for poultry, pigs, etc against my intended voyage: knowing, at the same time, that it would afford me an opportunity of seeing some parts of the country, between Montreal and the capital, whereof my knowledge, until then, could be only superficial, by seeing it from on board our ships, by conjectures formed from those places where I had been obliged to land with the troops, or from the country immediately in the neighbourhood of Quebec. As I was my own commander, not pressed in point of time, and had not any thing to apprehend from either shore, the colony being now restored to peace and tranquillity, I was more at leisure to make such observations respecting this valuable conquest as I can with certainty communicate to the public, and which the reader may depend on.

I cannot take upon me to determine either the extent or boundaries of Canada, or the source of the river St Lawrence which runs through it; the former are variously fixed by French historians and geographers, while the latter is pretended to be derived from remote northern and north-western lakes, as yet unknown to Europeans: these chimerical absurdities seem to be now adopted by British writers, and consequently it is not improbable they will be thus transmitted to latest posterity; however, leaving these matters to more competent judges, and that I may not exceed the limits prescribed to myself, I shall confine my narrative of this country from Lake Ontario, the most natural source of this truly majestic river, to its gulph or entrance at Cape Ray on the island of Newfoundland, and to the lands and settlements immediately in view of this navigation, which I look upon to be the most interesting parts of this colony: the extensive forests backward of them being, to this day, chiefly in their rude primitive state, uninhabited and unfrequented, except by the savage aborigines and other chasseurs, or hunters, whose accounts are generally extravagant and erroneous. The entrance is formed by Cape Ray, beforementioned, on the north-east and north cape; on the Island of Cape Breton on the south-west, which is about one hundred leagues from Quebec, thence to les Trois Rivières, reputed the half-way to Montreal, thirty-three leagues; and, from Montreal to the north-east point of Lake Ontario, it is also by computation near seventy leagues: but there is another entrance into this river from the sea, which is north about, through the straits of Belle Isle; this, however, being very unsafe, is seldom frequented, except when heretofore French ships, or perhaps vessels carrying on a contraband trade with the enemy, wanted to avoid our men-of-war or frigates cruising in the gulph.

The islands in this long extent of river are almost innumerable, and many of them are inhabited and well-cultivated, particularly the Isles of Coudre and Orleans, below Quebec; those of Ignatius, Teresa, Montreal, and Jesus, with some of lesser note in that district, and several others to the south-west of them in the Lake St Francis, of which St Peter's is the principal; but, Montreal and Orleans being the most considerable, it may be necessary to say something of them. The former is near forty miles in length, and about thirteen, or four leagues and an half, in breadth where widest: the soil is exceedingly rich and good, producing all kinds of European grain, and vegetables in great abundance, with variety of common garden fruits; but the south side of it is the most inhabited, consequently the best culti-vated; and, besides the settlements or parishes which are numerous, the island is adorned with private villas for the retirement of the more opulent merchants, and others, in the summer season. There are no Indian inhabitants on Montreal, neither are they any where desirous of settling on islands, which, I am informed, proceeds from an hereditary distrust, lest they should at any time be surprised and cut off by Europeans.

By the situation of this second place of consequence in Canada, they are exceedingly well supplied with all kinds of fresh-water fish, some of which are unknown to us, being, I am told, peculiar to the lakes and rivers of this country; they have likewise neat black cattle, horses, pigs and poultry in plenty; and, from the neighbouring shores, they are supplied with the greatest variety of game imagin-able, in the different seasons; nor are the inhabitants beholden to the main river for their water, the island abounding with delightful soft springs, which form a multiplicity of pleasant rivulets. I have already said so much of that fertile and beautiful garden, the Island of Orleans, in the course of this work, that it only remains to be told, besides five parishes into which it is divided, there are several gentlemen's seats; and yet its extent does not exceed twenty-one miles, by near four where it is broadest.

The navigation of the river has been also treated of; but it may be proper to add, that, though king's ships, who have been once up to Quebec, may venture there a second time without pilots, their remarks being generally more accurate than those of trading vessels, yet strangers should, by no means, venture of themselves upon hearsay, or the reports of others; and, with respect to the upper parts from the capital to Montreal, it is true there is water enough for ships not drawing more than eleven feet, yet the navigation is both difficult and perplexing, the channel running sometimes by the north, at others by the south coasts; and, in tacking from one shore to the other, obstructions are frequently met with, such as rocks and shoals of sand or mud, which if, the Canadians may be credited (and it is not improbable), are frequently removed from one part of the river to another by the immense floats of ice that roll up and down with the currents at the breaking up of the winters. To this I shall subjoin that, as these currents are remarkably rapid in most places, all ships and vessels intended for this voyage should be extremely well provided with good and sufficient ground-tackle, and have it always in readiness, whether sailing in company or otherwise. There are no cataracts between Quebec and Montreal, as some writers have advanced, except a strong ripple at what are called the Rapids of Richelieu, between Jacques Cartier and Deschambault; but these are not of the least consequence, for, at high water, though the channel runs serpentine, yet there is a sufficient depth for a forty-gun ship.

It is true there are frequent interruptions in the navigation from Montreal upwards, particularly between that island and Lake St Francis; but the others, between the lake and l'Isle Royale, are more frightful than dangerous. Sloops, or barges of equal burden, cannot work higher up than Montreal, neither can they come farther down from Lake Ontario than to l'Isle Royale; but the intermedial difficulties may be surmounted by flat-bottomed boats, canoes or other small vessels. There are great variety of safe and commodious bays and harbours in this river, after clearing the islands of Cape Breton and St John; of which the principal are Chaleur, Gaspée, Tadousac, Chaudiere, and a great many others needless to be recited; but the haven of Quebec exceeds all the rest, where a hundred ships of the line may ride in the greatest safety. Upon the whole, this is a most valuable river, and, when you are a little way advanced within the gulph, you are no longer clouded with those fogs so endemial to the coasts of Nova Scotia, Cape Breton and Newfoundland, but what are usually met with at certain seasons in more moderate climates.

The lower part of the country, from the entrance, is generally wild, uncultivated and, on the south side, covered with dark impenetrable woods, mostly pine and dwarf spruce, with stupendous rocks and barren mountains, which form a most dismal prospect; while the north, for several leagues, is low, marshy, covered with strong reeds and rushy grass, close forests appearing at some distance to the northward of them. The first settlement you meet with, after clearing the frontiers of Nova Scotia, is at St Barnaby, on the south shore, about thirty leagues within the gulph, where we were regaled with a prospect of an open, seemingly fertile and civilised country; and, upon reviewing my observations and minutes of the numerous parishes from thence upwards, till you arrive at the settlements opposite to Montreal, I find them in general rich, open and well cultivated, producing corn, flax and vegetables; stocked with horned cattle, sheep, horses, swine and poultry; exceedingly well watered by innumerable tributary rivers, rivulets and smaller brooks, which disembogue themselves into the river St Lawrence, and are plentifully stored with salmon, eels and other fish peculiar to these waters.

The north country does not make so promising an appearance, there being no improvements or settlements until you reach what are called the King's Farms at Mal Bay, near the river Saguenny, haven of Tadousac: there the lands have undergone cultivation, the soil is kind and grateful for the labour and industry bestowed upon it; but the country east and north-east of these farms remains in its primitive state, *rudis indigestaque moles*, with lofty and steep banks to the river: the lands on the south side also rise gradually high and steep, after you clear the woody island of Anticosti, with trees and under-wood on the face of the declivities; and continue so, for the most part, on both coasts, all the way upwards. From Mal Bay to Cape Tourmente, an extent not less than thirty miles, is mountainous and barren; but then, doubling this cape, you are agreeably surprised with a pleasant settlement, called St Paul's; the country there, and from that parish upwards, being in general clear, fertile and well improved, in like manner as the lands on the south coast, and intersected by a multiplicity of rivers and streams, whose waters are swallowed up by the river St Lawrence.

I am of opinion the south country deserves the preference, for the goodness of its soil; but neither the one coast, or the other, are uniformly fruitful, there being some exceptionable tracts on both

U

sides, which must be the case in a territory of so considerable an extent: and, in many parishes, one meets with coppices and small parcels of forest, perhaps designedly left by the inhabitants for fuel, shelter and various other necessary purposes. The lands on the coasts, from Montreal to Lake St Francis, are capable of great improvements: at present much cannot be said for them, being very woody, with a cold, spungy soil; but, from this lake to that of Ontario, north and south, the ground is much better, producing variety of excellent timber for ship-use, with good grass and little or no under-wood. The numerous islands you meet with are, in general, well cultivated and rich, particularly the island of Jesus above Montreal, St Peter's, etc etc being inhabited by Canadians, who are in the government and diocese of Quebec, as are likewise part of the lands north and south, interspersed, however, with many tribes of Indians, who are bad farmers, husbandry being intirely out of their sphere; the French have no settlements farther west than the Cedars, about half-way between Ontario and Lake St Francis; the country round the former, and on the principal rivers flowing into it, being inhabited by the aborigines, mostly Iroquois, whose chief employment, when they are not at war, is hunting and fishing.

It is computed there are above a hundred thousand souls in this colony, and, whether that number is confined to Canada proper, which, according to a modern British writer, does not exceed five hundred miles in length from N E to S W and two hundred miles in breadth, I cannot determine; but I presume the different tribes of Indians, who reside in this immense tract of country, are all included. From the Island of Coudre, below Quebec, to that of Montreal, the country on both sides of the river is so well settled and closely inhabited as to resemble almost one continual village; the habitations appear extremely neat, with sashed windows, and, in general, washed on the outsides with lime, as are likewise their churches, which are all constructed upon one uniform plan and have an agreeable effect on the traveller or passenger; but, upon entering their houses, you are strangely disappointed, being quite emblematical of the painted sepulchres we read of in Holy Writ; for the peasantry, as well as the lower trade's-people, mechanics etc here, as in France, are intolerably dirty, as well as deceitful, ridiculously fantastic and very ignorant: these pecularities may be likewise, with great aptness, ascribed to many others in superior stations; but, in enumerating the properties of the bulk of the people of any particular country, persons liberally educated, who are possessed of plentiful fortunes and endowed with generous polite sentiments, should, nevertheless, be exempted from these and all national reproaches. The women are not handsome nor fair, but sprightly and agreeable, and so complaisant to Britain's brave sons that, vanity apart, it may be hoped the next generation will, in all respects, be considerably improved; and, with regard to the complexions of the ladies of Canada, like those of their mother-country, all defects of nature are supplied, as much as possible, by art. The winter climate, for above six months, is exceedingly cold, four of which are truly rigorous; but, when once it sets in severe and the pores of the body are braced up, a person does not much regard it afterwards; for you have generally a serene atmosphere, except when a snow-storm sets in, and that seldom continues above twenty-four hours, during which time it is incessant.

The stoves that are used in this country are incomparably well adapted to the climate, and contribute, in a great measure, to soften the rigour of that long-frozen season; these, with all other utensils and materials of cast-iron, are made at a foundry contiguous to the Trois Rivières. I think these inventions would be exceedingly useful if fixed up in the halls of the old mansion-seats of the nobility and gentry of Great Britain, as the heat may be conveyed by pipes to the most remote apartments, which would not only preserve these buildings, with their furniture, from decay, but prevent those fatal accidents that frequently happen by fires, in the absence of the family, by the carelessness of servants. They stand upon a square frame of the same metal, about six or eight inches from the ground; and, if it is a boarded floor, the place where it is to be fixed should be first covered with leaves of sheet-iron; as should likewise the edges of the holes in wooden partitions where the pipes are conveyed from one room to another; which renders every thing perfectly safe.

The summers are generally pleasant, except for two months, when it is exceedingly hot, in July and August, with violent thunderstorms; but yet so prolific is this season, that the farmer expects to reap the fruits of his labour within four months after the seed is put into the ground; and the forwardness of vegetation in their gardens is really surprising. Great quantities of tobacco are planted in this colony, which is generally used by the poorer and meaner sort of people; but, from their not knowing how to cure or manufacture it properly, it is wretched insipid stuff, which they twist up into ropes, like hay, near two inches round, and afterwards make it into rolls of an immoderate size; I tasted it once for curiosity, and thought it had not better flavour than common weeds or cabbage-leaves dried: but, I presume, it will not be thought advisable to encourage the Canadians in the culture of this plant, lest it should, in process of time, become prejudicial to our own natural colonies, those of Virginia and Maryland in particular.

There are various kinds of timber to be met with in this country, such as red and white oak, black and white birch, fir and pine-trees of different species, maple, alder, cedar, bitter cherry, ash, chesnut, beech, hazel, black and white thorn, apple, pear, plum-trees, and an infinity of other non-descripts; besides a great choice of shrubs, particularly the capillaire, which grows not unlike fern and has no main stalk, but shoots up its leaves from the root, and its seeds grow in tufts on the back of the foliage, in like manner as fern; they have great plenty of it in the woods, and, I am informed, the inhabitants usually prepared great quantities of its syrup, which they sold to the merchants at Quebec, who exported it annually to France.

Canada does not, at present, produce sufficient corn for its own consumption, which may, in a great measure, be attributed to the want of people to cultivate the ground, the natives having been, for the most part, employed these fifteen years (even in times of profound peace between the two Crowns) in a military way, incroaching on their neighbours to aggrandise and extend their dominions, to the great neglect of the true interests of their country: and such as could be spared from that service were usually engaged in the fisheries on the coasts of Nova Scotia, Cape Breton, Labrador, etc as the principal part of their diet consists in the article of fish. For the future, it is to be hoped, every obstacle being removed and the grand system of their politics intirely changed, due attention will be paid to agriculture and trade, both by the Canadians themselves and their new masters, who are ever ready to grant all reasonable indulgences to an industrious and deserving people. In a word, the improvement of tillage should be the chief object, the lands in general being easy, kind, capable of producing all the necessaries and conveniences of life in great abundance; and the climate, notwithstanding its northerly situation, contributing thereto, to the intire gratification of its hardy and healthy inhabitants, who live to an extreme old-age.

The multifarious kinds of fish, wherewith the lakes and rivers abound, have been already mentioned. Besides these, and innumerable other benefits, they have variety of all sorts of game, bipeds as well as quadrupeds, in the greatest plenty; and finer poultry, with tame and wild pigeons, no other country can boast of: moreover, the Canadians have an excellent breed of black cattle, sheep, pigs and horses, with which the farms in general are plenteously stocked. In fine, this province, though mostly an inland country, has, by means of the river St Lawrence, the advantages of an extensive sea-coast, thereby affording as well a commodious exportation of its own produce as a reasonable importation of foreign commodities, and an easy conveyance from one part to another, even to the most remote corners of the colony. To conclude, Canada is a fruitful, pleasant, most valuable territory, and its warlike inhabitants, together with the national troops of France, were justly sensible thereof and of its great importance, having, from first to last, persevered, though deserted and destitute as they have been, in exerting the utmost activity, vigilance and bravery in its defence; furthermore, the acquisition of this immense tract of country completely secures to us the peaceable possession of Nova Scotia, together with the quiet enjoyment of the frontiers of all our numerous colonies to the southward; blessings, which I sincerely hope the British Americans, who have more or less woefully experienced a long reverse of fortune, will ever most gratefully and dutifully acknowledge to Divine Providence and their benign mother-country, their protector and most generous deliverer, to latest posterity.

# Biographical Index

Abercromby, Lieutenant-General James. A major in 1742, he became a major-general in 1756 and went to America in command of the 50th Regiment the same year. Commanded the 2nd Brigade in the expedition against Louisbourg in 1757 and, in December of that year, was made colonel-in-chief of the 60th Regiment. Following the recall to England of the Earl of Loudoun, he was appointed commander-in-chief of the British forces in America and, in July 1758, led the unsuccessful expedition against Montcalm's forces at Ticonderoga in which Lord Howe was killed. He was then recalled to England, being succeeded as commander-in-chief by General Amherst, became a lieutenant-general in 1759 and was made deputy governor of Stirling Castle in 1772. 21, 24, 71-2, 159, 290-1, 294-5.

Abraham, Plains of, 196, 230, 246

Acadia, 9, 29, 106, 112, 124, 178, 293

Albany, 26, 77-8, 103, 159-60, 169, 209, 281, 293-5

*Alcide*, 121, 142, 193

Allen's River, 48, 66

Amherst, Field-Marshal Lord Jeffrey. Born in 1717, he became an ensign in the Guards in 1731 and served as aide-de-camp to General Ligonier in Germany and also on the staff of the Duke of Cumberland. In 1758 he was given command, as a major-general, of the successful expedition which captured Louisbourg, and later the same year succeeded Abercromby as commander-in-chief of the British forces in America. Captured Fort Duquesne, Ticonderoga and Crown

Point and shared in the capture of Montreal. Knighted in 1761, he was appointed governor-general of British North America, but returned to England in 1763 and, in the same year, became governor of Virginia He was created Baron Amherst in 1776, was made a field-marshal in 1796 and died the following year. 9, 11-12, 71-2, 75, 77, 82-5, 89-9, 103, 113, 115-16, 118, 120-1, 128, 132, 144, 146, 150, 159-72, 177, 183-5, 192-4, 209, 271-2, 274, 276-7, 280, 287-90, 292, 295, 297-302

*Ann and Elizabeth*, 192-3

Annapolis River, 42

Annapolis Royal, 26, 34-5, 46-7, 51, 57, 60-1, 65, 73, 92, 97, 99, 102, 106, 111, 293-4

Aubrey, Monsieur, 210-11, 216

Point de Barille, 283-4

Barnaby's River, 58, 62, 122

Barré, Colonel, 83, 115, 226

Barrington, Lord, 10-11

Baye Verte, 32, 35, 39, 99

Beaumont, 134-6

Beauport, 130, 141, 146, 155, 179, 185, 194-5, 205, 259

Beau Sejour, 26, 31

Bic island, 122-3, 255

Boishébert, Charles des Champs de. Born in 1727, he was attached to the garrison at Quebec as regimental adjutant at the age of fifteen. In 1754 he was in command of the fort at the mouth of the St John river where he was attacked by Monckton a few days after the surrender of Beauséjour in 1755. Unable to resist, he destroyed the fort and moved higher up the river, but later the same year led a success-

311

Lorette, 231, 236, 239-40, 242-3, 260
Loring, Captain, 169, 213-15
Loudoun, John Campbell, Earl of. Born in 1705, he joined the army in 1727. At the outbreak of the 1745 rebellion, he raised the 54th Regiment in support of George II, but it was nearly entirely wiped out at the battle of Preston. In 1755 he became colonel-in-chief of the 60th Regiment, and the following year was appointed governor-in-chief of Virginia and commander-in-chief of the British forces in America. He was present at Louisbourg in 1757, but was superseded in his command the following year and recalled to England. He served as second-in-command in Portugal in 1762, and was promoted to general in 1770. He died in 1782. 17, 20-1, 26-7, 29-30, 38, 71, 294
Louisbourg, 8, 9, 19, 20, 23-6, 29, 30, 33, 38, 70-6, 81, 85, 90-3, 104, 113-22, 140, 147, 155, 174, 186, 193, 196, 198, 202, 204, 250, 264, 276, 280, 294, 298
Lunenburg, 43-4, 293

M'Cartney, Captain, 243-4
McDonell, Captain, 239-40, 247
M'Kellar, Major, 115, 130, 247
Maitland, Captain, 115, 226
Malone, Captain, 290-1
Maryland, 212, 308
Massachussetts, 20, 68
Mayass [Maillard's] Hill, 43, 49, 50, 53, 64-8, 76
*Medway*, 121, 192-3
Mohawk, river, 9, 159, 213
Monckton, General Robert. Born in 1726, he joined the army in Flanders in 1742 and was present at Fontenoy in 1745. Elected an MP in 1751, he was sent to Nova Scotia in the following year and, in 1754, was appointed lieutenant-governor of Annapolis Royal. In 1755 he captured the French forts

of Beauséjour and Gaspereau and, in 1759, was second-in-command of Wolfe's expedition against Quebec, when he was wounded. In 1761 he was promoted to major-general and appointed governor of New York. Later the same year he commanded the land force that sailed with Rodney to capture Martinique, Grenada, St Lucia and St Vincent. Returning to England in 1763, he became governor of Berwick-on-Tweed in 1765, governor of Portsmouth in 1778 and also represented Portsmouth in parliament from 1779 until his death in 1782. 71, 92-3, 96, 104, 113, 115-16, 134-5, 147, 150-1, 153, 157, 171, 179, 181-7, 191-200, 226, 295-7
Monroe, Colonel, 35, 36, 294
Montcalm, Louis Joseph de Montcalm Gozon, Marquis de. Born in 1712, he entered the army as an ensign at the age of nine. He became a captain in 1729 and, after a period of distinguished service, was promoted brigadier-general in 1756 and sent to Canada. In the same year he captured Fort Oswego, following this up by capturing Fort William Henry in 1757. In 1758 he completely defeated Abercromby at Ticonderoga and thus succeeded in keeping the British forces at bay despite his quarrels with the French governor-general, the Marquis de Vaudreuil. In 1759 he defended Quebec against Wolfe until the battle of the Plains where he was twice wounded. He died the following day. 8, 17, 30, 36, 72, 132, 138, 145-6, 150, 152, 171-2, 178-80, 189, 192, 194, 197, 199, 201, 203, 209, 294, 296
Montgomery, Colonel, 107, 161, 164, 214
Montmorency, 128, 130, 132, 139, 144, 146, 149, 153, 155, 171, 176, 179-81, 185-6, 192
Montreal, 9, 113, 132, 141, 151, 172,